HODDER GIBSON
Model Papers
WITH ANSWERS

D0716138

PLUS: Official SQA 2015 Past Paper
With Answers

Higher for CfE
History

Model Papers & 2015 Exam

Hodder Gibson Study Skills Advice – General	– page 3
Hodder Gibson Study Skills Advice – Higher for CfE History	– page 5
MODEL PAPER 1	– page 9
MODEL PAPER 2	– page 29
MODEL PAPER 3	– page 49
2015 EXAM	– page 69
ANSWER SECTION	– page 89

HODDER
GIBSON
AN HACHETTE UK COMPANY

This book contains the official SQA 2015 Exam for Higher for CfE History, with associated SQA approved answers modified from the official marking instructions that accompany the paper.

In addition the book contains model papers, together with answers, plus study skills advice. These papers, some of which may include a limited number of previously published SQA questions, have been specially commissioned by Hodder Gibson, and have been written by experienced senior teachers and examiners in line with the new Higher for CfE syllabus and assessment outlines, Spring 2014. This is not SQA material but has been devised to provide further practice for Higher for CfE examinations in 2015 and beyond.

Hodder Gibson is grateful to the copyright holders, as credited on the final page of the Answer Section, for permission to use their material. Every effort has been made to trace the copyright holders and to obtain their permission for the use of copyright material. Hodder Gibson will be happy to receive information allowing us to rectify any error or omission in future editions.

Hachette UK's policy is to use papers that are natural, renewable and recyclable products and made from wood grown in sustainable forests. The logging and manufacturing processes are expected to conform to the environmental regulations of the country of origin.

Orders: please contact Bookpoint Ltd, 130 Park Drive, Milton Park, Abingdon, Oxon OX14 4SE. Telephone: (44) 01235 827720. Fax: (44) 01235 400454. Lines are open 9.00–5.00, Monday to Saturday, with a 24-hour message answering service. Visit our website at www.hoddereducation.co.uk. Hodder Gibson can be contacted direct on: Tel: 0141 848 1609; Fax: 0141 889 6315; email: hoddergibson@hodder.co.uk

This collection first published in 2015 by
Hodder Gibson, an imprint of Hodder Education,
An Hachette UK Company
2a Christie Street
Paisley PA1 1NB

Typeset by Aptara, Inc

Printed in the UK

A catalogue record for this title is available from the British Library

ISBN: 978-1-4718-6078-2

3 2 1

2016 2015

Introduction

Study Skills – what you need to know to pass exams!

Pause for thought

Many students might skip quickly through a page like this. After all, we all know how to revise. Do you really though?

Think about this:

"IF YOU ALWAYS DO WHAT YOU ALWAYS DO, YOU WILL ALWAYS GET WHAT YOU HAVE ALWAYS GOT."

Do you like the grades you get? Do you want to do better? If you get full marks in your assessment, then that's great! Change nothing! This section is just to help you get that little bit better than you already are.

There are two main parts to the advice on offer here. The first part highlights fairly obvious things but which are also very important. The second part makes suggestions about revision that you might not have thought about but which WILL help you.

Part 1

DOH! It's so obvious but …

Start revising in good time

Don't leave it until the last minute – this will make you panic.

Make a revision timetable that sets out work time AND play time.

Sleep and eat!

Obvious really, and very helpful. Avoid arguments or stressful things too – even games that wind you up. You need to be fit, awake and focused!

Know your place!

Make sure you know exactly **WHEN and WHERE** your exams are.

Know your enemy!

Make sure you know what to expect in the exam.

How is the paper structured?

How much time is there for each question?

What types of question are involved?

Which topics seem to come up time and time again?

Which topics are your strongest and which are your weakest?

Are all topics compulsory or are there choices?

Learn by DOING!

There is no substitute for past papers and practice papers – they are simply essential! Tackling this collection of papers and answers is exactly the right thing to be doing as your exams approach.

Part 2

People learn in different ways. Some like low light, some bright. Some like early morning, some like evening / night. Some prefer warm, some prefer cold. But everyone uses their BRAIN and the brain works when it is active. Passive learning – sitting gazing at notes – is the most INEFFICIENT way to learn anything. Below you will find tips and ideas for making your revision more effective and maybe even more enjoyable. What follows gets your brain active, and active learning works!

Activity 1 – Stop and review

Step 1

When you have done no more than 5 minutes of revision reading STOP!

Step 2

Write a heading in your own words which sums up the topic you have been revising.

Step 3

Write a summary of what you have revised in no more than two sentences. Don't fool yourself by saying, "I know it, but I cannot put it into words". That just means you don't know it well enough. If you cannot write your summary, revise that section again, knowing that you must write a summary at the end of it. Many of you will have notebooks full of blue/black ink writing. Many of the pages will not be especially attractive or memorable so try to liven them up a bit with colour as you are reviewing and rewriting. **This is a great memory aid, and memory is the most important thing.**

WATCH YOUR TIME

With this section it is important to keep an eye on time. You will need to build in reading time and thinking time before you start to write. It is also important to look at the number of marks that are on offer. The *"evaluate the usefulness"* question is worth six marks and *"comparison"* question is worth five marks. The *"how fully"* question is worth nine marks. You also need to think about the essays that you are going to have to complete after you do this section. This part of the exam should take no more than one hour to complete. This then leaves you with 40 minutes for each of the essays.

The "evaluate the usefulness" question

This question asks you to judge a primary source. It will ask you to *"Evaluate the usefulness of Source X in describing/explaining/illustrating a historical event/development."* You are given instructions to use the source's origin, purpose and content as well as relevant recall that has not been mentioned in the presented source.

Four marks are available for evaluations that make use of who the author was, the type of source, its purpose and when it was written as part of your judgement.

Two marks are available for relevant evaluations of the source content.

Two marks are available for identifying information that has been missed out but would have made the source more reliable. Remember, you only need to make six points to gain full marks.

The biggest problem with this sort of question is when people do not read the question carefully. As a result, the source is simply described when what the marker is looking for is some link with the 'usefulness' of the source in answering the question. So the trick is to identify information that is relevant to the answer and then comment on it. You need to do both things to be sure of the mark.

The "comparison" question

This question will ask you to compare two sources. It will ask you to, *"Compare the views of Sources X and Y about an event/issue, etc"*. You are given instructions to comment on the sources overall and then in detail.

The two sources contain four different points that agree or disagree with each other. You have to identify the area they agree or disagree about and then illustrate this difference by selecting relevant phrases from the sources that show this. The overall comparison refers to the general areas of agreement and disagreement that are mentioned and explained in your answer. You do not need specific detail from the sources to make an overall comparison, but you do need to mention in general

ways what the two sources are about and in what ways they agree or disagree.

Each individual point of comparison gains one mark and the overall comparison gains up to two marks. A single comparison is when the area of similarity or difference is mentioned and then illustrated using relevant compared content from the two sources. Overall comparison marks are awarded when the specific areas of similarity/difference are summarised.

The biggest problem with this sort of question is when people make what are known as "ghost comparisons". You will get NO MARKS for "ghost comparisons". In other words, no marks for writing *"Source B says ... but Source C makes no mention of this"*.

The "how fully" question

This question tests your knowledge on one specific area of mandatory content listed as part of the course. You can see what these areas are in the Higher History Course support notes.

The question will be worded as follows, *"How fully does Source X describe/explain/illustrate a historical event/development"*. The source will contain four points that are relevant to the question asked and three marks are available for finding three of those points, then explaining what these points mean in your own words and why the point is relevant to the question. You then need to include information not covered in the source, but would help give a fuller understanding of the issue in the question. This part of the question is worth up to seven marks.

The biggest problem with this sort of question is, again, people not reading the question carefully then writing irrelevant information in your answer. You will get no marks for just listing factual information even if it is "correct" information. You will need at least six relevant points of recalled information if you want to get full marks. Like the evaluation question, you need to identify relevant information then link it to the question with relevant comment. This shows that you have interpreted the information rather than just copied it.

Section 2 and 3 – British History and European and World History

Sections 2 and 3 are assessed by extended responses, often referred to as essays. These extended responses are worth 20 marks each.

In the British section, there are five periods of history to choose from. You only have to study one of them and your learning centre will have chosen which topic you will study. You only have to write ONE EXTENDED RESPONSE from a choice of three questions in the British section.

In the European and World section, there are nine topics to choose from. You only have to study one topic, but some learning centres choose to teach more than that.

You only have to write ONE EXTENDED RESPONSE from a choice of three questions. If you have studied more than one topic, you still only write one extended response but from a wider choice of questions.

The SQA gives detailed advice on the course content in their Higher History Course Support Notes: http://www.sqa.org.uk/files_ccc/CfE_CourseUnitSupportNotes_Higher_SocialStudies_History.pdf

The SQA also gives detailed advice on the examination in the Specimen Question Paper they have produced, which is included in this book.

Extended responses

The SQA uses the term 'extended responses' rather than essays but this book will use the word 'essays' because that is the word most teachers and learners use. To be successful you must:

- **structure** your answer correctly
- **use relevant knowledge** in your answer
- **analyse and evaluate** this information in order to answer the question effectively.

Structure – the introduction

The introduction is awarded up to two marks. To ensure you get two marks you need to do three things.

1. Your introduction must include context. That means you must set the scene by describing the "back story" of the question. In a couple of sentences, describe the historical situation that the question is based on.

2. You need to give a line of argument. Now, this will depend upon the question asked. The easiest way to do this is to use the words of the question directly in the argument. So, if a question asks, *"How important were the reports of Booth and Rowntree in causing the Liberal reforms of 1906–14?"*, a relevant line of argument might be, *"the reports of Booth and Rowntree were important to an extent in causing the Liberal reforms of 1904–14, but they were not the only reason"*. This is a basic line of argument.

3. You will also need to identify the main headings or factors that you are going to explain in the main body of your essay. These can be done in a list or, more effectively, treated separately. This shows that you understand the topic and are showing the marker what you are going to develop as part of your answer.

A good introduction is well worth taking time over. It shows the direction that the essay is going to take and will help settle you and give you confidence before you develop the main part of the essay. It will also give you a guide to refer back to if you get half way through the essay and wonder what comes next.

Structure – the conclusion

The conclusion is worth up to two marks. In order to gain two marks you will need to do the following three things.

1. Your conclusion must be based on the information you have mentioned in the main part of the essay. Do not introduce new information in the conclusion.

2. In the conclusion, you summarise the arguments that you have created in the main part of your essay. This should show balance which means you should try to look at both sides of the argument – for example, how much the idea in the question was responsible for something and how far other things were responsible.

3. You then need to come to an overall judgement which directly answers the main question. The last sentence must refer back to the specific question asked as well as provide a judgement on that question if you are to get a good mark.

Knowledge

There are **six** marks given for the use of accurate and relevant knowledge in the main part of the essay. Your knowledge has to be relevant to the question asked and you must USE the information to help answer the question. For example, if a question asked how democratic Britain was by 1918, relevant knowledge on the franchise would be to say that by 1918 women aged over 30 who were graduates or married to a householder had gained the vote in national elections, but women under this age could not vote.

Reading the question carefully is important here as irrelevant information is not awarded any marks. Good essays will contain much more than six marks of accurate and relevant knowledge because detailed knowledge is essential for success in developing analysis and evaluation.

Analysis and evaluation

In total, there are 10 marks for analysis and evaluation and there are three different things to do to build up your marks.

1. Basic analysis

   You will get a mark each time you make a simple comment that makes a basic judgement about your information. In a question about the reasons why unification was achieved in Germany, a comment may be made such as *"The Zollverein was very important to German unification because it made people realise the advantages of states joining together"*. You have mentioned the Zollverein, which is knowledge, and you have made a simple judgement about its importance. Make this sort of comment 4 times in your essay and you will get 4 marks.

2. Getting more marks

   If you can develop your simple comment a bit more to link it to the factor you are writing about, then that is worth an extra mark. For example, in a question about the Liberal reforms, a simple comment about old-age pensions would be, *"Old-age pensions were an attempt to help people too old to work. It shows how the Liberals tried to help people who were poor through no fault of their own"*. To develop it further you must link to the factor you are writing about – in this case the factor is helping the old. Here is how you could do it – *"In fact the pensions were below the poverty line created by Rowntree and only given to people of good character aged over 70, therefore, the Liberals only partly eased the problem of poverty in old age"*. If you make that sort of developed comment twice, that will gain you an extra 2 marks.

3. Evaluation

   There are up to four marks awarded for the way in which you evaluate the knowledge to answer the question posed. Evaluation is where you make judgements on the factors that are relevant when answering an essay question.

   For example, for an essay on the unification of Germany, a number of factors will be looked at, including the development of nationalism, the rise of Prussian economic and military power, the weakness of Austria and the role of Bismarck.

Each factor can be evaluated by saying that it is important in some way. Better answers may put in some judgement as to the relative importance of a factor and even try to link them with each other. For example, *"without the growth of nationalist feeling that Germans should live together, Bismarck's job would have been much harder to complete"*. This is evaluation.

Beware!

The biggest problem with essay writing happens when people write descriptive essays or try to repeat an essay they did well in class. You must react to the wording of the question asked. The quality of evaluation and analysis is what makes an essay. If this is carefully linked to the question asked, then the mark will be good.

Timing again

It is very important to keep an eye on time in the examination. You should aim to have at least forty minutes put aside to answer each essay. You are expected to do a lot in these forty minutes. It is far better to write two essays of the same length rather than one long essay and one short essay. Two consistent essays will always score more marks than one good and one poor essay.

Good luck!

In the exam, THINK before you put pen to paper. You will have worked hard to get to this stage. Don't panic! Keep calm, read the questions carefully and decide what the question wants you to do. Then just follow the process described above.

Model Paper 1

Whilst this Model Paper has been specially commissioned by Hodder Gibson for use as practice for the Higher (for Curriculum for Excellence) exams, the key reference documents remain the SQA Specimen Paper 2014 and SQA Past Paper 2015.

HODDER GIBSON
LEARN MORE

National
Qualifications
MODEL PAPER 1

History

Duration — 2 hours and 20 minutes

Total marks — 60

SECTION 1 — SCOTTISH — 20 marks

Attempt ONE Part

SECTION 2 — BRITISH — 20 marks

Attempt ONE question from the Part you have chosen

SECTION 3 — EUROPEAN AND WORLD — 20 marks

Attempt ONE question from the Part you have chosen

Write your answers clearly in the answer booklet provided. In the answer booklet you must clearly identify the question number you are attempting.

Use **blue** or **black** ink.

Before leaving the examination room you must give your answer booklet to the Invigilator; if you do not you may lose all the marks for this paper.

SECTION 1 — SCOTTISH

Attempt ONE Part

PARTS

A.　The Wars of Independence, 1249—1328　　　　　　　Page 3

B.　The Age of the Reformation, 1542—1603　　　　　　Page 5

C.　The Treaty of Union, 1689—1740　　　　　　　　　Page 7

D.　Migration and Empire, 1830—1939　　　　　　　　Page 9

E.　The Impact of the Great War, 1914—1928　　　　　Page 11

SECTION 2 — BRITISH

Attempt one question from the Part you have chosen

PARTS

A.　Church, State and Feudal Society, 1066—1406　　Page 13

B.　The Century of Revolutions, 1603—1702　　　　　Page 13

C.　The Atlantic Slave Trade　　　　　　　　　　　　Page 13

D.　Britain, 1851—1951　　　　　　　　　　　　　　Page 14

E.　Britain and Ireland, 1900—1985　　　　　　　　Page 14

SECTION 3 — EUROPEAN AND WORLD

Attempt one question from the Part you have chosen

PARTS

A.　The Crusades, 1071—1204　　　　　　　　　　　　Page 15

B.　The American Revolution, 1763—1787　　　　　　Page 15

C.　The French Revolution, to 1799　　　　　　　　　Page 15

D.　Germany, 1815—1939　　　　　　　　　　　　　　Page 16

E.　Italy, 1815—1939　　　　　　　　　　　　　　　Page 16

F.　Russia, 1881—1921　　　　　　　　　　　　　　　Page 16

G.　USA, 1918—1968　　　　　　　　　　　　　　　　Page 17

H.　Appeasement and the Road to War, to 1939　　　Page 17

I.　The Cold War, 1945—1989　　　　　　　　　　　　Page 17

SECTION 1 — SCOTTISH — 20 marks

Part A — The Wars of Independence, 1249–1328

Study the sources below and attempt the questions which follow.

Source A: from a letter by Bishop William Fraser to Edward I, November 1290.

> Your ambassadors and the Scottish ambassadors who had been sent to you and also some nobles of the Kingdom of Scotland met at Perth. But a sad rumour echoed among the people that our lady was dead and because of this the kingdom of Scotland is troubled and the community perplexed. When the rumour was heard and published, Sir Robert Bruce, who previously did not intend to come to the meeting, came with a large retinue to confer with some who were there. We do not yet know what he intends to do or how he intends to act. Because of that there is a fear of a general war and a large-scale slaughter unless the Most High, through your active involvement and good offices, administer a quick cure.

Source B: from Richard Oram, *Kings and Queens of Scotland* (2006).

> Balliol certainly now assumed the bearing of king, yet he remained aware that he would have to impress the feudal lord of his lands in England if he wanted to secure the Kingdom of Scotland. On St Andrew's day 1292, John was inaugurated as King of Scots on the Stone of Destiny at Scone. Yet the ceremony was overseen by Edward's officials rather than the traditional Scottish earls and churchmen. Worse, within a matter of two months, John — again summoned to Northern England — crumbled under the demand that he renew his homage to Edward as Scotland's overlord. It was this regime that undoubtedly prepared John for further confrontations with Edward I over appeals from Scottish courts that the English king insisted he answered for at Westminster.

Source C: from a contemporary English chronicle.

> William Wallace was an outcast from pity, a robber, a sacrilegious man, a man who burnt alive boys in schools and churches in great numbers. Wallace had collected an army of Scots but had seen that he could not resist the powerful army of the King, and so fled himself from the battle at Falkirk, leaving his people to be slain by the sword. Wallace was at last taken prisoner by the King's servants and brought to London, as the King ordained that he should be formally tried. He was put to a most cruel, but amply deserved, death. His head was fixed on a stake and set on London Bridge. His four quarters thus divided, were sent to the four quarters of Scotland. Behold the end of a merciless man whom his mercilessness brought to this end.

SECTION 1 — SCOTTISH (continued)

Source D: from Alan Macquarrie, *Kingship and Nation* (2004).

> Neither William Wallace nor his father, the laird of Elderslie, had signed the Ragman Rolls, and so were outlawed. He escaped capture by the English garrison of Lanark with the help of his mistress, who was killed in the process. In revenge, Wallace killed the Sheriff of Lanark and set himself up as head of a band of outlaws. The Battle of Falkirk was a victory for the English mounted knights and the Welsh archers, who wore down the schiltrons by repeated cavalry charges and discharges of arrows. Wallace escaped and rescued the survivors as best he could. He remained at liberty until betrayed by Sir John Stewart of Mentieth. After his trial he was dragged for miles at the tail of a horse to Smithfield where he was put to death by being strangled, and dismembered.

Attempt all of the following questions.

1. How fully does **Source B** describe the relationship between John Balliol and Edward I?

   Use the source and recalled knowledge.

   9

2. Evaluate the usefulness of **Source A** as evidence of why the Scots asked Edward to resolve the succession crisis in Scotland.

   In reaching a conclusion you should refer to:
   * *the origin and possible purpose of the source;*
   * *the content of the source;*
   * *recalled knowledge.*

   6

3. Compare the views of **Sources C** and **D** about the life and death of William Wallace.

   Compare the content overall and in detail.

   5

[Now go on to Section 2 starting on *Page thirteen*]

SECTION 1 — SCOTTISH — 20 marks

Part B — The Age of the Reformation, 1542–1603

Study the sources below and attempt the questions which follow:

Source A: from a contemporary History of the Scottish Reformation by John Knox.

> The Archbishop of St Andrews, apprehended that Blessed Martyr of Christ Jesus, Walter Myln, a man of old age, who he most cruelly put to death by fire in St. Andrews, on 28th April, 1558. Immediately after Myln's death, a new strength of purpose developed among the whole people. In the meantime, the town of Perth embraced The Truth. This provoked the Queen Regent to a new fury; in which she willed the Lord Ruthven, Provost of that town, to suppress all Protestant religion there. On 2nd of May 1559, arrived John Knox from France. He went to Dundee, where he earnestly asked the brethren of Perth, "That he might be permitted to assist them, and to preach the reformed faith amongst them". This was granted to him; therefore he departed to Perth with them; where he began to preach.

Source B: from Jenny Wormald, *Mary Queen of Scots* (1988).

> At about 2am on 10th February 1567, the house was blown up. Darnley escaped into the garden, where his body was found: he had been smothered by, it was suspected, the Douglas kinsmen of the Earl of Morton. Mary should have been in strict mourning, instead she attended a wedding the day after Darnley's murder. She allowed Darnley's father Lennox to accuse Bothwell of the murder and bring him to trial. It was a farce. Whoever else was involved, it is significant that no one doubted the principal conspirator was Bothwell. On 15th May, she married Bothwell, a Protestant. Mary had always insisted on her right to her personal Catholicism, whatever happened to anyone else in Scotland, and had created considerable problems by doing so. The end was now very near.

Source C: from the records of the General Assembly of the Kirk of Scotland, 1597.

> Meeting at Perth, according to his Majesty's request, and concerning the articles proposed by the King. The brethren, after long conference and mature deliberation agree as follows: The Assembly ordains that no minister shall criticise his Majesty's laws but should seek remedy from his Presbytery, Synod or General Assembly which will present his complaints to his Majesty and report on his Majesty's answer. No man's name should be rebuked from the pulpit, unless his fault be well known and in public. Every Presbytery should watch that each minister's doctrine is agreeable with God's word. No meetings should be held by ministers without his Majesty's knowledge and consent, apart from the Kirk Session, Presbytery and Synod meetings. In all principal towns ministers should not be chosen without the consent of their own flock and his Majesty.

SECTION 1 — SCOTTISH (continued)

Source D: from Gordon Donaldson, *Scotland: James V to James VII, History of Scotland* (1965).

> A general assembly met in February at Perth and not, as the previous assembly had appointed, in April at St Andrews. It was hard to raise objections if the king chose to bring forward the date of the assembly, but when his right to do this was admitted it was equally hard to challenge his right to postpone an assembly. It was equally hard to challenge the king's power to name the place of meeting. The assembly of 1597 conceded that ministers should not be appointed in the chief towns without the consent of the king, and passed various measures curbing the freedom of ministers in the course of their sermons, to attack the laws, to censure individuals and comment on politics.

Attempt all of the following questions.

4. How fully does **Source B** explain why Mary, Queen of Scots lost her throne?

    Use the source and recalled knowledge.   9

5. Evaluate the usefulness of **Source A** as evidence of the growth of Protestantism in Scotland before the Reformation of 1560.   6

    In reaching a conclusion you should refer to:
    - *the origin and possible purpose of the source*
    - *the content of the source;*
    - *recalled knowledge.*

6. Compare the views of **Sources C** and **D** about James VI's attempts to control the Kirk.   5

    Compare the content overall and in detail.

[Now go on to Section 2 starting on *Page thirteen*]

SECTION 1 — SCOTTISH — 20 marks

Part C — The Treaty of Union, 1689–1740

Study the sources below and attempt the questions which follow.

Source A: from a speech by John Dalrymple, Earl of Stair, in Parliament, 1706.

> We followed the example of other nations and formed the Company of Scotland to trade with the West Indies. We built ships and planned a colony on the isthmus of Darien. What we lacked were not men or arms, or courage, but the one thing most needful: we lacked the friendly co-operation of England. The pitiful outcome of that enterprise is too sad a story to be told again. Suffice it to say that the English did not treat us as partners or friends or fellow subjects of a British king. They treated us as pirates and enemy aliens. We were exposed to the hostile rivalry of Spain, encouraged by England. Our colony was sacked. We suffered every cruelty an enemy can inflict.

Source B: from Daniel Defoe, *History of the Union* (1709).

> Many members of Parliament knew that the standing of Scotland in the British Parliament would only be that of a province of England. Also, they knew that Cornwall would send almost as many members to Parliament as the whole of Scotland, and this was an example of Scotland's subjection. This was a general complaint, but was very widespread. The people cried out that they were Scotsmen and they would remain Scotsmen. They condemned the word "British" as fit only for the Welsh, who had already been made the subjects of the English. Scotland had always had a famous name in foreign courts, and had enjoyed privileges and honours there for many years, bought with the blood of their ancestors. The common people went about the streets crying "no union", and called those *negotiators* traitors, and threatened them to their faces.

Source C: from T. M. Devine, *The Scottish Nation: 1700-2007* (2006).

> The "New Party", soon to be known as "Squadrone Volante", had emerged out of the Country Party in 1704. As events were to prove, this group of around two dozen members was to have a key role in the outcome of the union vote. Crucial in carrying the treaty as a whole was Article XV, which dealt with the "Equivalent". This was an attractive inducement to the Squadrone Volante, the small party whose support the Court Party had to retain in order to achieve ultimate success, so finely balanced was the overall position in Parliament. Some of the Equivalent was to be used to compensate the investors in the ill-fated Darien Company. Among the most significant of these were members of the Squadrone. The formidable political management machine of the Court Party contrasted with the disarray of the parliamentary opposition.

SECTION 1 — SCOTTISH (continued)

Source D: from Christopher A. Whately, *The Scots and the Union* (2007).

> With around twenty-five Squadrone MPs, the government could carry the union, and did. Squadrone votes proved critical in securing approval for several of the articles which, had they been defeated, would have brought the union process to a shuddering halt. In part the Court's success was achieved by political management, which was to spur court-minded MPs into attending and voting for a cause many were at best sympathetic to, and only in a few cases seriously enthusiastic about. There were MPs however who voted consistently for the articles without benefiting at all from the Equivalent — eight of these were associated with the Squadrone. If the purpose of the Equivalent had been to bribe MPs, the outcome was disappointing. Support for union depended on much more than material gain.

Attempt all of the following questions.

7.   How fully does **Source B** explain the arguments for and against the Treaty of Union?   **9**

    Use the source and recalled knowledge.

8.   Evaluate the usefulness of **Source A** as evidence of worsening relations between Scotland and England between 1690 and 1705.   **6**

    In reaching a conclusion you should refer to:

    • *the origin and possible purpose of the source;*
    • *the content of the source;*
    • *recalled knowledge.*

9.   Compare the views of **Sources C** and **D** about the reasons for the passing of the Treaty of Union.   **5**

    Compare the content overall and in detail.

[Now go on to Section 2 starting on *Page thirteen*]

SECTION 1 — SCOTTISH — 20 marks

Part D — Migration and Empire, 1830–1939

Study the sources below and attempt the questions which follow.

Source A: from Angus Nicholson, Canada's Special Immigration Agent in the Highlands of Scotland, 1875.

> All the competing Emigration Agencies formerly reported on, are still at work as actively as ever. The New Zealand and Australian authorities are particularly alert, the streets of every town and village being always well ornamented with their bills and posters offering free passages and other inducements to emigrants. Not only so, but nearly all newspapers being subsidised by means of their advertisements, are doing their full share in the same direction. It has to be noted that a considerable number of potential recruits have been diverted from Canada to New Zealand as a result of the latter's offer of free passages. It is extremely difficult for us to attract emigrants when these territories are offering free passages while we expect the emigrants to pay their own fares to Canada.

Source B: from Martin J Mitchell, *Irish Catholics in the West of Scotland, in his "New Perspectives on the Irish in Scotland"* (2008).

> The prevailing view about Catholic Irish in nineteenth-century Scotland is that they were despised by the bulk of the native population, and as a result formed separate and isolated communities in the towns in which they settled in significant numbers. Some historians have highlighted sectarian riots and disturbances in Scotland in the nineteenth century as proof that there was considerable Protestant working class hostility towards the Catholic Irish community. However, if these incidents are looked at more closely, most of the incidents did not involve Scottish workers, but were instead "Orange" and "Green" disturbances involving Protestant Irish and Catholic Irish immigrants. The available evidence states or suggests that most Scottish workers were not participants—they remained aloof and let the two immigrant groups continue their old battles.

Source C: from Jock Phillips and Terry Hearn, *Settlers: New Zealand Immigrants from England, Ireland and Scotland, 1800–1945* (2008).

> The vast majority of Scots who emigrated to New Zealand came from around Edinburgh or Glasgow, playing important roles in her economic development. Not surprisingly, the Dunedin entrepreneurs, like the clothing magnates John Ross and Robert Glendinning, or the Burt Brothers who established a nationwide plumbing firm, were Scottish. Scots were also over-represented among those noted for their contribution to education and even more strongly among those involved in science and health. Otago saw the first high school for girls open in 1871 thanks to the daughter of an iron-merchant from Angus—the first headmistress was also a Scot! The Scottish education system of 1872 was the model for New Zealand's Education Act of 1877 and the fact that Otago had for a long time the only medical school in the country, and the strong links that school established with Edinburgh, helps to explain the continuing impact of Scots-born people in both the health and scientific fields.

SECTION 1 — SCOTTISH (continued)

Source D: from James Adam, *Twenty-Five Years of an Emigrant's Life in the South of New Zealand*, (1876).

> A gentleman who thirteen years ago was a draper's assistant in Scotland now owns the finest retail business in Dunedin, employs fifty hands and pays £250 weekly in wages. The enterprise of the Dunedin merchants has done much for the commerce and prosperity of Otago. The Scot has certainly made his mark on this land, not only in commerce but also in the field of education, setting up schools throughout the area. Several of the Scots' descendants have also become doctors, administering to the health of the local population in a most efficient manner. In 1862, another born Scot from Edinburgh, arrived in Dunedin to conduct a geological survey of Otago and three years later he was appointed to found the Geological Survey of New Zealand, managing New Zealand's premier scientific society.

Attempt all of the following questions.

10. How fully does **Source B** illustrate the experience of immigrants in Scotland?   9

    Use the source and recalled knowledge.

11. Evaluate the usefulness of **Source A** as evidence of the reasons for Scottish migration and emigration.   6

    In reaching a conclusion you should refer to:
    • *the origin and possible purpose of the source;*
    • *the content of the source;*
    • *recalled knowledge.*

12. Compare the views of **Sources C** and **D** about the contribution of Scots to the economic growth and development of the Empire.   5

    Compare the content overall and in detail.

[Now go on to Section 2 starting on *Page thirteen*]

SECTION 1 — SCOTTISH — 20 marks

Part E — The Impact of the Great War, 1914–1928

Study the sources below and attempt the questions which follow.

Source A: from the diary of Private Thomas McCall, Cameron Highlanders describing the attack at Loos, September, 1915.

> The soldier lying next to me gave a shout, saying, "My God! I'm done for". His mate next to him asked where he was shot. He drew himself back and lifted his wounded pal's kilt, then gave a laugh, saying, "Jock, ye'll no die. Yer only shot through the fleshy part of the leg!" We moved on towards the village of Loos, where machine guns were raking the streets and bayonet-fighting was going on with Jerry (slang for Germans). Prisoners were being marshalled in batches to be sent under guard down the line. I came to a little restaurant. By the noise going on inside I thought they were killing pigs. I went inside and opened a door where blood was running out from underneath. I saw some Highlanders busy, having it out with Jerry with the bayonet.

Source B: from Nicholas Morgan, *In War's Wake*, (1984).

> During the four years of the war, recruitment to the armed forces from Scotland came to nearly a quarter of the adult male population, a higher percentage than any other country in the UK. Scottish forces suffered disproportionately higher losses than their English counterparts. Wartime, in particular, revolutionised the position of women in the economy, but women's war-work, whether unskilled tasks such as shell-filling or the more skilled jobs, was intended to be temporary. In 1918 women demonstrated in Glasgow, protesting against their enforced removal from the workplace. The slaughter remained to haunt a nation. Grey granite war memorials sprang up in cities, towns and especially villages throughout the country, where lists of names often paid testimony to rural communities that were never to recapture the strength of their pre-war years.

Source C: from Trevor Royle, *The Flowers of the Forest: Scotland and the First World War* (2006).

> The Clyde in 1913 launched 750,000 tons of shipping but by the end of the 1920s the Clyde was launching merely 56,000 tons of shipping, and 69 per cent of insured workers in the Scottish shipbuilding trade were unemployed. In 1913, Scotland employed 140,000 miners but 20 years later the coal industry was finding work for only 80,000 hands and producing a third less coal. In 1913 Scottish unemployment was well below 10% but in the 1920s it never fell below 10%. The Dundee jute trade was deeply depressed and in the late 1920s the value of Scottish farming was falling while it was still rising in England, and in the fishing industry the numbers of those employed and the value of the catch were both steadily dropping.

SECTION 1 — SCOTTISH (continued)

Source D: from Edwin Muir, *Scottish Journey* (1935)

> By 1928 the story in Scotland was one of general economic decline. Between 1921 and 1923 shipbuilding on the Clyde dropped from 500,000 tons to 170,000 mainly as a result of cancellations. Coal production suffered as a result of falling international markets, especially in Eastern Europe and the same fate for the same reason hit the fishing industry. Jute production in Dundee was adversely affected by declining orders, shrinking markets and worker's strikes. In 1921 a census carried out by the Board of Agriculture showed the number of male farm workers had fallen a great deal. According to the Board's findings the decline was not restricted to any particular part of the country but was widespread throughout Scotland. Soon machine age farming would change the face of farming forever.

Attempt all of the following questions.

13. How fully does **Source B** describe the impact of war on Scottish society?   **9**

    Use the source and recalled knowledge.

14. Evaluate the usefulness of **Source A** as evidence of the experience of Scots on the Western Front.   **6**

    In reaching a conclusion you should refer to:
    - *the origin and possible purpose of the source;*
    - *the content of the source;*
    - *recalled knowledge.*

15. Compare the views of **Sources C** and **D** about the economic effect of the war on Scotland.   **5**

    Compare the content overall and in detail.

[Now go on to Section 2 starting on *Page thirteen*]

MARKS

SECTION 2 — BRITISH — 20 marks

Part A — Church, State and Feudal Society, 1066–1406

16. *The nobility received all of the benefits from the feudal structure while the peasants received none.*
   How valid is this view of medieval society?   **20**

17. To what extent did David I increase the centralisation of royal power during his reign?   **20**

18. How successfully did King John of England increase royal authority during his reign?   **20**

Part B — The Century of Revolutions, 1603–1702

19. *Religion was the most important cause of the challenge to the authority of King James I in England.*
   How valid is this view?   **20**

20. To what extent did religious issues bring about the English Civil War?   **20**

21. How important were the actions of James II in causing the Revolution of 1688–1689?   **20**

Part C — The Atlantic Slave Trade

22. To what extent were Britain's military victories in the wars of the eighteenth century the main reason for the development of the Atlantic Slave Trade?   **20**

23. *Fear of slave resistance and revolt determined how slaves were treated.*
   How valid is this view?   **20**

24. To what extent was hostile propaganda the major obstacle to the abolition of the slave trade?   **20**

SECTION 2 — BRITISH (continued)

Part D — Britain, 1851–1951

25. How important was the role of pressure groups in Britain becoming more democratic between 1851 and 1928?

20

26. *Changing attitudes in British society towards women was the major reason why some women received the vote in 1918.*
How valid is this view?

20

27. To what extent did the Liberal's social reforms from 1906 to 1914 fail to deal with the real problems facing the British people?

20

Part E — Britain and Ireland, 1900–1985

28. *The response of Unionists to the Home Rule Bill was the main reason for the growth of tension in Ireland up to 1914.*
How valid is this view?

20

29. How important was British conduct during the Anglo-Irish War in preventing a peace settlement in Ireland between 1918 and 1921?

20

30. How important were political differences between the Protestant and Catholic communities in contributing to the developing crisis in Northern Ireland up to 1968?

20

[Now go on to Section 3 starting on *Page fifteen*]

MARKS

SECTION 3 — EUROPEAN AND WORLD — 20 marks

Part A — The Crusades, 1071–1204

31. *The Pope's desire to channel the military power of the knightly class was the main reason for calling the First Crusade.*
How valid is this view?   20

32. *The success of the Crusaders was due to divisions amongst the Muslim states.*
How valid is this view of the First Crusade?   20

33. To what extent can it be argued that Richard I was a greater military leader than Saladin?   20

Part B — The American Revolution, 1763–1787

34. To what extent was disagreement over the frontier the key issue between Britain and the colonies by 1763?   20

35. To what extent were the views of Edmund Burke typical of British opinion towards the conflict with the American colonists in the period between 1763 and 1781?   20

36. How important was French intervention to colonial victory in the American War of Independence?   20

Part C — The French Revolution, to 1799

37. To what extent did the Third Estate have the greatest cause for complaint under the Ancien Regime?   20

38. To what extent was Louis XVI responsible for the failure of constitutional monarchy in 1792?   20

39. *The constitution of 1795 was the main reason for Napoleon's coup of 1799.*
How valid is this view?   20

SECTION 3 — EUROPEAN AND WORLD (continued)

Part D — Germany, 1815–1939

40. How important were cultural factors in the growth of national feeling in Germany between 1815 and 1850?   **20**

41. To what extent was resentment towards Prussia among the German states the main obstacle to German unification by 1850?   **20**

42. How important were economic factors in the rise to power of the Nazi Party between 1920 and 1933?   **20**

Part E — Italy, 1815–1939

43. How important was the role of Mazzini in the growth of Italian nationalism between 1815 and 1850?   **20**

44. How important was the influence of Austria in preventing the unification of Italy between 1815 and 1850?   **20**

45. To what extent did Mussolini achieve power by 1925 as a result of the weaknesses of Italian governments?   **20**

Part F — Russia, 1881–1921

46. *The Tsar had a secure grip on power in the years before 1905.*
How valid is that view?   **20**

47. To what extent was the power of the Tsarist state weakened in the years between 1905 and 1914?   **20**

48. How important was Bolshevik propaganda in the success of the 1917 October revolution?   **20**

MARKS

SECTION 3 — EUROPEAN AND WORLD (continued)

Part G — USA, 1918–1968

49. To what extent was racism the main reason for changing attitudes towards immigration after 1918?   20

50. *The weakness of the US banking system was the main reason for causing the Great Depression of the 1930s.*
How valid is this view?   20

51. How important was the emergence of effective organisations to the development of the Civil Rights campaigns after 1945?   20

Part H — Appeasement and the Road to War, to 1939

52. To what extent does disappointment over the terms of the Peace Settlements of 1919 explain the aggressive nature of fascist foreign policies in the 1930s?   20

53. To what extent does British public opinion explain the policy of appeasement between 1936 and 1938?   20

54. *Munich was a triumph for British foreign policy.*
How valid is this view?   20

Part I — The Cold War, 1945–1989

55. How important were ideological differences between east and west in the emergence of the Cold War up to 1955?   20

56. *The Cuban Crisis of 1962 was a direct consequence of the domestic pressures on Khrushchev.*
How valid is this view?   20

57. How important was the danger of Mutually Assured Destruction in forcing the superpowers into attempts to manage the Cold War?   20

[END OF MODEL PAPER]

Model Paper 2

Whilst this Model Paper has been specially commissioned by Hodder Gibson for use as practice for the Higher (for Curriculum for Excellence) exams, the key reference documents remain the SQA Specimen Paper 2014 and SQA Past Paper 2015.

HODDER
GIBSON
LEARN MORE

National Qualifications
MODEL PAPER 2

History

Duration — 2 hours and 20 minutes

Total marks — 60

SECTION 1 — SCOTTISH — 20 marks

Attempt ONE Part

SECTION 2 — BRITISH — 20 marks

Attempt ONE question from the Part you have chosen

SECTION 3 — EUROPEAN AND WORLD — 20 marks

Attempt ONE question from the Part you have chosen

Write your answers clearly in the answer booklet provided. In the answer booklet you must clearly identify the question number you are attempting.

Use **blue** or **black** ink.

Before leaving the examination room you must give your answer booklet to the Invigilator; if you do not you may lose all the marks for this paper.

SECTION 1 — SCOTTISH

Attempt ONE Part

PARTS

A.   The Wars of Independence, 1249–1328   Page 3

B.   The Age of the Reformation, 1542–1603   Page 5

C.   The Treaty of Union, 1689–1740   Page 7

D.   Migration and Empire, 1830–1939   Page 9

E.   The Impact of the Great War, 1914–1928   Page 11

SECTION 2 — BRITISH

Attempt one question from the Part you have chosen

PARTS

A.   Church, State and Feudal Society, 1066–1406   Page 13

B.   The Century of Revolutions, 1603–1702   Page 13

C.   The Atlantic Slave Trade   Page 13

D.   Britain, 1851–1951   Page 14

E.   Britain and Ireland, 1900–1985   Page 14

SECTION 3 — EUROPEAN AND WORLD

Attempt one question from the Part you have chosen

PARTS

A.   The Crusades, 1071–1204   Page 15

B.   The American Revolution, 1763–1787   Page 15

C.   The French Revolution, to 1799   Page 15

D.   Germany, 1815–1939   Page 16

E.   Italy, 1815–1939   Page 16

F.   Russia, 1881–1921   Page 16

G.   USA, 1918–1968   Page 17

H.   Appeasement and the Road to War, to 1939   Page 17

I.   The Cold War, 1945–1989   Page 17

SECTION 1 — SCOTTISH — 20 marks

Part A — The Wars of Independence, 1249–1328

Study the sources below and attempt the questions which follow.

Source A: from the Treaty of Birgham (1290).

> Having considered the peace of both kingdoms, we have granted in the name of our lord (Edward I) that the rights and liberties of Scotland shall be preserved. We promise that the kingdom of Scotland shall remain separate and divided from the kingdom of England and that it shall be free and independent. We grant that no tenant in chief of the king of Scotland shall be forced to go outside the kingdom to do homage or fealty. No parliament shall be held out with the kingdom and borders of Scotland on matters concerning that kingdom. No one of the kingdom of Scotland shall be held to answer out with that kingdom for any agreement entered into, or for any crime committed, or in any other cause contrary to the laws and customs of that kingdom.

Source B: from GWS Barrow, *Robert Bruce* (1988).

> The whole course of the negotiations which culminated in the Treaty of Birgham, shows the guardians above all anxious to do nothing that might impair the 'rights' or the integrity of Scotland. The Treaty of Birgham was the high-water-mark of the endeavour by the Guardians and the community. The treaty envisaged two feudal kingdoms, England and Scotland ruled separately though in harmony by a king and queen. The Scottish kingdom was to remain, as the Scots had demanded, free and without subjugation. Elections to the clergy in Scotland were to be free of external interference and tenants in chief of the Scots Crown need do homage for their lands in Scotland only, persons in Scotland who had been accused of a crime or sued at law should not have to answer in a court outside their country.

Source C: from the Chronicle of Walter of Guisborough, 1296.

> All that day and the next our king was expecting the burgesses of Berwick to come to his peace but they would not accept the peace which he offered. Twenty-four English warships attacked Berwick but were driven back. When these things were told to our king he ordered them to sound the bugles and enter the city. When the city was taken they killed more than 8,000 of the enemy. On the same day the men of strength who were in the castle garrison surrendered. The king kept their captain Lord William Douglas until the end of the war. He allowed two hundred men who were with him to go free carrying their arms having first taken an oath from them that they would never lift a hand against him or the kingdom of the English.

Page three

SECTION 1 — SCOTTISH (continued)

Source D: from Richard Oram, *The Kings and Queens of Scotland* (2006).

> After Bannockburn, Robert overcame his remaining Scottish opponents and took their lands. This gave him extensive resources with which to reward his supporters and subjects in order to secure their loyalty. Robert also intensified his attacks on northern England both in search for cash and to force Edward II to recognise Bruce's kingship of a free Scotland. By 1323 Bruce attempted to secure peace for Scotland, even negotiating a peace with Edward II's lieutenants in northern England. Yet faced with the English King's refusal to give up Scotland, Robert had to settle for a long uneasy truce in 1323. Robert worked hard to ensure a relatively stable inheritance for his son. A new mutual defence agreed with France in 1326 was part of this, but a full peace, between England and an independent Scotland was still his ultimate goal.

Attempt all of the following questions.

1. How fully does **Source D** explain the reasons for the ultimate success of Bruce in maintaining Scotland's independence?

   Use the source and recalled knowledge.

   9

2. Evaluate the usefulness of **Source C** as evidence of the relationship between John Balliol and Edward I.

   In reaching a conclusion you should refer to:
   - *the origin and possible purpose of the source;*
   - *the content of the source;*
   - *recalled knowledge*

   6

3. Compare the views of **Sources A** and **B** about the Scots attempts to protect their independence through the Treaty of Birgham.

   Compare the content overall and in detail.

   5

[Now go on to Section 2 starting on *Page thirteen*]

SECTION 1 — SCOTTISH — 20 marks

Part B — The Age of the Reformation, 1542–1603

Study the sources below and attempt the questions which follow.

Source A: from *The Treaty of Edinburgh*, 1560.

> At Edinburgh on 6 July 1560 the following terms are agreed between France and England. All military forces of each party shall withdraw from the realm of Scotland, and all warlike operations in England, Ireland and Wales shall cease. And since the realms of England and Ireland belong by right to Queen Elizabeth, no other is allowed to be named king or queen of England or Ireland. It is therefore agreed that the most Christian King Francis and Queen Mary shall abstain from using or carrying the title or arms of the kingdom of England or Ireland. And King Francis and Queen Mary will fulfil all those things which were granted by their representatives to the nobility and people of Scotland provided that the nobility and people of Scotland fulfil and observe what was contained in those conventions and articles.

Source B: from Rosalind K Marshall, *John Knox* (2000).

> Mary of Guise died shortly after midnight on 11 June 1560. Elizabeth I had already sent William Cecil to Newcastle to negotiate with French envoys and he now moved to Edinburgh. A truce was arranged between England and France and the Treaty of Edinburgh was signed on 6 July. The principal clause stated that all foreign soldiers were to withdraw from Scotland. Francis II and Mary, Queen of Scots, would abstain from displaying the English arms with those of Scotland. Since the Scots had spontaneously and freely professed and acknowledged their obedience and loyalty towards their most Christian king and queen, Francis and Mary would fulfil all their obligations in the treaty. Everything relating to religion would be referred to the Scots Parliament, and after the treaty had been signed John Knox held a service of thanksgiving in St Giles.

Source C: from Sir James Melville, *The Murder of Riccio, 9 March 1566*.

> David Riccio obtained the position of secretary to Mary, and got her Majesty's attention, which caused him to be so envied and hated that some of the nobility would ignore him. The King, Darnley, probably gave his consent too easily to the slaughter of seigneur Riccio, which the Lords of Morton, Ruthven, Lindsay and others had devised, so that they could be masters of the court and hold the parliament. When the murderers entered, seigneur Riccio clutched the Queen and cried for mercy; but George Douglas drew out the King's dagger and struck him with it. He gave screams and cries and was roughly removed from the Queen, who could not get him safe, neither by threat or entreaty. He was forcibly dragged out of the room, and slain and her Majesty was kept captive.

SECTION 1 — SCOTTISH (continued)

Source D: from Ian B. Cowan, *The Scottish Reformation* (1982).

> The way the partnership between Kirk and society worked in post-Reformation Scotland was different from the pre-Reformation era. In some respects the role of the church in society had been greatly reduced because secular forces undertook duties that had previously been the preserve of the Catholic Church. The right of a congregation to choose its own minister was asserted in the Second Book of Discipline. The place of music in the services of the Kirk and in the life of the people was to suffer as a result of the Reformation. The character of the Kirk was established in the immediate post-Reformation era when circumstances forced the victorious reformers to adopt a compassionate attitude towards the representatives of the old faith. In this respect the Scottish Reformation was to produce little of the intolerance that characterised the Reformation in England.

Attempt all of the following questions.

4. How fully does **Source D** explain the impact of the Reformation on Scotland?

   Use the source and recalled knowledge.

   9

5. Evaluate the usefulness of **Source C** as evidence of Mary's difficulties in ruling Scotland.

   In reaching a conclusion you should refer to:
   - *the origin and possible purpose of the source;*
   - *the content of the source;*
   - *recalled knowledge*

   6

6. Compare the views of **Sources A** and **B** about the changes brought in by the Treaty of Edinburgh in 1560.

   Compare the content overall and in detail.

   5

[Now go on to Section 2 starting on *Page thirteen*]

SECTION 1 — SCOTTISH — 20 marks

Part C — The Treaty of Union, 1689–1740

Study the sources below and attempt the questions which follow:

Source A: from Christopher A. Whatley, *The Scots and the Union* (2006).

> In the 1690s Scotland was tipped over the edge of an economic abyss that was to have profound political consequences for the nation's history. Factors included a series of harvest failures and the effects of England's war with Scotland's ally France, particularly the damaging loss of French trade. The erection of protective tariffs by countries overseas blocked the export of certain Scottish goods. Finally, there was the disaster of Darien, Scotland's ambitious scheme to establish a colony in South America. As it happened, the outcome – eventually – was incorporating union with England, but the decade of crisis might equally have produced a very different result.

Source B: from Daniel Defoe, *History of the Union* (1709).

> Since the Union of the Crowns in 1603, and in a hundred years of joint monarchy with England, the Scots had been very sensitive to the sinking economic condition of their nation. They were aware of the damage both to trade and to the wealth of the inhabitants of the country. This was plainly owing to the loss of Scottish ministers' presence at Court in London, the disadvantages of tariffs and the influence the English had over their Kings. It was just as plain that one way for the Scots to restore themselves was in terms of incorporating union and alliance with England. There would be advantages for Scottish commerce of free access to English and empire markets. Without incorporating union, the Scottish economy would remain unstable. It was either union, or a return back to their separate self-existing state.

Source C: is from a petition from Stirling Town Council to the Scottish parliament, 18 November 1706.

> We have considered the Union of Scotland and England as contained in the articles of the treaty. We desire true and continued peace and friendship with our neighbours in England. However, we judge it our duty to the nation and parliament to state that this treaty will prove ruinous to our manufacturing industry, since the new freedom of trade will never balance the new insupportable burden of taxation. The treaty will deprive us, and the rest of the royal burghs in this nation, of our fundamental right of being represented in the legislative power. Thus, an ancient nation, so long and gloriously defended by patriots, will be suppressed as our dear parliament is extinguished and we are brought under a burden which we will never be able to bear, with fatal consequences which we tremble to think about.

SECTION 1 — SCOTTISH (continued)

Source D: is from Paul Henderson Scott, *The Union of 1707* (2006).

> One irony of the Union is that it did not in the end extinguish Scotland as a nation; it retained its own distinctive identity, attitudes and ideas, and its traditions were so strong that they were not easily eradicated. The consequences of the Treaty in this respect were not as harmful as they might have been, although it did exert a strong Anglicising influence. Nevertheless, the guarantees to the Scottish legal system in the Treaty and to the Church in the Act of Security for the Kirk had more influence on Scotland than the distant British Parliament. English and Scottish historians have concluded that the continuation of the Scottish systems of education and local government were a significant achievement of Union.

Attempt all of the following questions.

7. How fully does **Source D** explain the effects of the Union up to 1740?   9

   Use the source and recalled knowledge.

8. Evaluate the usefulness of **Source C** as evidence of attitudes towards the union in Scotland.   6

   In reaching a conclusion you should refer to:
   * *the origin and possible purpose of the source;*
   * *the content of the source;*
   * *recalled knowledge*

9. Compare the view s of **Sources A** and **B** about worsening relations between Scotland and England between 1690 and 1705.   5

   Compare the content overall and in detail.

[Now go on to Section 2 starting on *Page thirteen*]

SECTION 1 — SCOTTISH — 20 marks

Part D — Migration and Empire, 1830—1939

Study the sources below and attempt the questions which follow.

Source A: from the Quarterly Journal of Agriculture 1832–34.

> I have not the slightest hesitation in declaring, that it appears to me as plain as the sun at noonday, that a farmer in Scotland, occupying a farm that does not pay him, distressed as he must be, struggling from morning to night with mental anxiety and worry pressing upon his mind and yet after all quite unable to support his family or better their circumstances - I say that a farmer continuing to remain in Scotland even when unemployed while so much land lies in Canada to occupy acts the part of an insane person. In a short time there will be no cheap land to be procured about these parts. The best way for my brothers to lay out their money here is in buying land which is every year rising in value.

Source B: from the *Scotsman*, 20 Feb 1923, 'Emigration boom in the Hebrides'.

> Great interest is being taken in the scheme of the Ontario government to emigrate young men and women between 18 and 23 to Canada. The Ontario agent finds that he could treble the number he is authorised to enlist owing no doubt to the depressed state of trade in Lewis, the lack of employment generally and the inability of the farmers to satisfy the hunger of the families. Immediately on landing employment will be found for farmers and the women can find employment in domestic work. The pay is good as experienced men can at the very start earn £5 to £6 per month. The men also have the prospect of becoming owners of their own farms once again.

Source C: adapted from *New Arrivals* by Tony Jaconelli in *Our Glasgow Story*.

> My family left our warm village in Italy in 1921 to work in some place called Scotland. School was a nightmare for me but my brother Giacomo, a name quickly shortened to Jack, enjoyed school life. He was a quick learner and always able to take care of himself. A few times I found myself surrounded by classmates chanting at me because I was a foreigner. Jack scattered them and they stopped bothering me completely. Our family moved a couple of times in an effort to improve our lot. Domenico took a job in the largely Italian trade of terrazzo tile workers and most of my brothers followed him into the trade. Meanwhile, I eventually lost all trace of my mother tongue and developed a strong Glasgow accent. In no time at all I was a complete Glaswegian.

SECTION 1 — SCOTTISH (continued)

Source D: from ed. T.M. Devine, *Irish Immigrants and Scottish Society in the Nineteenth and Twentieth Centuries* (1991).

> The immigration of the Irish into Scotland changed the population balance of several lowland towns, especially Glasgow, Greenock, Dundee, Paisley and Airdrie. Scotland's industrialisation was made easier because employers had access to a huge reservoir of Irish labour which was not only cheap, but was willing to move anywhere and do anything to find work. The huge construction schemes of the nineteenth-century cities and the roads, railways, docks and harbours that supported Scotland's industrial revolution depended on this vast labour supply. However, the Irish were seen by many Scots as a threat to the Scottish way of life. The Irish presence is also vital to an understanding of Scottish culture as the Catholic Irish and their descendants have played such an influential role in the evolution and shaping of Scottish society ranging from literature to music and on to football.

Attempt all of the following questions.

10. How fully does **Source D** explain the effects of migration and Empire on Scottish society?

    Use the source and recalled knowledge.

    9

11. Evaluate the usefulness of **Source C** as evidence of the assimilation of immigrants into Scottish society.

    In reaching a conclusion you should refer to:
    - *the origin and possible purpose of the source;*
    - *the content of the source;*
    - *recalled knowledge*

    6

12. Compare the views of **Sources A** and **B** about the reasons for Scottish migration to Canada.

    Compare the content overall and in detail.

    5

[Now go on to Section 2 starting on *Page thirteen*]

SECTION 1 — SCOTTISH — 20 marks

Part E — The Impact of the Great War, 1914–1928

Study the sources below and attempt the questions which follow.

Source A: by John Jackson, *Private 12768: Memoir of a Tommy* (2004) writing about the Battle of Loos.

> The situation at Hill 70 was serious. A third time the order was given to attack that awful hillside, but the enemy were too many for us and again we fell back, truly we were holding to the motto of the regiment 'A Cameron never can yield'. As the evening drew on we made a fourth and final attempt to win and hold the ridge. This time we meant to do or die. To the sound of the pipes and led by our brave old colonel, bareheaded and with no other weapon than his walking stick, we made for the top of Hill 70 through murderous rifle and machine gun fire, while shells crashed all around us. We made the top but now we were desperate for the promised reinforcements but no help could we see.

Source B: by Philip Gibbs, official British wartime correspondent on the Western Front for the *Daily Chronicle,* writing about the Battle of Loos.

> By seven-forty the two assaulting brigades of the 15th Division had left the trenches and were in the open. Shriller than the scream of shells above them was the skirl of pipes, going with them. The orders of the Scottish troops, were to go "all out," and to press onto Hill 70. With the promise of reinforcements to follow, they trudged on to Hill 70. For a time there was a kind of Bank Holiday crowd on Hill 70. The German machine gunners, knowing that the redoubt on the crest was still held by their men, initially dared not fire. Then the quietude of Hill 70 was broken by a new bombardment from German guns. "Dig in," said the officers. "We must hold on at all costs until the reinforcements come up." None came and they were forced to withdraw.

Source C: from *The Glasgow Herald* 29th October 1915

> The first attempt to put into force the eviction notices which have been issued against Glasgow tenants who are participating in the 'Rent Strikes' was made yesterday afternoon in Merryland Street, Govan. As has been the custom since the beginning of the movement against increased rents, a demonstration of the 'strikers' was held at the time when the eviction notice became operative. While Mrs Barbour of the Glasgow Women's Housing Association, was addressing those who had assembled, two sheriff officers arrived and endeavoured to gain admission to the house. As soon as it was known that it was proposed to evict the tenant the demonstrators determined to resist. Most of them were women, and they attacked the officers and their assistants with peasmeal, flour, and whiting. A woman was arrested on a charge of assaulting one of the officers.

SECTION 1 — SCOTTISH (continued)

Source D: from W. Hamish Fraser, *Scottish Popular Politics From Radicalism to Labour* (2000).

> The war years also showed that support for Scottish home rule had not really abated. The policy of the STUC was to call on the Parliamentary Labour Party to support 'the enactment of a Scottish Home Rule Bill'. The same spirit of nationalism forced Arthur Henderson and the Labour leadership in London, much against their better judgement, to concede a separate Scottish Council of Labour with a considerable amount of autonomy. At the same time, the war undermined even further the organisation of Scottish Liberalism, but also much of its moral authority. The more radical elements were disenchanted by Lloyd George's political tactics and by his gung-ho determination to accept nothing less than unconditional surrender. Liberalism was thrown into disarray while the ILP was able to emerge as the natural successor to advanced liberal radicalism.

Attempt all of the following questions.

13. How fully does **Source D** describe the impact of the war on political developments in Scotland?

    Use the source and recalled knowledge.

    9

14. Evaluate the usefulness of **Source C** as evidence of the impact of the war on Scottish women.

    In reaching a conclusion you should refer to:
    - *the origin and possible purpose of the source;*
    - *the content of the source*
    - *recalled knowledge.*

    6

15. Compare the views of **Sources A and B** about the experience of Scots on the Western Front.

    Compare the content overall and in detail.

    5

    20

[Now go on to Section 2 starting on *Page thirteen*]

MARKS

SECTION 2 — BRITISH — 20 marks

Part A — Church, State and Feudal Society, 1066–1406

16. To what extent was the role of the Church in medieval Scotland and England confined to religion?

20

17. How successful was King John in his attempts to increase royal authority?

20

18. How important was the growth of towns in causing the decline of feudal society?

20

Part B — The Century of Revolutions, 1603–1702

19. To what extent were Charles I's policies in Scotland between 1625 and 1642 effective?

20

20. How important were religious issues in causing the Revolution of 1688–89?

20

21. *Financial reform was the most significant change brought about by the Revolution Settlement.*
     How valid is this view?

20

Part C — The Atlantic Slave Trade

22. To what extent was the slave trade the major factor in the development of the British economy in the eighteenth century?

20

23. *The slave trade was too important to the British economy to allow it to be abolished.*
     How valid is this view?

20

24. How important was the campaign organised by the Anti-Slavery Society in bringing about the abolition of the slave trade?

20

MARKS

SECTION 2 — BRITISH (continued)

Part D — Britain, 1851–1951

25. *Britain was still far from being a democratic country by 1928.*
    How valid is this view?   20

26. To what extent did the Liberal reforms of 1906 to 1914 make a significant
    improvement to the lives of the British people?   20

27. *The Labour government of 1945 to 1951 met the needs of the people 'from the
    cradle to the grave'.*
    How valid is this view?   20

Part E — Britain and Ireland, 1900–1985

28. To what extent did World War One change political attitudes towards British rule in
    Ireland?   20

29. How important were economic issues in contributing to the developing crisis in
    Northern Ireland up to 1968?   20

30. How important were the religious and communal differences between both
    communities in preventing peace in Ireland between 1968 and 1985?   20

[Now go on to Section 3 starting on *Page fifteen*]

MARKS

SECTION 3 — EUROPEAN AND WORLD — 20 marks

Part A — The Crusades, 1071–1204

31. How important were religious factors in the decision of Europeans to go on crusade?   **20**

32. *While Richard was a greater military leader, Saladin was a better diplomat.*
How valid is this view?   **20**

33. To what extent had the crusading ideal declined by the Fourth Crusade in 1204?   **20**

Part B — The American Revolution, 1763–1787

34. How important was the rejection of the Olive Branch petition in the colonists' declaration of independence in 1776?   **20**

35. How important was the colonists' advantage of fighting on home ground in their eventual victory in the American Revolution?   **20**

36. To what extent was the American Constitution of 1787 an answer to the problems highlighted by the experience of British rule?   **20**

Part C — The French Revolution, to 1799

37. To what extent did revolution break out in France in 1789 as a result of the economic crisis of 1788–9?   **20**

38. To what extent did the increasing intervention of the army in politics bring about Napoleon's coup of 1799, which created the Consulate?   **20**

39. *The Bourgeoisie gained most from the French Revolution.*
How valid is this view?   **20**

MARKS

SECTION 3 — EUROPEAN AND WORLD (continued)

Part D — Germany, 1815–1939

40. To what extent had nationalism grown in Germany by 1850?   20

41. To what extent were the weaknesses of the Weimar Republic the major reason for the rise of the Nazi Party between 1920 and 1933?   20

42. *Through their economic policies the Nazis gave the people what they wanted.* How valid is this as a reason for the Nazis maintaining power between 1933 and 1939?   20

Part E — Italy, 1815–1939

43. To what extent had nationalism grown in Italy by 1850?   20

44. How important was the appeal of fascism in Mussolini's achievement of power in Italy by 1925?   20

45. How important was the use of fear and intimidation in maintaining Fascist control over Italy between 1922 and 1939?   20

Part F — Russia, 1881–1921

46. How important was working class discontent in causing the 1905 revolution in Russia?   20

47. To what extent did the Bolsheviks gain power due to the weaknesses of the Provisional Government?   20

48. How important was the use of terror by the Reds in allowing them to win the Civil War?   20

MARKS

SECTION 3 — EUROPEAN AND WORLD (continued)

Part G — USA, 1918–1968

49. How important were the activities of the Ku Klux Klan as an obstacle to the achievement of civil rights for black people before 1941?   20

50. How important was the emergence of effective black leaders in the growing demand for Civil Rights between 1945 and 1968?   20

51. To what extent did the Civil Rights campaigns of the 1950s and 1960s result in significant improvements in the lives of black Americans?   20

Part H — Appeasement and the Road to War, to 1939

52. To what extent did fascist powers use diplomacy to achieve their aims?   20

53. *The Munich agreement of 1938 was a reasonable settlement under the circumstances.* How valid is this view?   20

54. To what extent did the occupation of Czechoslovakia in March 1939 lead to the outbreak of World War Two six months later?   20

Part I — The Cold War, 1945–1989

55. To what extent did the Soviet Union control Eastern Europe up to 1961?   20

56. To what extent were the superpowers' attempts to manage the Cold War between 1962 and 1985 prompted by the economic cost of the arms race?   20

57. How important was the role of Gorbachev in ending the Cold War?   20

[END OF MODEL PAPER]

Model Paper 3

Whilst this Model Paper has been specially commissioned by Hodder Gibson for use as practice for the Higher (for Curriculum for Excellence) exams, the key reference documents remain the SQA Specimen Paper 2014 and SQA Past Paper 2015.

HODDER GIBSON
LEARN MORE

National
Qualifications
MODEL PAPER 3

History

Duration — 2 hours and 20 minutes

Total marks — 60

SECTION 1 — SCOTTISH — 20 marks

Attempt ONE Part

SECTION 2 — BRITISH — 20 marks

Attempt ONE question from the Part you have chosen

SECTION 3 — EUROPEAN AND WORLD — 20 marks

Attempt ONE question from the Part you have chosen

Write your answers clearly in the answer booklet provided. In the answer booklet you must clearly identify the question number you are attempting.

Use **blue** or **black** ink.

Before leaving the examination room you must give your answer booklet to the Invigilator; if you do not you may lose all the marks for this paper.

SECTION 1 — SCOTTISH

Attempt ONE Part

PARTS

A. The Wars of Independence, 1249—1328   Page 3

B. The Age of the Reformation, 1542—1603   Page 5

C. The Treaty of Union, 1689—1740   Page 7

D. Migration and Empire, 1830—1939   Page 9

E. The Impact of the Great War, 1914—1928   Page 11

SECTION 2 — BRITISH

Attempt one question from the Part you have chosen

PARTS

A. Church, State and Feudal Society, 1066—1406   Page 13

B. The Century of Revolutions, 1603—1702   Page 13

C. The Atlantic Slave Trade   Page 13

D. Britain, 1851—1951   Page 14

E. Britain and Ireland, 1900—1985   Page 14

SECTION 3 — EUROPEAN AND WORLD

Attempt one question from the Part you have chosen

PARTS

A. The Crusades, 1071—1204   Page 15

B. The American Revolution, 1763—1787   Page 15

C. The French Revolution, to 1799   Page 15

D. Germany, 1815—1939   Page 16

E. Italy, 1815—1939   Page 16

F. Russia, 1881—1921   Page 16

G. USA, 1918—1968   Page 17

H. Appeasement and the Road to War, to 1939   Page 17

I. The Cold War, 1945—1989   Page 17

SECTION 1 — SCOTTISH — 20 marks

Part A — The Wars of Independence, 1249–1328

Study the sources below and attempt the questions which follow.

Source A: from Alan Young, *Robert the Bruce's Rivals: The Comyns, 1212–1314* (1997).

> Behind the legal arguments, there were clearly intense political manoeuvrings. The Comyn family used all their power and influence as the dominant political group to support the candidature of their relative, John Balliol. Balliol's success would both maintain and even increase Comyn power. This must be set beside the ambitions of the Bruce family who were determined to stake their claim to power and were prepared to take advantage of every opportunity that came along in order to turn this claim into reality. Even before the Maid's death in September 1290 Bruce had tried to increase his territorial power in the north. In the winter of 1290–1291, Bruce had also presented himself as the rightful heir. During the "Great Cause" he put forward a case that he was the recognised successor of Alexander II.

Source B: from The Chronicle of John of Fordun, 1350.

> In March 1296, the King of England, being strongly stirred up, marched in person, with a large force, on Scotland. Upon the town of Berwick, sparing neither sex nor age, the aforesaid King of England, put to the sword some 7500 souls. On 27 April, in the same year, was fought the battle of Dunbar, where Patrick of Graham and many Scottish nobles fell wounded in defeat, while a great many other knights fled to Dunbar Castle. However, up to 70 of them, including William, Earl of Ross, were betrayed by the warden of the castle and handed over to the King of England, like sheep offered to the slaughter. In this, Balliol's war, all the supporters of Bruce's party were generally considered traitors to their King and country.

Source C: from Michael Penman, *The Scottish Civil War* (2002).

> King John must have feared the danger from within his borders from disappointed Scottish nobles who preferred to side with the English King, this of course included the Bruces. For Edward in early 1296 the campaign to Scotland was carried out from the outset by using the full force of England's experienced army. On 30 March his large army made a swift example of the town of Berwick, slaughtering over 7000 inhabitants. When a small Scottish force attempted to relieve the besieged castle of Dunbar, King John was absent. In the ensuing battle at Dunbar on 27 April the Scots were defeated resoundingly by a small English force led by Surrey. Edward then progressed north unhindered. The Scots leaders soon lost all stomach for the fight.

MARKS

SECTION 1 — SCOTTISH (continued)

Source D: from The Chronicle of Walter of Guisborough, around 1300.

> Meanwhile two friars were sent to the Scots, to see if they wanted to embrace the peace which the English offered. Wallace replied, "Tell your men that we have not come for peace but are ready for the fight, to free our kingdom." There was not a more suitable place to put the English into the hands of the Scots. When the Scots saw that they could win, they came down from the hill. Sending men with pikes, they seized the end of the bridge so that no Englishman could cross or return. Among the English nobles cut down by the Scottish pikemen there fell Lord Hugh de Cressingham. The Scots hated him and cut his hide into little bits for he was a bonny man and pretty fat, and they called him not the King "treasurer" but his "treacherer".

Attempt all of the following questions.

1. How fully does **Source A** illustrate the succession problem in Scotland, 1286–1296?   **9**

    Use the source and your own knowledge.

2. Evaluate the usefulness of **Source D** as evidence of the growth of Scottish resistance to King Edward, 1296–1297.

    In reaching a conclusion you should refer to: **6**
    *   *the origin and possible purpose of the source;*
    *   *the content of the source;*
    *   *recalled knowledge.*

3. Compare the views of **Sources B** and **C** about the subjugation of Scotland by Edward I.   **5**

    Compare the content overall and in detail.

[Now go on to Section 2 starting on *Page thirteen*]

SECTION 1 — SCOTTISH — 20 marks

Part B — The Age of the Reformation, 1542–1603

Study the sources below and attempt the questions which follow.

Source A: from Alec Ryrie, *The Age of Reformation: 1485–1603* (2009).

> In December 1557 the Protestant nobles of the Lords of the Congregation sent Mary of Guise a set of ambitious but not impossible requests. They asked to be allowed to host Protestant sermons on their estates and they also wanted prayers in the vernacular to be used in parish churches. She gave the petitioners what they felt was a fair hearing, and promised to lay the question before the parliament. A settlement seemed possible. However, Knox had returned to Scotland and on 11th May had preached an inflammatory sermon at Perth which triggered a full-scale riot. Guise regarded this as an act of rebellion and the Protestant Lords mobilised to defend themselves. More or less by accident, a religious rebellion had broken out. Guise's mishandling of the situation in 1559 eventually united most of the political nation against her.

Source B: from a letter from Mary, Queen of Scots to the Archbishop of Glasgow, 11 February 1567.

> This last night 9th February, the house in which the King was lodged was in an instant blown in the air, whilst he was lying sleeping in his bed, with such force, that of the whole lodging there is nothing remaining. It must have been done by force of gunpowder and appears to have been a mine. It is not yet known who carried out this deed and in what manner. At any rate, we believe it was intended for us as well as for the King; for we lay the most part of the last week in the same lodging, and were there attended by the lords that were in town that same night at midnight. It was only by chance that we did not stay the night, by reason of some masque in the abbey (of Holyrood).

Source C: from Alison Weir, *Mary, Queen of Scots, and the Murder of Lord Darnley* (2008).

> In the aftermath of Darnley's death there was much speculation as to who was implicated in the murder and how exactly it was carried out. Two people were formally accused of it. These two people were the Earl of Bothwell and the Queen herself. While the Protestant Lords disliked Darnley, they may have seen the murder as an opportunity to rid themselves of Bothwell. The Lords of the Council concluded that the Old Provost's Lodging and the Prebendaries' Chamber had been blown into the air by the force of the powder. However, the whole matter remains a mystery. In addition, from about 4pm until Mary returned to Holyrood around midnight, Bothwell was in attendance on her, and conspicuously dressed in a masquing costume. It is very unlikely that he made himself so visible by walking up and down the Canongate.

SECTION 1 — SCOTTISH (continued)

Source D: from The Second Book of Discipline (1578).

> It is proper for kings and princes to be called lords over their subjects, whom they govern civilly. However, it is proper for Christ alone to be called Lord and Master in the spiritual government of the Kirk. All others who hold positions in the Kirk should not become powerful, and should not be called lords, for they are ministers and servants. Sometimes these men are called pastors, because they feed their congregation; sometimes episcopi or bishops, because they watch over their flock; sometimes ministers, by reason of their service and office; and sometimes they are called elders, because they take care of the spiritual government, which ought to be most dear unto them. It is Christ's proper office to command and rule in his Kirk, through his Spirit and word, by the ministry of men.

Attempt all of the following questions.

4. How fully does **Source A** explain the reasons for the Reformation of 1560?   **9**

   Use the source and recalled knowledge.

5. Evaluate the usefulness of **Source D** as evidence of the efforts of the Kirk to maintain its independence.   **6**

   In reaching a conclusion you should refer to:
   * *the origin and possible purpose of the source;*
   * *the content of the source;*
   * *recalled knowledge.*

6. Compare the views of **Sources B** and **C** about the events which brought Mary's marriage to Darnley to an end.   **5**

   Compare the content overall and in detail.

[Now go on to Section 2 starting on *Page thirteen*]

SECTION 1 — SCOTTISH — 20 marks

Part C — The Treaty of Union, 1689–1740

Study the sources below and attempt the questions which follow.

Source A: from a speech by Andrew Fletcher in the Scottish Parliament, 1703.

> Since the Union of the Crowns, government ministers of England have ruined us by extending great lands and pensions to Scotsmen of the royal court to make them willing instruments of the English. The principal offices in the Scottish government are given to such men whom English ministers know will be submissive to their intentions. We appear to the rest of the world more like a conquered province than a free and independent people. It can be proved that the English court has bribed Scots so that they are now masters of us at our own cost. This is the cause of our poverty, misery and dependence upon England. We have been so long poor, miserable and dependent that we have neither the heart nor the courage to free ourselves.

Source B: from Paul Henderson Scott, *The Union of 1707* (2006).

> As the terms of the treaty became known there was an impressive reaction from all over the country, with a flood of Addresses to parliament. All of those Addresses were strongly opposed to the union and there was none in favour. There had been no previous instance of such a unanimous expression of the views of the people on an important political issue. It showed the strength of national feeling and widespread literacy and awareness of the issues in the union debate. The Addresses protested against the union as "contrary to the honour and independence of the Kingdom". This is especially remarkable at a time when democracy did not exist in any state and when it was widely held that people who were not landowners or Members of Parliament had no right to express views on matters of government policy.

Source C: from Christopher A. Whatley, *The Scots and the Union* (2006).

> Ninety-plus Addresses against the union streamed into parliament over a period of just over eight weeks from the beginning of November. The similarity of much of the language in most of the Addresses suggests they were the result of a campaign by the Country party. Yet what is striking is that the very act of signing the Addresses indicates that the signatories had common concerns. The Addresses spoke in defence of Scotland's honour and independent sovereignty, as embodied in its parliament and the "fundamental laws and constitution of this kingdom". The Addresses reveal not only how widespread public opposition to union was but also much about its nature. Signatures were made on behalf of the illiterate, so we cannot be sure that those represented in the Addresses were fully aware of what was being said about the union on their behalf.

SECTION 1 — SCOTTISH (continued)

Source D: English agent, Daniel Defoe, reporting on the Treaty debates in the Scottish Parliament, 30 December 1706.

> The surprise offer of the Equivalent compensation provided for shareholders of the Company had various effects on Scots people. The Darien investment was a dead weight upon many who had wanted their money returned. The money had been long spent, and generally speaking investors had abandoned themselves to despair and thought it to be lost forever. So entirely had they given up hope of reimbursement, that they would be willing to sell their stock at one tenth of its value once the union was concluded. However, after all this, to find that the whole amount would be returned with interest was a happy surprise to a great many, and took the edge off the opposition which some Scots would otherwise have expressed towards union. In particular, those in the Squadrone Volante will now be persuaded to vote in favour of union.

Attempt all of the following questions.

7. How fully does **Source A** explain the reasons for worsening relations with England after 1690?   9

   Use the source and recalled knowledge.

8. Evaluate the usefulness of **Source D** as evidence of the passage of the Union through the Scottish parliament.   6

   In reaching a conclusion you should refer to:
   * *the origin and possible purpose of the source;*
   * *the content of the source;*
   * *recalled knowledge.*

9. Compare the views of **Sources B** and **C** about attitudes towards union in Scotland.   5

   Compare the content overall and in detail.

[Now go on to Section 2 starting on *Page thirteen*]

SECTION 1 — SCOTTISH — 20 marks

Part D — Migration and Empire, 1830–1939

Study the sources below and attempt the questions which follow.

Source A: from James Hunter, *Glencoe and the Indians* (1996).

> Incessant rain had made it impossible for the population of the west coast to harvest the peat on which they depended for domestic fuel. In this extremity the poor people were, in some places, forced to burn their huts and cottages. In such situations, the crofts to which the mass of Highlanders had been driven as a result of earlier clearances had long since proved incapable of providing adequately for their occupants. Crofting families survived on a diet consisting largely of potatoes. When that crop failed, as it did regularly, hunger became a severe problem. Landlords, practically none of whom now felt any responsibility for the Highlander's fate, simply organised more evictions in order to create still more sheep farms. People thus deprived of their crofts had little alternative but to go elsewhere.

Source B: from *The Ayr Advertiser*, 1849.

> The Irish have been driven by the increasing poverty in their own country to emigrate to Scotland. By their hard work railways have been formed and new and important sources of wealth opened up. However, the Irish, during the past ten years, have absolutely inundated this country. They have also swallowed up our rapidly increasing Poor Rates, have directed charity away from its proper channels, and have filled our jails. By their greatest numbers they have lessened wages or totally deprived thousands of the working people of Scotland of that employment which legitimately belonged to them. Lastly, there can be no doubt that their contact with the Scotch has not been for the benefit morally or intellectually of the latter. Let us redouble our efforts not to keep Scotland for the Scotch, for that is impossible; but to keep Scotland — Scotch!

Source C: adapted from evidence about the poor in Edinburgh contained in the "Report on the State of the Irish Poor in Great Britain", 1836.

> We are of the opinion that evils said to arise from Irish immigration have been considerably magnified. However, the wave of Irish immigration that washes over us each year should be restricted and this principally because the Catholic Irish who invade us are of a class which interferes materially with the wants and needs of the labouring poor, particularly in their dependence on adequate funds within the Poor Rates. In general, our own poor are far superior to the newcomers in point of sober and moral habits. We have no doubt that the work of this parish could be done, and the harvest got in, without the competition from Irish labourers whose presence forces down the wages to be earned from this work.

MARKS

SECTION 1 — SCOTTISH (continued)

Source D: written by David Laing to his sister in Scotland, 19 February, 1873. Laing emigrated from Edinburgh and settled in Canada after he left the army.

> Dear Sister,
> I have read your letter 20 times over since I received it. I am prospering in life now but I am so lonely. The boys are all grown up men and are working on the same railway I do. I was promoted on the first of April, am foreman of a gang of 20 men receiving all the stores and material. We have 86 locomotive engines to keep in repair and 400 miles of rails to keep in good repair so that the produce of this land can reach the ports and then across the world. Our foremen are nearly all Scots and many of the working men also. I fear that without these men there would be no railway, no prosperity and no trade in this part of the world.

Attempt all of the following questions.

10. How fully does **Source A** explain the reasons for the migration of Scots?   9

    Use the source and recalled knowledge.

11. Evaluate the usefulness of **Source D** as evidence of the impact of the contribution of Scots to the economic growth and development of the Empire.   6

    In reaching a conclusion you should refer to:
    • *the origin and possible purpose of the source;*
    • *the content of the source;*
    • *recalled knowledge.*

12. Compare the views of **Sources B** and **C** about the experience of Irish immigrants in Scotland.   5

    Compare the content overall and in detail.

[Now go on to Section 2 starting on *Page thirteen*]

SECTION 1 — SCOTTISH — 20 marks

Part E — The Impact of the Great War, 1914–1928

Study the sources below and attempt the questions which follow.

Source A: A diary entry from Private Moir of the Queen's Own Cameron Highlanders: Loos, September 29, 1915.

> We were relieved on Sunday morning, after holding our own against the Germans' repeated counterattacks, but we were not out an hour when the lot that came in lost one of the trenches that we had taken. On Monday we had another charge and got the trench back before coming out of the trenches yesterday with about 70 or 80 of us surviving, out of the 1100 originals. Sir John French came along just as we were leaving our old billets and he gave us a few words of praise. He told us he never knew the Camerons to fail in anything they had ever put their hands to and that was why he chose Camerons for his bodyguard.

Source B: from William Kenefick, *War Resisters and Anti-Conscription in Scotland: an Independent Labour Party Perspective* (1999).

> Scots responded in great numbers to the call to arms at the outbreak of war in 1914 and by December 1914, 25% of the male labour force of western Scotland had signed up. However it was being reported throughout the press from as early as October that the numbers enlisting were falling slightly and even a slight fall in recruitment meant that the topic of conscription was raised. The Glasgow Herald reported in December 1914 that if voluntarism did not work then conscription was the only alternative. The Daily Record ran similar articles promoting support for conscription. Despite the National Registration Act, recruitment levels fell to around 80,000 per month by January 1916 and conscription became a reality.

Source C: from Trevor Royle, *The Flowers of the Forest* (2007).

> Within a day of the declaration of war, the recruiting office in Edinburgh's Cockburn Street was doing brisk business and, by the end of August 20,000 recruits had been processed. In Glasgow six thousand men enlisted over the very first weekend of war. However, the number of volunteers began to fall off in 1915. There were increasing concerns that compulsory military service would be introduced and anti-conscription rallies had been held in Glasgow since the end of 1915, one meeting being addressed by committed anti-war protestors Sylvia Pankhurst and John MacLean. The National Registration Act of July 1915 required all persons to register for possible service but the national registration scheme was unworkable and recruitment continued to fall and, though long resisted, compulsory service became inevitable resulting in the Military Services Act of 1916.

MARKS

SECTION 1 — SCOTTISH (continued)

Source D: from Following the Fishing accounts of Annie and James Watt who worked with the herring fishing fleets 1914–1920.

> All the years that we worked, up till the end of the First World War, the price we got for a barrel of herring was 4 pence, this money was vital for many families. Thousands of barrels were shipped to Germany, Poland and Russia. Things were never as good with the herring after the war. The price went up to six pence for a time then they took it down to three pence. Costs had risen and the men couldn't pay for the gear, the fuel and the wage. Things were that bad that they couldn't pay us for gutting the herring so we went on strike. One curer we worked for went broke. That was David Buchan. He was one of the richest curers in Peterhead. He'd a big house and everything, but he lost the lot.

Attempt all of the following questions.

13. How fully does **Source A** describe the involvement of Scots on the Western Front? 9

    Use the source and recalled knowledge.

14. Evaluate the usefulness of **Source D** as evidence of the economic difficulties faced by Scotland after 1918. 6

    In reaching a conclusion you should refer to:
    - *the origin and possible purpose of the source;*
    - *the content of the source;*
    - *recalled knowledge.*

15. Compare the views of **Sources B** and **C** about recruitment and conscription in Scotland. 5

    Compare the content overall and in detail.

[Now go on to Section 2 starting on *Page thirteen*]

MARKS

SECTION 2 — BRITISH — 20 marks

Part A — Church, State and Feudal Society, 1066–1406

16. To what extent was the secular church more important than the regular church in the Middle Ages?   20

17. *The need to develop 'Law and Order' was the main factor in the development of centralised monarchy.*
    How valid is this view on the reign of Henry II?   20

18. How important were changing social attitudes in causing the decline of feudal society?   20

Part B — The Century of Revolutions, 1603–1702

19. *The policies of Charles I led to problems ruling Scotland.*
    How valid is this view?   20

20. How important was the role of the Army in the failure to find an alternative form of government between 1649 and 1658?   20

21. How successfully did the Revolution Settlement of 1688–1702 address the key issues between the Crown and Parliament?   20

Part C — The Atlantic Slave Trade

22. How important was the slave trade in the development of the British economy in the eighteenth century?   20

23. *African societies benefited from their involvement in the slave trade.*
    How valid is this view?   20

24. To what extent was the decline in the economic importance of slavery the main reason for the abolition of the slave trade?   20

MARKS

SECTION 2 — BRITISH (continued)

Part D — Britain, 1851–1951

25. To what extent can Britain be described as a fully democratic country by 1918? **20**

26. To what extent did the Liberal government of 1906–1914 introduce social reform due to the social surveys of Booth and Rowntree? **20**

27. *The social reforms of the Labour government of 1945–1951 failed to deal effectively with the needs of the people.*
How valid is this view? **20**

Part E — Britain and Ireland, 1900–1985

28. *The decline of the Nationalist Party was the most significant impact of World War One on Ireland.*
How valid is this view? **20**

29. How important were divisions in the Republican Movement in causing the outbreak of the Irish Civil War? **20**

30. To what extent was the British government policy of Direct Rule the main obstacle to peace in Northern Ireland between 1968 and 1985? **20**

[Now go on to Section 3 starting on *Page fifteen*]

MARKS

SECTION 3 — EUROPEAN AND WORLD — 20 marks

Part A — The Crusades, 1071–1204

31. To what extent was peer pressure the main reason for going on crusade?   20

32. How important were divisions amongst the crusaders in bringing about the fall of Jerusalem in 1187?   20

33. *By the Fourth Crusade in 1204 the Crusading Ideal was dead.*
How valid is this view?   20

Part B — The American Revolution 1763–1787

34. *Disputes over taxation was the main reason for the outbreak of the American colonists' revolt against British rule in 1776.*
How valid is this view?   20

35. *French intervention changed the whole nature of the American War of Independence.*
How valid is this view?   20

36. To what extent did the American Constitution successfully address the issues raised by the experience of rule by Britain?   20

Part C — The French Revolution, to 1799

37. How important was the role of the bourgeoisie in the collapse of royal authority in France by 1789?   20

38. How important was the threat of counter-revolution as a cause of the Terror between 1792 and 1795?   20

39. To what extent did the peasants gain most from the French Revolution by 1799?   20

MARKS

SECTION 3 — EUROPEAN AND WORLD (continued)

Part D — Germany, 1815–1939

40. *By 1850 political nationalism had made little progress in Germany.*
    How valid is this view?   20

41. How important was the attitude of foreign states in the achievement of German unification by 1871?   20

42. *Propaganda was crucial to the maintenance of power by the Nazis between 1933 and 1939.*
    How valid is this view?   20

Part E — Italy, 1815–1939

43. To what extent was the idea of nationalism well established in Italy in the years before 1850?   20

44. To what extent was the unification of Italy by 1870 the result of foreign intervention?   20

45. How important was the use of propaganda in maintaining Fascist power in Italy between 1922 and 1939?   20

Part F — Russia 1881–1921

46. To what extent was Bloody Sunday responsible for the 1905 Revolution in Russia?   20

47. To what extent did working class discontent cause the outbreak of the February Revolution in 1917?   20

48. *The role of Trotsky was the main reason why the Reds won the Civil War.*
    How valid is this statement?   20

MARKS

SECTION 3 — EUROPEAN AND WORLD (continued)

Part G — USA 1918–1968

49.   To what extent were divisions within the black community the main obstacle to achieving civil rights before 1941?   **20**

50.   How effective was the New Deal in solving America's problems in the 1930s?   **20**

51.   *The Civil Rights Movement of the 1950s and 1960s met the needs of black Americans*
How valid is this view?   **20**

Part H — Appeasement and the Road to War, to 1939

52.   To what extent did Fascist governments use military threat and force in pursuing their foreign policies from 1933?   **20**

53.   *British foreign policy was a complete failure in containing the spread of Fascist aggression up to March 1938.*
How valid is this view?   **20**

54.   To what extent was the outbreak of war in September 1939 brought about by the failure of British diplomacy and relations with the Soviet Union?   **20**

Part I — The Cold War, 1945–1989

55.   *The Soviet Union effectively controlled Eastern Europe in the years up to 1961.*
How valid is this view?   **20**

56.   To what extent were the difficulties faced by the US military the reason why America lost the war in Vietnam?   **20**

57.   *The economic weakness of the Soviet Union led to the end of the Cold War.*
How valid is this view?   **20**

[END OF MODEL PAPER]

National Qualifications 2015

X737/76/11 **History**

FRIDAY, 1 MAY
1:00 PM – 3:20 PM

Total marks — 60

SECTION 1 — SCOTTISH — 20 marks

Attempt ONE Part

SECTION 2 — BRITISH — 20 marks

Attempt ONE question from the Part you have chosen

SECTION 3 — EUROPEAN AND WORLD — 20 marks

Attempt ONE question from the Part you have chosen

Write your answers clearly in the answer booklet provided. In the answer booklet you must clearly identify the question number you are attempting.

Use **blue** or **black** ink.

Before leaving the examination room you must give your answer booklet to the Invigilator; if you do not you may lose all the marks for this paper.

[BLANK PAGE]

DO NOT WRITE ON THIS PAGE

SECTION 1 — SCOTTISH

Attempt ONE Part

PARTS

A.   The Wars of Independence, 1249–1328   Page 4

B.   The Age of the Reformation, 1542–1603   Page 6

C.   The Treaty of Union, 1689–1740   Page 8

D.   Migration and Empire, 1830–1939   Page 10

E.   The Impact of the Great War, 1914–1928   Page 12

SECTION 2 — BRITISH

Attempt one question from the Part you have chosen

PARTS

A.   Church, State and Feudal Society, 1066–1406   Page 14

B.   The Century of Revolutions, 1603–1702   Page 14

C.   The Atlantic Slave Trade   Page 14

D.   Britain, 1851–1951   Page 15

E.   Britain and Ireland, 1900–1985   Page 15

SECTION 3 — EUROPEAN AND WORLD

Attempt one question from the Part you have chosen

PARTS

A.   The Crusades, 1071–1204   Page 16

B.   The American Revolution, 1763–1787   Page 16

C.   The French Revolution, to 1799   Page 16

D.   Germany, 1815–1939   Page 17

E.   Italy, 1815–1939   Page 17

F.   Russia, 1881–1921   Page 17

G.   USA, 1918–1968   Page 18

H.   Appeasement and the Road to War, to 1939   Page 18

I.   The Cold War, 1945–1989   Page 18

SECTION 1 — SCOTTISH — 20 marks

Part A — The Wars of Independence, 1249–1328

Study the sources below and attempt the questions which follow.

Source A: from Michael Brown, *The Wars of Scotland 1214–1371* (2004)

> In March 1286 Scotland's leaders gathered for the funeral of Alexander III. There would be no crowning of a new king to balance the burial of the old. Alexander III's sudden death had brought the male line of the royal dynasty to an end. A measure of the problems now facing the Scottish leaders was the desire for "advice and protection" from Edward I, which would later lead to demands for recognition of Edward's authority over the Scottish realm. Six Guardians were appointed in response to the vital need to carry on the day-to-day running of the government in the absence of a royal leader. The belief that the queen, Yolande of Dreux, was carrying the dead king's child turned out to be mistaken. The young child Margaret of Norway was now the only descendant of King Alexander III.

Source B: from Fiona Watson, *Under the Hammer* (1998)

> John Balliol was enthroned at Scone on St Andrew's Day, 1292. Within another month King John had sworn homage for the kingdom of Scotland for a second time. However, it would be foolish to ignore the fact that John's reign was overshadowed by Edward I's determination, right from the start, to enforce the widest possible interpretation of his rights as overlord of Scotland. English influence was noticeable at a number of levels. King John was left in no doubt that he personally could, and would, be called to answer for the actions of the Scottish courts, in the presence of Edward I and the English parliament. For example, only one week after King John's enthronement, Edward I had heard a court appeal on behalf of a Scottish merchant, Roger Bartholomew who complained against a decision taken by the Scottish courts.

Source C: from Michael Prestwich, *Edward I* (1988)

> Any doubts about John Balliol's position must have been resolved on 26 December 1292 when King John did homage to the King of England which clearly recognised Edward I's overlordship of the realm of Scotland. Edward I was not however content with a mere recognition of his overlordship: he was determined to exercise his authority to the full. It was the question of appeals to Edward I's court that was the first test of Edward I's strength and King John's weakness. Edward I made it clear that he intended to hear any appeal cases brought to him as overlord of Scotland, when and where he chose. Furthermore, if need be, Edward I would even summon King John to appear before him in England to answer legal claims and complaints in person.

MARKS

SECTION 1 — SCOTTISH (continued)

Source D: from The Chronicle of Lanercost, August 1314

> In August 1314, Edward Bruce, James Douglas, John Soules and other nobles of Scotland, under the authority of Robert Bruce, invaded England by way of Berwick with cavalry and a large army. They devastated almost all Northumberland with fire and they burned the towns of Brough, Appelby and Kirkoswald in Cumberland and other towns here and there on their route through Durham and into Yorkshire as far south as Richmond. But the people of Coupland, fearing their return and invasion, sent messengers and paid much money to the Scottish King to escape being burned by them in the same way as they had destroyed other towns. Passing near the priory of Lanercost, the Scottish forces then re-entered Scotland.

Attempt all of the following questions.

1. How fully does **Source A** describe the succession problem in Scotland 1286–1296?   9

   Use the source and your own knowledge.

2. Compare the views of **Sources B** and **C** about the relationship between John Balliol and Edward I.   5

   Compare the sources overall and in detail.

3. Evaluate the usefulness of **Source D** as evidence of the reasons for the ultimate success of Robert Bruce in maintaining Scotland's independence.   6

   In making a judgement you should refer to:
   - *the origin and possible purpose of the source*
   - *the content of the source*
   - *your own knowledge*

[Now go on to SECTION 2 starting on *Page fourteen*]

MARKS

SECTION 1 — SCOTTISH — 20 marks

Part B — The Age of the Reformation, 1542–1603

Study the sources below and attempt the questions which follow.

Source A: from M. Lynch, *Scotland a New History* (1991)

> The Reformation of 1560 was sparked off by a riot in Perth in which the town's Catholic religious houses were sacked. By July groups of nobles, lairds and burgesses, which made up a cross-section of society, had attacked a series of towns in central Scotland, including St Andrews and Dundee, and had entered Edinburgh.
>
> After returning to the capital from France and Geneva, Knox was installed as its first Protestant minister on the seventh of the month. There had been a change of Regent in October 1559 and a provisional government had also been established. This pleased Knox and his followers as they were unhappy with Mary of Guise's heavy taxation and her pro-French policies. Also pleasing was the support of England and the arrival of an English army in March 1560 which proved to be a decisive factor.

Source B: from T. Booher, *The life and impact of Scottish Reformer John Knox* (2012)

> Mary Queen of Scots returned from France after her husband had died. She returned on the condition that she would not take part in the forbidden Catholic mass. She agreed not to, but went back on her word upon arrival attending mass at Holyrood Chapel. She also upset many of the Scots nobility by surrounding herself with French servants. However, it was events in her personal life that were to cause her the most harm. Most notable was her secret marriage to the Earl of Bothwell, who was suspected of murdering her previous husband Lord Darnley. This led to further distrust towards Mary. Knox had five meetings with Mary Queen of Scots, criticising her marriages. From this time on, Knox was able to teach and preach in relative safety, until his death in 1572.

Source C: from J.E.A. Dawson, *Scotland Re-formed 1488–1587* (2009)

> On her return Mary's half-brother James Stewart, Earl of Moray, advised she settle into her natural place at the head of the kingdom without rocking the religious boat. Mary surrounding herself with French servants did not go down well with the Scottish nobility. Her choice of husbands also caused shock waves, particularly her marriage to Bothwell. She ignored advice and attended mass at Holyrood on her arrival, to many Protestants' disgust. Problems and distrust were also caused by many other errors of judgment. Such events did not go unnoticed by Knox who held five meetings with the queen to show his disapproval of the goings-on in her personal and public life.

MARKS

SECTION 1 — SCOTTISH (continued)

Source D: from the Second Book of Discipline (1578)

> We must have respect to the poor members of Jesus Christ's kingdom, who sadly multiply amongst us. The Kirk belongs to the poor as much as it does everyone else and our duty is to help them. We also call for the liberty of the election of persons called to the ministry to be in the hands of the congregation. As for the Kirk rents, we desire the order to be admitted and maintained with the sincerity of God's word and practice of the purity of the Kirk of Christ. Doctors will be appointed in universities, colleges, and schools to open up the meaning of the scriptures in every parish, and teach the basics of religion.

Attempt all of the following questions.

4. How fully does **Source A** explain the reasons for the Reformation of 1560?   9

   Use the source and your own knowledge.

5. Compare the views of **Sources B** and **C** about Mary's difficulties in ruling Scotland.   5

   Compare the sources overall and in detail.

6. Evaluate the usefulness of **Source D** as evidence of the impact of the Reformation on Scotland.   6

   In making a judgement you should refer to:
   - *the origin and possible purpose of the source*
   - *the content of the source*
   - *your own knowledge*

[Now go on to Section 2 starting on *Page fourteen*]

SECTION 1 — SCOTTISH — 20 marks

Part C — The Treaty of Union, 1689—1740

Study the sources below and attempt the questions which follow.

Source A: from The History Today Companion to British History (1995).

> The Darien Scheme was a plan for the foundation of a Scottish colony, to be called New Caledonia, on the Darien area of Panama, Central America. The colony was to be managed by the Company of Scotland, founded in 1695. The chief object was to promote Scottish trade. It was hoped that the colony might provide a market for Scottish goods. There was English political opposition because of the threat to the English-owned East India Company. English sabotage was blamed for underfunding and mismanagement of the scheme. King William was held responsible for encouraging Spanish opposition in Central America, which led to the scheme's failure. Anglo-Scottish relations were strained and this was shown by anti-English riots in Edinburgh.

Source B: from a pamphlet by Seton of Pitmedden, *Scotland's great advantages by a Union in England*, (1706).

> With union, England will secure its old and dangerous Scots enemy to be its friend, and this ensures peace for the English. Scotland will no longer be threatened by its powerful neighbour, nor conquered by foreign enemies. Our brave and courageous Scotsmen will join a British fleet and army and we will be secured by their protection. Our burgh merchants will take our manufactures to England and return with profits. English merchants will have free access to all our seas and ports and will have the same privileges as citizens of Scotland. We Scots will be the same among them, and can travel to plantations in the colonies with greater assurance than ever before. We will see our craftsmen's lives improve as a result of union. Our land will be better cultivated and manured.

Source C: from a speech by Lord Belhaven in Parliament, November 1706

> When I think about union, my mind is crowded with sad thoughts:
>
> I think I see a free kingdom losing power to manage its affairs. I think I see the royal burghs losing all the branches of their old commerce and trades in the face of English competition. I think I see our valiant and brave Scottish soldiers at home asking for a small pension, or left to beg, once their old regiments are broken, while young English soldiers form part of the standing British army. I think I see the honest industrious craftsman loaded with new taxes, drinking water instead of ale. I think I see the backbroken farmer, with his corn wasted upon his hands, because his land is worthless.
>
> Are these not very affecting thoughts?

SECTION 1 — SCOTTISH (continued)

Source D: from a Jacobite leaflet, *The Miserable State of Scotland* (1723)

> Before the union we had to pay no taxes other than those raised by the Scots parliament, and these were not high, and were spent by the government in Scotland. Now we have not only a Land Tax, but a Salt Tax, Malt Tax, Window Tax, Leather Tax, a Candle Tax, a Soap Tax, a Starch Tax, and Paper Tax. In addition, our import custom duties are now set at English rates which are three times what we used to pay before union, and these have been set by parliament in London to be raised for the next 99 years! There are many reasons for bringing back the old Scots parliament whose incorporation into the English parliament the Scots were bullied and bribed into accepting.

Attempt all of the following questions.

7. How fully does **Source A** explain worsening relations between Scotland and England?　9

   Use the source and your own knowledge.

8. Compare the views of **Sources B** and **C** about attitudes towards union with England.　5

   Compare the sources overall and in detail.

9. Evaluate the usefulness of **Source D** as evidence of the effects of union to 1740.　6

   In making a judgement you should refer to:
   - *the origin and possible purpose of the source*
   - *the content of the source*
   - *your own knowledge*

[Now go on to Section 2 starting on *Page fourteen*]

SECTION 1 — SCOTTISH — 20 marks

Part D — Migration and Empire, 1830—1939

Study the sources below and attempt the questions which follow.

Source A: from James Hunter, *The Last of the Free* (1999)

> It is unarguable that following the collapse of the kelp trade landlords were looking for change. Many landlords were of the view, by the 1840s, that it could only be of benefit to them to rid their land and properties of people. They attempted to do this following the hardship of the famine period, perhaps the most far-reaching occurred on Barra, South Uist and Benbecula. Those islands belonged to John Gordon of Cluny. Gordon chartered a fleet of five ships in order to transport 1,700 people from his Hebridean properties to Canada. Similarly, other landlords contributed to the cost of fares to encourage families to emigrate. More than 16,000 people were helped to emigrate from the Highlands and Islands between 1847 and 1857.

Source B: from a speech by Mr R. Smillie, who was President of the Scottish Miners' Federation in May 1903.

> The Scottish Miners' Federation represents about 85—90% of miners in Scotland. Figures show that 1,320 aliens (foreign workers) are working underground in Lanarkshire out of a total employment figure of 31,000. Some of these aliens may never have seen a coalmine before their arrival in Scotland. The Federation has complained about the employment of aliens in the mines on the grounds of safety. Their lack of English language is a hazard to themselves and fellow workers. There has been action over the past months as many British miners are idle, while aliens are employed. Preference, it seems, has been given to the foreigner. There is also a widespread belief that the foreigners are being used to bring wages down. Although aliens in the mining industry are described as Poles about 90% are Lithuanian.

Source C: from Robert Duncan, *The Mineworkers* (2005)

> The Lithuanians first came to work in North Lanarkshire coalmines in the early 1890s. They were the focus of considerable concern largely because of their ignorance of coal mining. Until the early 1900s at least there is evidence that Lithuanian labour was used to cut wages. As one would expect, the expressed view of the mining employers was usually complimentary about the hardworking and reliable foreign workers. Contrary to the evidence from the miners' union, the employers were also adamant that the foreign workers did not present additional dangers to safety. They claimed adequate provision was made to instruct them in their duties, including translations of mining regulations into their own language. It is difficult to work out just what proportion of foreign mine workers were involved in accidents as many Lithuanians adopted Scots names so records are unclear.

MARKS

SECTION 1 — SCOTTISH (continued)

Source D: from a letter by a Scottish politician to the editor of *The Scotsman* newspaper on 4th July 1938.

> Dear Sir — The upcoming Empire Exhibition will be a welcome opportunity to showcase the industrial might of Glasgow and the west of Scotland created by the Empire. A meeting of the Empire Development Conference is to be held during the exhibition. The intention of the meeting is to encourage emigration from Britain "to populate the empty spaces of the Empire". Many Scots feel that renewed emigration would be entirely contrary to Scotland's interests. The primary need for Scotland is reconstruction at home so that Scotland's "empty spaces" can be populated once more. It is more than time that a firm check was put on the drain from Scotland of her best types. For far too long Scotland's best have been drawn away by the opportunities that the Empire has presented.

Attempt all of the following questions.

10. How fully does **Source A** explain the reasons for Scottish migration?

    Use the source and your own knowledge.

    9

11. Compare the views of **Sources B** and **C** about the reactions of Scots to immigrants.

    Compare the sources overall and in detail.

    5

12. Evaluate the usefulness of **Source D** as evidence of the impact which the Empire had on Scotland.

    In making a judgement you should refer to:
    * *the origin and possible purpose of the source*
    * *the content of the source*
    * *your own knowledge*

    6

[Now go on to Section 2 starting on *Page fourteen*]

SECTION 1 — SCOTTISH — 20 marks

Part E — The Impact of the Great War, 1914—1928

Study the sources below and attempt the questions which follow.

Source A: from a letter by Private Howard, a soldier in the 7th Cameron Highlanders.

> On the morning of the 25th we had given the Germans gas but it came back on us. I got a dose but it didn't knock me out. On we went. German shells were falling amongst us and time and time again I was knocked off my feet but I wasn't struck. A pal of mine, a fellow Cameron Highlander from Paisley, was lying alongside me when he gave a groan. He pointed to his left arm. I cut off his tunic and shirt sleeves. A bullet had got him on the arm and blood gulped out and the smell of it was sickening. I got out my field dressing to help him but before I had finished I was drenched in his blood. My pal I am glad to say managed alright.

Source B: from T. Royle, *The Flowers of the Forest, Scotland and the First World War* (2006).

> In the streets women carried placards stating: "We are fighting the Prussians in Partick". Unusually, the strikers were supported by their employers who did not want productivity slowed down by factors outside their control. Matters came to a head when a mass meeting was held in Glasgow's George Square on 17 November to protest against the prosecution of 18 tenants due to appear in court for refusing to pay rent increases. By then the rent strikes had escalated, with men taking their own wildcat strike action at Fairfield's and Beardmore's. Rebellion was in the air but the strikes ended the following month when the government rushed through the Rent Restriction Act. It was a victory for what would later be known as "people power".

Source C: from a pamphlet by Councillor A. McBride of the Glasgow Labour Party Housing Association (1921).

> Our committee organised demonstrations with banners demanding the Government to take action. We informed the Secretary for Scotland Mr McKinnon-Wood that the people desired that the rents should not be increased above the pre-war standard. Rents were still soaring and events were rapidly approaching a crisis. With the summoning of a number of munitions workers to attend court the most dramatic incident of the struggle happened. Men engaged in work on the Clyde stopped working and marched in their thousands with those summoned to the court. As a result of this daring innovation in Rent Eviction trials, the cases were dismissed and the Rent Strikers won a fight which justified the wisdom of the Glasgow Labour Party Housing Committee. A few days after this an Act to limit rent increases was introduced by the Government.

SECTION 1 — SCOTTISH (continued)

Source D: from an editorial comment made in the *Glasgow Herald* newspaper, 1st February 1919.

> It is impossible not to be upset by the disgraceful proceedings of yesterday in George Square and other parts of the city. In the scenes of violence and bloodshed there have been no fatalities to report but 53 people were injured by the throwing of missiles or the use of the baton. David Kirkwood, one of the strike leaders, and a member of the ILP, is under arrest on the charge of inciting the mob. It has been known from the first that the strike movement is controlled by a small section of the Clyde Workers' Committee who are pressing for a 40 hour week. Many works on Clydeside have been closed due to picketing by crowds numbering several hundreds of strikers that can only be called organised intimidation. The revolutionary activities of these Bolshevists have damaged Glasgow's reputation.

Attempt all of the following questions.

13. How fully does **Source A** describe the experience of Scots on the Western Front?   9

    Use the source and your own knowledge.

14. Compare the views of **Sources B** and **C** about the events of the Rent Strikes.   5

    Compare the sources overall and in detail.

15. Evaluate the usefulness of **Source D** as evidence of political developments in Scotland after the war.   6

    In making a judgement you should refer to:
    * *the origin and possible purpose of the source*
    * *the content of the source*
    * *your own knowledge*

[Now go on to Section 2 starting on *Page fourteen*]

MARKS

SECTION 2 — BRITISH — 20 marks
Attempt ONE question

Part A — Church, State and Feudal Society, 1066—1406

16. To what extent was religion the main role of the Church in medieval society?

20

17. *King John of England successfully increased royal authority.*
     How valid is this view?

20

18. *The Peasants' Revolt was the main reason for the decline of feudal society.*
     How valid is this view?

20

Part B — The Century of Revolutions, 1603—1702

19. *The policies of Charles I led to problems ruling Scotland.*
     How valid is this view?

20

20. To what extent were James II's attempts at absolutism the main cause of the Revolution of 1688—89?

20

21. To what extent did the Revolution Settlement of 1688—1702 alter the balance of power between the monarchy and parliament?

20

Part C — The Atlantic Slave Trade

22. How important was the slave trade in the development of the British economy in the eighteenth century?

20

23. *The power of vested interests was the most important obstacle to the abolition of the slave trade.*
     How valid is this view?

20

24. To what extent was the decline in the economic importance of slavery the main reason for the abolition of the slave trade?

20

MARKS

SECTION 2 — BRITISH (continued)

Part D — Britain, 1851–1951

25. *Britain was a fully democratic country by 1918.*
    How valid is this view?   20

26. *The Liberal reforms of 1906 to 1914 failed to improve the lives of the British people.*
    How valid is this view?   20

27. To what extent did the reforms of the Labour Government of 1945–1951 meet the needs of the British people?   20

Part E — Britain and Ireland, 1900–1985

28. *The First World War totally changed the political situation in Ireland.*
    How valid is this view?   20

29. *Economic issues were the reason for the crisis that developed in Northern Ireland by 1968.*
    How valid is this view?   20

30. How important were economic differences as an obstacle to peace, 1968–1985?   20

[Now go on to Section 3 starting on *Page sixteen*]

MARKS

SECTION 3 — EUROPEAN AND WORLD — 20 marks
Attempt ONE question

Part A — The Crusades, 1071–1204

31. To what extent do religious motives explain why many Christians from different classes went on Crusade to the Holy Land?

    20

32. *Richard and Saladin were both great military and diplomatic leaders during the Third Crusade.*

    How valid is this view?

    20

33. To what extent had the crusading ideal declined by the time of the Fourth Crusade in 1204?

    20

Part B — The American Revolution, 1763–1787

34. To what extent did the punishment of Massachusetts contribute to the colonists' moves towards independence by 1776?

    20

35. How important was the role of George Washington in the colonists' victory in the War of Independence?

    20

36. *The American Constitution addressed the key political issues in the new United States.*

    How valid is this view?

    20

Part C — The French Revolution, to 1799

37. How important was the influence of the Enlightenment as a reason for the French Revolution in 1789?

    20

38. *The role of Sieyes was the reason for the establishment of the Consulate.*

    How valid is this view?

    20

39. *The Clergy gained most from the French Revolution.*

    How valid is this view?

    20

MARKS

SECTION 3 — EUROPEAN AND WORLD (continued)

Part D — Germany, 1815—1939

40. *By 1850 supporters of nationalism had made significant progress in their aims.*
    How valid is this view?

    20

41. How important was resentment towards the Treaty of Versailles as a reason why the Nazis had achieved power by 1933?

    20

42. How important was the use of fear and terror as a reason why the Nazis were able to stay in power, 1933—39?

    20

Part E — Italy, 1815—1939

43. *Between 1815 and 1850, there was a real growth in nationalist feeling in Italy.*
    How valid is this view?

    20

44. To what extent were economic difficulties the reason why the Fascists achieved power in Italy by 1925?

    20

45. How important were Mussolini's economic and social policies in maintaining Fascist power in Italy between 1922 and 1939?

    20

Part F — Russia, 1881—1921

46. How important was military defeat in the war against Japan in causing the 1905 Revolution in Russia?

    20

47. How important was the appeal of the Bolsheviks in the success of the October Revolution of 1917?

    20

48. How important was the role of Trotsky in the victory of the Reds in the Civil War?

    20

MARKS

SECTION 3 — EUROPEAN AND WORLD (continued)

Part G — USA, 1918–1968

49. To what extent was a lack of political influence the main obstacle to the achievement of Civil Rights for black people up to 1941?

20

50. How important was the role of Martin Luther King in the development of the Civil Rights campaign, after 1945?

20

51. To what extent did the Civil Rights Movement meet the needs of black Americans, up to 1968?

20

Part H — Appeasement and the Road to War, to 1939

52. *Military agreements, pacts and alliances were the most important method used by Germany and Italy to pursue their foreign policies from 1933.*

How valid is this view?

20

53. *The Munich Agreement of 1938 was a reasonable settlement under the circumstances.*

How valid is this view?

20

54. How important was the Nazi-Soviet Pact in causing the outbreak of war in 1939?

20

Part I — The Cold War, 1945–1989

55. *Soviet policy towards Eastern Europe up to 1961 was very effective.*

How valid is this view?

20

56. To what extent was the economic cost of the arms race the reason why the superpowers attempted to manage the Cold War, 1962–1985?

20

57. To what extent did the actions of President Reagan lead to the end of the Cold War?

20

[END OF QUESTION PAPER]

HIGHER FOR CfE | ANSWER SECTION

SQA AND HODDER GIBSON HIGHER FOR CfE HISTORY 2015

GENERAL MARKING PRINCIPLES FOR HIGHER FOR CfE HISTORY

The specific Marking Instructions are not an exhaustive list. Other relevant points should be credited.

(i) For credit to be given, points must relate to the question asked. Where candidates give points of knowledge without specifying the context, up to **1 mark** should be awarded unless it is clear that they do not refer to the context of the question.

eg *Some soldiers on the Western Front suffered from trench foot as they were unable to keep their feet dry.* (**1 mark for knowledge**, even though this does not specify that it relates to the Scottish soldiers)

(ii) Where marks are awarded for the use of knowledge, each point of knowledge must be developed, eg by providing additional detail, examples or evidence.

(iii) There are four types of question used in this Paper, namely:

    A. Evaluate the usefulness of Source . . .

    B. Compare the views of Sources . . .

    C. How fully does Source . . .

    D. Extended response questions using a range of stems, including 'how important', 'how successful', 'how valid', 'to what extent'. These require candidates to demonstrate knowledge and understanding and to apply their skills of analysis and evaluation in order to answer the question asked.

(iv) For each of the question types (in iii above), the following provides an overview of marking principles and an example of their application for each question type.

A Questions that ask candidates to *Evaluate the usefulness of a given source as evidence of* . . . (6 marks)

Candidates must evaluate the extent to which a source is useful by commenting on evidence such as the author, type of source, purpose, timing, content and omission.

Up to the total mark allocation for this question of 6 marks:

- a maximum of **4 marks** can be given for evaluative comments relating to author, type of source, purpose and timing
- a maximum of **2 marks** may be given for evaluative comments relating to the content of the source
- a maximum of **2 marks** may be given for evaluative comments relating to points of significant omission

Example:

Source A is useful as evidence of Scottish involvement on the Western Front because it is from a diary of an officer from the Black Watch who will be well informed about the Scots military involvement at the Battle of Loos. (**1 mark for origin: authorship**) *As it is a diary it is also useful as it will give an eyewitness view of the battle.* (**1 mark for origin: purpose**) *The source was written at the end of October 1915 which makes it useful because it was in the immediate aftermath of the battle.* (**1 mark for origin: timing**)

The content is about the men his battalion lost in the attack. This is useful as the deaths of 19 officers and 230 men shows the losses Scots took. (**1 mark for content**) *It is also useful as the Black Watch were part of 30,000 Scots who attacked at Loos, showing a lot of Scottish involvement.* (***1 mark for a point of context***)

However, the source does not give other ways in which Scots were involved on the Western Front. General Douglas Haig who was Scottish made a large contribution to the war as he was Commander in Chief of British Forces after 1915. (***1 mark for a point of significant omission***)

B Questions that ask candidates to *Compare the views of two sources* (5 marks)

Candidates must interpret evidence and make direct comparisons between sources. Candidates are expected to compare content directly on a point-by-point basis. They should also make an overall comparison of the viewpoints of the sources.

Up to the total mark allocation for this question of 5 marks:

Each point of comparison will be supported by specific references to each source and should be awarded **1 mark**.

An overall comparison which is supported by specific references to the viewpoint of each source should be awarded **1 mark**. **A second mark** should be awarded for a development of the overall comparison.

Examples:

Sources A and B agree that Cressingham was killed and skinned by the Scots after the battle. Source A says Cressingham, a leader amongst the English knights, was killed during the battle and later skinned. Source B agrees when it says 'the treacherer Cressingham was skinned following his death during the battle'. (***1 mark for a point of comparison supported by specific reference to each source***)

Sources A and B agree that William Wallace and Andrew Murray were leaders of the Scottish army at Stirling and that the Scots were victorious. (***1 mark for overall comparison***) *However, they disagree about the importance of the English mistakes made by Warrenne.* (***a second mark for developing the overall comparison***)

C Questions that ask *How fully does a given source explain/describe* . . . (9 marks)

Candidates must make a judgement about the extent to which the source provides a full description/explanation of a given event or development.

Up to the total mark allocation for this question of 9 marks:

- candidates should be given **up to 3 marks** for their identification of points from the source that support their judgement; each point from the source needs to be interpreted rather than simply copied from the source
- candidates should be given **up to 7 marks** for their identification of points of significant omission, based on their own knowledge, that support their judgement
- a maximum of **2 marks** may be given for answers in which no judgement has been made

Example:

Source B gives a fairly good explanation of the reasons why people left Scotland. The source mentions the potato famine in the Highlands in 1846 which led to large numbers of people leaving rather than starving. (**1 mark for interpreting the source**) *It mentions specifically how landlords evicted crofters to make way for sheep farming in order to make their land profitable.* (**1 mark for interpreting the source**) *It also talks about the terrible living conditions which drove people to look for a better life abroad.* (**1 mark for interpreting the source**)

However, the source does not mention all the reasons why people left Scotland. It fails to mention the decline of the kelp industry which forced many Scots to look for work elsewhere. (**1 mark for a point of significant omission**) The problems of the fishing industry led to hardships for many Scots. When the herring industry declined due to loss of markets after the war, people left Scotland. (**1 mark for a point of significant omission**) Others, such as handloom weavers from the Western Isles, left as they couldn't compete with the new factories in the towns and cities of the Central Belt. (**1 mark for a point of significant omission**)

D Extended response questions (20 marks)

Historical context

Marks can be awarded for answers which describe the background to the issue and which identify relevant factors. These should be connected to the line of argument.

Conclusion(s)

Marks can be awarded for answers which provide a relative overall judgement of the factors, which are connected to the evidence presented, and which provide reasons for their overall judgement.

Eg *This factor was clearly more significant in bringing about the event than any other factor because ....*

While conclusions are likely to be at the end of the essay, they can also be made at any point in the response.

Use of evidence

Marks can be awarded for evidence which is detailed and which is used in support of a viewpoint, factor or area of impact.

For knowledge/understanding marks to be awarded, points must be:

- *relevant to the issue in the question*
- *developed (by providing additional detail, exemplification, reasons or evidence)*
- *used to respond to the demands of the question (ie explain, analyse, etc)*

Analysis

Analysis involves identifying parts, the relationship between them, and their relationships with the whole. It can also involve drawing out and relating implications.

An analysis mark should be awarded where a candidate uses their knowledge & understanding, to identify relevant factors such as political, social, economic, religious, etc (although they do not need to use this terminology), or which explore aspects within these, such as success vs failure; different groups, such as elderly vs youth; or different social classes **and** clearly show at least one of the following:

- links between different components
- links between component(s) and the whole
- links between component(s) and related concepts
- similarities and consistency
- contradictions and inconsistency
- different views/interpretations
- the relative importance of components
- understanding of underlying order or structure

Examples of relationships between identified factors could include:

- Establishing contradiction or inconsistencies within factors
  Eg *While they were successful in that way, they were limited in this way.*

- Establishing contradiction or inconsistencies between factors
  Eg *While there were political motives for doing this, the economic factors were against doing this.*
- Establishing similarities and consistencies between factors
  Eg *In much the same way as this group were affected by this development, this group were also affected in this way.*
- Establishing links between factors
  Eg *This factor led to that factor.* OR *At the same time there was also ...*
- Exploring different interpretations of these factors
  Eg *While some people have viewed the evidence as showing this, others have seen it as showing ...* OR *While we used to think that this was the case, we now think that it was really ...*

Evaluation

Evaluation involves making a judgement based on criteria. Candidates will make reasoned evaluative comments relating to, for example:

- The extent to which the factor is supported by the evidence
  Eg *This evidence shows that X was a very significant area of impact.*
- The relative importance of factors
  Eg *This evidence shows that X was a more significant area of impact than Y.*
- Counter-arguments including possible alternative interpretations
  Eg *One factor was ... However, this may not be the case because ...* OR *However, more recent research tends to show that ...*
- The overall impact/significance of the factors when taken together
  Eg *While each factor may have had little effect on its own, when we take them together they became hugely important.*
- The importance of factors in relation to the context
  Eg *Given the situation which they inherited, these actions were more successful than they might appear.*

Marks can be awarded for developing a line of argument which makes a judgement on the issue, explaining the basis on which the judgement is made. The argument should be presented in a balanced way making evaluative comments which show their judgement on the individual factors and may use counter-arguments or alternative interpretations to build their case.

Example:

'The social reforms of the Labour government of 1945–1951 failed to deal effectively with the needs of the people.'

How valid is this view?

*In 1945, Clement Atlee, the leader of the Labour Party won a landslide victory against the Conservatives. (**background to the issue**) He immediately set out to try to deal with the needs of the British people but whether he did or not has caused much debate. The Labour Party looked to the Beveridge Report as a blueprint for change. It highlighted five social evils that would have to be tackled to meet the needs of the people: want, disease, ignorance, squalor and idleness. (**factors identified**) It was these evils that Labour set out to tackle and did so with varying success. (**connects factor to line of argument**)*

Want was one of the first social evils to be tackled. The National Insurance Act of 1946 was introduced to allow those too sick to work or those unemployed to maintain a basic subsistence. *(1 mark for knowledge used to support a factor)* In theory, this sorted out a great deal of problems. However, the only way to get the benefits when sick or unemployed was to pay 156 weekly contributions. That's three years' worth. What if the person was too sick to work so couldn't contribute the 156 payments in the first place? *(1 mark for analysis of aspects within a factor)* This meant that although the Labour government met the needs of many workers, there was still a large portion of people that did not receive this help and therefore Labour failed to meet the needs of some people. *(1 mark for evaluating an individual factor which is linked to other evaluative comments and recognises the question)*

One of Labour's biggest successes in meeting the needs of the people was the National Health Service (NHS). The NHS was free, comprehensive and universal. *(1 mark for knowledge used to support a factor)* It allowed everyone in the country to have access to medical attention. *(1 mark for knowledge used to support a factor)* Many diseases that had been rampant before the NHS died out and the medical needs of the people had been met. However, the NHS was a victim of its own success as Labour was not prepared for the numbers of people using it. *(1 mark for analysis of aspects within a factor)* This meant that not only did they have to charge for some areas such as dental and eye care, *(1 mark for knowledge used to support a factor)* they used funds from different government areas as the costs were too high compared to what was originally thought. *(1 mark for knowledge used to support a factor)* This also meant less money going towards meeting the needs of people in other areas. *(1 mark for analysis of relationship between factors)*

Education was seen as a good way to close the gap between lower and upper classes, and so meet the needs of the people. The Education Act made it so that children had to stay in school until the age of 15. *(1 mark for knowledge used to support a factor)* This meant they got a better education and were more likely to get better jobs. Labour also implemented the 11+ exam which pupils sat at the age of 11 to decide what type of school they would go to. The high scorers would go to the grammar schools and the others to secondary modern schools. *(1 mark for knowledge used to support a factor)* This was meant to allow working-class children to reach greater potential. However, the system was still biased towards the upper class and therefore did not meet the needs of all of the people. *(1 mark for evaluating an individual factor which is linked to other evaluative comments and recognises the question)*

During the war, millions of houses had been destroyed and a third of all remaining houses were damaged to an extent. *(1 mark for knowledge used to support a factor)* This meant Labour would have to focus on building more houses to meet the needs of the people. With the housing problem before the war being bad, Labour had a big task on their hands and aimed to build 200,000 houses a year. *(1 mark for knowledge used to support a factor)* However, Britain was lacking resources and manpower *(1 mark for analysis of aspects within a factor)* and so, even with the mass production of prefabricated houses, the housing needs of many people were not met. *(1 mark for evaluating an individual factor)*

Unemployment rates during this time were down massively compared to a decade before. The Beveridge Report had stated that unemployment would never fall below 3%, yet Labour smashed this and reached 2.5 %. *(1 mark for knowledge used to support a factor)* Many say that Labour met the needs of the people as they dropped unemployment this low which allowed people to live better lives. However, it is argued that it was only the country healing its wounds from the war that caused unemployment to drop. *(1 mark for analysis of different interpretations a factor)* So, during the time of the Labour government, the employment needs of the people were fulfilled. Whether it was down to Labour or not is debatable. *(1 mark for evaluating an individual factor)*

In conclusion, while Labour passed many acts that did help to meet the needs of the people, they did not fully meet their needs. However, what Clement Atlee and the Labour government did in the short span they had was truly amazing and helped set up the foundations of the system we have now which meets the needs of most of the people. *(2 marks for an overall judgement in relation to the issue)*

	Mark	0 marks	1 mark	2 marks
Historical context	2	Candidate makes one or two factual points but these are not relevant.	Candidate establishes two out of three from the background to the issue or identifies relevant factors or a line of argument.	Candidate establishes the background to the issue, identifies relevant factors and connects these to the line of argument.
Conclusion	2	No overall judgement is made on the issue.	Candidate makes a summary of points made.	Candidate makes an overall judgement between the different factors in relation to the issue.

Use of knowledge	6	No evidence is used to support the conclusion.	**Up to a maximum of 6 marks**, 1 mark will be awarded for each developed point of knowledge used to support a factor or area of impact. For a knowledge mark to be awarded, points must be: <ul><li>relevant to the issue in the question</li><li>developed (by providing additional detail, exemplification, reasons or evidence)</li><li>used to respond to the demands of the question (ie explain, analyse, etc)</li></ul>

Analysis	6	There is a narrative response.	**Up to a maximum of 6 marks**, 1 mark will be awarded for each comment which analyses the factors in terms of the question. **A maximum of 4 marks** will be awarded for comments which address different aspects of individual factors.

Evaluation	4	No evidence of an overall judgement being made.	**1 mark** should be awarded where the candidate makes an isolated evaluative comment on an individual factor that recognises the topic of the question.	**2 marks** should be awarded where the candidate makes isolated evaluative comments on different factors that recognise the topic of the question.	**3 marks** should be awarded where the candidate connects their evaluative comments to build a line of argument that recognises the issue.	**4 marks** should be awarded where the candidate connects their evaluative comments to build a line of argument focused on the terms of the question.

Detailed Marking Instructions for each question

SECTION 1: SCOTTISH

Question	General marking principles for this type of question	Max mark	Specific Marking Instructions for this question
1	Candidates must make a judgement about the extent to which the source provides a full description/ explanation of a given event or development.	9	*Candidates can be credited in a number of ways up to a maximum of 9 marks.* • candidates should be given **up to 3 marks** for their identification of points from the source that support their judgement; each point from the source needs to be interpreted rather than simply copied from the source • candidates should be given **up to 7 marks** for their identification of points of significant omission, based on their own knowledge, that support their judgement • a maximum of **2 marks** may be given for answers in which no judgement has been made
2	Candidates must evaluate the extent to which a source is useful by commenting on evidence such as the author, type of source, purpose, timing, content and omission.	6	*Candidates can be credited in a number of ways up to a maximum of 6 marks.* • a maximum of **4 marks** can be given for evaluative comments relating to author, type of source, purpose and timing • a maximum of **2 marks** may be given for evaluative comments relating to the content of the source • a maximum of **2 marks** may be given for evaluative comments relating to points of significant omission
3	Candidates must interpret evidence and make direct comparisons between sources. Candidates are expected to compare content directly on a point-by-point basis. **Up to the total mark allocation for this question of 5 marks:** A developed comparison will be supported by specific references to each source and should be given **1 mark**. An overall comparison will be supported by specific references to the viewpoint of each source and should be given **1 mark**.	5	*Candidates can be credited in a number of ways up to a maximum of 5 marks.* **Up to a maximum of 4 marks**, each developed comparison which is supported by specific references to each source should be given **1 mark**. An overall comparison will be supported by specific references to the viewpoint of each source and should be given **1 mark**.

SECTION 3: EUROPEAN AND WORLD

Question			General marking principles for this type of question	Max mark	Specific Marking Instructions for this question
1	A		**Historical context** **Up to 2 marks** can be awarded for answers which describe the background to the issue and which identify relevant factors.	2	*Candidates can be credited in a number of ways **up to a maximum of 2 marks**.* **2 marks** Candidate establishes the background to the issue, identifies relevant factors and connects these to the line of argument. **1 mark** Candidate establishes two out of three from the background to the issue or identifies relevant factors or a line of argument. **No marks** Candidate makes one or two factual points but these are not relevant.
	B		**Conclusion(s)** **Up to 2 marks** can be awarded for answers which provide a relative overall judgement of the factors, connected to the evidence presented and which provide reasons for their overall judgement. While conclusions are likely to be at the end of the essay they can also be made at the start or throughout the essay.	2	*Candidates can be credited in a number of ways **up to a maximum of 2 marks**.* **2 marks** Candidate makes an overall judgement between the different factors in relation to the issue. **1 mark** Candidate makes a summary of points made. **No marks** No overall judgement is made on the issue
	C		**Use of evidence** **Up to 6 marks** can be awarded for evidence which is detailed and which is used in support of a viewpoint, factor or area of impact.	6	*Candidates can be credited in a number of ways **up to a maximum of 6 marks**.* **1 mark** should be awarded for each point of knowledge used to support a factor. *For knowledge/understanding marks to be awarded, points must be:* • *relevant to the issue in the question* • *developed (by providing additional detail, exemplification, reasons or evidence)* • *used to respond to the demands of the question (ie explain, analyse, etc)*
	D		**Analysis** **Up to 6 marks** can be awarded for answers which move beyond description and explanation of relevant detail to comment on the factors. This can include, for example: • establishing links between factors • establishing contradiction or inconsistencies within factors • establishing contradiction or inconsistencies between factors • establishing similarities and consistencies between factors • exploring different interpretations of these factors	6	*Candidates can be credited in a number of ways **up to a maximum of 6 marks**.* **Up to a maximum of 6 marks, 1 mark** will be awarded for comments which analyse the factors in terms of the question. **A maximum of 4 marks** will be awarded for comments which address different aspects of individual factors.

Question		General marking principles for this type of question	Max mark	Specific Marking Instructions for this question
	E	**Evaluation** **Up to 4 marks** can be awarded for evaluative comments which show a judgement on the factors such as: • the extent to which the factor is supported by the evidence • the relative importance of factors • counter-arguments including possible alternative interpretations • the overall impact/ significance of the factors when taken together • the importance of factors in relation to the context	4	*Candidates can be credited in a number of ways up to a maximum of 4 marks.*

Candidates can be credited in a number of ways up to a maximum of 4 marks.

4 marks	**4 marks** should be awarded where the candidate connects their evaluative comments to build a line of argument focused on the terms of the question.
3 marks	**3 marks** should be awarded where the candidate connects their evaluative comments to build a line of argument that recognises the issue.
2 marks	**2 marks** should be awarded where the candidate makes isolated evaluative comments on different factors that recognise the topic of the question.
1 mark	**1 mark** should be awarded where the candidate makes an isolated evaluative comment on an individual factor that recognises the topic of the question.
No marks	No evidence of an overall judgement being made.

MODEL PAPER 1
SECTION 1: SCOTTISH

Part A: The Wars of Independence, 1249—1328

1. How fully does Source B describe the relationship between John Balliol and Edward I? (9)

Candidates may be credited in a number of ways up to a maximum of 9 marks.

A maximum of 2 marks may be given for answers which refer only to the source.

Possible points which may be identified in the source include:

- Balliol was aware that he needed to impress Edward if he wanted to secure the kingdom.
- John's inauguration as King of Scots was attended by English officials rather than the traditional Scottish nobles and churchmen.
- John was summoned, more than once, to Northern England by Edward and crumbled in face of demand he renew his homage to Edward as overlord.
- Edward insisted he hear appeals from Scottish courts at Westminster.

Possible points of significant omission may include:

- Edward had decided that the Treaty of Birgham was no longer valid, since the marriage had not gone through; he demanded that John agree to this.
- It was only a week into his reign when the Burgesses of Berwick appealed to Edward over a court decision made by the Guardians, that John had upheld.
- Other appeals were quick in coming, such as the damaging Macduff case.
- Scottish kings were not used to being summoned to appear before an English court.
- Alexander III had refused to do homage for Scotland.
- John had to agree to some English members of his government.
- Edward forced John to release him of any promise he made about Scottish autonomy.
- John did try to resist but he backed down in the face of threats.
- In 1294 Edward ordered John to bring Scottish troops to fight for him in France.
- This angered the Scottish nobles who had good trading relations with France.
- Nobles elected a council of Guardians to help John stand up to Edward.
- John sent envoys to treat with the French king in 1295; this was formally ratified in 1296 after Edward's invasion.
- April 1296 John sent Edward a list of grievances with Edward's handling of the issue of overlordship, it has been suggested he was forced to do this by the guardians.
- John decided to submit to Edward hoping for leniency: he surrendered at Kincardine.
- From this John was brought before Edward at Brechin and ceremoniously stripped of his royal regalia, his surcoat stripped from his body.
- Here John earned his nickname from English soldiers, Toom Tabard.
- John was taken as a prisoner to London.
- Any other valid point of explanation that meets the criteria described in the general marking principles for this kind of question.

2. Evaluate the usefulness of Source A as evidence of why the Scots asked Edward to resolve the succession crisis in Scotland. (6)

Candidates can be credited in a number of ways up to a maximum of 6 marks.

Examples of aspects of the source and relevant comments:

Aspect of the source	Possible comment
Author: William Fraser, Bishop of St Andrews	Useful as one of the six elected Guardians of Scotland.
Type of Source: Letter	More useful as honest articulation of concerns on the death of Alexander and subsequent power struggle in Scotland.
Purpose: To avoid civil war	Useful as an appeal to Edward in an attempt to avoid civil war in Scotland.
Timing: Contemporary	More useful as from the time of the Great Cause.
Content	**Possible comment**
• A sad rumour reverberated among the people that our lady was dead, because of this the kingdom of Scotland is troubled and the community perplexed.	Useful as illustrates concern at the death of the Maid of Norway, the last heir of Alexander.
• When the rumour was heard and published Sir Robert Bruce, who had not intended to come to the meeting came with a large retinue to confer with some who were there. Concern as his intentions are not known	Useful as illustrates problems of powerful magnates jockeying for position in the absence of strong leadership.
• Fear of a general war and a large-scale slaughter unless the Most High, through your active involvement and good offices, administer a quick cure.	Useful as shows the reasons for appealing to Edward to help sort out the succession crisis in Scotland.

Possible points of significant omission may include:

- Maid of Norway, only direct surviving blood relation to the dead Alexander III had died on reaching Orkney causing the succession crisis.
- Fraser believes that Edward should come to an understanding with Balliol, and this is the only way to avoid civil war.
- The Earls of Mar and Atholl were also collecting their army, which further led to fear of civil war.
- Scots were looking for Edward I to arbitrate between the two competitors.
- Fear that the guardianship would collapse.
- Alexander had had a good working relationship with Edward I of England.
- Edward I had a reputation as a statesman.
- Fraser's letter led to a reaction from the Bruce faction: letter of the seven earls.
- Balliol was also manoeuvring for the crown, he had established a close relationship with Bishop Bek, Edward's chief representative in Scotland.
- Desire of Edward to revive English claims of overlordship.

- The majority of Scots looked kindly on Edward's intervention, at least at the beginning.
- Any other relevant points.

3. **Compare the views of Sources C and D about the life and death of William Wallace?** (5)

Candidates can be credited in a number of ways up to a maximum of 5 marks.

Possible points of comparison may include:

Overall: Sources C and **D** both agree on Wallace about several events during his career. They agree that he started out as an outlaw, was defeated at Falkirk and was executed by Edward. However **Source C** paints Wallace in a very negative light demonstrating a lot of bias, whereas **Source D** offers a more balanced judgement of his career.

Source C	Source D
Wallace was an outcast, robber and sacrilegious man. Wallace was a cruel robber who burnt churches and killed school boys.	Wallace became an outlaw because his father did not sign the Ragman Roll, and the Sheriff of Lanark killed his mistress.
Wallace could not resist the power of the English army at Falkirk, and fled leaving his people to be slain.	Wallace's army was worn down by knights and archers, but he escaped after making sure that he rescued the survivors of his army.
Wallace was taken prisoner by Edward's servants and taken to London.	Wallace was betrayed by Sir John Stewart of Mentieth.
Wallace was executed, his head was placed on a stake on London Bridge and his body divided into four and sent to the 4 quarters of Scotland.	Wallace was put to death by being strangled and dismembered.

Part B: The Age of the Reformation, 1542—1603

4. **How fully does Source B explain why Mary, Queen of Scots lost her throne?** (9)

Candidates may be credited in a number of ways up to a maximum of 9 marks.

A maximum of 2 marks may be given for answers which refer only to the source.

Possible points which may be identified in the source include:

- Bothwell was regarded as the main suspect in the murder of Darnley.
- Mary failed to mourn for Darnley which did not look good.
- The trial of Bothwell was to prove to be a farce.
- Her marriage to Bothwell was Protestant which appeared hypocritical.

Possible points of significant omission may include:

- Handbills went up in Edinburgh showing that popular opinion blamed Bothwell and implicated Mary.
- On the day of Bothwell's trial, Edinburgh was full of his armed supporters. This resulted in even Darnley's father, Lennox failing to give evidence.
- Catholics disappointed by Mary's actions; Mary did little to help the Catholic faith in Scotland.
- Marriage to Bothwell by Protestant rites alienated Catholics at home and abroad.

- Mary had the difficult situation of being a Catholic monarch in a land which had become Protestant.
- Marriage to Darnley lost Mary the support of her half brother James Stewart, Earl of Moray and other nobles. This led to the Chase about Raid.
- Mary made a poor choice of husband in Darnley. His life style and his craving for power proved to be an embarrassment.
- Lack of attendance by Mary at Council Meetings was a likely cause of the Rizzio murder. Nobles feeling neglected.
- Mary's apparent closeness to Bothwell before the murder of Darnley heightened suspicion of her involvement.
- Murder of Darnley was a major blow to Mary's position but she may have survived if she had acted properly.
- The marriage to Bothwell was regarded as scandalous. Bothwell had just recently had his own marriage annulled.
- Bothwell was not a popular figure with many of the nobles.
- A sizeable number of the nobles felt strongly enough to form the Confederate Lords and rise to overthrow Mary.
- In 1567, Mary was forced to abdicate by the Lords of the Congregation.
- She abdicated in favour of her infant son, with Moray returning as Regent.
- In 1568, she escaped and raised troops but was defeated by Moray. This resulted in her escape to England.
- Mary naively hoped that Elizabeth would provide her with troops; instead she was imprisoned until her execution in 1587.
- Any other valid point of explanation that meets the criteria described in the general marking principles for this kind of question.

5. **Evaluate the usefulness of Source A as evidence of the growth of Protestantism in Scotland before the Reformation of 1560.** (6)

Candidates can be credited in a number of ways up to a maximum of 6 marks.

Examples of aspects of the source and relevant comments:

Aspect of the source	Possible comment
Author: John Knox	More useful as Knox was the leader of the Protestant Reformation in Scotland. Less useful as may be biased account.
Type of Source: Book	More useful as extensive five volume account of the Reformation.
Purpose: To provide account of events during the Reformation	More useful as it gives an insight into the Protestant view of the events of the Reformation. Less useful as source is likely to be biased in favour of the Protestant movement.
Timing: Contemporary	More useful as from the time of the growth of Protestantism in Scotland.

Content	Possible comment
• The death of Walter Myln increased fervour amongst the Protestants.	Useful as shows how the burning of Walter Myln by Roman Catholics at St Andrews led to pro-Protestant feeling.
• Perth was to become a Protestant town.	More useful as illustrates the growth of Protestantism.
• John Knox felt able to return to Scotland and openly preach in Perth.	More useful as shows that Protestant leaders felt able to preach in the open showing the extent of support for the new faith.

Possible points of significant omission may include:

• Knox had not been in Scotland at the time of Myln's death.
• There was a growing interest in Protestant ideas as bibles and other literature arrived from Europe.
• Acts of Parliament were passed to protect the Catholic Church in Scotland which indicates that Protestant ideas were becoming a threat.
• Impact of the preaching tour of George Wishart.
• Confidence had grown amongst the Scots Protestants after Elizabeth became Queen of England in 1558.
• By 1558 in some east coast burghs Protestant congregations were meeting and using the English Prayer book.
• The Beggars Summons — notices during winter of 1558–59 on Friary doors demanding that the Friars leave the friaries.
• Bonds had been entered into by some of the Scots nobility.
• Scottish Protestant Lords organised themselves as the Lords of the Congregation.
• Any other valid point of explanation that meets the criteria described in the general marking principles for this kind of question.

6. Compare the views of Sources C and D about James VI's attempts to control the Kirk. (5)

Candidates can be credited in a number of ways up to a maximum of 5 marks.

Possible points of comparison may include:

Overall: Source C agrees with **Source D** that King James used various methods to attempt to control the Kirk, although **Source C** also shows that the Kirk wished to control the doctrine of its ministers.

Source C	Source D
General Assembly met at Perth as the king had requested.	General Assembly met at Perth rather than St Andrews as ministers in the north more likely to support the King. The King could choose the place where the Assembly met.
The King had the right to choose the date when the General Assembly would meet.	No meeting to be held without the King's knowledge.
In all the main towns ministers to be chosen by the congregation and the King.	Ministers in the main towns should not be appointed without the consent of the King.
No minister was to criticise the King and no man's name was to be rebuked from the pulpit.	Restrictions were placed on ministers' sermons, in particular commenting on politics and censuring individuals.

Part C: The Treaty of Union, 1689–1740

7. How fully does Source B explain the arguments for and against the Treaty of Union? (9)

Candidates may be credited in a number of ways up to a maximum of 9 marks.

A maximum of 2 marks may be given for answers which refer only to the source.

Possible points which may be identified in the source include:

• Scotland would become a province of England.
• Subjection of Scotland: Cornwall would send almost as many members to Parliament as whole of Scotland.
• Scots wanted to remain known as Scots and not British.
• Scotland had fought for honour as a nation and was recognised by foreign countries.

Possible points of significant omission may include:

• The creation of 'Scotlandshire' was a genuine fear for opponents of union.
• 45 Scots MPs in the House of Commons was felt to be under-representation.
• Many cherished what Lord Belhaven called 'Mother Caledonia'.
• Opponents of union wanted Scotland to remain an independent nation.

Arguments against union:

• British parliament would favour English trade over Scottish.
• Fear of loss of European trade.
• Royal burghs would be deprived of rights.
• Manufacturers may be ruined.
• English currency, weights and measures might be introduced.
• Presbyterians feared a British parliament dominated by Anglican church with bishops' seats in the House of Lords.
• Fears of reduction in status of Scottish nobility in British parliament.
• Scots Episcopalians opposed union and Hanoverian succession — only Stuart dynasty might restore episcopacy to Scottish church.

Arguments for union:

• Advantages in commerce and trade.
• Economy would improve — national product would increase.
• Scotland's trade would catch up with other European nations' free trade with English colonies.
• Protection of being in Great Britain.
• Common interests already with England.
• Advantages of Scottish politicians being part of the court of the king in London.
• Hanoverian succession offered security to Protestantism thus reducing threat from Popery: compared with Edict of Nantes and persecution of Huguenots.
• Union reduced risk of war.
• Any other valid point of explanation that meets the criteria described in the general marking principles for this kind of question.

8. **Evaluate the usefulness of Source A as evidence of worsening relations between Scotland and England between 1690 and 1705?** (6)

Candidates can be credited in a number of ways up to a maximum of 6 marks.

Examples of aspects of the source and relevant comments:

Aspect of the source	Possible comment
Author: John Dalrymple, Earl Stair	More useful as an important noble in the pro-Union camp. Less useful as he is clearly biased.
Type of Source: Speech	More useful as articulates views of those in the pro-Union camp.
Purpose: To remind Scots of treatment by English during Darien/to support an incorporating union	More useful as illustrates the problems Scotland had in attempting to set up an Empire of their own.
Timing: Contemporary	More useful as view is from the time of debate over union with England.
Content	**Possible comment**
• Scotland suffered from a lack of co-operation from England.	Useful as illustrates problems of a hostile England to Scottish trade.
• England treated Scots as pirates and enemy aliens, not fellow British subjects.	Useful as shows poor treatment of Scots by English and by implication this would improve if in union as British subjects.
• England encouraged Spain to attack the Scots colony.	Useful as illustrates methods used by the English to oppose the Darien scheme.

Possible points of significant omission may include:

- King William objected to Darien as it threatened English trade.
- William influenced many English investors to withdraw from the Company, antagonised many Scots.
- William persuaded the Dutch to refuse to sell ships to the Scots.
- East India Company stopped foreign investment in Company of Scotland.
- William instructed English colonists in Jamaica not to offer help to the Scots.
- William was influenced by English foreign policy towards Spain and France.
- No security for Scotland from Union of the Crowns.
- King William firmly controlled Scotland to reduce threat of Jacobite rebellion.
- Glencoe Massacre (in which Stair himself had been complicit).
- England's war with France affected English dealings with Scotland.
- Jacobite plot to assassinate William further strained relations.
- Continued effects on trade of English Navigation Acts of the 1660s.
- Issues concerning the succession — Act of Settlement (England).
- Act of Security (Scotland) — threat to restore the Stuarts.
- Wool Act and Wine Act in Scotland.
- Alien Act in England threatening Scottish trade with England.
- Consequence of 1688–89 Revolution: Scottish Parliament — no longer willing to 'rubber stamp' decisions taken in England.

- Scotland's economic problems — seven ill years, no help from England.
- England's fear that France may use Scotland as 'back door' — threat of invasion.
- Influence of the English Court on Scottish government — Queen Anne would employ only those who would support the Hanoverian Succession.
- Distrust existing between Episcopalian Church and Presbyterian Church of Scotland.
- Captain Green executed in Leith.
- Covenanters still agitating for Covenant of 1638 to be observed.
- Any other valid point of explanation that meets the criteria described in the general marking principles for this kind of question.

9. **Compare the views of Sources C and D about the reasons for the passing of the Treaty of Union.** (5)

Candidates can be credited in a number of ways up to a maximum of 5 marks.

Possible points of comparison may include:

Overall: Source C and **Source D** agree that the Squadrone and political management were reasons for the passing of the Treaty of Union, but they differ on the importance of the Equivalent.

Source C	Source D
Squadrone had a key role in outcome of union vote.	Squadrone votes proved critical in securing approval for several articles.
The Equivalent was crucial in carrying the treaty.	The Equivalent did not bribe MPs — support for union depended on more than material gain.
The Equivalent was an inducement to the Squadrone Volante	Eight of Squadrone did not benefit from government patronage.
Formidable political management machine of Court Party.	Court's success achieved by political management.

Part D: Migration and Empire, 1830–1939

10. **How fully does Source B illustrate the experience of immigrants in Scotland?** (9)

Candidates may be credited in a number of ways up to a maximum of 9 marks.

A maximum of 2 marks may be given for answers which refer only to the source.

Possible points which may be identified in the source include:

- Poor relations highlighted — bigotry, prejudice, intolerance shown by Scots, for example.
- Immigrants blamed for Scotland's misfortunes.
- Immigrants caused disease, hardship and unemployment.
- Immigrants seen as a lower class than the native Scot.

Possible points of significant omission may include:

- Immigrants brought their own culture, religion.
- Immigrants used as 'scapegoats' for economic and social problems within Scotland.
- Immigrants inhabited the poorest parts of towns in general.

- Lack of assimilation by some immigrant groups, especially Irish Catholics.
- Irish Catholics frequently faced sectarian prejudice.
- Protestant Irish more readily accepted into Scottish society.
- Lithuanians seen as a threat initially, but eventually assimilated well.
- Italians assimilated fairly well, but did not integrate; not viewed as a threat to Scottish way of life.
- Jewish immigrants faced some hostility but not widespread: this group assimilated fairly easily, though maintaining their unique identity.
- More positive view of immigrants given by employers generally, possibly due to the fact they would work for lower wages and at any type of work.
- Immigrants still unable to join certain clubs, associations even after a long period of residence.
- Development of a Protestant backlash at the growth of Catholic immigrants generally, but especially on collapse of Scottish economy in 1920s and after 1920 Education Act.
- Any other valid point of explanation that meets the criteria described in the general marking principles for this kind of question.

11. Evaluate the usefulness of Source A as evidence of the reasons for Scottish migration and emigration. (6)

Candidates can be credited in a number of ways up to a maximum of 6 marks.

Examples of aspects of the source and relevant comments:

Aspect of the source	Possible comment
Author: Emigration Agent	More useful as it gives the views of an emigration agent representing Canada.
Type of Source: Report	More useful as source is official report so likely to be telling the truth.
Purpose: To highlight a problem in attracting emigrants to Canada	More useful as it highlights a problem that the Canadians have in attracting emigrants to Canada.
Timing: Contemporary	More useful as it is from the time when many Scots emigrated to foreign shores.
Content	**Possible comment**
• Emigration Agencies actively working to attract emigrants	More useful as it illustrates one of the methods used by countries in recruiting Scots to emigrate.
• New Zealand and Australian authorities' work is widespread, offering free passages and other inducements and diverting potential recruits from Canada	More useful as the source shows how different countries worked, in this case offering inducements to potential emigrants.
• Newspapers also push their cause as they gain revenue from their advertisements	More useful as source illustrates how newspapers also had an interest in encouraging Scots to emigrate.

Possible points of significant omission may include:

- Domineering landlords and lack of real opportunities encouraged emigration from the Highlands of Scotland.
- Inducements offered by foreign lands, e.g. free land in Canada.
- Use of free and assisted passages by many territories to encourage Scottish emigrants, e.g. to both agricultural and urban workers.
- The Highland Problem.
- The Highland Clearances.
- Failure of the kelp and herring industries.
- Effects of the Agricultural Revolution on farming and employment.
- Effects of Industrial Revolution on craftsmen.
- Sub-division of land into crofts.
- Harsh employment conditions on the land.
- Government schemes to assist emigration, e.g. Highland and Islands Emigration Society.
- Transport Revolution, i.e. from sail to steam ships.
- Attractions of the 'big city'-employment, better wages, easier work.
- Discovery of gold in the USA.
- Any other valid point of explanation that meets the criteria described in the general marking principles for this kind of question.

12. Compare the views of Sources C and D about the contribution of Scots to the economic growth and development of the Empire. (5)

Candidates can be credited in a number of ways up to a maximum of 5 marks.

Possible points of comparison may include:

Overall: Source C and **Source D** agree that emigrant Scots made a significant and positive contribution to the growth and economic development of the Empire, but while **Source C** is totally positive in the view **Source D** adds a note of caution that some Scots made a less than positive contribution to their adopted land although the numbers are relatively few.

Developed through detail:

Source C	Source D
Scots have played important roles in the economic development of New Zealand.	Enterprise of the Dunedin merchants has done much for the commerce and prosperity of Otago.
Scots noted for their contribution to education, the first high school for girls in Otago opened in 1871 due to the efforts of a Scot.	The Scot has made his mark in the field of education, setting up schools in the area.
Scots were strongly over-represented among those involved in health matters.	Several of the Scots' descendants became doctors administering to the health of the local population.
Otago had strong links with the Edinburgh medical school and Scots-born people had a continuing impact in the scientific field.	A Scot founded the Geological Survey Of New Zealand and managed New Zealand's premier scientific society.

Part E: The Impact of the Great War, 1914—1928

13. How fully does Source B describe the impact of war on Scottish Society? (9)

Candidates may be credited in a number of ways up to a maximum of 9 marks.

A maximum of 2 marks may be given for answers which refer only to the source.

Possible points which may be identified in the source include:

- Scottish recruitment was a 'higher percentage than any other country in UK'
- 'Scottish forces suffered disproportionately higher losses'.
- 'Wartime revolutionized the position of women in the economy'
- 'The slaughter remained to haunt the nation'.

Possible points of significant omission may include:

Recruitment:

- Recruitment and Conscription: By the end of the first week in September 1914, Glasgow was able to boast that it had recruited more than 22,000 men.
- By December 1914, 25% of the male labour force of western Scotland had already signed up.
- 13% of those who volunteered in 1914—15 were Scots.
- Young Scots urged to join the army through a mixture of peer pressure, feelings of guilt, appeals to patriotism, hopes for escapism and adventure, heroism, self-sacrifice and honour. For the unemployed, the army offered a steady wage.
- Kitchener's campaign was a huge success: examples such as by the end of August 20,000 men from the Glasgow area had joined up.
- In Scotland there were no official 'Pals Battalions' but in reality — the Highland Light Infantry/Tramway battalion; the 16th battalion/the Boys Brigade.
- In Edinburgh, Cranston's Battalion and McCrae's battalions became part the Royal Scots. McCrae's battalion was the most famous because of its connection with Hearts football club.

Casualty rates:

- The official figure given at the end of the war calculated that Scotland had suffered 74,000 dead.
- Huge sacrifice of Scots during the war: of 557,000 Scots who enlisted in the services, 26.4% lost their lives. One in five British casualties were Scottish.
- Campaigners for a national war memorial claimed the figure was over one hundred thousand.

Women in Wartime economy:

- Shift towards military and manufacturing employment and a temporary decline in some service industries.
- Number of women working increased from 593,210 in 1911 and 638,575 a decade later.
- Before the war less than 4,000 women worked in heavy industry in Scotland.
- Number of women employed in munitions in Scotland rose to 31,500 by October 1918.
- Many women workers were used for 'dilution' of labour
- Women worked as conductors on trams and buses, as typists and secretaries and nearly 200,000 women found work in government departments.

Remembrance:

- Collective national grief in Scotland.
- Also great pride in the achievement of the Scottish units.
- Local memorials were erected around the country.
- Scots wanted their own memorial in tribute to their special sacrifice: Edinburgh Castle houses the memorial and museum. It was officially opened in 1928. Over 148,000 Scottish names are carved on the national war memorial.
- The British Legion was set up and in 1921 the British Legion Scotland. Poppy Day started at the same time. The act of silence at 11am on 11 November started in 1919.
- Pacifism and Conscientious Objectors: People objected for religious, ethical or political reasons.
- DORA took industries, communications and resources under direct Government control, censorship of the press, imprisonment of war protestors, civilians could be tried under court martial, reduced hours of public houses etc
- Rent Strikes saw a prominent role played by women like Mary Barbour, Helen Crawfurd and Agnes Dollan.
- These women would even physically oppose evictions and won with the passing the Rent Restriction Act freezing rent levels and introducing state intervention in the private housing rental market for the first time.
- Any other valid point of explanation that meets the criteria described in the general marking principles for this kind of question.

14. Evaluate the usefulness of Source A as evidence of the experience of Scots on the Western Front. (6)

Candidates can be credited in a number of ways up to a maximum of 6 marks.

Examples of aspects of the source and relevant comments:

Aspect of the source	Possible comment
Author: Private Thomas McCall	Useful as McColl was present at the battle of Loos therefore has experience of events.
Type of Source: Diary	More useful as likely to be a truthful memory of events as a personal account.
Purpose: To record events during the battle of Loos	Useful as a gory account, so looks uncensored, but Less useful as may be a one-sided account.
Timing: Contemporary	More useful as contemporary account from the time of the battle of Loos.
Content	**Possible comment**
My god I am done for	Useful as it illustrates fear of death among Scottish soldiers.
He lifted his wounded pal's kilt then gave a laugh	Useful as it shows camaraderie of fighting as well as maintenance of distinct Scottish identity.
Machine guns were raking the street and bayonet fighting was going on.	Useful as it shows Scottish experience of fighting.

Possible points of significant omission may include:

- Military tradition of Scots: kilted regiments considered to be good soldiers.
- Scots contribution to battle of Loos: deserves to be called a Scottish battle owing to the large number of Scottish troops in action. 30,000 took part in the attack.

- One third of British casualties were Scottish at Loos.
- Loos was first taste of action for Kitchener's New Army volunteers.
- The 9th and 15th Scottish Divisions were to be involved in the attack.
- Experience of Scots in Trenches: conditions such as trench foot, rats, etc.
- Experience of fighting and its effects: bombardment, shellshock, etc.
- Battle of the Somme: 3 Scottish divisions 9th, 15th [Scottish] and 51st [Highland] took part as well as numerous Scottish battalions in other units: i.e. the Scots Guards in the Household Division. 51 Scottish infantry battalions took part in the Somme offensive at some time.
- Battle of Arras: Saw concentration of 44 Scottish battalions and 7 Scottish-named Canadian battalions, attacking on the first day, making it the largest concentration of Scots to have fought together.
- One third of British casualties were Scottish at Arras.
- Role in other battles, such as Cambrai and Third Ypres.
- Experience of Scottish women on Western Front: Scottish Ambulance Unit, etc as balance in question that asks only about "Scots on Western Front".
- Any other valid point of explanation that meets the criteria described in the general marking principles for this kind of question.

15. **Compare the views of Sources C and D about the economic effect of the war on Scotland.** (5)

Candidates can be credited in a number of ways up to a maximum of 5 marks.

Possible points of comparison may include:

Overall: Sources C and **D** agree that Scotland suffered economic decline in the post-war years in a number of key industries including shipbuilding, coal, jute and agriculture.

Source C	Source D
The Clyde in 1913 launched 750,000 tons of shipping but by the end of the 1920s the Clyde was launching merely 56,000 tons of shipping.	Between 1921 and 1923 shipbuilding ion the Clyde dropped (and) the Clyde was already beginning to pay for the artificial boom which had rescued it during the war years.
In 1913 Scotland employed 140,000 miners but 20 years later the coal industry was producing a third less coal.	Coal production suffered.
The Dundee jute trade was deeply depressed.	Jute production in Dundee was adversely affected by declining orders.
In the late 1920s the value of Scottish farming was falling.	According to the Board (of agriculture) the decline was not restricted to any particular part of the country but was widespread throughout Scotland.

MODEL PAPER 1
SECTION 2: BRITISH

Part A: Church, State and Feudal Society, 1066—1406

Candidates can be credited up to a maximum of 20 marks.

16. **'The nobility received all of the benefits from the feudal structure while the peasants received none.' How valid is this view of medieval society?**

Context
In medieval life the peasant class played an important part in feudal society. They made up the largest group within the feudal system. However, the peasant class did rely upon those above them in feudal society.

The peasant class
- The feudal term of villein or serf indicated a peasant who was not free to leave his home farm or village. They were bought and sold along with the land and were expected to work at least three days a week in the lord's lands without recompense and hand over the best of their produce in exchange for the rent of their farmland.
- Peasants tended to work hard, mostly in the agricultural sector. All the work had to be done by hand and this resulted in long hours of back-breaking work.
- Not all peasants received the same amount of good farming land, and often it was the case that land was rotated amongst the peasants.
- Accommodation was often very poor, especially for the lower strata of peasant society. Many peasants lived in poorly constructed one-bedroom dwellings, which they shared with their animals. A single hearth provided all the heat, lighting and cooking facilities.
- Firewood was at a premium: peasants were forced to pay a penny to their lord for the right to pick up fallen wood for the fires.
- Food was basic and, in times of famine, starvation was a real threat.
- Peasants played an important part of feudal society, beyond the need for a productive class working in agriculture. It was expected that peasants would run their own day-to-day lives without the need for the feudal lord's presence. Local reeves and bailiffs, appointed by the peasants or the lord himself, would act in his stead.

Other factors:
Landowners
- Held lands given by the king.
- Provided economic support through payment of taxes.

Nobles
- Had duties to perform for the king, usually military service.
- Barons relied on the loyalty of their followers and needed to ensure that they did not lose that authority.
- During the time of civil war or a weak monarch, barons could increase their position and political power.

Knights
- Tournaments trained knights in warfare, the chivalric code, and in being loyal to their feudal overlord.
- Chivalry for many knights meant more than just fighting. Many of the popular stories of the time centred on legends such as The Arthurian.

- Knights like William the Marshal saw his career as a way of becoming rich and famous.
- Knights were the warring class within medieval society.

Church

- Provided church services for baptism, marriage and death.
- Spiritual guidance through prayer .
- Provided social support such as hospitals, inns and education.
- Maintained employment in the village, eg the wool trade.
- Monks (the regular church) took direction from the Pope/king although they were cloistered and therefore detached from society.
- Priests (the secular church) were not restricted in their prayer and were in daily contact with society.

King

- Hoped to encourage loyalty to the monarch, eg Edward I.
- Monarchs required the church to maintain government records, laws and taxes.
- The king was supposed to offer protection, justice and guidance to his subjects.

Any other relevant factors.

Candidates can be credited up to a maximum of 20 marks.

17. To what extent did David I increase the centralisation of royal power during his reign?

Context

David I reigned from 1124–1153. He is credited with carrying out a Davidian Revolution in Scotland including his foundation of burghs, implementation of the ideals of Gregorian Reform, foundation of monasteries, Normanisation of the Scottish government, and the introduction of feudalism.

Development of the economy

- David introduced numerous monasteries, which helped to develop the wool trade, eg Melrose Abbey, and cultivate barren land.
- David granted charters to over 15 towns.
- Trade was encouraged with Germany, Scandinavia and France. David introduced the first Scottish coins to help promote trade.
- Introduction of feudal landholding.
- During his time in England, David became an admirer of the feudal landholding system. He introduced a form of military feudalism into areas of Scotland, notably the southwest, Lothian and the northeast. Noble families were given grants of land. In return they offered David their support, both politically and militarily.

Development of the royal government

- David created a small but loyal group that had specific roles to aid him in the running of his household and the kingdom. Sheriffs replaced thanes in the remote areas of the kingdom. They offered direct royal contact for those away from the traditional seat of power.

Development of the royal military forces

- The new feudal forces brought to David by his introduction of feudalism offered a significant advantage when dealing with the Celtic Mormaers. Traditionally it was the Mormaers who controlled the summoning of the common army of Scotland. Now David had an independent force loyal to him. However, this force often did not work well with the other elements of the Scottish forces, as seen at the disastrous Battle of the Standard.

Development of the justice system

- New Scottish barons were given the rights to hold their own courts within their fiefs. This was an obvious extension of the king's law, rather than reliance on the traditional Celtic courts led by Brechons, experts in the law. Eventually these Celtic courts died out and were replaced with sheriff courts. The gradual acceptance of the kings law led the way to the decrease of importance of the Mormaers and the acceptance of central control.

Development of the Church

- Started by David's mother Margaret, the introduction of the Roman Church at the expense of the Celtic one offered a significant boon to the development of royal authority. As the Church preached the divine grace of the king, it was hard to justify any rebellions against him.

Any other relevant factors.

Candidates can be credited up to a maximum of 20 marks.

18. How successfully did King John of England increase royal authority during his reign?

Context

King John was the youngest, and favourite, son of Henry II and Eleanor of Aquitaine. On the death of his elder brother Richard, he became King of England despite the claims of his nephew Arthur. He struggled to hold the widespread Angevin Empire together in the face of the challenges of the Capetian monarch of France and his own barons.

Royal finances

- John was more efficient in collecting taxes.
- Used wardships to raise cash.
- Introduced new taxes: eg 1207 tax on income and moveable goods.
- Improved quality of silver coinage.

Impact of the loss of Normandy

- Had an impact on the royal finances as it reduced John's income.
- The recovery of the royal lands north of the Loire became the focus of John's foreign policy and led to policies which eventually led to challenges to his authority.
- The need to fund warfare to recover Normandy led to the frequent use of Scutage to raise cash. It was used much more frequently than under Henry II and Richard, levied 11 times in 17 years.

Administration of government

- John filled many of the roles in the royal household with new men; especially from Poitou. This was not popular with the English barons.

Military power

- Established the Royal Navy.
- Extensive use of mercenaries rather than feudal service.
- Able to exert his military strength against the nobility and the French.
- John was an able military commander; ie when conflict started with France and his nephew Arthur, he defeated them and captured Arthur.
- His forces and his allies were decisively beaten at the Battle of Bouvines in 1214.

Law and justice

- Increasingly partial judgements were resented.
- John increased professionalism of local sergeants and bailiffs.
- Extended the system of coroners.

Relations with the Church

- John fell out with Pope Innocent III over the appointment of the Archbishop of Canterbury. Innocent insisted on the appointment of Langton which John opposed.
- Papel interdict laid on England and Wales for 6 years.
- In 1213 John made England a fief of the papacy.
- Noble uprising led by Archbishop of Canterbury.

Relations with the nobility

- Nobles refused to fight in France. This was especially true of the northern Barons who had little stake in France.
- Nobles felt their status was reduced by use of mercenaries.
- John became increasingly suspicious of the nobles.
- High cost of titles led to nobles becoming overly indebted.
- John took hostages to ensure nobles behaved. He showed he was prepared to execute children if the father opposed him.
- Relations worsened over the course of the reign, ending with Magna Carta and rebellion of many Barons.

John's personality

- He could be generous, had a coarse sense of humour and was intelligent.
- However, could also be suspicious and cruel: vicious in his treatment of prisoners and nobles.
- Arthur, his nephew, died in mysterious circumstances.
- Powerful lords like William de Braose fell from favour and were persecuted. William's wife and son were imprisoned and died. He died in exile in France.

Any other relevant factors.

Part B: The Century of Revolutions, 1603–1702

Candidates can be credited up to a maximum of 20 marks.

19. 'Religion was the most important cause of the challenge to the authority of King James I in England.' How valid is this view?

Context

James VI of Scotland became James I of England in 1603. He had been used to absolute rule in Scotland and expected the same in England. However, the English parliament would not accept the divine right of kings, and expected to wield some power itself.

Religion

- James I had a lifelong hatred of Puritanism; Puritans existed in large numbers in the House of Commons and were demanding church reform.
- The king feared moves towards Presbyterianism and rejected the Millenary Petition at the Hampton Court Conference of 1604, saying 'no bishops, no king', and vowing to maintain an Episcopalian Church of England.
- James I relaxed the Recusancy Laws against Roman Catholics, which revealed that there were more Roman Catholics than many in the House of Commons had feared.
- The Gunpowder Plot of 1605 increased tension and turned many against Roman Catholics.
- Parliament was horrified that the king allowed his son to marry a Roman Catholic French princess and allowed her to celebrate mass privately at court.

Other factors.
Finance

- James I wanted to exist financially independent of Parliament and manipulated the statute books to re-impose anachronistic laws which were designed merely to raise revenue.

- Fiscal devices such as monopolies and wardships were unpopular.
- The king alienated his natural allies in the House of Lords by selling honours and titles and appearing to devalue the status of the aristocracy.
- Increases in customs duties led to the Bates Case in 1606 which James I won, although Parliament declared the duties illegal in 1610.

Politics

- Parliament had been encouraged since the days of Henry VIII to make policy, and therefore its members felt they could criticise the Crown freely; however, James I asserted the divine right of kings as he claimed he had been accustomed to this in Scotland, which made his status as a foreigner more unattractive to the English Parliament.
- The House of Commons opposed James I to such an extent that the stability of the nation was affected.
- The king conceded defeat in the Goodwin Case which gave Parliament fresh impetus to challenge him further.
- James I attempted to curtail parliamentary freedom of speech by imprisoning outspoken MPs in the Tower of London when Parliament was dissolved.

Law

- James I attempted to control the court system by appointing judges who would favour the Crown; Parliament saw this as unfair and objected to the abuse of power.
- The king imposed martial law in towns where troops were preparing to embark on foreign campaigns; Parliament opposed this.
- The king billeted troops in the homes of civilians in order to enforce the law.

Ruling England and Scotland

- Parliament in London rejected the king's proposed union between Scotland and England as they felt he was making no attempt to understand the English constitution, which accorded greater powers to Parliament in London than were accorded in Edinburgh.
- James I sought to obtain greater taxation in Scotland, and employed members of loyal clans as government agents, at considerable expense, to extract payment of overdue taxes or fines.
- James I exerted his influence in the Highlands with force, giving permission for certain clans to attack clans who had not professed loyalty to him.
- As legitimate king of Scotland, James I (and VI) was carrying out a role into which he had been born; however, his position in trying to maintain rule over two kingdoms, and the dominance of England, meant Scotland proved to be more than a minor irritation in his attempts to achieve stability.

Any other relevant factors.

Candidates can be credited up to a maximum of 20 marks.

20. To what extent did religious issues bring about the English Civil War?

Context

Charles I was monarch of the three kingdoms of England, Scotland, and Ireland from 1625 until his execution in 1649. Charles believed in the divine right of kings and thought he could govern according to his own conscience. Many of his subjects opposed his policies.

Religious issues

- In 1628 Charles I made William Laud Archbishop of Canterbury. Laud wanted to stamp out Puritanism and believed in the authority and discipline of the Church and sacred status of clergy.
- Anyone who offended the Church was brought to trial.
- Laud's High Church policies were detested by all Puritans, including many MPs.
- Charles I authorised Laud's punishment of Puritan preachers and clamp-down on conventicles.
- Tight censorship of printed word to prevent criticism of High Church.
- 20,000 Puritans fled England to America in 10 years.
- In 1637 Laud imposed the Prayer Book in Scotland. Prayer Book fiercely opposed by members of Scottish Kirk.
- Thousands of Scots signed the National Covenant pledging to defend Presbyterianism.
- Charles I lost 1st and 2nd Bishops' Wars in 1639 and 1640 in attempt to enforce the Prayer Book.
- Charles I allowed Queen Henrietta Maria to celebrate Mass publicly at court with a representative of the Pope in attendance, which infuriated Puritans in Parliament.
- King influenced by wife who encouraged him to relax laws against Roman Catholics, Laud who encouraged him to promote High Church policies, and Thomas Wentworth whose work made king more absolute.

Other factors

Economic issues

- Charles I wanted to be financially independent, but resorted to anachronistic methods of raising revenue, such as forced loans, forest laws and distraint of knighthood. Methods unpopular with MPs.
- Tonnage and poundage tax allowed kings a share in profits from farm produce.
  Parliament only voted to grant this to Charles I for 1 year, but he continued to raise it without their consent.
- King used Court of Star Chamber to impose heavy fines on those committing crimes against royal policy.
- Charles used legal loopholes to sell monopolies to companies rather than individuals.
- In 1634 he re-imposed Ship Money and in 1635 extended the tax inland.
- Parliament opposed this, as there was no guarantee that it would always be used for ship-building.
- Financial crisis between 1640 and 1642, Charles I asked for Parliamentary funding for Bishops Wars. MPs took advantage, demanding abolition of prerogative courts and ship money, introduction of Triennial Act, and impeachment of Wentworth who was condemned to death.

Political issues

- Charles I believed in the Divine Right, treated promises to Parliament lightly, was a poor judge of character and surrounded by advisors unsuited to their positions.
- Parliament tried to introduce bills and Charles I disapproved.
- He imprisoned MPs who criticised his stance against them and some remained in prison for up to 11 years.
- The House of Commons antagonised the king by impeaching serving government ministers. Impeachments designed to show that ministers were responsible to Parliament as well as Crown.
- When Parliament was asked to support Charles I's foreign policy it drew up Petition of Right in 1628 and forced king to sign it.

- Although it reduced the king's powers, in 1629 Charles I dissolved Parliament because it criticised his levying of tonnage and poundage.
- Between 1629 and 1640 the "Eleven Years Tyranny" — Charles I ruled without Parliament. Threats of Scottish invasion in 1640–2 led to drastic action by Parliament in forming its own army.
- Rebellion in Ireland, hostilities broke out in Ireland as people rose up against ruthless policies imposed by Wentworth during 1630s.
- Political crisis, January 1642, Charles entered Commons to try and arrest 5 Puritan MPs, but they escaped.
- Civil War, Charles I left London for the north, joined by two-thirds of Lords and one-third of Commons, by March 1642 Parliament formed an army and the king responded by raising the standard at Nottingham.

Legal issues

- Charles I's use of Court of Star Chamber caused resentment in Parliament. MPs believed Star Chamber was being used as instrument for enforcing royal policy.
- In 1637 people were outraged by sentencing of 3 men to be pilloried, have ears cropped and be imprisoned for life merely for writing Puritanical pamphlets.
- The king allowed Archbishop of Canterbury to use Court of High Commission to put on trial anyone who opposed his religious policy and to persecute Puritans.
- Thomas Wentworth, Earl of Stafford, was king's chief minister from 1628. Wentworth used Council of the North to enforce ruthless "Thorough" policies in north of England, put down rebellions and influence justice system.
- In 1633 Wentworth was made Lord Deputy of Ireland. There he revived Ireland's fishing, farming and linen industries but this was merely to generate more money for the Crown and make the Irish subservient to the king.

Any other relevant factors.

*Candidates can be credited **up to a maximum of 20 marks**.*

21. How important were the actions of James II in causing the Revolution of 1688—1689?

Context

James II came to the throne in 1685. James was a Catholic and many politicians in England were deeply loyal to the Protestant Church of England. When James tried to restore Catholicism in England many Protestants in England began to plot to overthrow James.

James II

- James II, who practised Roman Catholicism, attempted to rule absolutely.
- Dismissed Parliament in 1685.
- Replaced Anglican advisors with Roman Catholic ones; placed Roman Catholics in important posts at Oxford and Cambridge Universities.
- Stationed 13,000-strong army outside London.
- Re-established Prerogative Courts in 1686 and used Suspending Powers to suspend laws against Roman Catholics.
- Used Dispensing Powers to dismiss these laws from statute books.

Other factors

Charles II

- Charles II, who had been exiled in France during Interregnum, had accepted limitations on his power when monarchy was restored in 1660. Prerogative law courts were abolished, non-parliamentary taxation was prohibited, and Triennial Act remained in place.

- Loopholes, however, meant the king could still make policy.
- Puritans lost power in House of Commons.
- Charles II initially did not try to abuse power. In turn, Parliament realised that the king could not live off his own finances and granted him taxation on alcohol.
- Nevertheless, towards the end of his reign Charles II ruled without Parliament for 4 years.
- Divine Right preached from pulpits. It seemed the old Stuart combative approach to rule was re-asserting itself over Parliament.

Religious issues

- Issue of church governance which arose before the Civil War had not been resolved. Many MPs fearful of continued Stuart dominance of Anglican Church policy.
- James II's promotion of Roman Catholics to key posts antagonised Presbyterians.
- Heir to the throne to be raised as a Roman Catholic.
- Divide between Episcopalians and Presbyterians in Scotland created hostility from Scottish Parliament towards monarchy.

Political issues

- Divine Right and absolutism as practised by Stuart monarchs continued to provoke resentment from MPs.
- Status of monarchy questioned by Parliament.
- Charles II's dismissal of Parliament resembled Charles I's 11-Year Tyranny.
- James II's use of Suspending and Dispensing Powers seen as an abuse by Parliament.
- Questions raised over control of the army.

The role of Parliament

- Parliament resented James II's abuses of power but took comfort from the thought that he would be succeeded by Protestant daughter Mary.
- However, the king married again and had son, to be raised as Roman Catholic.
- June 1688, Parliament wrote to Mary, by now married to Dutch Prince William of Orange, offering the Crown.
- William and Mary arrived in November with an army and on Christmas Day James II fled to France after his younger daughter Anne as well as leading generals declared support for Mary. William and Mary became joint sovereigns on February 13th 1689.
- There were no clear lines of authority.
  Questions existed over who held sway in religious matters; Parliament feared a monarch could try to impose Roman Catholicism on country.
  Still possible for a monarch to be financially independent of Parliament and manipulate succession in favour of Roman Catholic line.
- Both Charles II and James II had proved it was possible for a monarch to rule without Parliament, influence legislative and judicial procedure, control army for own means, and assert religious and political will on Scotland and Ireland.
- Parliament saw need to agree constitutional status for monarchy.
- With no Bill of Rights, any future monarchs, including William and Mary, could preach notions of Divine Right, absolutism and passive obedience.
- Future limitations on power of monarchy would have to be written into law.
- In 1689 Parliament drew up the Bill of Rights, which legalised the new relationship between Crown and Parliament.
  This would ensure no future king or queen could attempt absolutism.

- Bill of Rights would be part of a wider set of legal provisions for new order in the country. Settlement established that kings and queens should depend upon Parliament for finance, succession would be determined by Parliament and not the sitting monarch, judicial system would be controlled by Parliament, and no future monarch could rule without Parliament.

Part C: The Atlantic Slave Trade

Candidates can be credited up to a maximum of 20 marks.

22. **To what extent were Britain's military victories in the wars of the eighteenth century the main reason for the development of the Atlantic Slave Trade?**

Context
The Atlantic slave trade of the 18th century was a new kind of slavery and was on a scale much greater than ever before. West Indian plantation owners increasingly turned to African slaves for labour.

Military victories

- The Treaty of Utrecht, at the end of the war of the Spanish Succession gave the British the asiento or right to be the sole supplier of slaves to Spain's colonies in South America for a period of 30 years. The contract for this was given to the newly formed South Sea Company. Queen Anne was given 22.5% of the companies stock.
- In 1714 George I inherited her shares and purchased more. Although in 1720 massive speculation in the company's shares produced the 'South Sea Bubble' where shares crashed ruining many of the investors. Nevertheless the company survived and between 1715 and 1731 transported approximately 64,000 African slaves.
- The Seven Years War was chiefly an imperial war fought between Britain, France and Spain and many of the most important battles of the Seven Years War were fought at sea to win control of valuable overseas colonies.
- Britain emerged from the war as the leading European imperial power, having made large territorial gains in North America and the Caribbean, as well as India. Slave labour was necessary to exploit these gains.

Other factors
Importance of the slave trade to British economy

- Financial, commercial, legal and insurance institutions emerged to support the activities of the slave traders; slave traders became bankers, plantation owners became MPs, stately homes were built on the proceeds of the slave trade and many new businesses were financed by profits made from slave-trading.

Religious factors

- The Church of England had links to slavery through the United Society for the Propagation of the Gospel missionary organisations which had plantations and owned slaves; the Church of England supported the laws not to educate enslaved Africans; some Bible passages such as the Curse of Ham from Genesis were used to justify slavery; other Bible passages such as Exodus were banned in British colonies because they could be interpreted as being hostile to slavery.

Shortage of labour

- High death rate among native populations due to lack of resistance to diseases brought by European traders and colonists, and ill-treatment at the hands of colonists, created labour shortage in the West Indies.

- The failure to find alternative sources of labour: few colonists were willing to work on plantations as manual labour; there was a limit to the number of British criminals who could be sent as forced labour; limited number and timespan of indentured servants.
- Huge profits were to be made from trade in tropical crops such as sugar cane; this created increased demand for labour to work on plantations in the colonies.
- Tropical crops such as sugar cane required a large labour force to plant, look after, harvest and process in harsh, unpleasant conditions.

The legal position

- The status of slaves as property was long-established. It took a series of court cases from the 1770s that dealt with the rights of former slaves within the British Isles to challenge the legality of slavery and the slave trade, eg Granville Sharp's resolute campaign to prove the illegality of slavery in England that culminated in Lord Mansfield's decision in the Somerset case.

Racial factors

- Facing a labour shortage, colonists turned to the labour system developed in Spain, Portugal, and the Atlantic islands, ie the use of enslaved Africans; entrenched racism among merchants and landowners meant that enslaving African captives was accepted by colonists; the unequal relationship that was created as a consequence of the enslavement of Africans was justified by the ideology of racism — the belief that Africans were inferior to Europeans; many Europeans claimed that African captives would be executed in Africa if the slave trade was abolished and that African slaves benefited from being in the care of enlightened Europeans rather than African despots hostile to slavery.

Any other relevant factors.

*Candidates can be credited **up to a maximum of 20 marks**.*

23. 'Fear of slave resistance and revolt determined how slaves were treated.' How valid is this view?

Context

Slaves were abducted people from Africa. Naturally they resented being stolen from their previous lives. Some enslaved people took opportunities to resist or fight back in differing ways.

Safety and the fear of revolt

- Both on slave ships and plantations there was a constant fear of a slave revolt.
- On ships, security was paramount, as crews were heavily outnumbered by their cargoes. This meant that slaves were kept under decks for long periods. It also meant that they were usually shackled for the whole passage.
- As the number of revolts in slave ships grew so did the cost as larger crews were required.
- On plantations, there was fear of slave resistance, both overt and otherwise.
- Harsh legal codes were enacted by island assemblies (dominated by planters) covering the treatment/punishment of runaways as well as those who resisted openly.
- Escaped ex-slaves called Maroons raided plantations, killed militia and freed slaves. Due to the inability of the planters to crush them they entered into a Treaty with them which gave them some toleration in return for leaving the slave system alone.

- **Other factors**

Humanitarian concerns

- Humanitarian concerns had little impact on the treatment of slaves in Africa or on the Middle Passage. Participants were not in daily close contact with slaves and did not get to know them personally.
- The West Indian plantations, on the other hand, were small communities. Where members of the owner's family were present, bonds of affection did grow between slaves and free. Where such personal ties did not exist, there was less moderation of the brutalities of slavery.

Religious concerns

- Slave traders/owners were able to point to the existence of slavery in the Bible, and use this as a justification for the institution.
- Slave traders/owners claimed that slaves were being exposed to Christianity; enslavement was therefore good for them, as it gave them a chance of eternal salvation.
- Some participants were religious and moderated their treatment of slaves accordingly.

Financial considerations

- In essence, the slave trade and the institution of slavery were commercially based. Most participants entered the trade or owned or worked the plantations as a means of income. Financial considerations were usually paramount.
- The debate over 'loose' or 'tight' pack on board slave ships had little to do with humanitarianism. In loose pack, slaves were treated better and had better conditions, but the prime motivation was to transport as many slaves as possible to the auctions in the West Indies, alive.
- To extract as much work from slaves as possible on the plantations, slaves were often beaten or worse.
- As slaves were property, bought and paid for, they were valuable. On the other hand, they were cheap enough to work, or beat, to death. This was known as 'wastage'.

Racism and prejudice

- There was ignorance of African culture and achievements. Africans were regarded by some Europeans as almost another species. This was used as an excuse for extreme brutality.

Any other relevant factors.

*Candidates can be credited **up to a maximum of 20 marks**.*

24. To what extent was hostile propaganda the major obstacle to the abolition of the slave trade?

Context

As the campaign to abolish the slave trade grew in size and influence so did the campaign by 'vested interests' to keep slavery.

Propaganda against abolition

- The pro-slavery lobby issued pamphlets to try to counter the arguments of the abolitionists.
- Supporters of slavery and the slave trade could try to claim that the enslaved on plantations were treated at least as well as the working classes in Britain.
- Abolitionists were accused of being radicals sympathetic towards the increasingly extreme revolutionaries in France.
- To be pro-abolition was seen as being unpatriotic as a result.
- Abolition, it was argued, would lead to the loss of the West Indian colonies to France or America.

- Other factors

Events in France

- War with Revolutionary France from 1793, also took people's attention away from the abolition campaign.
- It encouraged the belief among many MPs that the abolitionist cause was associated with revolutionary ideas. eg Clarkson openly supported the French Revolution.
- Radicals used the same tactics as abolitionists to win public support – associations, petitions, cheap publications, public lectures, public meetings, pressure on Parliament; some abolitionists were linked to radicals and therefore they had to be resisted because of fear that events in France might be repeated in Britain.
- In 1794 the radical (Jacobin) national Convention voted to end slavery in the French Colonies. British government became suspicious of radicals as represented by mass petitions.
- Slave rebellion in Saint-Domingue—Abolition was associated with this symbol of brutal violence and in turn led to an exaggerated, general fear of slave revolts. Toussaint l'Ouverture was denounced. This was linked to fears of Jacobinism.
- Slave violence played into the hands of the slave lobby, confirming their warnings of anarchy. Britain suffered humiliation when it attempted to take the rebel French Colony and was beaten by disease and the ex-slave army.

Attitude of successive British governments

- These were influenced by powerful vested interests such as MPs and merchants from London, Liverpool and Bristol; abolitionists found it easier to win support from general public, most of whom could not vote, than persuade MPs to vote for abolition.
- Belief of slave owners and their supporters that millions of pounds worth of property would be threatened by the abolition of the slave trade.
- The slave trade was necessary to provide essential labour on the plantations; there was fear that abolition would ruin the colonies.

The importance of the slave trade to the British economy

- The trade generated finance; West Indian colonies were an important source of valuable exports to European neighbours.
- Taxes would have to be raised to compensate for the loss of trade and revenue.
- Abolition would help foreign rivals such as France as other nations would fill the gap left by Britain.
- British cotton mills relied on cheap, slave-produced cotton.
- British consumers benefited from cheap, slave-produced sugar.
- Ports like Liverpool, Bristol and Glasgow also benefited.
- Names like Kingston Bridge and Jamaica Street show the importance of the trade in Glasgow.

Fears over national security

- Abolition could destroy an important source of experienced seamen it was argued, thus there was a possibility that Britain would lose its advantage over its maritime rivals.
- On the other hand, the Triangular Trade was arguably a graveyard for British seamen.

Any other relevant factors.

Part D: Britain 1851–1951

Candidates can be credited up to a maximum of 20 marks.

25. How important was the role of pressure groups in Britain becoming more democratic between 1851 and 1928?

Context

By the mid-19th century changes to Britain's economy (industrialisation) were resulting in social change, such as the demand for literacy. Such changes brought about increasing demands for political change.

Pressure groups

- The 1867 Reform Act was passed amongst considerable popular agitations; before them the Reform League and Reform Union had been active.
- The suffragists and suffragettes were influential in gaining the franchise for women.
- Role of trade unions may also be considered.
- There was debate about the methods which should be adopted, whether direct action or peaceful protest would be more effective.
- Large-scale meetings, eg Hyde Park.

Other factors

The effects of industrialisation and urbanisation

- Urbanisation and growing class identity within an industrial workforce and the spread of socialist ideas led to demands for a greater voice for the working classes.
- The growth of the Labour party offered a greater choice.
- Demographic change, including rapid urbanisation, sparked demands for redistribution of seats.
- The growing economic power of middle-class wealth-creators led to pressure for a greater political voice.
- Basic education, the development of new, cheap, popular newspapers and the spread of railways helped to create an awareness of national issues.
- After 1860 the fear of the 'revolutionary mob' had declined. Skilled working men in cities were more educated and respectable. That was an argument for extending the vote in 1867.

Changing political attitudes

- Political reform was no longer seen as a threat. In the USA and in Europe, struggles were taking place for liberty and a greater political say for the people. Britain tended to support these moves abroad, making it logical for this to happen in Britain too.
- The growing influence of the Liberal Party in challenging older vested interests — the Liberal Party opposed the power of the old land-owning aristocracy, eg the secret ballot to assist working-class electorate to use their political voice to promote social reforms.
- Politicians combined acceptance of changes which they suspected were unavoidable while ensuring that their own party political interests would be protected.
- The death of former PM Palmerston represented the changing tone of politics as the reactionary ideas of the early 19th century gave way to new ideologies.
- The veto of the unelected chamber was removed partly as result of the 1910 elections fought on the issue of 'peers vs people' and the financing of social reform to help the poor, especially in urban areas.

Party advantage

- In 1867 the Conservative Party became the government after 20 years out of power. To an extent the Reform Act could be seen as 'stealing the Liberal's clothes' to gain support.

- The Corrupt and Illegal Practices Act of 1883 limited the amount of spending on elections; the Liberals believed the advantage held by wealthier Conservative opponents would be reduced.
- By placing the reforms of 1883 and 1884 close to the next election, the Liberals hoped to gain advantage from grateful new voters in towns more fairly represented after the redistribution of seats.

The effects of the First World War

- The war necessitated more political change. Many men still had no vote but were conscripted to fight from 1916.
- As further reform for males was being considered, fears of a revival of the militant women's campaign, combined with a realisation of the importance of women's war work led to the Representation of the People Act of 1918 which gave votes to more men and some women.
- The role of women can be overstated as the eventual franchise was for women aged over 30. Many munitions workers were younger than this.
- It could also be argued that the war provided an opportunity for the coalition government to give women the vote. No one political party was able to claim it was behind the idea.

The effects of examples of developments abroad

- In a number of foreign countries there was a wider franchise for men than in Britain; in others women could also vote. Neither development had threatened the established social order.

Any other relevant factors.

Candidates can be credited up to a maximum of 20 marks.

26. **'Changing attitudes in British society towards women was the major reason why some women received the vote in 1918.' How valid is this view?**

Context
Throughout the 19th century more and more men were given the right to vote yet there was no sign of the right to vote in national elections being given to women. This gave rise to the women's suffrage movements.

Changing attitudes towards women

- The campaigns for women's suffrage can be seen within the context of changing attitudes within society towards women in the late 19th and early 20th centuries.
- The historian Martin Pugh stated that 'their participation in local government made women's exclusion from national elections increasingly untenable'.
- Millicent Fawcett argued that wider social changes were vital factors in the winning of the franchise.
- Women became increasingly active in public affairs — town councils, Boards of Guardians, members of political organisations.
- Educational opportunities slowly opened up to women: University, medical school, etc. Professions opened up to women: Law, Medical profession.
- Legal developments giving women rights over property: 1882 Married Women's Property Act, etc.

Other factors

The importance of the Great War

- Britain declared war on Germany on 4 August 1914 and two days later the NUWSS suspended its political campaigning for the vote. Undoubtedly the sight of women 'doing their bit' for the war effort gained respect and balanced the negative publicity of the earlier Suffragette campaign.

- A WSPU pro-war propaganda campaign encouraged men to join the armed forces and women to demand 'the right to serve'.
- Women's war work was important to Britain's eventual victory. Over 700,000 women were employed making munitions.
- The creation of a wartime coalition also opened the door to change.
- The traditional explanation for the granting of the vote to some women in 1918 has been that women's valuable work for the war effort radically changed male ideas about their role in society and that the vote in 1918 was almost a thank you for their efforts. But the women who were given the vote were 'respectable' ladies, 30 or over, not the younger women who worked long hours and risked their lives in munitions factories.
- Another argument about the 1918 act is that it only happened because politicians grew anxious to enfranchise more men who had fought in the war but lost their residency qualification to vote and women could be 'added on' to legislation that was happening anyway.
- The war acted more as a catalyst, but the tide was flowing towards female suffrage before it started.

The NUWSS

- The NUWSS believed in moderate, 'peaceful' tactics to win the vote such as meetings, pamphlets, petitions and parliamentary bills. Membership remained relatively low at about 6,000 until around 1909 but grew to 53,000 by 1914 as women angered by the Suffragettes' campaign found a new home.

The WSPU – the Suffragettes

- Emmeline Pankhurst formed the Women's Social and Political Union (WSPU) in 1903.
- WSPU adopted the motto 'Deeds Not Words'. The new strategy gained publicity with noisy heckling of politicians. Newspapers immediately took notice. The Suffragettes had achieved their first objective – publicity.
- Violent protest followed, e.g. window smashing campaign and arson attacks aimed to provoke insurance company pressure on the Government.
- The prisons filled with Suffragettes. Women used starvation as a political weapon to embarrass the government. In response the government introduced the Prisoner's Temporary Discharge for Ill Health Act — the Cat and Mouse Act.
- The actions of the Suffragettes mobilised opinion for and against. It can be argued that were it not for the Suffragette campaign, the Liberal Government would not even have discussed women's suffrage before World War One.
- But for opponents the militant campaign provided an excellent example of why women could not be trusted with the vote.

Example of other countries

- By 1913 many states in the USA, in Scandinavia, Finland (1906) and countries in the British Empire, such as New Zealand (1893) had given the vote to women. This had not caused the disasters that had been predicted. In fact, most countries believed giving women the vote had helped them.

Any other relevant factors.

Candidates can be credited up to a maximum of 20 marks.

27. To what extent did the Liberal's social reforms from 1906 to 1914 fail to deal with the real problems facing the British people?

Context

The Liberal government 1906–1914 marked a transition point between the laissez faire attitudes of 19th century governments and the more socially interventionist governments that came to power in the mid 20th century.

Social problems

- The problems could be summarised as poverty, especially among the 'deserving poor' of the old, the young, the sick and the unemployed.

The young

- The Provision of School Meals Act allowed local authorities to raise money to pay for school meals but the law did not force local authorities to provide school meals.
- Medical inspections (1907) for children were made compulsory but no treatment of illnesses or infections found was provided until 1911.
- The Children's Charter (1908) Act banned children under 16 from smoking, drinking alcohol, or begging. New juvenile courts were set up for children accused of committing crimes. Remand homes were opened for children awaiting trial and borstals for children convicted of breaking the law. Probation officers were employed to help former offenders in an attempt to avoid re-offending.
- The time taken to enforce all legislation meant the Children's Charter only helped improve conditions for some children.

The old

- Pensions Act 1908: people over 70 were given between 1 shilling and 5 shillings a week depending on any income they might have. Once a person over 70 had an income above 12 shillings a week, their entitlement to a pension stopped. Married couples were given 7/6d. Levels of benefits were low.
- Few of the elderly poor lived until their 70th birthday. Many of the old were excluded from claiming pensions because they failed to meet qualification rules.
- Nevertheless there was a high uptake and many people were grateful for their pension — 'Thank God for that Lord George'. (Thinking the helpful Lloyd-George surely had to be a Lord!)

The sick

- The National Insurance Scheme of 1911 applied to workers earning less than £160 a year. Each insured worker got 9 pence in benefits from an outlay of 4 pence — 'ninepence for fourpence'.
- Only the insured worker got free medical treatment from a doctor. Other family members did not benefit from the scheme.
- The weekly contribution was in effect a wage cut which might simply have made poverty worse in many families. It helped some who had previously got no help.

The unemployed

- The National Insurance Act (part 2) only covered unemployment for some workers in some industries and like part 1 of the Act, required contributions from workers, employers and the government. For most workers, no unemployment insurance scheme existed.
- There were other reforms which could be argued helped meet 'problems', eg working conditions.

- In 1906 the Workman's Compensation Act covered a further six million workers who could now claim compensation for injuries and diseases which were the result of working conditions.
- In 1908 miners secured an eight-hour working day.
- In 1909 the Trade Boards Act tried to protect workers in the sweated trades like tailoring and lace making by setting up trade boards to fix minimum wages.
- In 1911 a Shops Act limited working hours and guaranteed a weekly half-day holiday.

Limitations

- Aspects of poverty such as housing were not dealt with, posing the argument that Liberal reforms were not entirely successful in dealing with poverty and need.

Any other relevant factors.

Part E: Britain and Ireland, 1900–1985

Candidates can be credited up to a maximum of 20 marks.

28. "The response of Unionists to the Home Rule Bill was the main reason for the growth of tension in Ireland up to 1914." How valid is this view?

Context

Since 1801, when Ireland joined the Union of Great Britain, there had been opposition from some groups to rule from London. By 1900 the desire for Home Rule had increased and was causing a political problem for Britain.

Unionist responses to the Home Rule Bill

- Setting up of the UVF was example of the willingness to use violence to further the cause of those opposed to Home Rule and an indication of the extent in the breakdown in peace in Ireland.
- Signing of the Solemn League and Covenant in Belfast at Town Hall, to the world's press, 250,000 Ulstermen pledged themselves to use 'all means necessary' to defeat Home Rule.
- The role of Carson and Craig. Sir Edward Carson's theatrical political performances caught the public imagination and brought the case of the Unionists to the nation.
- Orange and Ulster Unionist groups were revived.
- The Curragh Mutiny.

Other factors

Nationalist responses to the Home Rule Bill

- The Irish Volunteer Force (IVF) was set up. Members from the Gaelic League, the Gaelic Athletic Association, Sinn Fein and the IRB all joined hoping to use the IVF for their own purposes. By May 1914 it had 80,000 members, which also shows the extent in the breakdown in the willingness for peace in Ireland as a result of the Home Rule Bill.
- In 1913 a third private army was set up called Irish Citizen Army, under the leadership of James Connolly, a socialist. It had two clear aims. To gain independence for Ireland and set up a socialist republic, for working class of all religions to join up with to improve their lives.
- Minority opinions take different view: support for Irish Republic from groups like the Irish Republican Brotherhood — Connolly's views; supporters of a workers republic: Griffith; or Sinn Fein; Pearse and his supporters. Very much minority views at this time.

- **The British position in Ireland**
- In 1865 Gladstone wanted Home Rule and when the Liberals were re-elected in 1892 Gladstone introduced the Second Home Rule Bill but the House of Lords, dominated by Conservatives, were opposed to Home Rule and wanted to maintain the Union. The Bill was rejected.
- Support for the Unionists from British politicians like Bonar Law and the Conservative Party. In 1908 Bannerman was replaced as Prime Minister by Asquith who, by the end of 1909, declared that he was a supporter of Home Rule.
- After 1910 the Liberals needed the help of the Irish Nationalists to run the country as they would not have a majority otherwise so passed the third reform bill. With the support of John Redmond, the leader of the Nationalists, a Bill was passed to reduce the power of the House of Lords, which was dominated by Conservatives, from being able to block a Bill to only being able to hold up the passing of a Bill for two years.
- As a result, the Home Rule Bill for Ireland, which was previously blocked by the House of Lords, could now be passed.

The Irish cultural revival and re-emergence of Irish Republicanism

- In 1884 the Gaelic Athletic Association was set up 'for the preservation and cultivation of our national pastimes.' And games like Gaelic football and hurling became very popular. In 1883 the Gaelic League was also set up whose aim it was to revive, and preserve the Irish language and Gaelic literature.
- Setting up of Sinn Fein (Ourselves) by Arthur Griffith in 1904 to boycott all things British and for the Irish to set up their own parliament in Ireland, which Griffith thought would force the British Government to collapse.
- IRB was revived with Thomas Clarke recruiting young men in Dublin for the movement. These two groups both wanted an Ireland separate from Britain and both willing to use force.

Redmond and Home Rule

- Redmond believed that Home Rule Bill would lead to greater unity and strength in the Empire, which was supported by the majority in the south but vehemently opposed by those in Ulster. He also believed it would end ill-will, suspicion and disaffection in Ireland, and between Britain and Ireland.
- He believed Ireland would be happy, prosperous, united and loyal.
- Ireland would be peaceful at this time and could give up hostility towards Britain.
- Britain would be willing to treat Ireland equally, as part of the empire.
- Redmond's Party consistently strong throughout Southern Ireland, where there was strong support for Home Rule.

Distinctive economic and religious features of the Northern Counties

- Ulster was mainly Protestant and feared that a government lead by Dublin would see the imposition of laws on Northern Ireland based on Catholic faith, which they were opposed to.
- Ulster was worried they would lose the benefits they enjoyed economically from being part of the British Empire, such as the linen industry and the shipbuilding industry.

Any other relevant factors.

Candidates can be credited up to a maximum of 20 marks.

29. How important was British conduct during the Anglo-Irish War in preventing a peace settlement in Ireland between 1918 and 1921?

Context

Tension in Ireland over the issue of Home Rule faded slightly with the outbreak of World War One. Those tensions exploded with the Easter Rising. The violence that followed made a return to peace unlikely.

British conduct during the Anglo-Irish War

- Formation of the Black and Tans composed largely of World War I veterans, employed as auxiliaries by the Royal Irish Constabulary from 1920 to 1921 to suppress revolution in Ireland. Although it was established to target the Irish Republican Army, it became notorious for its numerous attacks on the Irish civilian population.
- Black and Tans used wholesale violence, theft, drunken rampages, attacks on villages such as the burning of Balbriggan, village creameries were burnt down and houses were destroyed.
- In March 1920 RIC men shot dead the Lord Mayor of Cork as well as murdering suspects, or "Shinners" as they were known, often on the merest of evidence, for being in the wrong place at the wrong time.
- Black and Tans fired in to the crowd killing 12 people and injuring 60 at Croke Park where there was a Gaelic football match was taking place. The sacking of Cork City by the Black and Tans.
- RIC members were instructed to challenge Irish civilians from ambush and shoot them if they did not obey the RIC officers.
- RIC officers were encouraged to shoot suspicious looking people. If innocent people were killed then this could not be helped. No RIC officers were to get in to trouble for shooting people.
- Regular British Army also committed atrocities such as burning the towns of Mallow and Fermoy, but the Irish did not distinguish between them and the Black and Tans.
- The best houses in local areas were taken and used, with the occupants evicted, if the local police station had been burned or destroyed, turning the Irish people against the British and increasing tension.

Other factors
Role of IRA

- The IRA campaign also prevented peace in Ireland as their attacks on British troops and men working for Britain escalated the violence.
- Ambush, assassination, the disappearance of opponents, the sabotage of enemy communications and the intimidation of local communities to not support the British forces.
- Attacks on British troops.
- Attacks on G-men (detectives concentrating on IRA atrocities).
- Attempted assassination of Lord French (Viceroy).
- Flying Columns: mobile IRA squads used in ambushes of RIC and army.
- Role of IRA leaders, particularly Michael Collins.

The General Election of 1918

- The success of Sinn Fein in this election, who opposed British rule, meant that Ireland would only want peace if Ireland gained independence from Britain.
- Sinn Fein won 73 seats, compared to winning none in 1910, showing increased resentment of British Rule.

- Sinn Fein membership had now reached 112,000. 34 were in prison, one had been deported, two were ill and 7 were absent on Sinn Fein business, so there was only 25 present when they held their first public meeting in January 1919. This meant control of the movement largely moved to the IRB and the IVF.
- Ballot boxes being stuffed and the 'dead' voting.
- There were some complaints by soldiers that they did not get voting papers and these men were more likely to vote Nationalist rather than Sinn Fein. Moreover there were no Nationalist candidates in 26 of the constituencies, which helped the Sinn Fein party.
- Ulster Unionists won an extra 10 seats and now had 26 seats in Westminster, making partition increasingly likely.

The Declaration of Independence and the Dail

- Republicans lead by Sinn Fein, did not attend Westminster, met at the Mansion House in Dublin and declared themselves 'Dail Eireann' thus increasing division between Ireland and Britain.
- De Valera was made the President of Ireland, Arthur Griffith Vice President, Michael Collins was made the Minister of Finance which again caused division as these men were vehemently opposed to British Rule in Ireland.
- Most local councils in Ireland, except for those in Ulster, recognised the rule of this new assembly, as opposed to British Rule.
- By 1921 1,000 Sinn Fein law courts had been set up and Collins raised £350,000 and many people paid their taxes to the Minister of Finance, Collins, rather than the British Government.
- Dail failed to meet very regularly as many of its members were unable to meet but worked as couriers – carried communication between the different people in hiding but Irish were willing to even obey this rather than have British rule.
- Law and order maintained though as Dail relied on 'alternative' courts, presided over by a priest or lawyer and backed up by the IRA. This system won the support of the Irish communities as well as the established Irish legal system but contravened British rule.
- Dail had won the support of the masses, the Catholic Church and professional classes in Ireland thus increasing division between Ireland and Great Britain as even the influential people of Ireland were moving away from British rule.
- Dail wrested power away from Britain to a reasonable extent due to military wing of the Dail.

Any other relevant factors.

*Candidates can be credited **up to a maximum of 20 marks.***

30. **How important were political differences between the Protestant and Catholic communities in contributing to the developing crisis in Northern Ireland up to 1968?**

Context
Religion had divided the Irish population for centuries. The mainly Protestant Northern Ireland wanted to remain part of the United Kingdom whereas the Catholics in Northern Ireland hoped to be united with the rest of Ireland.

Political differences

- Parliament in Northern Ireland opened June 1921, it had limited control and could be overruled by Westminster.
- James Craig, the first Prime Minister, refused to speak to the Boundary Commission.
- A third of Ulster was Catholic and wanted unification; the Protestant two thirds did not want it.

- There was only on average 10 or 12 Nationalists in parliament whereas there was an average of 40 Unionists so Nationalists' views were rarely listened to.
- In Westminster there were 10 or 12 Unionists to 2 Nationalists.
- Unionist support increased after De Valera in 1932 called for a Republic 'in fact' and banned Governor General, and the right to appeal to Privy Council External Relations Act passed.
- In 1959 Eire became a Republic, which heightened Unionist fears about the pressure to end partition.
- In April 1951 Eire leader Browne was forced to resign after party leaders insisted he respect the Catholic Church's stance on matters, Unionists were worried about Catholic rule if Ireland unified.
- Unionists had fears about giving Catholics fairer treatment so the Orange Order and UVF revived.

Other Factors
Economic Issues

- De Valera's economic war with Great Britain worried Unionists that Great Britain might abandon them. Depression in the 30s saw unemployment of over 25% for Catholics, but Protestants were mainly employed.
- The South was poor, so the North was financially better off as part of the United Kingdom.
- The North benefited greatly economically from helping Great Britain during WWII, eg factories, farms. Unemployment fell to 5%, even some from the south were employed, eg aircraft and ship building. Ulster shared mainland British suffering during war, eg rationing.
- WWII underlined the economic and strategic importance of Ulster to Britain.
- Ulster benefited greatly from being part of the British Welfare state, payments were 50%–67% higher than those in the south for Unemployment benefit.
- Britain gave extra money to Ulster to set up a Welfare state: 1961–63 £60m average, £160m by 1972.
- In the 1950s Eire had one of the poorest standards of living in Western Europe.

Cultural Differences

- In 1923 the Education Act was amended, but the Catholic Church retained control over Catholic schools. Protestants refused to acknowledge cultural identity of Catholics.
- In Eire Irish language was used in government and taught in schools.
- The Gaelic League and other language groups sprung up. Irish music and dance thrived. Gaelic football and hurling were more popular than soccer, rugby and cricket in Eire.

The Unionist Ascendancy in Northern Ireland

- Ulster was not willing to sever links with Britain, but wanted to ensure Unionist control.
- B Specials set up and RUC; both were issued with guns.
- Special Powers were introduced — internment, prohibit meetings, special courts, death penalty.
- Votes in local Councils were restricted to householders and property owners so Catholics were ruled out.
- Boundaries were redrawn to secure Unionist councillors (gerrymandering).
- Proportional Representation was abolished to reduce Catholic influence in politics.
- Unionist Councillors favoured Protestants for housing and job vacancies.
- Revival of Orange Orders in 60s; Protestants favoured in 70s.

- Role of Brookeborough: Ulster Unionist leader and Prime Minister of Northern Ireland, 1943—1963: kept Unionists largely unified.

Continuing Threat of the IRA

- The Catholics in the North turned to the IRA to defend them from Orange rioters.
- The IRA shootings, Kevin O'Higgins assassination, a Garda barracks attack led to the Public Safety Act.
- During the war they attacked mainland Britain, eg Coventry.
- Upsurge in violence in 50s but came to nothing and ended by 1962, a failure after which they were divided.

Issues of Civil Rights

- Catholics set up NICRA for equal rights, as young Catholics benefited from better education.
- Campaign for Social Justice set up, 1966 nationalists commemorate Easter Rising in Belfast. June 1966 Ian Paisley starts a riot by taking his supporters into a Catholic area.
- Coalisland to Dungannon march, Peaceful Civil Rights march charged by police in 1968. In October 1968 police in Londonderry attack NICRA march with violence, which was captured by the media. Homeless Citizens League, Derry Citizens Action Committee (John Hume) set up.
- Devlin's People's Democracy Belfast—Londonderry march attacked by RUC and B Specials.
- Well-known Nationalists and IRA members were seen in Civil Rights marches.

Any other relevant factors.

MODEL PAPER 1
SECTION 3: EUROPEAN AND WORLD

Part A: The Crusades, 1071—1204

Candidates can be credited up to a maximum of 20 marks.

31. "The Pope's desire to channel the military power of the knightly class was the main reason for calling the First Crusade." How valid is this view?

Context

Fear of the expansion of Islam was a reason for the calling of the First Crusade. The Pope in Western Europe feared Islamic expansion and saw himself as the saviour of Eastern Christianity. There was already fear from the South, and the Moorish threat in Spain. There was a real fear that the Islamic threat had to be stopped in the East before it threatened Western Christianity.

Arguments for the importance of the Pope's desire to channel the military power of the knightly class:

- The introduction of Norman feudalism across Western Europe had created the knightly class. Their dedication to learning the arts of war had created a culture based around the skills of fighting. Even tournaments had come to be seen as integral part of the culture and as entertainment.
- However, for knights to use their skills in anger was a sin.
- Pope Urban had long considered how he could turn the nature of Western knighthood to a less aggressive, less damaging activity.
- Urban saw the Crusade as a way to channel this aggression in a way that would be of benefit to Christianity.
- Urban was well aware of the growing political instability of Italy. Northern Italy with its growing urban centres and rich Lombard provinces was a tempting target for both the Norman knights and the German Emperors.
- By calling a crusade the Pope could channel this aggression away from Italy and the Church while at the same time exerting a moral control over the armed knights. This was a simple step from the already successful 'Peace of God' and 'Truce of God' attempts by the church in the 1020s.

Other factors

Fear over the expansion of Islam

- Pope Urban used the fear of Islamic expansion in his famous speech at Clermont in 1095. He pointed to the successful Reconquista in Spain. El Cid had only captured Valencia from the Moors in 1094.
- He pointed to the threat of the Turks to Byzantium, eg the Battle of Manzikert 1071, a topic that was already talked about across Europe. He claimed that the loss of Anatolia had 'devastated the Kingdom of God'.
- He detailed claims of Turkish activities such as torture, human sacrifice and desecration.

Threat to Byzantium

- The Seljuk Turks had been threatening the Empire for decades
- There was fear in Europe that if Byzantium was allowed to fall then the expansion of this new aggressive Islamic group into central Europe would be inevitable.
- Alexius, Emperor of Byzantium, was seen as a bulwark against this eventuality and his letter asking for help was taken very seriously in Western Europe.

The development of Christianity

- The new style of pope, influenced and trained at the monastery of the Cluny, heralded a shift in the emphasis of Christianity. No longer were popes to be subservient to the monarchs or warlords of Europe.
- Popes now actually challenged kings and demanded the right to appoint priests, bishops and cardinals as they saw fit. This led to the development of the Investiture Contest and this power struggle between the Pope and the Holy Roman Emperor, directly affected Pope Urban, possibly influencing his decision.
- The new millennium had brought in a period of religious zeal.

The Great Schism

- The papacy was anxious to re-join the two halves of the Christian church.
- Since the Great Schism of 1054, where the Pope of Rome and Patriarch of Constantinople excommunicated each other, it had been the goal of every Pope to become head of the Greek Orthodox Church.
- Now the Crusade seemed to offer Pope Urban the opportunity to achieve this.

Development of Mediterranean trade

- The development of trade within the Mediterranean Sea had been in the hands of ambitious cities in Italy, notably Venice, but also Pisa and Genoa. By 1095, Venice had bound its future to Byzantium.
- Their preferential trade agreements with Constantinople for silk, spices and other luxury goods meant that they were keen to see Byzantium saved from the expansion of the Turks.

Papal authority and the Investiture Contest

- By 1075 the relationship between the Church and the Holy Roman Emperor, the church's supposed protector, had deteriorated badly.
- Pope Gregory VII had excommunicated Henry IV and Henry invaded Rome.
- Henry IV, the Holy Roman Emperor, had been locked in a power struggle with Urban over the Investiture contest, which had led to popes, including Urban, fleeing Rome. This was part of an ongoing struggle between the Church and State over the appointment of Bishops.
- The desire of the reforming popes (trained at Cluny) was to firmly establish the dominance of the papacy in this area.
- The papacy was anxious to re-join the two halves of the Christian church. Since the Great Schism of 1054, where the Pope of Rome and Patriarch of Constantinople excommunicated each other, it had been the goal of every pope to become head of the Greek Orthodox Church.
- The Crusade seemed to offer Pope Urban the opportunity to achieve this. A papacy that was able to accomplish this would be less vulnerable to the problems that had plagued the Papacy in the previous decades.
- Byzantium was home to the Orthodox church, saving it would help re-establish cordial relations with the eastern Christians.

Any other relevant factors.

Candidates can be credited up to a maximum of 20 marks.

32. 'The success of the Crusaders was due to divisions amongst the Muslim states?' How valid is this view of the First Crusade?

Context

In 1095 Pope Urban II proclaimed the First Crusade with the stated goal of restoring Christian access to holy places in and near Jerusalem. Following the first crusade there was an intermittent 200-year struggle for control of the Holy Land. As a result of the First Crusade, four main crusader states were created in the Middle East

Arguments for the importance of the division amongst Muslim states

- The Islamic response to the First Crusade was slow in getting under way. During the crusade Muslim leaders were more willing to fight among themselves than join forces against the common enemy. In fact many did not even realise that this was a common enemy. Kilij Arslan, for example, expected the 'Princes' Crusade' to be no more of a concern than Peter the Hermit's followers. Thus he was off raiding his Muslim neighbours when Nicaea came under attack.
- Kerbogha's army abandoned him at the battle of Antioch in 1098. Many had feared that his victory would allow him to gain a semblance of authority over the other Seljuk Turkish leaders. There was tension in his army as the Turks mistrusted the Arab-speaking Muslims and the different tribes of nomads. The lack of unity was clear among the divisions of Ridwan of Aleppo and Duquaq of Damascus.
- The fundamental division of Muslim between the Fatimids and the Seljuks is illustrated in the Egyptians seizure of Jerusalem. The Egyptian army used siege engines to reduce the walls of Jerusalem in a siege that lasted 6 weeks. This not only damaged the defences of the city but reduced the number of defenders available. The Fatimids even sent embassies to the crusaders offering them Jerusalem in exchange for an alliance against the Seljuks.
- For the Muslims this was not seen as a holy war, at least at the outset. To them, unifying to face the Christians was a more dangerous idea than the crusaders themselves.
- Religious divisions between Sunni and Shiite Islam.

Other factors

Military importance of the knight

- The First Crusade had been unexpected by local Muslim leaders. Those that had witnessed the ineptitude of the People's Crusade expected Christian knights to be as inept in combat.
- However Christian knights were often ferocious fighters, used to long campaigns in Europe, whereas the knights of the East were seen as gentlemen of culture and education.
- The mounted tactics of the knights were relatively unknown in the east and the sight of the largest concentration of knights in history assembled on the field was a truly awesome sight. This full frontal charge of the knights was in contrast to the tactics deployed by the Islamic forces. Their hit and run horse archers were not prepared for this aggressive style. Crusading knights used aggressive combat tactics, and utilised heavier armour and barding for their horses.
- The constant fighting of the 12th century had well prepared the organised and disciplined knightly classes for warfare. Many, such as Raymond of Toulouse, had combat experience against the Moors in Spain.

Misunderstanding of the Crusaders' intent

- Muslims misunderstood the threat of the Western knights. Many saw this as another expedition from Byzantium and thought them soldiers of Alexius.
- Such raids had occurred before; however, this was different. Here the Christians had an ideological motivation not yet encountered by the Islamic leaders.

Help from Byzantium

- The First Crusade was the only crusade to have significant support from Constantinople. Even though Alexius's army did not participate in the Crusade itself, they did cause problems, diverting a lot of Muslim resources.
- Alexius also provided much needed supplies at the sieges of Antioch and Jerusalem.

Religious fervour

- The sheer determination of the crusaders helped them through incredible hardships during their passage through the Taurus Mountains and at the sieges of Antioch and Jerusalem. Because they believed God would help them, they attempted the impossible, where most armies would have surrendered, eg Battle of Antioch and the belief in the Holy Lance.
- The Muslims did not really understand this idea of a 'Holy War' they assumed the crusaders were after land and territory and therefore they tended to underestimate what the crusaders could achieve.

Any other relevant factors.

Candidates can be credited up to a maximum of 20 marks.

33. To what extent can it be argued that Richard I was a greater military leader than Saladin?

Context

Saladin and Richard the Lionheart are two names that tend to dominate the crusades. Both have gone down in medieval history as great military leaders.

Arguments to suggest that Richard was a greater military leader than Saladin

- Richard had established himself as an able leader prior to the crusade.
- Richard was good at motivating troops, and his arrival at the siege of Acre galvanised the troops in a way that Philip had been unable to do.
- Even when confined to his bed due to illness he was still able to direct the operations.

Victories

- While journeying to the Holy Lands, Richard captured Cyprus.
- Richard, despite being lured into a trap, won the Battle of Arsuf with an impressive charge of knights that routed Saladin's men.
- Saladin was defeated in battle and it helped raise morale; the great defeat of Hattin had been erased from the minds of the crusaders.
- Richard won the Battle of Jaffa against overwhelming odds.
- Saladin had failed to defeat Richard in battle, and he lost control of his men at Jaffa; they refused to obey his orders.

Use of tactics

- Richard took his time to march to Jerusalem.
- He organised his men into well defended columns, marching down the coastal route using his fleet to carry plenty of supplies. This way he was able to protect his vulnerable supply line from Turkish raids.
- Richard was enough of a military tactician to realise that he did not have the men to capture Jerusalem.

- Richard always lined up with the Templars in battle which was seen as the fiercest part of the fighting.

Arguments to suggest Richard was able to exploit Saladin's mistakes

- Saladin's decision to spare the crusaders at Tyre, in order to allow them a safe haven to board ships for the west, was a grave military error. Conrad was able to successfully take over the defence of the city and use it as a base for the third crusade.
- Saladin was unable to keep his large army in the field for the whole year round. Many men were needed back on the farms, or were only expected to provide a certain numbers of days service.
- **The fall of Acre to Richard's forces:** The Battle of Arsuf, where Richard was outnumbered 3 – 1, and his men had fallen into Saladin's ambush. Richard held his men together and his all out cavalry charge smashed the Muslim forces.
- Saladin should have been able to capture or kill Richard at Jaffa; however, he failed to keep control of his men, who were reluctant to fight Richard due to his growing reputation as an unbeatable opponent.

Arguments to suggest that Saladin was a greater military leader than Richard

- Saladin brought effective military leadership and central authority to Egypt and Syria for the first time.
- In 1168, while Caliph of Egypt, he destroyed the combined crusader/Byzantium invasion fleet/ army at the port city of Damietta. In 1170 he followed this up with an attack on Gaza, massacring the Christian inhabitants of the city.
- Saladin's victory at the Battle of Hattin (1187) was all consuming. The military orders were devastated, King Guy had been captured, many of the nobles executed or taken into slavery. One by one the great forts and cities fell to Saladin's army. The capture of Jerusalem in 1187 made Saladin the hero of Islam. The eventual negotiated surrender saved much bloodshed.

Use of tactics

- In 1180 Saladin had successfully limited the attacks from Outremer by negotiating a peace treaty with Baldwin IV. Saladin's tactics leading up to Hattin were masterly. He provoked Guy of Lusignan into an unnecessary sally to aid a castle that was not seriously threatened. He avoided a pitched battle till the crusaders were debilitated by heat and thirst, then further disabled them by lighting fires.

Any other relevant factors.

Part B: The American Revolution, 1763—1787

Candidates can be credited up to a maximum of 20 marks.

34. To what extent was disagreement over the frontier the key issue between Britain and the colonies by 1763?

Context

By 1763, Britain had ruled the 13 American colonies for over a century. The harmony with Britain which colonists had once held had become indifference during the Whig Ascendancy of the mid-1700s. The ascendancy of George III in 1760 was to bring about further change in the relationship between Britain and America.

Land claims/The Proclamation of 1763

- Quarrels arose after individual colonists and land companies unwittingly violated treaties agreed between Britain and Indian tribes.

- The Royal Proclamation of 1763 was issued October 7, 1763, by King George III following Great Britain's acquisition of French territory in North America after the end of the French and Indian War/Seven Years' War.
- The purpose of the proclamation was to organise Great Britain's new North American empire and to stabilise relations with Native North Americans through regulation of trade, settlement, and land purchases on the western frontier.
- The proclamation created a boundary line (often called the proclamation line) between the British colonies on the Atlantic coast and American Indian lands (called the Indian Reserve) west of the Appalachian Mountains.
- The proclamation line was not intended to be a permanent boundary between white and American Indian lands, but rather a temporary boundary which could be extended further west in an orderly, lawful manner.
- The proclamation outlawed private purchase of Native American land, which had often created problems in the past; instead, all future land purchases were to be made by Crown officials 'at some public Meeting or Assembly of the said Indians'. Furthermore, British colonists were forbidden to move beyond the line and settle on native lands, and colonial officials were forbidden to grant lands without royal approval.
- The proclamation gave the Crown a monopoly on all future land purchases from American Indians.
- Almost immediately, many British colonists and land speculators objected to the proclamation boundary, since there were already many settlements beyond the line (some of which had been temporarily evacuated during Pontiac's War), as well as many existing land claims yet to be settled. Indeed, the proclamation itself called for lands to be granted to British soldiers who had served in the Seven Years' War.
- Prominent American colonists joined with land speculators in Britain to lobby the government to move the line further west.

Other factors

The Seven Years' War

- The war highlighted the status of the colonies as territories to be fought over by imperial powers. Britain, France and Spain all viewed America as a potential possession. The British fought the Seven Years' War which prevented the colonies being ruled by France. Victory in 1763, and the acquisition of Canada, should have made British rule more secure, but the removal of the French threat meant that many colonists saw less need for British protection.

Old colonial system

- Britain treated colonies merely as a source of revenue, and plundered valuables from America. Those in New England and the Middle Colonies objected to being used as a dumping ground for British goods. Wealthy Southern plantation owners objected to members of the British government attempting to control them. Frontiersmen were frustrated at British attempts to prevent them from going beyond the Frontier. However, being part of the Empire meant protection from the British Army against the French and Indians.

Navigation Acts

- Passed in 1650s, these stated that colonists could only sell their goods to the British, could only buy goods from the British, and could only use British shipping. Royal Navy enforced the Acts by patrolling east coast of colonies for rogue Dutch, French or Spanish ships.

- However, the acts gave colonists a guaranteed market. During the Whig Ascendancy in mid-1700s many colonists were able to ignore the Acts as the Royal Navy was unable to enforce them as strictly.

Political differences

- The colonies were more advanced politically than Britain, each having its own elected Assembly which passed local laws and raised local taxes, and so they resented the lack of representation in the British Parliament which sought to control their lives. However, the British Empire provided an order to the existence of the colonies.
- Britain acted out the role of Mother Country. Britain appointed a governor for each colony, whose payment by the colony ensured an element of control for the colonists over the governor.

George III

- When George III ascended the throne in 1760 he oversaw a re-imposition of British rule over the colonies. This was seen as tantamount to foreign invasion by many colonists who had acted in an independent spirit during the Whig Ascendancy.
- Colonies had their own militia and did not feel the British Army was required in America. However, George III aimed to ensure the security of the colonies by maintaining a British military presence and together with Parliament planned an economic strategy to raise money from the colonists to pay for this.

Neglect by Britain

- During the Whig Ascendancy, colonist assemblies had assumed powers which should have been exercised by governors, and they resented Parliament's attempts to reverse this trend.

Any other relevant factors.

Candidates can be credited up to a maximum of 20 marks.

35. **To what extent were the views of Edmund Burke typical of British opinion towards the conflict with the American colonists in the period between 1763 and 1781?**

Context

By 1763 opinion was divided over the actions of the British government to control their American colonies. Some observers hoped the colonists would think twice before commencing what would be a bloody and unfortunate war while others saw the colonists as rebels who needed to be brought into line.

Edmund Burke

- Burke studied the American situation and took colonists demands seriously.
- He made speeches in House of Commons, citing the common bond of 'Englishness' which existed between Britain and America, and urging Parliament to 'loosen the reins' on colonists or lose America for good.
- However, Burke's views were dismissed as alarmist by many Parliamentarians.

Other factors

George III

- George III, popular in Britain, sacked Grenville after the Stamp Act and appointed Pitt (Earl of Chatham) as Prime Minister.
- He supported Parliament's right to tax colonies. He asserted his view that problems in America were 'localised' in New England, and declared colonies to be in 'rebellion 'after 1775.
- However, the king's actions led colonists to call him a tyrant, and critics in Britain, notably Burke, believed his actions to have accelerated the move to war.

Parliament
- In the House of Lords, Lord Sandwich and others disregarded warnings of impending crisis and seriously underestimated colonists' forces.
- However, as well as Burke and Chatham, others such as John Wilkes spoke in favour of radical change in policy towards America.

Earl of Chatham
- He had been Prime Minister during the Seven Years' War and again in mid-1760s when he repealed the Stamp Act. He became more aware of the colonists' plight in his final years, and repeatedly warned of the impending situation in America.
- However, Chatham's warnings fell on deaf ears, as Parliament ignored his pleas for conciliation and his assertion that America could not be beaten if war broke out.

Thomas Paine
- Paine had been in America since November 1774, making republican speeches and meeting with colonists. He published 'Common Sense' in January 1776 and it sold 100,000 copies in America, and more than that in Britain and Europe.
- However, Paine was a radical, too radical for many colonists.
- Some in Britain read his work out of fascination rather than because they agreed with him. In America, many who may have been influenced by 'Common Sense' were already considering independence after rejection of the Olive Branch Petition.

British cotton industrialists
- Mill owners, including some MPs, wanted speedy resolution to the crisis to ensure continued supply of raw materials from colonies.
- Cotton workers — Mill workers wanted trade to be maintained in order to preserve jobs. Scotland and Ireland — some Scots and Irish sympathised with colonists' resentment of 'English' rule and understood their calls for greater autonomy.

Any other relevant factors.

Candidates can be credited up to a maximum of 20 marks.

36. How important was French intervention to colonial victory in the American War of Independence?

Context
After the Declaration of Independence in 1776, Britain and the 13 American colonies went to war for five years on land and another two at sea. British troops surrendered at Yorktown in 1781, and Britain recognised American independence in 1783.

Franco-American Alliance
- France entered the war and took the conflict to Europe.
- Britain was forced to re-assign its military resources to defend itself and the Empire.
- French contribution to the colonists' cause took many forms — men, ammunition, training, supplies, and uniforms, fighting Britain around the world.
- However, France was not persuaded until February 1778 to make its alliance with America, by which time the Continental Army was already starting to make progress in the war in the colonies.
- The entry of France into the war may have encouraged Spain and Holland to follow suit within the next two years.
- French intervention on the part of Admiral de Grasse preceded the final British surrender at Yorktown.

- However, the war had been taking place for over eighteen months by the time France entered.
- France's main contribution was at sea rather than on land.

Other factors
British military inefficiency
- On several occasions British generals did not act appropriately to orders received. Orders from London were misinterpreted.
- One example was Howe marching south to Brandywine instead of north into New England, thus isolating Burgoyne who subsequently surrendered his forces at Saratoga.
- Petty jealousies obstructed co-operation amongst British military leaders.
- Changes in personnel holding high office hindered progress.
- However, in many instances the British were forced into bad decisions by the tactics of Washington's army.

Distance between Britain and the colonies
- This caused a delay in communications between London and the military generals, with orders from Britain often overtaken by events by the time they reached America.

George Washington
- Washington was an inspirational leader, a self-made Virginian whose choice as Commander of the Continental Army gave heart to many.
- He fought guerrilla warfare effectively.
- He taught his troops to fire accurately from distance in open battle.
- He had experience of the British Army during the Seven Years' War.
- His speeches to troops offered them the incentive of independence if they won the war.
- However, Washington benefited from luck on several occasions, such as when inefficiency led the British into traps or when the French arrived at Yorktown.

Land war fought on American soil
- This gave the Continental Army an advantage, as the colonists' knowledge of the theatre of war meant they handled the terrain better than the British. Local people burned their crops rather than let them fall into British hands, reducing potential supplies for the British.

Role of other foreign powers
- Spanish and Dutch entry into the war — they stretched British resources even further and made the British less effective in the colonies.
- Armed League of Neutrality — Russian, Danish and Swedish willingness to fire on the Royal Navy placed extra pressure on Britain.

Any other relevant factors.

Part C: The French Revolution, to 1799

Candidates can be credited up to a maximum of 20 marks.

37. To what extent did the Third Estate have the greatest cause for complaint under the Ancien Regime?

Context
By the late 18th century the grievances of the bourgeoisie were seen as a serious challenge to the Ancien Regime. The bourgeoisie had grown considerably in number but had little or no influence on state policy-making, yet they were expected to contribute to taxation whereas the nobility and clergy were not.

The role of the Third Estate — the bourgeoisie

- The bourgeoisie — often individually wealthy — nonetheless resented the privileges and exemptions enjoyed by the First and Second Estates. Although they had displayed their talents in business, the law and in education, members of the bourgeoisie were denied access to political power and suffered higher tax burdens than their social 'superiors'.
- Businessmen were particularly bitter about trade barriers, different regional weights and measures and restrictive trade and working practices which inhibited the free inter-flow of trade and industrial expansion. Intellectually astute, they had taken on board the ideas of the Philosophes which had called for a more rational, fair and equal society where privileges, exemptions and restrictive practices would be ended.
- Although they had displayed their talents in business, the law and in education, members of the bourgeoisie were denied access to political power and suffered higher tax burdens than their social 'superiors'.
- It is hardly surprising that the bourgeoisie were at the head of revolutionary political, social and economic change during 1788 and 1789.

The peasantry

- The peasants laboured under a hugely unfair burden of taxation. Their grievances were compounded by the failure of the grain harvest in 1789. This hit agricultural incomes and the economic crisis peaked at the point when the political future of France was being decided in the newly-formed National Assembly (June).
- The ending of feudalism (August 1789) also had much to do with peasant discontent reaching its peak during the 'Great Fear' in the countryside in July.

The urban workers

- The economic crisis in agriculture hit manufacturing in 1789 when rising bread prices cut the demand for manufactured goods.
- Lay-offs and falling incomes intensified revolutionary fervour in the great cities such as Paris.
- Overall, the greatest threat to the Ancien Regime came from the bourgeoisie but the influence of other social groups cannot be ignored.

Role of the clergy

- The clergy was split into the upper and lower clergy. The upper clergy were almost wholly exempt from the payment of taxes and were tenacious in holding onto the privilege. The Catholic Church owned 10% of land in France and extracted tax (the tithe) from the peasantry in order to fund the Church's operations.
- The lower clergy often sympathised with the peasants in their parishes who suffered under an enormous burden of taxation relative to income and this precipitated tensions within the hierarchy of the Church. It also explains why some of the clergy were prepared to lead protests against the Ancien Regime on behalf of their parishioners — eg in drawing up Cahiers des Doleances in preparation for the meeting of the Estates-General in 1789. The Cahiers revealed a catalogue of discontent and provided a platform from which an attack on the privilege, venality and exemption from taxation rife in the Ancien Regime — privileges and exemptions enjoyed by the upper clergy — could be launched.
- Moreover, attempts to increase government income through a land tax levied on the Church and the nobility were met by bitter opposition in the Assembly of Notables among whose number the upper clergy were prominent. This precipitated a financial crisis and the convocation in 1788 of the Estates-General. This decision led directly to the attack on privilege which culminated in the collapse of the Ancien Regime in 1789 with the establishment of the National Assembly in June, the end of feudalism in early August and the Declaration of the Rights of Man in late August.

Role of the nobility

- Like the clergy, the nobility were almost wholly exempt from taxation. As a result they, too, have to accept a considerable degree of culpability for the Revolution.
- The nobility was split — between the traditional Nobles of the Sword and the more recently ennobled Nobles of the Robe. The former gained access — often through birth rather than merit — to the highest and most lucrative offices of the State, Church and the Army.
- The 'old' nobility sought to protect these privileges against the 'new' nobility — and, indeed, the bourgeoisie. Clearly this precipitated tension and a desire for change.
- Many of the leaders of the movement which sought revolutionary change in 1788 and 1789 were drawn from the ranks of the lesser nobility. Their intellect, organisation and education made them formidable opponents of the Ancien Regime — often in alliance with the numerically larger bourgeoisie. It is also worth noting that the Assembly of Notables (bitter opponents of reform) counted many of the traditional nobility among their number.

Any other relevant factors.

Candidates can be credited up to a maximum of 20 marks.

38. To what extent was Louis XVI responsible for the failure of constitutional monarchy in 1792?

Context

Louis XVI was a direct descendant of a line of kings who believed in the Divine Right to rule and resented any limitations to his power. It was therefore difficult for him to fully embrace the changes that would be required to rule as a Constitutional Monarch

Role of Louis

- Even before the outbreak of revolution in July 1789, Louis had shown himself incapable of making the strong decisions necessary to save the monarchy by dismissing Finance Minister Calonne in the face of opposition from the nobility to the major tax reforms needed to save France from bankruptcy.
- After the Declaration of the Rights of Man in August 1789, Louis failed to openly endorse its principles and in the weeks ahead seemed to be preparing for a counter-revolution through the build-up of troops at Versailles. This aroused considerable suspicion and, even at this early stage, made the achievement of a constitutional monarchy unlikely.
- The so-called March of the Women which forced the Royal family back from Versailles into the Tuileries indicates how Louis' actions during July to September had robbed the monarchy of much support.
- In June 1791 the royal family attempted to escape the Revolution by slipping across the border. They were stopped at Varennes and returned to Paris. The mistrust generated by his persistent ambivalence towards the Revolution brought a significant upsurge of support — particularly in Paris — for a Republic. Although not the end of the monarchy, Louis' actions in June 1791 made its demise increasingly certain.

- Even before his veto on decrees against 'refractory' clergy and émigrés in December, Louis' actions during 1791 had done the monarchy immeasurable harm. His lukewarm support for the reforms of the Constituent Assembly had generated popular hostility in Paris from the spring of 1791 onwards.

Other factors

- **The** émigrés promoted anti-revolutionary sentiment abroad which damaged the monarchy at home.
- The Declaration of Pillnitz (August 1791) in which Austria and Prussia threatened to intervene against the Revolution had been inspired by the king's émigré brothers. This intensified suspicion of the monarchy.

The National Assembly's decision to introduce the Civil Constitution of the Clergy

- This caused great controversy in a traditionally Catholic country and created deep divisions which polarised the Revolution. The monarchy — since it was historically associated with the Church — was irrevocably damaged in the eyes of the radicals who exploited the king's unease over the Civil Constitution for their own ends.
- Louis' failure to openly endorse this and his support for émigré nobles (many of whom had left France in the aftermath of the Civil Constitution of the Clergy) increased the hostility of large sections of the population towards the monarchy.

The Declaration of War (April 1792) and the Manifesto of the Duke of Brunswick (July 1792)

- These events radicalised the Revolution to the point where the position of the monarchy became impossible because of the king's identification with the enemy.
- This was Louis' own fault but it should be remembered that France declared war on Austria in April 1792 and it suited the radical anti-monarchists who thought that a successful war would bring them increased support at home and prove a decisive blow to the monarchy.
- The final overthrow of the monarchy in August 1792 had become inevitable under the pressures exerted by the war.

Any other relevant factors.

Candidates can be credited up to a maximum of 20 marks.

39. "The constitution of 1795 was the main reason for Napoleon's coup of 1799." How valid is this view?

Context
When Austria declared war on France in 1799 Napoleon and the republic's best army was in Egypt. When Napoleon returned to France he was hailed as the country's savior and he began to plot his route to power.

The Constitution of 1795

- Policy-makers framed a new constitution which sought to reconcile the bitterness of the preceding years by imposing checks and balances against the emergence of one dominant individual, group or faction. In so doing, many historians argue that the new constitution was a recipe for instability in the years that followed.
- A bi-cameral legislature was established wherein each chamber counter-balanced the power of the other. By doing so it inhibited strong and decisive government.
- To ensure continuity, the new Convention was to include two-thirds of the outgoing deputies from the old. This enraged sections of the right who felt that the forces of left-wing radicalism still prevailed in government. The resulting mass protests in October 1795 were put down by the army under Bonaparte.

- The principle of using extra-parliamentary forces to control the State had been established with Bonaparte right at the heart of it. It was to prove a dangerous precedent.
- Annual elections worked against consistent and continuous policy-making.
- So did the appointment of an Executive — the Directory — one of whose members rotated on an annual basis.
- Again, the counter-balance between the legislature and the executive may have been commendable but it was to prove inherently unstable in practice.

Other factors
Role of Napoleon Bonaparte

- Napoleon's swift rise through the military had not gone unnoticed by people like Sieyes. He was a popular war hero owing to successful campaigns in Italy against the Austrians and Egypt against the Mamlukes.
- He had shown himself willing to put down the mob in Paris as well: 'the whiff of grapeshot'. Yet he was unwilling to be a pawn and had political ambitions of his own.

The context of government in 1794/5

- In the late summer of 1794 France was emerging from two years of increasing radicalisation and resulting bitterness between opposing factions.
- The Jacobins under Robespierre had been overthrown and a 'White Terror' was soon to sweep the country in revenge for the excesses of the radical left during the Terror.
- France had been torn apart by civil war, threatened by foreign armies egged on by émigré nobles seeking to overthrow the Revolution and riven by religious conflict occasioned by the State's opposition to the primacy of the Catholic church.

Increasing intervention of the army in politics

- Even before the 1795 constitution was ratified the army had been used to quell sans-culottes insurgents who sought to invade the Convention and to repel an émigré invasion at Quiberon.
- Napoleon's use of a 'whiff of grapeshot' to put down the disturbances in October merely underlined the parlous nature of politics at the time.
- The deployment of the army in May 1796 to put down the left-wing Babeuf Conspiracy was followed by the Coup of Fructidor in September 1797 when the first 'free' Convention elections (where the two-thirds majority rule did not apply) returned a royalist majority.

Role of Sieyes

- Afraid that France would descend into anarchy as a result of the on-going political conflict and deeming the 1795 constitution unworkable, Sieyes enlisted the aid of Bonaparte in mounting a coup against it. The Convention, the Directory and the legislative councils had run their course and few, if any, mourned their passing.

Any other relevant factors.

Part D: Germany, 1815—1939

Candidates can be credited up to a maximum of 20 marks.

40. How important were cultural factors in the growth of national feeling in Germany between 1815 and 1850?

Context

In 1815 'Germany' was not a unified state but a loose confederation made up of 39 separate states with their own rulers and systems of government. However, the development of a more modern industrialised economy in

Germany after 1815 created conditions for greater unity and led to a growth of national feeling.

Cultural factors

- The main unifying force was language — 25 million Germans spoke the same language and shared through it the same culture and literature.
- Writers and thinkers (eg Heine, Fichte, Goethe, Brothers Grimm, Schiller, Hegel) encouraged the growth of a German consciousness.

Other factors
Economic factors

- Urbanisation and industrialisation in the German states led to frustration at the political fragmentation of Germany which can be argued to be the most important obstacle to German economic development.
- Middle-class businessmen called for a more united market to enable them to compete with foreign countries.
- Prussian economic expansion proceeded steadily in the 19th Century. Prussia's gain of territory on the River Rhine after 1815 (leading to a drift in power away from Austria and towards Prussia as the latter began to build on the rich resources such as coal and iron deposits) meant it had good reason to reach an agreement with neighbours to ensure relatively free travel of goods and people between its lands in the east and the west.
- Businessmen complained that tax burdens were holding back economic development. Prussia created a large free-trade area within Prussia herself which aided the needs of businessmen.
- The Zollverein was the 'mighty lever' of German unification. By 1836, 25 of the 39 German states had joined this economic free-trade area (Austria was excluded).
- Railway/road development from the 1830s onwards ended the isolation of German states from each other. They enabled the transport and exploitation of German natural resources. Economic co-operation between German states encouraged those seeking a political solution to the issue of German unity.

Political factors

- Ideas of the French Revolution appealed to the middle classes in the German states. German princes had stirred national feeling to help raise armies to drive out the French, aiding the sense of a common German identity with common goals.

Growth of liberal political beliefs.

- The 1848 Revolutions in Germany raised consciousness greatly even though they failed.

Military factors

- The impact of the Napoleonic wars meant many Germans saw that Napoleon/France had been able to conquer the separate, autonomous German states before 1815 due to their divisions.
- Growth of Burschenschaften pre-1815 dedicated to driving French from German soil — zealous but lacking a clear idea of how best to accomplish the task.

Any other relevant factors.

Candidates can be credited up to a maximum of 20 marks.

41. To what extent was resentment towards Prussia among the German states the main obstacle to German unification by 1850?

Context

German nationalism, the desire for a united Germany, was already in existence in 1815 as a response to the ideas of the French Revolution and due to resentment of French domination under Napoleon. However, the lack of popular support for nationalism — especially amongst the peasants — and the political repression coordinated by Metternich meant there were still many factors unfavourable to German nationalism.

Prussia and North German States.

- Northern German states were mostly Protestant and southern states mainly Catholic. Generally, the northern states looked to Prussia for help and protection while the southern states looked to Austria. Many German states were suspicious of the motives of Prussia within 'Germany', believing it was striving to dominate the area.
- Jealousy existed among many German states towards Prussia — economic success of Prussia was envied.
- Prussian military strength was both admired and looked upon with trepidation by many German states.

Other factors
Particularism

The leaders of the German states also obstructed unification — protective of their individual power and position. They wanted to maintain the status quo that would safeguard this for them.

Austrian strength

- The states within 'Germany' had been part of the moribund Holy Roman Empire, traditionally ruled by the Emperor of Austria.
- Post-1815 the chairmanship of the Bund was given to Austria on a permanent basis, partly as she was considered to be the major German power.
- Metternich opposed liberalism and nationalism by using the weapons of diplomacy and threats of force. Use of the police state, repression and press censorship.
- Smaller German states were in awe of the power and position of the Austrian Empire.
- Austrian control over the administration and management of the empire, stamping authority on the Bund.
- Karlsbad Decrees and the Six Articles.
- Post-1815 Austrian military strength and bureaucracy continued to decline in effectiveness; there was a shift in balance of power between Austria and Prussia.
- Treaty of Olmutz, 1850 — signalled the triumph of Austria and humiliation of Prussia. German nationalism was now a spent force apparently.

Weakness of nationalism

- Nationalists were divided over which territory should be included in any united Germany; grossdeutsch and kleindeutsch arguments.

Failure of the Frankfurt Parliament

- Lack of clear aims and without an armed force to enforce its decisions. Lack of decisive leadership. Divisions among the 'revolutionaries' regarding aims and objectives.
- Self-interest among German rulers led to opposition to the actions at Frankfurt.

- Popular apathy – most Germans had little desire to see a united Germany, nationalism affected mainly the educated/business classes.

Attitude of foreign states

- There were Foreign concerns over the idea of a united Germany.
- None of the Great Powers wanted to see the creation of a strong Germany which might upset the balance of power. Britain, Russia, Austria and France were all happy to see the German states weak and divided.

Any other relevant factors.

Candidates can be credited up to a maximum of 20 marks.

42. How important were economic factors in the rise to power of the Nazi Party between 1920 and 1933?

Context

After defeat in the First World War, Germany became a Republic. The Weimar Republic faced many problems in its short life and by 1934 it was replaced by the Nazi dictatorship.

Economic factors

- 1922/23 hyperinflation — severe effects on the middle classes, the natural supporters of the Republic; outrage and despair at their ruination.
- Difficulties faced by farmers in Schleswig-Holstein gave the Nazis their first electoral breakthrough in 1928.
- The Great Depression of 1929 — arguably without this the Republic might have survived.
- Germany's dependence on American loans showed how fragile the recovery of the late 1920s was. The pauperisation of millions again reduced Germans to despair. Propaganda posters with legends such as 'Hitler — unsere letzte hoffnung' struck a chord with many. The Depression also polarised politics in Germany — the drift to extremes led to a fear of Communism, which grew apace with the growth of support for the Nazis.

Other factors

Weakness of the Weimer

- The Constitution/Article 48 ('suicide clause') — arguably Germany was too democratic. 'The world's most perfect democracy — on paper.
- The Treaty of Versailles — acceptance by the Republic of hated terms.
- A Republic without Republicans was 'a Republic nobody wanted' — lack of popular support for the new form of government after 1918.
- Lack of real, outstanding Weimar politicians who could strengthen the Republic, Stresemann excepted.
- Lukewarm support from the German Army and the Civil Service for the Weimar.
- Inability (or unwillingness) to deal effectively with problems in German society by the Republic.
- Lack of authority.

Weaknesses and mistakes of opponents

- Alliance of the new government and the old imperial army against the Spartacists — lack of cooperation between socialist groups — petty squabbling rife.
- Divisions among those groups/individuals who purported to be supporters of the new form of government, eg the socialists.
- Political intrigue — roles of von Schleicher and von Papen.

Role of Adolf Hitler and appeal of the Nazis after 1928

- Hitler's oratory — ability to put into words the outrage and frustrations of millions of Germans over a variety of issues.
- The Storm Troopers (SA) — Hitler's contribution to the setting up of the private army of the Nazi Party. To a worried middle-class they looked like the only political party willing to take on the Communists.
- Post 1925 — Hitler's decision to improve the efficiency of the Nazi Party, develop the effectiveness of its organisation, especially its propaganda machine.
- Hitler's uncompromising stance against the Treaty of Versailles struck a chord with millions of Germans.
- Hitler's alliance with Hugenberg offered the Nazi Party widespread publicity — propaganda. Hitler' s ruthlessness/pragmatic approach — for example, in his hard-headed negotiations with von Papen.
- Hitler's policies — something for everyone, despite often contradictory policies.
- Hitler gave people somebody to blame for their problems: November Criminals, Jews, etc.

Any other relevant factors.

Part E: Italy, 1815–1939

Candidates can be credited up to a maximum of 20 marks.

43. How important was the role of Mazzini in the growth of Italian nationalism between 1815 and 1850?

Context

The origins of Italian nationalism can be traced back to the Renaissance and the writings of Machiavelli who urged Italians to seize Italy from the 'barbarians'. However, the ideas of Mazzini and his anti-Austrian views led to the development of a more political nationalism in the 19th century.

Role of Mazzini

- Radical nationalist Mazzini not only inspired dreams of a united, democratic Italian republic through his written works, but also formed an activist movement — 'Young Italy' — whose aim was to make these dreams a reality.

Other factors

Economic factors

- Economic factors were not important directly. Wealth lay in land (landowners were often reactionary) and trade (where the educated bourgeoisie were more receptive to ideas of liberalism and nationalism).
- The election of a new, seemingly reformist, Pope, Pius IX, in 1846 inspired feelings of nationalism particularly amongst businessmen and traders as he wished to form a customs union.
- Tariff walls between the Italian states and the disorganised railway system prevented economic development of Italy, which did lead businessmen to be interested in unification.

Cultural factors

- The Risorgimento was inspired by Italy's past. Poets such as Leopardi glorified and exaggerated past achievements, kindling nationalist desires. Poets and novelists like Pellico inspired anti-Austrian feelings amongst intellectuals, as operas such as Verdi's 'Nabucco' and Rossini's 'William Tell'.
- There was no national Italian language — regional dialects were like separate languages. Alfieri inspired Italian language based on Tuscan. The poet and novelist Manzoni wrote in Italian. Philosophers spread ideas of nationalism in their books and periodicals.

- Moderate nationalists such as Gioberti and Balbo advocated the creation of a federal state with the individual rulers remaining but joining together under a president for foreign affairs and trade. Gioberti's 'On the moral and civil primacy of the Italians' advocated the Pope as president whilst Balbo, in his book 'On the hopes of Italy', saw the King of Piedmont/Sardinia in the role.
- Military weakness. The French Revolution led to a realisation that, individually, the Italian states were weak. The fragmentation of Italy in the Vienna Settlement restored Italy's vulnerability to foreign invasion.

Effects of the French Revolution and Napoleonic wars

- Italian intellectuals had initially been inspired by the French Revolution with its national flag, national song, national language, national holiday and emphasis on citizenship
- Napoleon Bonaparte's conquest inspired feelings of nationalism — he reduced the number of states to three; revived the name 'Italy'; brought in a single system of weights and measures; improved communications; helped trade, inspiring desire for at least a customs union.
- Napoleon's occupation was hated — conscription, taxes, looting of art.

Resentment of Austria

- After the Vienna settlement in 1815, hatred of foreign control centred on Austria. The Hapsburg Emperor directly controlled Lombardy and Venetia; his relatives controlled Parma, Modena, Tuscany. Austria had strong ties to the Papacy and had alliances with other rulers. Conscription, censorship, the use of spies and the policy of promotion in the police, civil service and army only for German speakers was resented.
- Austrian army presence within towns like Milan and the heavily garrisoned Quadrilateral fortresses ensured that Italians could never forget that they were under foreign control and this inspired growing desire for the creation of a national state.

Secret societies

- The growth of secret societies, particularly the Carbonari, led to revolts in 1820, 1821, 1831. Also Young Italy and their revolts in the 1830s.

Any other relevant factors.

Candidates can be credited *up to a maximum of 20 marks*.

44. How important was the influence of Austria in preventing the unification of Italy between 1815 and 1850?

Context

By 1850 the forces of nationalism had grown in Italy. The Revolutions of 1849–9 showed this, but it also illustrated the tensions within the nationalist movement and the continued strength of the Austrians.

Influence of Austria

- Following the Vienna Settlement the Austrian Emperor, Francis I, had direct control of Lombardy and Venetia. Relatives of the Austrian Hapsburg Emperor controlled Parma, Modena and Tuscany (Central Duchies). Austria had agreements with the other states. Lombardy and Venetia were strictly controlled — censorship, spies, conscription (8 years), policy to employ German speakers (Austrian) in law, police, army civil service so controlled others (non Austrian).
- The Austrian army was common sight in major cities and in the Quadrilateral fortress towns on Lombard/Venetian border (Verona, Peschiera, Legnano, and Mantua).

- The Austrian army was sent in by Metternich to restore order following the Carbonari-inspired revolts in 1820, 1821 and 1831.
- Austria had a first-class commander, Radetsky. In 1848 Charles Albert's army won two skirmishes, but Radetsky awaited reinforcements then defeated Albert at Custozza forcing an armistice. Radetsky re-took Milan in August. After Albert's renewal of war, Radetsky took just three days to defeat him again (Novara). He then besieged Venetia until the Republic of St Mark surrendered on 22 August 1849. Austrians re-established control across northern and central Italy.

Other factors
Popular indifference

- Patriotic literature inspired intellectuals and students but did not reach the vast majority of the population who were illiterate (90% in some areas). The mass of the population were indifferent to nationalist ideas.

Geography

- Geographical difficulties hindered the spread of nationalist ideas. It also led to problems of economic development: the industrial north and the rural south.

Attitudes of Italian rulers

- Individual rulers were opposed to nationalism. Pope Pius IX denounced nationalism in 1848.

Nationalist divisions/weakness

- Secret societies lacked clear aims, organisation, leadership, resources and operated in regional cells.
- The Young Italy movement was dead by 1850.
- Moderate nationalists feared extremists like Mazzini.
- The 1848/49 revolutions showed that nationalist leaders did not trust one another (Manin and Charles Albert) or would not work together (C. Albert and Mazzini).

Failure to capitalise on Austrian weakness in 1848

- There was division between those desiring liberal changes within existing states and those desiring the creation of a national state.

Any other relevant factors.

Candidates can be credited up to a maximum of 20 marks.

45. To what extent did Mussolini achieve power by 1925 as a result of the weaknesses of Italian governments?

Context

Italy was a new country formed by 1871. When it entered the First World War the Italians expected great rewards. They were disappointed when it became clear Italy would not benefit from their involvement in the war.

Weaknesses of Italian governments

- Parliamentary government was weak and ineffective.
- The Liberals had no party structure and a narrow support base.
- Coalitions were corrupt; Bribery was commonplace (trasformismo).
- New parties with a wider support base threatened existing political system.
- Universal male suffrage and PR worsened the situation resulting in unstable coalitions.
- Giolitti made an electoral pact with Mussolini (1921). The fascists gained 35 seats then refused to support the government.
- The Liberals fragmented into at least four different factions grouped around former PMs.

- Once Mussolini was PM these groups felt they could control him and believed he could tame the extreme fascists. The majority of 'liberals' supported the Acerbo Law. Aventine Secession played into Mussolini's hands.

Weak governments failed to deal with Italy's internal problems.

- Coalitions failed to deal with Italy's growing post WWI economic problems:
  - foreign loans and massive national debt
  - spiralling inflation
  - low wages
  - food shortages
  - escalating unemployment, strikes, demonstrations and occupation of factories
  - violence of both socialist and fascists.

They did little to support the police as law and order broke down and fears of civil war/ revolution grew.

The government did not stop D'Annunzio's seizure of Fiume. Government ineffective over 'Biennio Rosso'.

Other factors

Weaknesses of the monarchy

- The king caved in over the 'March on Rome'.

Socialist weaknesses

- Revolutionary socialists dominated the leadership of PSI (socialists) and they refused involvement in 'liberal' coalitions.
- Biennio Rosso frightened the middle/upper classes who feared communism. In the 1919 elections PSI did well but could not form government. It split into moderates, radicals and communists in 1921.
- In 1922 the General Strike failed. Moderates failed to join an anti-fascist coalition. In 1925 Mussolini banned socialist parties.

PPI weaknesses

- Pope Pius XI constantly undermined Sturzo's PPI. PPI was divided over its attitude to fascism — the right preferred fascism over socialism. The left were anti-fascist. Mussolini exploited this by including two right wing PPI in his coalition.
- Pius directly negotiated with Mussolini over existing problems between church and state, and effectively sidelined Sturzo. PPI officially abstained over Acerbo Law. Pope rejected PPI involvement in the anti-fascist coalition of 1924.
- By 1926 Mussolini had banned all opposition parties.

Appeal of fascism

- Fascism promised strong government.
- Squadristi violence was directed against socialism so gained support of elites and middle classes.
- Violence showed fascism was strong and ruthless.
- Appeal to nationalism, capitalising on the resentment towards the Paris Peace Settlement.

Mussolini's skills

- He seized his opportunities and changed political direction offering support to conservative elites: Pope; king; army.
- He kept fascist policies vague to attract support from different groups.
- He copied D'Annunzio's tactics – direct action; flags, banners, salutes, songs – fascism seemed dynamic.
- He used 'piazza politics' and his newspaper effectively.
- He outmanoeuvred fascist extremists.

Any other relevant factors.

Part F: Russia, 1881–1921

Candidates can be credited up to a maximum of 20 marks.

46. "The Tsar had a secure grip on power in the years before 1905." How valid is that view?

Context

Opposition groups were kept weak in the Tsarist state before 1905. The main reasons for making this possible were the 'Pillars of Autocracy'. Each of these 'Pillars' strengthened the Tsar's position, and made it almost impossible for opposition groups to challenge the state.

Opposition groups

- Opposition groups, eg Social Democrats (supported by industrial workers) and Liberals (who wanted a British-style parliament), were fairly weak. However, these groups were not powerful or popular enough to effect change.
- There were various revolutionary groups like the Social Revolutionaries (supported by peasants seeking land reform). Moreover these groups were further weakened by the fact they were divided and disorganised.
- The leaders were often in prison or in exile.

The 'Pillars of Autocracy'

- **The Church** helped to ensure that the people, particularly the peasants, remained loyal to the Tsar. They preached to the peasants that the Tsar had been appointed by God and that they should therefore obey the Tsar. Ensured the peasants were aware of the Fundamental Law.
- **The Fundamental Law** stated 'To the emperor of all Russia belongs the supreme and unlimited power. God himself commands that his supreme power be obeyed out of conscience as well as out of fear'. This was the basis of the Tsarist state.
- **The army** was controlled by the officers who were mainly upper-class, conservative and loyal to the Tsar. They ensured that the population and the peasantry in particular, were loyal to the Tsar. They crushed any insurgence and were used to enforce order in the country and loyalty to the Tsar.
- **The secret police (Okhrana)** was set up to ensure loyalty to the Tsar and weed out opposition to the Tsar. They did this by spying on all people of society irrespective of class. Those showing any sign of opposition to the Tsar were imprisoned or sent into exile. Large numbers were exiled.
- **The civil service** mainly employed middle-class people, therefore ensuring the loyalty of that class. The civil service was responsible for enforcing laws on censorship and corruption and controlling meetings which made it very difficult for the revolutionaries to communicate.

Censorship

- This controlled what people could read, what university lecturers could say, access to schools, and limited the number and type of books available in libraries.

Russification

- This was the policy of restricting the rights of the national minorities in the Russian Empire by insisting that Russian was the first language. As a result, law and government were conducted throughout the Russian Empire in the Russian language. This maintained the dominance of the Russian culture over that of the minorities.
- State intervention in religion and education.
- Treated subjects as potential enemies and inferior to Russians.

Zubatov unions

- Organised by the police, these were used to divert the attention of the workers away from political change by concentrating on wages and conditions in the factories, thus reducing the chances of the workers being influenced by the revolutionary groups. Unions in 1903 became involved in strikes and so were disbanded due to pressure.

Any other relevant factors.

Candidates can be credited up to a maximum of 20 marks.

47. To what extent was the power of the Tsarist state weakened in the years between 1905 and 1914?

Context

By 1905 Russia's problems had led to open opposition to the Tsarist state. Poor military performance in the war with Japan exposed the social, economic and political weaknesses of the state.

October Manifesto

- The Duma received legislative powers, ie agree to new laws.
- The electorate was widened, and promised freedom of speech, to have meetings and liberty of conscience.
- This split the revolutionary forces with the moderate liberals accepting it.
- On the face of it there was change, but...
- Duma (parliament) granted to buy off the middle classes.
- Before Duma met, the Tsar took back much of the power he had conceded.
- He announced the 'Fundamental Laws' whereby the Supreme autocratic power belonged to the Tsar, in that no law could be passed without his approval.
- The Duma had two chambers. The first house was elected and the second house (state council) would be largely dominated by the Tsar and could veto lower chamber proposals.
- The Tsar could appoint and dismiss ministers who were not responsible to the Duma.
- The Tsar could dissolve the Duma, but had to call elections for a new one.
- Article 87 meant the Tsar could issue decrees 'in exceptional circumstances' when the Duma was not sitting.

The Duma

- 1st Duma: Lasted from April to June 1906. Dismissed for demanding a full democratic parliament. 'Vyborg Group' of liberals who resisted were arrested and banned from future elections.
- 2nd Duma: Lasted from Feb to June 1907. Few liberals in this Duma as most of them were part of the 'Vyborg Group'. Closed due to the Tsar's resentment to criticism of the administration of the army, thus showing power of Tsarist state.
- 3rd Duma: Lasted from 1907 to 1912. The rich dominated it and only 1 man in 6 could now vote. This Duma was very right wing and was accused of merely rubber-stamping Tsarist policies, however it helped Stolypin bring about Land Reform which was disliked by the nobles, questioned ministers, discussed state finances, and made proposals to modernise the army, showing that Tsarist policy could change, but was it weakened?
- 4th Duma: Lasted from 1912 to 1914. It was of a similar make-up to the 3rd Duma. It also criticised the government at times, such as it's handling of the Lena goldfield strike and the very heavy-handed style of the government in repressing working class protest, but although critical did it weaken the Tsarist State? Dissolved itself at the start of WWI.

Stolypin cracked down on revolutionaries

- Government ministers in reality helped the Tsar in some ways: role of Stolypin.
- Many of the revolutionaries were stamped out.
- Stolypin set up tribunals, which sentenced to death every terrorist captured by the secret police.
- There was a reduction in opposition to the Tsar and his running of the country.
- The Soviets were crushed in 1905 as they were a focal point of opposition to the Tsar.

Agricultural Reforms

- Stolypin introduced these important reforms to win the support of the peasants. Redemption payments were ended. Peasants were given complete freedom to leave the Mir and they could turn their holdings in to their own property, this was to produce a rich class of peasants and help farming.
- These reforms reduced opposition to the Tsar as the peasants became loyal to the Tsar and allowed him to rule as he wished.

June 1907 Electoral Law Change

- Franchise was restricted to favour the gentry and urban rich at the expense of the workers, peasants and nationalities, which tended to reinforce Tsarist power.
- The Army remained loyal to the Tsar. After 1905 this enabled the Tsar to repress opposition such as revolutionaries.

Any other relevant factors.

Candidates can be credited up to a maximum of 20 marks.

48. How important was Bolshevik propaganda in the success of the 1917 October revolution?

Context

Previous limited reform was not enough to save Tsarist rule from the stresses of fighting in World War 1. Those same stresses severely weakened the Provisional government through the summer of 1917.

Bolshevik Propaganda

- Lenin returned to Russia announcing the April Theses, with slogans such as 'Peace, Land and Bread' and 'All Power to the Soviets' which were persuasive and appealed to important groups such as the workers and peasants.
- Lenin talked of further revolution to overthrow the Provisional Government and his slogans identified the key weaknesses of the Provisional Government.

Other factors

The Provisional Government lacked authority

- The Provisional Government was an unelected government; it was a self-appointed body and had no right to exercise authority.

The Petrograd Soviet

- The old Petrograd Soviet re-emerged and ran Petrograd. The Bolsheviks kept attending the Petrograd Soviet when most of the others stopped doing so and this gave them control of the Soviet, which they could then use against the Provisional Government.
- The Petrograd Soviet undermined the authority of Provisional Government especially when relations between the two worsened.
- Order No. 1 of the Petrograd Soviet weakened the authority of the Provisional Government as soldiers were not to obey orders of Provisional Government that contradicted those of the Petrograd Soviet.

The War
- The Provisional Government gave in to the pressure of the army and from the Allies to keep Russia in the War.
- Remaining in the war helped cause the October revolution and helped destroy the Provisional Government as the misery it caused continued for people in Russia.

Workers
- The workers were restless as they were starving due to food shortages caused by the war.
- The shortage of fuel caused lack of heating for the workers in their living conditions.
- The shortage of food and supplies made the workers unhappy and restless.

The Land Issue
- All over Russia peasants were seizing nobles' land and wanted the Provisional Government to legitimise this.
- The failure of the Provisional Government to recognise the peasants' claims eroded the confidence in the Provisional Government.
- Food shortages caused discontent, and they were caught up by revolutionary slogans such as 'Peace, Land and Bread'.

The July Days
- The Bolsheviks staged an attempt to seize power, rising in support of the Kronstadt sailors who were in revolt. The revolt was easily crushed by the Provisional Government but showed increasing opposition to the Provisional Government, especially from the forces.
- The revolt also showed that the Provisional Government was still reasonably strong and able to crush opposition such as the Bolsheviks who now appeared to be weakened.

Kornilov affair
- General Kornilov, a right wing general, proposed to replace the Provisional Government with a military dictatorship and sent troops to Petrograd.
- Kerensky appealed to the Petrograd Soviet for help and the Bolsheviks were amongst those who helped.
- Some Bolsheviks were armed and released from prison to help put down the attempted coup.
- The Bolsheviks did not return their weapons to the Provisional Government after they defeated Kornilov.
- Bolsheviks were able to act as protectors of Petrograd.

Any other relevant factors.

Part G: USA, 1918—1968

Candidates can be credited up to a maximum of 20 marks.

49. To what extent was racism the main reason for changing attitudes towards immigration after 1918?

Context
Within the USA, changing attitudes towards immigration had been growing during the 19th and early 20th centuries. Many Americans felt their way of life was being challenged by immigrants from Southern and Eastern Europe.

Prejudice and racism
- Changing nature of immigrants. Old immigrants were WASPs mainly from the North and West of Europe. New immigrants were mainly from Southern and Eastern Europe. New immigrants were Catholic or Jewish — this worried WASP America.
- New immigrants were unfamiliar with democracy — this was viewed as a threat to the American Constitution.

- New immigrants continued to wear traditional dress and looked out of place.
- Nativism — small town values and eugenics. Pseudo science arguing immigrants from southern and eastern Europe are inferior people. The Nordic superior race — Madison Grant.
- State-sanctioned sterilization of 'inferior' mothers.
- Rebirth of KKK appealing to 100% Americanism.

Other factors

Fear of revolution
- Russian revolution in 1917 had established the first communist state committed to spreading revolution and destroying capitalism.
- 'Red Scare' 1919 and it looked as if revolution was imminent.
- Palmer Raids, August 1919.

Isolationism
- The 1920 Alien Land Law in California built on the 1913 Alien Land Law. It was firmly aimed at Japanese immigrants and it prohibited their ownership of agricultural land or being allowed a long-term lease. Aimed to discourage immigrants from the east.
- At the beginning of the First World War American public opinion was firmly on the side of neutrality.
- Wanted to keep out of foreign problems and concentrate solely on America.
- President Wilson — America should not become involved in Europe's 'civil war'.
- When the war ended, most Americans wanted a return to isolationism.
- Would not join the League of Nations; many Senators were concerned that if the USA joined, it might soon get dragged into another European war.

Social fears
- Immigrants congregated with people from their own culture in ghettos.
- Immigrants were blamed for high crime rates in cities, particularly those cities with high levels of immigrants, eg Sacco-Vanzetti case.
- Immigrants blamed for spread of organised crime, especially the Mafia.
- Prohibition boosted image of gangster and names such as Al Capone confirmed public expectation of immigrant involvement.

Economic fears
- Trade unions believed that anything they did to improve conditions or wages was wrecked by Italian or Polish workers who were prepared to work longer hours for lower wages.
- 1919 strikes — new immigrants were used as 'strike-breakers'. This caused huge resentment and an increase in the desire to stop immigrants coming into the country.

The effects of the First World War
- Many immigrants during the First World War had sympathies for their mother country.
- Many German immigrants had supported the German side in the war and society was split when the USA joined the war against Germany.
- Irish Americans were suspected of being anti-British.
- Many citizens felt hostile to anything foreign such as imported goods.

Any other relevant factors

Candidates can be credited up to a maximum of 20 marks.

50. **"The weakness of the US banking system was the main reason for causing the Great Depression of the 1930s." How valid is this view?**

Context
In the 1920s the USA experienced an economic boom but how real was it? By 1930 the USA entered a period of prolonged economic and social depression.

Weakness of the US banking system
- Major problem was lack of regulation.
- Banking system was made up of hundreds of small, state-based banks.
- When one bank collapsed it often led to a 'run' on other banks, resulting in a banking collapse and national financial crisis.

Other factors
Saturation of the US market
- New mass-production methods and mechanisation meant that production of consumer goods had expanded enormously.
- Cars, radios and other electrical goods had flooded the market and more was being made than people could buy.
- By 1929 those who could afford consumer goods had already bought them.
- Throughout the 1920s business had benefited from low tax policies. The result of this was that the bottom 40% of the population received only 12.5% of the nation's wealth.
- In contrast, the top 5% owned 33% of the nation's wealth. Therefore, domestic demand never kept up with production.

Results of the First World War on European economies.
- All European states, except Britain, placed tariffs on imported goods. US economy could not expand its foreign markets.

Economic boom of the 1920s
- Republican administration's policy of Laissez-Faire.
- Failure to help farmers who did not benefit from the 1920s boom.
- Low capital gains tax encouraged share speculation which resulted in the Wall Street Crash.
- The Depression was also due to the actions — or inactions — of President Hoover.

Wall Street crash
- Atmosphere of uncertainty in October 1929 and shareholders began to sell their stocks.
- 24 October 1929 — Black Thursday.
- 29 October 1929 — Black Tuesday.
- Share collapse caused panic.
- Stock market crash did play a role in the Depression but its significance was as a trigger. Collapse of credit, and of confidence.

Any other relevant factors.

Candidates can be credited up to a maximum of 20 marks.

51. **How important was the emergence of effective organisations to the development of the civil rights campaigns after 1945?**

Context
Before and after 1945 the USA was a racist society to a large extent. Black Americans faced hostility due to racist attitudes. Such racism was underpinned by legal sanction, social attitudes and organisations that persecuted black Americans.

Effective black organisations formed
- 1957 — Martin Luther King and other black clergy formed the Southern Christian Leadership Conference (SCLC) to coordinate the work of Civil Rights groups. King urged African Americans to use peaceful methods.
- 1960 a group of black and white college students organised the Non-violent Coordinating Committee (SNCC) to help the Civil Rights movement.
- They joined with young people from the SCLC, CORE and NAACP in staging sit-ins, boycotts, marches and freedom rides.
- Combined efforts of the civil rights groups ended discrimination in many public places including restaurants, hotels and theatres.

The emergence of effective black leaders
- Martin Luther King.
- Malcolm X.
- Stokely Carmichael.

Other factors
Effects of the Second World War
- Black soldiers talked about the 'Double-V-Campaign': Victory in the war and victory for Civil Rights at home.
- A. Philip Randolf is credited with highlighting the problems faced by black Americans during World War Two.
- March on Washington.
- Roosevelt's response — Executive order 8802.
- Roosevelt also established the Fair Employment Practices Committee to investigate incidents of discrimination.
- Creation of the Congress of Racial Equality (CORE) in 1942. Beginning of a mass movement for civil rights.

Evidence of continuing racial discrimination
- The experience of war emphasised freedom, democracy and human rights yet in the USA Jim Crow laws still existed and lynching went unpunished.
- The Emmet Till murder trial and its publicity.

Legal changes
- Education: 1954 Brown v Board of Education of Topeka.
- Supreme Court decision 1954 opened the door to more change.
- Little Rock Central High School.
- Transport: 1955 Rosa Parks and the Montgomery Bus Boycott.

Any other relevant factors.

Part H: Appeasement and the Road to War, to 1939

Candidates can be credited up to a maximum of 20 marks.

52. **To what extent does disappointment over the terms of the Peace Settlements of 1919 explain the aggressive nature of fascist foreign policies in the 1930s?**

Context
Fascist belief was founded on the idea of national unity. It totally opposed the idea of internal class division. In the cases of Italy and Germany it was also expansionist in outlook. Mussolini looked to create a new Roman Empire while Hitler sought living space for the 'excess' German population.

The Peace Settlements of 1919
- Determination to revise/overturn Paris Peace Settlement, German resentment of war guilt, reparations, disarmament, lost territory. Italian resentment of failure to gain control of Adriatic.
- Germany's desire to seek revenge for its defeat in WWI.

Other factors

Rise of dictatorships

- Lack of restraining internal political powers on Hitler and Mussolini

Economic difficulties after 1929

- Legacy of Germany and Italy's post-WW1 economic difficulties such as labour unrest, unemployment and inflation.
- The impact of the world economic crisis 1929–32 on the German and Italian economies intensified international competition and protectionism.
- Italy used aggressive foreign policies to distract from internal economic difficulties.
- Continuing economic problems in the 1930s. Needs of re-armament and domestic consumption.
- Economic imperatives; the need for additional resources leading to aggressive, expansionist foreign policies, eg Italy in Abyssinia, German drive to the east.

Fascist ideology

- Pathological hatred of communism, anti-Soviet crusade; contempt for democracy.
- Militarism — fascist glorification of war; Prussian/German military traditions.
- Extent to which foreign policies driven by Hitler's and Mussolini's own beliefs, personalities, charismatic leadership.
- Irredentism, eg Hitler's commitment to the incorporation of all Germans within the Reich.
- Mussolini's 'Roman' ambitions in the Mediterranean and Africa; Hitler's ambitions in Eastern Europe and Russia — Lebensraum.

Weakness of the League of Nations

- Failure of the League. Divided response of other powers, eg British appeasement, French political divisions, US isolationism, mutual suspicion of Soviet Russia; relative weakness of successor states in Eastern Europe.
- Example of success of Japan in Manchuria and Italy in Abyssinia in defiance of League.

The British policy of appeasement

- British appeasement to an extent encouraged both Germany and Italy to increase their demands and do so increasingly forcefully.
- British attempts to bring Mussolini into their camp resulted in the Hoare-Laval Pact, which produced a popular outcry when the terms were leaked. Mussolini saw that Britain and France were not opposed in principle to gains for Italy in East Africa and he was able to defy sanctions and keep Abyssinia.
- Hitler knew of British reservations about some terms of the Versailles Treaty and was able to play on these, increasingly realising that he would not be stopped, eg re-armament, the re-occupation of the Rhineland and then the Anschluss.

Any other relevant factors.

*Candidates can be credited **up to a maximum of 20 marks**.*

53. To what extent does British public opinion explain the policy of appeasement between 1936 and 1938?

Context

Britain was keenly aware that it was not fully prepared for war. Therefore Britain's foremost aim was the maintenance of peace. Up to March 1938, this was largely achieved.

Conflicts that did occur were on the periphery of Europe/the Mediterranean.

Public opinion

- Early Nazi foreign policy justifiable — 'only going in own front garden' — Rhineland 1936.
- Peace Pledge Union — 11 million signatures for anti-war position.
- Peace Ballot 1935.
- Fulham by-election often used as evidence for appeasement support — questionable. Oxford Union debate — no strong support to fight for King and Country.
- Fear of bombing — as seen in newsreels (Guernica 1937) and also 'Things to Come' movie.
- Fear of return to horrors of Great War and also new technology fears — gas bombing of civilians.
- There are more important issues to spend money on.
- Many felt European problems were not our concern.
- Distractions of the Abdication crisis.

Other factors explaining the policy of appeasement between 1936 and 1938

- Military weakness.
- Run-down state of armed forces following WW1.
- Army: conscription ended post-WW1, scaled right down in size.
- Navy: not so run-down but not fully maintained; many obsolete ships.
- Air Force: lack of adequate air defences and fear of aerial bombing.
- Multiple threats — Japan in the East, Italy in the Mediterranean and North Africa, Germany in Central Europe.
- Warnings of Chiefs-of-Staff: Britain could not fight three enemies at same time.
- Exaggerated assessments of German military strength.

1919 Peace Settlement was seen as too harsh on Germany

- Sympathy for Germany's genuine grievances.
- British reluctance to enforce Treaty provisions and preference for policy of making concessions.
- Economic difficulties — impact of 1929–32 economic crisis and depression, reluctance to further damage international trade and commerce.

Fear of communism — suspicion of Soviet Russia;

- Nazi Germany seen as a buffer and destabilising the Nazi regime might lead to questions over communist revolution in Germany.
- Perceived lack of reliable allies (but there are doubts as to how reliable Britain was as an ally herself).
- Other general worries.
- Failure of League of Nations, eg Manchuria, Abyssinia.
- French political divisions, military weakness and Maginot mentality.
- US isolationism.
- Mutual suspicions vis-a-vis Soviet Russia.
- Relative weakness of Eastern European successor states.
- Doubts over commitment of Empire and the Dominions in event of war.
- Italy also appeased in vain attempt to prevent alliance with Germany.
- Belief that Hitler would moderate views in power and be reasonable.
- Chamberlain's personal convictions and control of foreign policy.

Any other relevant factors.

Candidates can be credited up to a maximum of 20 marks.

54. "Munich was a triumph for British foreign policy." How valid is this view?

Context

In the years before 1938 it was clear that Hitler had ambitions to move Nazi power eastwards. Hitler called this policy Lebensraum. His ultimate goal was Russia but Czechoslovakia stood in his way.

British Prime minister Chamberlain felt that he was the main that could bring peace to Europe.

Arguments for and against the settlement; differing views of the Munich settlement.

Munich a victory?

- Hitler himself was dissatisfied by Munich – felt 'robbed' of a war with the hated Czechs. Czechoslovakian defences were effectively outflanked anyway following the Anschluss.
- Britain and France were not in a position to prevent German attack on Czechoslovakia in terms of:
  - geography — difficulties of getting assistance to Czechoslovakia
  - public opinion — reluctant to risk war over mainly German-speaking Sudetenland.
  - military unpreparedness for wider war — especially Britain's air defences
  - lack of alternative, unified international response to Hitler's threats: failure of League of Nations
  - French doubts over commitments to Czechoslovakia
  - US isolationism
  - mutual suspicion of Soviet Russia
  - strong reservations of rest of British Empire and Dominions concerning support in event of war.
- Attitudes of Poland and Hungary — willing to benefit from dismemberment of Czechoslovakia.
- Munich bought another year for rearmament which Britain put to good use.

Munich a defeat?

- A humiliating surrender to Hitler's threats.
- Another breach in the post-WW1 settlement.
- A betrayal of Czechoslovakia and democracy.
- Czechoslovakia wide open to further German aggression — destruction of Czechoslovakia, March 1939.
- Further augmentation of German manpower and resources.
- Furtherance of Hitler's influence and ambitions in Eastern Europe.
- Further alienation of Soviet Union.
- Poland left further exposed.
- A British, French, Soviet agreement was a more effective alternative.

Any other relevant factors.

Part I: The Cold War, 1945–1989

Candidates can be credited up to a maximum of 20 marks.

55. How important were ideological differences between east and west in the emergence of the Cold War up to 1955?

Context

The wartime alliance had always been one of convenience owing to the common enemy of Nazism. America had not recognised the Soviet communist government's legitimacy until 1933. As the Second World War came to an end the tensions between a capitalist America and her allies and communist Russia became all too clear.

Ideological differences

- Impact of 1917 Bolshevik revolution in Russia on relations with the Western powers: Soviet withdrawal from WW1, involvement of West with anti-Bolshevik Whites: ideological differences between communism and capitalism.
- Fears in the West that communism was on the march led President Truman to the policy of containment. British power was in retreat: WW2 had been expensive so the British aimed to reduce their world commitments, specifically in Greece where civil war raged between communists and royalists.
- Fear of similar problems in Italy when allied troops left; activities of Mao in China.
- Truman acknowledged world dividing into two hostile blocs in his speech to support free peoples and proposals to oppose totalitarian regimes — exemplified by the Marshall Plan.
- Fulton speech by Churchill. Creation of competing military alliances: NATO and Warsaw Pact further polarised the world.
- The Soviet Union rejected the Western economic model and set up its own economic bloc: Comecon.

Other factors

- Tensions within the war-time alliance.
- WW2: suspicion of USSR by allies because of Nazi-Soviet Pact of 1939.
- Tensions within the wartime alliance as the defeat of Nazism became clear.
- Soviet Union felt they had done the bulk of the land fighting and wanted security for the USSR.
- Yalta conference: Stalin determined to hang on to land gained and create a series of sympathetic regimes in Eastern Europe.
- The USA wanted to create a free trade area composed of democratic states. Soviet actions in Poland, Romania, Bulgaria, etc, in creating pro-communist regimes and Allied actions in Western Europe and Greece further increased tensions.

The US decision to use the atom bomb

- One aim of the use of atom bombs on Hiroshima and Nagasaki was to impress the USSR and make them ready to make concessions in Eastern Europe.
- Stalin knew about the Manhattan project and refused to be intimidated and in fact it made him even more suspicious of the USA.

The arms race

- Stalin was determined to make the Soviet Union a nuclear power as soon as possible; the development of the arms race.
- The British and the French were also developing their independent nuclear deterrents which, realistically, were only aimed at the USSR.
- Development of technologies to deliver nuclear weapons.

Disagreements over the future of Germany

- The Potsdam Conference and policy over Germany whereby the allied sectors remained free as compared to Soviet sector which was stripped of assets as reparations. The economic status of Germany: creation of Bizonia in West.
- Contrast between the developing capitalist West and centrally-controlled East: introduction of Deutschemark in West led to the Berlin Blockade in 1949.

The crisis over Korea

- Stalin encouraged communist North Korea to invade capitalist South. This led to American-led UN intervention on behalf of the South, and resultant Chinese intervention. Soviet and American pilots fought each other across Korea. Stalemate along 38th parallel. The Cold War had been sealed with a Hot War.

Any other relevant factors.

Candidates can be credited up to a maximum of 20 marks.

56. "The Cuban Crisis of 1962 was a direct consequence of the domestic pressures on Khrushchev." How valid is this view?

Context

In 1962 the Cold War was at its height. Tensions between America and Russia meant that the political futures of the respective leaders of those two countries depended on how strong each could show himself to be and neither wanted to 'blink first' if it came to a face-to-face showdown.

Domestic pressures of Khrushchev

- Ongoing deadlock over Berlin and criticism of Khrushchev at home over cuts in the armed forces, economic failures and the issues surrounding de-Stalinisation, Hungary 1956, etc.
- Khrushchev believed a foreign policy coup would help improve matters for him at home.
- Khrushchev aware of need to raise the Soviet standard of living and to greatly expand his country's space program. He sought to increase international standing of USSR and his own authority.
- Khrushchev became premier after outmanoeuvring rivals. He needed to maintain authority.
- Khrushchev wanted to avoid war with the Western nations and, at the same time, increase economic competition between communist and non-communist countries. The policy, known as peaceful co-existence, caused bitter quarrels between the Soviet Union and China.
- Khrushchev needed to maintain his status in communist bloc.
- Khrushchev worried that if the Soviet Union lost the arms race it might invite a first strike from the United States. Soviet missiles placed in Cuba would solve that problem.

Other factors

Miscalculation by Khrushchev.

- Khrushchev felt that Kennedy was a weak president after the Bay of Pigs, June 1961. Summit in Vienna to discuss Berlin. USA did little to oppose construction of Berlin Wall. Khrushchev felt that Kennedy lacked power and support to make concessions over the arms race. Events were to prove him wrong.
- Khrushchev had been advised that the installation could be done secretly and that the Americans would not discover the missiles until long after. The advice was wrong.

Ideological reasons

- Khrushchev was sympathetic to Castro. Some historians argue that he wanted to use Cuba as a launch pad for revolution in Central America. Missile deployment would provide protection for the revolution.

American policy over Cuba

- Domestic pressures for Kennedy as an explanation for the Cuban Crisis of 1962.
- In 1960 Kennedy became President. He promised tougher defence polices and progressive health, housing, and Civil Rights programs. But Kennedy won by just over 100,000 votes. He lacked a reliable majority in congress.

- Kennedy needed to show he had strength and determination to gain respect and support.
- Kennedy was already embarrassed by Bay of Pigs fiasco where 1400 Cuban exiles landed and were crushed by Castro's army.
- Argument that this forced Castro to start preparing to defend himself against another attack and drew him closer to Khrushchev and the Soviet Union.
- Castro asked for significant conventional military aid.
- Kennedy was under some pressure from CIA to continue to destabilise Castro's Cuba.
- America was very sensitive about the presence of a communist state so close to Florida.
- American aggression seemed to be confirmed by the United States practising the invasion of a Caribbean island with a dictator named Ortsac: Operation Mongoose overseen by Robert Kennedy.

The nuclear arms race

- The Soviets wanted to place nuclear missiles in Cuba because they were trying to balance out the number of nuclear arms between themselves and the United States.
- The United States had placed their Jupiter missiles in Turkey and now the USSR felt very threatened. Kennedy had originally placed the Jupiter missiles in Turkey in 1961 because the United States had feared the possible nuclear capabilities of the Soviet Union. These missiles became a major threat to the Soviets because they were capable of striking anywhere in the USSR.
- Counter view that the missiles were obsolete.
- In order to defend themselves, and let the United States know what it was like to be surrounded by a deadly threat, the Soviets placed missiles in Cuba.

Any other relevant factors.

Candidates can be credited up to a maximum of 20 marks.

57. How important was the danger of Mutually Assured Destruction in forcing the superpowers into attempts to manage the Cold War?

Context

As part of the Cold War, each side raced to build the latest in weapons of mass destruction. The world worried if a sudden crisis between East and West would cause one or other leaders to 'press the button' and start a nuclear war.

Mutually Assured Destruction

- The development of vast arsenals of nuclear weapons from 1945 by both superpowers as a deterrent to the other side; a military attack would result in horrific retaliation.
- So many nuclear weapons were built to ensure that not all were destroyed even after a first-strike, and this led to a stalemate known as MAD. Arms race built on fear.
- The threat of nuclear war seemed very close on the discovery of Soviet nuclear missiles in Cuba in 1962. Before Khrushchev backed down, nuclear war was threatened.
- It also illustrated the lack of formal contact between the superpowers to defuse potential conflicts.
- Introduction of a 'hot-line' between the Kremlin and White House in order to improve communication between the superpowers.
- Khrushchev and Kennedy also signed the Limited Nuclear Test Ban Treaty, the first international agreement on nuclear weapons.

Other factors

The importance of verification

- Some historians think Arms Control would never have taken root, but for the ability of the sides to verify what the other was doing.
- American development of surveillance technology (U2 and satellites) meant that nuclear weapons could be identified and agreements verified.
- Example of U2 flight over Cuba where Anderson photographed nuclear sites.
- Also U2 and satellite verification to make sure the Soviets were doing as promised at the negotiating table.

Economic reasons

- Developments in technology raised the costs of the arms race.
- The development of Anti-Ballistic Missile technology and costs of war led to SALT 1, and the ABM treaty.
- Limiting MIRV and intermediate missile technology led to SALT 2.
- The cost of 'Star Wars' technology also encouraged the Soviet Union to seek better relations.
- Khrushchev's desire for better relations between the superpowers in the 50s and 60s was, in part, about freeing up resources for economic development in the USSR. He hoped this would show the superiority of the Soviet system.
- Gorbachev wanted to improve the lives of ordinary Russians and part of this was by reducing the huge defence budget, eg Intermediate Nuclear Forces Treaty, December 1987.

Co-existence and détente

- Policies of co-existence and détente developed to defuse tensions and even encourage trade.
- Role of others like Brandt in West Germany in defusing tension through their policies of Ostpolitik.
- However there were also times of great tension between the superpowers.
- The Second Cold War — Soviet invasion of Afghanistan in 1979 and the advent of the Reagan presidency led to poor relations between the superpowers.
- New technology allowed both sides to continue to develop powerful armaments despite agreements. Intermediate and battlefield nuclear technology for example.

Any other relevant factors.

MODEL PAPER 2
SECTION 1: SCOTTISH

Part A: The Wars of Independence, 1249—1328

1. How fully does Source D explain the reasons for the ultimate success of Bruce in maintaining Scotland's independence? (9)

Candidates can be credited in a number of ways up to a maximum of 9 marks.

A maximum of 2 marks may be given for answers which refer only to the source.

Possible points which may be identified in the source include:
- Robert rewarded his followers from lands of his enemies and thus ensured their loyalties.
- Robert raided northern England to try to force the English king to negotiate.
- Robert negotiated an uneasy truce with England in 1323.
- Robert negotiated a mutual defence treaty with France in 1326 as part of his policy to ensure a stable inheritance for his son.

Possible points of significant omission may include:
- Bannockburn represented a major victory for Robert, it was the start of his fearful reputation as a great warlord who couldn't be beaten.
- Bannockburn had more of an impact on domestic politics in Scotland than any real long-term military benefits. Robert passed legislation forbidding nobles holding land in both England and Scotland.
- Robert took land from the disinherited at Cambuskenneth and shared it among his supporters to gain their loyalty.
- The war in the north of England was a significant and often overlooked aspect of the Scottish Wars.
- As well as the 1315 invasion, Robert attacked England no fewer than 5 times (1316, 1318, 1322, 1323 and 1328).
- The campaign of 1322 was particularly impressive and culminated in the battle Old Byland, which almost saw a repeat of Bannockburn and the capture of Edward II.
- In 1320 the Declaration of Arbroath, a rebuttal to the papal decrees against Robert, was dispatched to Rome along with other letters. It is often seen as a key defence against English insistence that the papacy intervene on their behalf. By 1323 papal attitude to Scotland had significantly improved.
- The campaign of 1328, following the murder of Edward II by Isabella and Mortimer is a final decisive move by Robert.
- He re-opened his Irish campaign with a new army invading Ulster, at the same time his most trusted lieutenants raided northern England, skilfully running rings around Mortimer and the young newly crowned Edward III.
- Robert's announcement that he intended to annex Northumbria eventually forced Isabella and Mortimer to sign the Treaty of Edinburgh 1328.
- Edward Bruce invaded Ireland to take war to the English and create a pan-Celtic alliance. Overran Ulster quickly, but became bogged down.
- **Any other** valid point of explanation that meets the criteria described in the general marking principles for this kind of question.

2. Evaluate the usefulness of Source C as evidence of the relationship between John Balliol and Edward I. (6)

Candidates can be credited in a number of ways up to a maximum of 6 marks.

Examples of aspects of the source and relevant comments:

Aspect of the source	Possible comment
Author: Walter of Guisborough	More useful as account is based on personal observation and experience. Less useful as author is English so may be biased.
Type of Source: Chronicle	Useful as written by an educated author.
Purpose: Record of events during Scottish wars	Useful as considered to be a relatively reliable record of events. Possible bias as the priory suffered during the wars so less useful.
Timing: Written in the early 14th century	Source is more useful as it dates from the time when relations between Balliol and Edward were very strained.
Content	**Possible comment**
• When the city was taken more than 8,000 were killed.	Useful as it shows the savagery of the English forces unleashed by Edward. Also, corroborated by other sources.
• Taking of hostages like Lord William Douglas.	More useful as it shows method used by Edward with the aristocracy as he had to gain their loyalty.
• Taking of oaths of loyalty from two hundred men.	More useful as shows another method used by Edward to ensure loyalty from Scots, further developed on his 'tour' through a defeated Scotland after Dunbar.

Possible points of significant omission may include:

- Despite the Scots early confidence, and the fortification of Berwick, the city fell quickly to Edward's more professional and experienced army.
- The garrison of the castle surrendered under the laws of chivalry and Edward allowed them to go, but the townsmen and Burghers were slaughtered.
- Edward forced the women and children to abandon their homes and re-populated Berwick with people from Northumbria.
- The Earl of Surrey defeated the Scottish army at Dunbar, many Scottish knights and nobles were captured.
- Edward I captured important castles such as Roxburgh, Edinburgh and most importantly Stirling, there was no attempt at resistance at Stirling.
- Edward's march northward to Elgin, and the acceptance of oaths of loyalty from nobles along the way (Ragman's Roll).
- King John's humiliating surrender at Kincardine Castle (Tomb Tabard).
- Edward's removal of the Stone of Destiny and Scottish legal documents to prevent an inauguration of a future king.
- The appointment of the Earl of Surrey as lieutenant of Scotland.
- **Any other** valid point of explanation that meets the criteria described in the general marking principles for this kind of question.

3. Compare the views of Sources A and B about the Scots attempts to protect their independence through the Treaty of Birgham. (5)

Candidates may be credited in a number of ways up to a maximum of 5 marks.

Possible points of comparison may include:

Overall: Both sources generally agree that the Scottish Guardians were concerned about maintaining the independence of Scotland.

Source B offers a more detailed summary of how the kingdom would function under a dual monarchy and seems to suggest more optimism than the frank statements of the actual treaty.

Source A	Source B
No one of the kingdom of Scotland shall be held to answer out with that kingdom for any agreement entered into, or for any crime committed, or in any other cause contrary to the laws and customs of that kingdom.	Persons in Scotland who had been accused of a crime or sued at law should not have to answer in a court outside their country.
The rights and liberties of Scotland shall be preserved.	The guardians above all were anxious to do nothing that might impair on the royal dignity or the integrity of Scotland.
We promise that the kingdom of Scotland shall remain separate and divided from the kingdom of England.	The treaty envisaged two feudal kingdoms: England and Scotland ruled separately.
We explicitly grant that no tenant in chief of the king of Scotland shall be forced to go outside the kingdom to do homage or fealty.	Tenants in chief of the Scots Crown need do homage for their lands in Scotland only.

Part B: The Age of the Reformation, 1542–1603

4. How fully does Source D explain the impact of the Reformation on Scotland? (9)

Candidates can be credited in a number of ways up to a maximum of 9 marks.

A maximum of 2 marks may be given for answers which refer only to the source.

Possible points which may be identified in the source include:

- There was a new religious fervour demonstrated by support for Presbyterian beliefs.
- Congregations had the right to choose their own minister.
- The place of music in the lives of people generally and in Kirk services was to suffer.
- There remained a compassionate attitude towards representatives of the Catholic faith.

Possible points of significant omission may include:

- Great emphasis was laid upon attendance at both daily and Sunday services and every effort made to ensure that no possible diversions existed which might detain a congregation from their duties.
- The *Second Book of Discipline* led indirectly to a regular meeting of ministers from 10 to 20 parishes for discussion of doctrine, which became the presbytery.

- It proved impracticable to dispossess the Catholic clergy of their benefices so they were allowed to retain two-thirds of their revenues for life.
- Concessions made to Catholic clergy, on the grounds of old age or ill health.
- James VI was reluctant to enforce anti-Catholic laws.
- The General Assembly continued to ask the king to take action against Catholic nobles and Jesuit ministries.
- The Kirk Sessions of Protestant Scotland were to become guardians of moral and religious matters, replacing the Catholic church's congregational organisations.
- The elaborate interiors of Catholic Churches were replaced with plain, whitewashed parish kirks.
- Assistance given to the poor from the friaries ended. New plans to help the poor by the Presbyterian church faced difficulty and were hard to enforce.
- Catholic saints' days and festivals were no longer publicly observed.
- Literary works and Kirk sermons were published in English rather than Latin.
- Many of the issues prevalent within the Catholic Church prior to the Reformation remained, such as: attendance; poverty of some parishes; and poor quality of preaching.
- Social/economic factors.
- **Any other** valid point of explanation that meets the criteria described in the general marking principles for this kind of question.

5. Evaluate the usefulness of Source C as evidence of Mary's difficulties in ruling Scotland. (6)

Candidates can be credited in a number of ways up to a maximum of 6 marks.

Examples of aspects of the source and relevant comments:

Aspect of the source	Possible comment
Author: James Melville	More useful as Melville was a trusted member of Mary's household. Less useful as may be biased.
Type of Source: From memoir	More useful as personal account of Melville's life and experiences.
Purpose: To give an account of Riccio's death	The source is more useful as it can be considered to be an accurate account. Although one of Mary's household, Melville, had warned Mary about her favouritism towards Riccio.
Timing: Contemporary	More useful as contemporary to events and murder of Riccio is considered to be a turning point in Mary's reign.

Content	Possible comment
• David Riccio as Mary's secretary was envied and hated by the nobility.	Useful as it shows the dislike of Riccio by the Scottish nobility.
• Mary's husband, Darnley, agreed to the murder of Riccio which Scottish Lords had planned so that they could control the court and parliament.	Useful as it shows the involvement of Darnley, the fickle second husband of Mary.
• Mary was unable to save Riccio and was kept captive.	Useful as it illustrates the changing power relationship in Scotland and the fact that the nobles felt they could act in this way.

Possible points of significant omission may include:

- Mary's marriage to Darnley was unpopular amongst nobles and members of her household.
- As the Queen's husband, Darnley wanted the 'crown matrimonial' in order to become joint ruler with her. Mary refused as he was unfit to rule.
- Darnley became resentful and joined a plot to murder Mary's secretary, Riccio.
- Darnley's uncle took Darnley's knife to strike the first blow. He left the knife in Riccio's body to show that Darnley was involved in the murder.
- During the struggle, Mary was seized and threatened with a pistol. Her life was in danger and so was the life of her unborn child.
- Throughout Mary's reign, rivalry between noble families was one of the main sources of trouble for the Queen.
- Religion was a major problem for Mary. People were expected to follow their ruler's religion. Scotland had just had a Protestant revolution, but its Queen was a Catholic.
- Queen Elizabeth viewed Mary, her cousin and heir, with suspicion. However, Mary feared that Elizabeth might assist Scottish Protestants to rise against her.
- Opposition to Mary's marriage to Lord Darnley led to the Chaseabout Raid. The (noble) rebels sought help from Elizabeth who refused and they fled to England. Mary demonstrated her authority over her nobles; yet she also lost the support of many powerful and potentially dangerous men.
- While some nobles hoped to benefit from her death, others planned to imprison her and make her child their ruler because they would gain from another minority.
- **Any other** valid point of explanation that meets the criteria described in the general marking principles for this kind of question.

6. Compare the views of Sources A and B about the changes brought in by the Treaty of Edinburgh in 1560. 5

Candidates may be credited in a number of ways up to a maximum of 5 marks.

Possible points of comparison may include:

Overall: Sources A and **B** look at the changes brought about by the Treaty of Edinburgh of 1560. Overall, the sources agree about the changes brought about by this treaty signed between England and France.

However, **Source A** says that the Scots nobles and people had to fulfil and observe the terms set out in the treaty while **Source B** says that the king and queen were obliged to fulfil their treaty obligations due to the Scots' obedience and loyalty.

Source A	Source B
All warlike operations shall cease.	Truce arranged between England and France.
All military forces of each party shall withdraw from the realm of Scotland.	All foreign soldiers were to withdraw from Scotland.
King Francis and Queen Mary shall abstain from using or carrying the title or arms of the kingdom of England or Ireland.	Francis II and Mary, Queen of Scots, would abstain from displaying the English arms with those of Scotland.
Francis and Mary will fulfil all those things which were granted to the nobility and people of Scotland provided that the nobility and people of Scotland fulfil and observe what was contained in those conventions and articles.	Francis and Mary would fulfil all their treaty obligations since the Scots had spontaneously and freely professed and acknowledged their obedience and loyalty towards their king and queen.

Part C: The Treaty of Union, 1689–1740

7. How fully does Source D explain the effects of the Union up to 1740? (9)

Candidates can be credited in a number of ways up to a maximum of 9 marks.

A maximum of 2 marks may be given for answers which refer only to the source.

Possible points which may be identified in the source include:

- Scotland would not be extinguished; it retained identity, attitudes, ideas; traditions were not eradicated.
- Treaty did exert strong Anglicising influence.
- Guarantees to Scottish legal system and Church had influence on Scotland.
- Continuation of Scottish systems of education and local government were a significant achievement of the Union.

Possible points of significant omission may include:

- Scottish tradition still evident in culture, music, art, literature, law, religion, education; Scottish Enlightenment, Scott, Smith, Hume, Burns.
- Influence of English agricultural techniques and innovations.
- Political effects: 1711 – parliament banned Scottish peers with English titles.
- Highland clans divided between Hanoverian and Jacobite loyalties.
- 1713 – motion repeal Act of Union defeated by 4 votes.
- Whig election victory in 1715 led to government delaying Malt Tax.

- 1725 – Secretary of State for Scotland replaced by Home Secretary.
- Economic effects: Scottish industry could not compete with English competition; only small number of Scots engaged successfully with colonies.
- Taxes led to increases in smuggling and loss of revenue for government.
- Paper industry failed; Scottish linen industry suffered.
- Merchant shipping benefited, particularly trade with Baltic and Caribbean.
- Tobacco industry developed in Glasgow.
- Agriculture improved; increased investment; 1727 – Royal Bank of Scotland.
- 1730s – favourable economic climate; industries such as linen recovered.
- Jacobite reaction: Jacobites led national sentiment in literature and songs.
- 1708 – abortive French-sponsored invasion by the Old Pretender.
- Jacobite rising of 1715; Earl of Mar played leading role; Battle of Sheriffmuir in November 1715 claimed as victory by both government and Jacobites.
- 1716 – Disarming Act banned holding of weapons by Highlanders.
- 1719 – failed attempt at rising in north-west Scotland by Earl Marischal.
- Other effects: claims of the unpopularity of union made vocally by opponents.
- 1712 – House of Lords became court of appeal for Scottish cases.
- 1724 – outbreak of fence-smashing by levellers; 1725 – Shawfield riots in response to Malt Tax; 1736 – Porteous riots in Edinburgh.
- Military road-building; establishment of forts in Highlands.
- 1710 – Tories in parliament failed to remove Church of Scotland's privileges; 1711 – Greenshields case; 1712 – Toleration Act and Patronage Act.
- 1722 – Marrow affair in Church of Scotland; 1733 secession from state church.
- **Any other** valid point of explanation that meets the criteria described in the general marking principles for this kind of question.

8. Evaluate the usefulness of Source C as evidence of attitudes towards the union in Scotland? (6)

Candidates can be credited in a number of ways up to a maximum of 6 marks.

Examples of aspects of the source and relevant comments:

Aspect of the source	Possible comment
Author: Stirling Town Council	Useful as gives the view of a Scottish Town Council and many represented their views in this way.
Type of Source: Petition	Useful as it gives a detailed account of the reasons for opposing union. Less useful as it is a one-sided source.
Purpose: To articulate view of council on proposed union	Useful as it shows the methods that were used to try to influence the debate over union.
Timing: 18 November 1706	Useful as it was written prior to the passing of the Act of Union so gives a contemporary account of common views at the time.

Content	Possible comment
• Treaty will bring insupportable taxation which will ruin manufacturing.	Useful as it shows commercial concerns about an increase in taxation for Scottish businesses.
• Burghs will lose right to be represented in legislative power.	Useful as it shows concerns about loss of special burgh rights which was common from town councils.
• Scotland will be suppressed as its parliament is extinguished with fatal consequences.	Useful as it illustrates broader concerns about the status of Scotland within the union caused by the loss of their own Parliament.

Possible points of significant omission may include:
- Royal burghs would be deprived of rights.
- Fear of loss of European trade.
- British parliament would favour English trade over Scottish.
- Attitudes against union:
  - English currency, weights and measures to be introduced.
  - Public opinion against union.
  - Reduction in status of Scottish nobility in British parliament.
  - Scots Episcopalians opposed union and Hanoverian succession- only Stuart dynasty might restore episcopacy to Scottish church.
  - Protestants feared a British parliament dominated by Anglican Episcopalian church with bishops' seats in the House of Lords.
  - Scots liberties at risk.
- Attitudes for union:
  - Advantages in commerce and trade.
  - Economy would improve — national product would increase.
  - Scotland's trade would catch up with other European nations'.
  - Free trade with English colonies.
  - Protection of being in Great Britain.
  - Common interests already with England.
  - Advantages of Scottish politicians being part of the court of the king in London.
  - Hanoverian succession offered security to Protestantism.
  - Threat from 'Popery' reduced.
  - Property preserved.
- **Any other** valid point of explanation that meets the criteria described in the general marking principles for this kind of question.

9. Compare the views of Sources A and B about worsening relations between Scotland and England between 1690 and 1705. (5)

Candidates may be credited in a number of ways up to a maximum of 5 marks.

Possible points of comparison may include:

Overall: Source A and **Source B** agree that Scotland's economy was affected by England; **Source A** attributes this to a combination of factors and **Source B** suggests that English actions were responsible.

Source A	Source B
Scotland tipped over the edge of an economic abyss.	Scots aware of sinking economic condition of their nation.
English wars leading to damaging loss of French trade.	Damage both to trade and wealth of Scotland.
Protective tariffs blocked the export of certain Scottish goods.	Problems owing to the disadvantages of tariffs.
Outcome was incorporating union with England.	One way for Scots to restore themselves was incorporating union and alliance with England.

Part D: Migration and Empire, 1830–1939

10. How fully does Source D explain the effects of migration and Empire on Scottish society? (9)

Candidates can be credited in a number of ways up to a maximum of 9 marks.

A maximum of 2 marks may be given for answers which refer only to the source.

Possible points which may be identified in the source include:
- The movement of the Irish changed the population balance of several lowland towns.
- A huge reservoir of Irish labour which was ready and willing to move anywhere and do anything to find work.
- Huge construction schemes of the nineteenth century relied on this vast labour.
- The Irish presence is vital to an understanding of Scottish culture as Catholic Irish have played such an influential role in the evolution and shaping of Scottish society, ranging from literature to music and on to football.

Possible points of significant omission may include:
- Details of economic contribution of Irish immigrants to railway building and infrastructure such as Glasgow underground system as well as role in Jute industry.
- Development of Celtic, Edinburgh Hibernian, Dundee United, etc.
- The Education (Scotland) Act 1918 allowed Catholic schools into the state system funded through education rates. It also gave the schools the right to give Catholic religious instruction and select their own teachers. Resentment in Scotland for 'Rome on the Rates'.
- One in four immigrants from Ireland were Protestant and brought their own distinct culture which had an impact in Scotland, especially through the Orange Lodge.
- Large numbers of poorer Jews arrived between 1880 and 1914 — by 1919 over 9,000 lived in Glasgow alone. Most lived in the Gorbals and maintained a separate identity — eg spoke Yiddish, the Jewish language.
- Jewish immigrants tended to work in particular jobs such as peddling and hawking (selling door to door).
- Sweated labour was associated with immigrants and Jews in particular: tailoring and cigarette making.
- Impact of Lithuanians to the economy, through the coal-mining industry around Coatbridge.
- In 1861 there were about 120 Italians in Scotland; by 1901 the Italian population was 4,051.
- Italians were usually found in catering trades, especially ice cream and fish and chips.

- Italian businesses met with success — the number of Italian cafes/takeaways in Glasgow increased (1903—89, 1905— 337), broadening the average Scots social experience.
- In addition to catering, Italians became established as hairdressers — they established the College of Italian Hairdressers in Glasgow in 1928 adding another distinct contribution to Scotland.
- Role of Empire in making Scots rich.
- Role of Empire as a market for Scottish goods and emigrants.
- Empire helped the export-orientated Scottish economy to develop, at least up until 1914, especially in production of shipping, locomotives, etc.
- Empire as a source of competition to Scottish economy: farm produce from Australia, Jute mill development in India, etc.
- **Any other** valid point of explanation that meets the criteria described in the general marking principles for this kind of question.

11. Evaluate the usefulness of Source C as evidence of the assimilation of immigrants into Scottish society.   (6)

Candidates can be credited in a number of ways up to a maximum of 6 marks.

Examples of aspects of the source and relevant comments:

Aspect of the source	Possible comment
Author: Tony Jaconelli	Useful as Jaconelli directly experienced life as an Italian immigrant in Scotland.
Type of Source: Memoire	Useful as a personal account of experience which reflects the broader experience of many Italians on arrival in Scotland. Less useful as account may have changed over time.
Purpose: To recount experience of life in Glasgow	Useful as it is a record of how one immigrant was treated in Glasgow in the 1920s.
Timing: Contemporary	Useful as a contemporary account at a time when many Italians were coming to Scotland.
Content	**Possible comment**
• I found myself surrounded by classmates chanting at me because I was a foreigner.	Useful as shows how assimilation was difficult when you were 'different'.
• Our family moved house a few times in an effort to improve our lot.	Useful as it illustrates the aspirational nature of many Italian immigrant families.
• In no time at all I was a complete Glaswegian.	Useful as it illustrates how one immigrant Italian eventually fitted in.

Possible points of significant omission may include:

Italians:

- Assimilation of Italians helped by popularity of ice cream parlours and fish and chip shops.
- Young Italians soon adopted local speech patterns due to frequency of contact in catering trade.

- Some tension between Catholic Italians and Presbyterian Scots. Italian cafes criticized by Scottish Presbyterian church leaders for opening on the Sabbath.
- Italian café owners also met with criticism from local people who claimed the cafés were sometimes the scenes of unruly behaviour. A Glasgow Herald article claimed ice cream parlours were morally corrupt and reported the 'ice cream hell'.
- There was a greater degree of acceptance of Italian cafes from the Temperance Movement as the cafés chose not to sell alcohol.

Catholic Irish:

- Often resented as competition for jobs.
- Blamed for spread of diseases and poverty.
- Catholic Irish workers were also accused of being strike-breakers and being willing to work for less money than Scottish workers.
- Often blamed for being 'benefit scroungers', claiming poor relief after 3 years residence.
- The Education (Scotland) Act 1918 allowed Catholic schools into the state system funded through education rates. It also gave the schools the right to give Catholic religious instruction and select their own teachers.
- The Catholic Irish had a shared experience with the Scottish worker in that they were affected by industrialisation and urbanisation, as well as fighting together during the First World War.
- Even into the 1930s Catholic Irish faced persecution, sometimes organised by the Church of Scotland.

Protestant Irish:

- Irish Protestants had a lot in common with the average Scot — long-term and deeply embedded cultural interaction between Ulster and lowland Scotland.
- Much easier assimilation because of religion.
- The first Scottish Orange Lodge opened in 1800 in the weaving centre of Maybole in Ayrshire. The growth of the lodge system in Scotland shows the spread of Irish Protestantism

Jews:

- Prejudice and discrimination affected the Jews in Scotland — The Daily Record — Aug 1905 'Alien Danger: Immigrants infected with loathsome disease'.
- Anti-semitism was never that widespread, possibly owing to low numbers of Jewish immigrants in relation to other groups.
- Very few Jews received any help from local poor relief. It was members of the Jewish community that helped each other, eg The Glasgow Jewish Board of Guardians and the Hebrew Ladies' Benevolent Society in 1901 were dealing with 500 cases of needy Jews.

Lithuanians:

- Between the 1860s and 1914 about 7,000 Lithuanians decided to settle in Scotland.
- Scots complained about the Lithuanians being dirty and immoral but soon most were accepted.
- Settlements in mining areas of central Scotland such as Coatbridge.
- At first Lithuanians were used as strike breakers but soon Lithuanians joined with the local workers and joined the strikes.
- Many Lithuanians integrated by changing surnames to Scottish names.
- During the Great War Lithuanians between 18 and 41 faced the choice of conscription into the British Army or

deportation for military service in Russia. Of the 1,800 Lithuanians who were called up, 700 joined the British Army and 1,100 chose to be deported to Russia.

- **Any other** valid point of explanation that meets the criteria described in the general marking principles for this kind of question.

12. Compare the views of Sources A and B about the reasons for Scottish migration to Canada. (5)

Candidates may be credited in a number of ways up to a maximum of 5 marks.

Possible points of comparison may include:

Overall: Both sources agree about the push factor of poverty and the pull factor of prosperity. Although almost a hundred years apart, both sources remark on the poverty of life in rural Scotland with high unemployment and the difficulty of providing for families. In contrast, both sources comment on the opportunities to be had in Canada, particularly the availability of employment and land for farming.

Source A	Source B
Occupying a farm that does not pay him.	The pay is good as experienced men can at the very start earn £5 to £6 a month.
Quite unable to support his family.	The inability of the crofts to satisfy the hunger of the families.
So much land lies in Canada to occupy.	The men also have the prospect of becoming tenant farmers and, later, on owners of their own farms.
A farmer continuing to remain in Scotland even when unemployed.	Lack of employment generally.

Part E: The Impact of the Great War, 1914—1928

13. How fully does Source D describe the impact of the war on political developments in Scotland? [9]

Candidates can be credited in a number of ways up to a maximum of 9 marks.

A maximum of 2 marks may be given for answers which refer only to the source.

Possible points which may be identified in the source include:

- The war years showed that support for Scottish home rule continued.
- Arthur Henderson and the Labour leadership in London were forced to concede a separate Scottish Council of Labour.
- The war undermined the organisation of Scottish Liberalism, but also much of its moral authority.
- The ILP was able to emerge as the natural successor to liberal radicalism.

Possible points of significant omission may include:

- Home rule still prominent. In September 1918 the Scottish Home Rule Association formed.
- The Labour Party manifesto of 1918 included a commitment to home rule for Scotland.
- The ILP MPs from Clydeside elected in November 1922 were committed to home rule.
- Initial instances of radicalism after war: 1919 — George Square.

- In the 1922 election, Labour made the breakthrough as the second political party.
- ILP members activities — involved in resisting the Munitions Act of 1915; in opposing the introduction of the dilution of labour; and anti-conscription.
- The ILP in Scotland had many women prominent in the party such as Mary Barbour, Agnes Dollan and Helen Crawfurd.
- It was difficult for Home Rule to make progress in Westminster parliament.
- Private members' home rule bills failed.
- Support for home rule waned within the Labour Party.
- Glasgow University Scottish National Association formed in 1926.
- In 1927 John McCormack and Roland Muirhead formed the National Party of Scotland. It distanced itself from the Labour Party. Drew support from intellectuals like Hugh McDiarmid.
- Some Liberals and Conservatives formed the Scottish Party at the end of the 1920s and proposed some form of devolution in an effort to attract Liberal and Unionist supporters.
- The Labour Party emerged as an important political force with seven seats in Scotland, winning as many votes as the Conservatives. Continued success in the 1922 election.
- The role of Manny Shinwell, Willie Gallacher, John MacLean.
- In Scotland the ILP was to the fore, campaigning on major issues. Membership increased.
- Clydeside ILP MPs confronted Conservatives and Liberals, even leadership of PLP MPs on issues of poverty and unemployment.
- The Conservative Party was strengthened as they worked hard to gain middle-class support, helped by Presbyterian churches. Scottish legal system also had strong links with the Conservatives.
- **Any other** valid point of explanation that meets the criteria described in the general marking principles for this kind of question.

14. Evaluate the usefulness of Source C as evidence of the impact of the war on Scottish women. (6)

Candidates can be credited in a number of ways up to a maximum of 6 marks.

Examples of aspects of the source and relevant comments:

Aspect of the source	Possible comment
Author: Journalist at the Glasgow Herald	Useful as an informed and accurate view of one event during the rent strikes.
Type of Source: Newspaper	Useful as it is an account of a rent strike in Glasgow, but is aimed at a wider audience. Less useful as it is only one event in one city.
Purpose: To report on the opposition in Glasgow to rent increases	Useful as it provides a detailed account of how the rent strikers and Mary Barbour in particular acted.
Timing: 29th October, 1915	Useful as it is a contemporary source at the beginning of the rent strikes in Glasgow, illustrating the effective methods that were used.

Content	Possible comment
• Reports on the first attempt to enforce eviction of a woman in Merryland Street, Glasgow who had not been paying her rent.	Useful as shows the problem of women falling into rent arrears and how the landlords reacted.
• Role of Mrs Barbour of the GWHA addressing demonstration of strikers.	Useful as it illustrates methods used by Mary Barbour in leading the rent strikes in Govan, Glasgow.
• Details methods used by demonstrators, mainly women.	Useful as it provides detail of the willingness of the demonstrators to use direct action to get their way.

Possible points of significant omission may include:

- Rent Strikes took place following large increases in rents and increased cost of living. Women at home with men away were particularly vulnerable.
- Rent strikes began in May 1915; 25,000 tenants joined the movement by the end of the year.
- Rent strikes saw a prominent role played by women — formation of tenants' strike committees, Glasgow Women's Housing Association and many local 'Women's Housing Associations'.
- Roles of Mary Barbour, Helen Crawfurd, Agnes Dollan and Jessie Stephens.
- Agitation, rent strikes and role of women in other areas such as Aberdeen and Dundee.
- Migration of thousands of workers into munitions districts had led to acute housing shortages.
- War led to women being more involved in local politics and changing male attitudes.
- The war led to dilution of labour and the employment of more women, for example, at Gretna in the huge munitions works.
- Anti-war groups formed like the No Conscription League: leading role of women in these groups.
- Role of women as workers on the land, etc.
- Conscientious objection.
- Loss and remembrance.
- **Any other** valid point of explanation that meets the criteria described in the general marking principles for this kind of question.

15. Compare the views of Sources A and B about the experience of Scots on the Western Front. (5)

*Candidates may be credited in a number of ways **up to a maximum of 5 marks**.*

Possible points of comparison may include:

Overall: Source A and **Source B** offer some similar and some contrasting opinions on the experience of Scots on the Western Front with regard to the taking of Hill 70. **Source A** reflects the tenacity and dogged determination required by Scots during a long and difficult attack, while **Source B** skirts over difficulties and gives the impression of an easier, successful attack. Both agree that the pipes played during the attack and that no reinforcements arrived.

Source A	Source B
A third time we **charged** on that awful hillside but the enemy, with his reserves at hand, were too many for us and again we fell back.	They **trudged** on to Hill 70. (No sense here of urgency or charging.)
We made for the top of Hill 70 through murderous rifle and machine gun fire.	For a time there was a kind of Bank Holiday crowd on Hill 70 as the German machine gunners initially dared not fire.
We made for the top to the sound of the pipes and led by our brave old colonel.	Shriller than the scream of shells was the skirl of the pipes going with them.
We were desperate for reinforcements but no help could we see.	We must hold on until the reinforcements arrive. None came.

MODEL PAPER 2
SECTION 2: BRITISH

Part A: Church, State and Feudal Society, 1066-1406

Candidates can be credited up to a maximum of 20 marks.

16. To what extent was the role of the Church in medieval Scotland and England confined to religion?

Context
The Roman Catholic Church emerged from the fall of Rome to play a central role in daily life in medieval Western Europe. Although the Church was there to ensure people's salvation it served a broader role as well. Through its religious sacraments, it marked the important stages of life. It also fulfilled a role in social and economic development, and even in politics.

Religious role
- The medieval church offered the people the hope of salvation. The church promised that in the afterlife things would improve, assuming that your soul was pure and free of sin. This offered a certain amount of social control but offered comfort and stability, providing answers to difficult questions.
- Church services such as christenings, marriages and burials were an important part of everyday life. The church also celebrated holy days.
- Religion offered a certain amount of understanding about the world. The existence of God helped to explain not only how the world worked but in a society without the benefit of science, the unexplained could often be frightening.
- The importance of saints, relics and pilgrimages not only reinforced the power of God, but pilgrimage especially provided a way of opening new horizons and helping expand medieval Europe and trade.
- Monasteries provided hope for a greater salvation through a life of prayer and devotion.

Social role
- The church often provided alms to the poor, offering the only real poor relief available.
- The church provided basic education for lay people, notably sons and daughters of nobility. The church, particularly the monasteries, helped develop architecture, art and music. Universities provided degrees in theology, medicine and arts.
- Church hospitals provided free medical care, especially for lepers.
- The church provided a social centre for rural and urban life; games and music were common after Sunday services.

Economic role
- Monasteries made significant contributions to the economic development of the 12th century.
- They helped to cultivate many barren areas of England and Scotland.
- Some monasteries helped to fund and maintain important trades, such as the wool trade in Scotland.

Political role
- The church legitimised monarchs.
- The papacy was a European power, able to influence other monarchs through the threat of excommunication and interdict.
- Monarchs required the help of the clerics to run the government, count taxes and write laws.
- In England the church was part of the feudal structure, able to raise armies to defend their lands, as the Bishop of Durham did at the Battle of the Standard in 1138.

Any other relevant factors.

Candidates can be credited up to a maximum of 20 marks.

17. How successful was King John in his attempts to increase royal authority?

Context
King John was the youngest, and favourite, son of Henry II and Eleanor of Aquitaine. On the death of his elder brother Richard, he became King of England despite the claims of his nephew Arthur. He struggled to hold the widespread Angevin Empire together in the face of the challenges of the Capetian monarch of France and his own barons.

Impact of the loss of Normandy
- Had an impact on the royal finances as it reduced John's income.
- The recovery of the Royal lands north of the Loire became the focus of John's foreign policy and led to policies which eventually led to challenges to his authority.
- The need to fund warfare to recover Normandy led to the frequent use of Scutage to raise cash. It was used much more frequently than under Henry II and Richard, levied 11 times in 17 years.

Royal finances
- John was more efficient in collecting taxes.
- Used wardships to raise cash.
- Introduced new taxes: eg 1207 tax on income and moveable goods.
- Improved quality of silver coinage.

Administration of government
- John filled many of the roles in the royal household with new men; especially from Poitou. This was not popular with the English barons.

Military power
- Established the Royal Navy.
- Extensive use of mercenaries rather than feudal service.
- Able to exert his military strength against the nobility and the French.
- John was an able military commander; ie when conflict started with France and his nephew Arthur, he defeated them and captured Arthur.
- His forces and his allies were decisively beaten at the Battle of Bouvines in 1214.

Law and justice
- Increasingly partial judgements were resented.
- John increased professionalism of local sergeants and bailiffs.
- Extended the system of coroners.

Relations with the Church
- John fell out with Pope Innocent III over the appointment of the Archbishop of Canterbury. Innocent insisted on the appointment of Langton which John opposed.
- Papal interdict laid on England and Wales for 6 years.
- In 1213 John made England a fief of the papacy.
- Noble uprising led by Archbishop of Canterbury.

Relations with the nobility
- Nobles refused to fight in France. This was especially true of the northern Barons who had little stake in France.

- Nobles felt their status was reduced by use of mercenaries.
- John became increasingly suspicious of the nobles.
- High cost of titles led to nobles becoming overly indebted.
- John took hostages to ensure nobles behaved. He showed he was prepared to execute children if the father opposed him.
- Relations worsened over the course of the reign, ending with Magna Carta and rebellion of many Barons.

John's personality

- He could be generous, had a coarse sense of humour and was intelligent.
- However, could also be suspicious and cruel: vicious in his treatment of prisoners and nobles.
- Arthur, his nephew, died in mysterious circumstances.
- Powerful lords like William de Braose fell from favour and were persecuted. William's wife and son were imprisoned and died. He died in exile in France.

Any other relevant factors.

Candidates can be credited up to a maximum of 20 marks.

18. How important was the growth of towns in causing the decline of feudal society?

Context

The decline of feudalism happened as the previous order of society where land was exchanged for economic or military service was challenged. Economic developments, which changed the relationship between peasants and lord as well as the development of new ways to trade and pay for labour/service led to its decline.

The growth of towns

- Townsmen had different rights than those living in the countryside.
- Many had the rights to hold their own courts, and these were seen as free from feudal interference.
- Towns could buy a charter, granting Burgh status, allowing them to freely trade with overseas merchants. Burgesses could buy and sell their holdings.
- A villein who lived in the town for a year and a day would become a freeman.
- The development led to the creation of a sort of middle class gentry in the fifteenth century, the mediocre or middling sort.

Other factors:
Gradual decline in the old feudal manor economy

- With markets for their goods fluctuating considerably, many nobles came to understand their weak economic position. For some it was better to let their peasants become tenants who rented their land than to continue as their feudal protector.
- Without the need for a feudal lord and protector, there was little need for serfs or villeins. It was easier to hire laborers, and relying on fixed rates of income from rents or salaries became more common.

Changing social attitudes

- Peasants who could afford to purchase or rent extra land could propel themselves upwards on the social ladder.
- The de la Poles family in Hull rose from traders to become royal bankers, and the Pastson family rose out of serfdom to become country gentry.
- Social commentators like Peter Idley complained that it had become impossible to tell the difference between 'knave and knight', because they dressed alike.

The growth of trade/mercantilism

- It has been argued that the feudal structure and serfdom hampered entrepreneurial merchants in England and Scotland. Many found the freedom of burgh life allowed them to develop trade without the burden of labour services or restrictions in movement.
- Others discovered that sheep were a far more profitable resource than peasants could ever be, leading to development of mercantile skills.
- Development of an affluent merchant class

The Black Death

- The decline in the population meant that the survivors, particularly of the lower classes, could demand and often received better wages for their labour. Wage levels in England roughly doubled. Indeed, the shortage of labourers is often seen as causing the decline of serfdom in Western Europe.
- Parliament in England attempted to halt this decline by passing the 'Statute of Labourers' in 1351, but it wasn't very effective and was mostly ignored.
- Landowners for the first time needed to negotiate for their serfs' services, leading to higher wages and better living conditions for those that survived.
- The Black Death led to the old feudal relationship between lord and serf disappearing.

The Peasants' Revolt

- In England the attempts of the The Statute of Labourers in 1351 to force peasants back into serfdom were widely and strongly resisted. The extent of the revolt and the impressive way in which it was organised shows that the old feudal consensus had broken down.
- The Peasant's Revolt was a reaction to the attempts to force peasants to return to the old ideas of labour services.

Any other relevant factors.

Part B: The Century of Revolutions, 1603—1702

Candidates can be credited up to a maximum of 20 marks.

19. To what extent were Charles I's policies in Scotland between 1625 and 1642 effective?

Context
Charles I succeeded his father James I in 1625 and ruled over both England and Scotland until 1642. He continued to reign in Scotland until his death in 1649 at the hands of the English Parliament. During this time there were considerable challenges facing the king in his attempts to enforce his policies in Scotland.

Political policy

- Charles I's policies took power and land from Scottish nobles.
- The king did not visit Scotland until 1633 when he was crowned there.
- The king appointed bishops rather than nobles to Scottish Privy Council.
- John Spottiswoode appointed Chancellor; first non-secular official in this position since Reformation.
- Charles I gave increasing power to bishops, undermining status of Scottish nobility.
- The Stuart notion of the Divine Right of Kings was brought to an end by Scots opposition to Charles I's attempts to impose his will on the Scottish people.

Religious policy

- Charles I introduced William Laud, the Archbishop of Canterbury, to Scotland in 1633.

- Laud proceeded to oversee Anglican practice in Scottish churches.
- Many resented influence of Laud.
- The king approved of unification of churches without consulting Privy Council.
- The 1635 Book of Canons declared that the monarch had authority over the Church of Scotland and introduced a new Service Book, a Scottish bishops' variation of the English Prayer Book.
- On 23 July 1637 the English Prayer Book was read at St. Giles Cathedral by Dean John Hanna who subsequently had a stool thrown at him by a serving woman, Jenny Geddes.
- In the chaos that ensued, the Bishop of Edinburgh was shouted down by the crowd in support of Geddes.
- Across Scotland people declared their opposition to the Service Book, placing Charles I's Privy Council in a difficult position, caught between king and his rivals.

The Covenanters

- In Scotland the Covenanting movement challenged Charles I over religious policies and was politically active
- Covenanters wanted to preserve Presbyterianism in Scotland.
- The National Covenant was signed in 1638.
- The Covenant was designed to promote a church free from monarchical meddling.
- Charles I failed to suppress Covenanters, contributing to outbreak of the War of the Three Kingdoms.
- During the war, English Parliament's treaty of alliance with Scottish Covenanters — the Solemn League and Covenant of 1643 — was a key feature of positive change in the fortunes of king's enemies.

First Bishops' War

- The first Bishops' War took place in 1639.
- Charles I could not raise enough money to fight the war effectively; was forced to agree to truce in June as part of Pacification of Berwick.
- As well as conceding military failure, truce gave Scots religious freedoms.
- Charles I's inability to put down the Scots brought an end to his 'Eleven Years' Tyranny' in England.
- The king recalled Parliament in 1640 to request revenue to continue war with Scotland.
- This 'Short Parliament' lasted one month as the king dissolved it rather than debate his role during the Eleven Years' Tyranny as condition of Parliamentary granting of funds.

Second Bishops' War

- The second Bishops' War was a continuation of the first but ended in equal humiliation for Charles I in the Treaty of Ripon of October 1640.
- Treaty cost England the price that the Scottish Parliament had to pay for its forces.
- Defeat by Scots forced the king to recall Parliament, this time after being advised to do so by a grouping of peers known as Magnum Concilium.
- This 'Long Parliament' was to last longer than the previous one, but still represented a downturn in the king's fortunes, as the English Civil War shortly followed.

Any other relevant factors.

Candidates can be credited up to a maximum of 20 marks.

20. How important were religious issues in causing the Revolution of 1688—89?

Context

The Revolution of 1688—89 was caused by James II's religious tolerance and Catholicism which concerned many of the English political elite. The combination of English Parliamentarians and the Protestant William of Orange led to the Revolution of 1688—9.

Religious issues

- Issue of church governance which arose before Civil War had not been resolved.
- Many MPs fearful of continued Stuart dominance of Anglican Church policy.
- James II's promotion of Roman Catholics to key posts antagonised Presbyterians.
- Heir to the throne to be raised as a Roman Catholic.
- Divide between Episcopalians and Presbyterians in Scotland created hostility from Scottish Parliament towards monarchy.

Other factors
Political issues

- Divine Right and absolutism as practised by Stuart monarchs continued to provoke resentment from MPs.
- Status of monarchy questioned by Parliament.
- Charles II's dismissal of Parliament resembled Charles I's 11-Year Tyranny.
- James II's use of Suspending and Dispensing Powers seen as an abuse by Parliament.
- Questions raised over control of the army.

Lines of authority Crown and Parliament

- There were no clear lines of authority.
- Questions existed over who held sway in religious matters; Parliament feared a monarch could try to impose Roman Catholicism on country.
- Still possible for monarch to be financially independent of Parliament and manipulate succession in favour of Roman Catholic line.
- Both Charles II and James II had proved it was possible for monarch to rule without Parliament, influence legislative and judicial procedure, control army for own means, and assert religious and political will on Scotland and Ireland.
- Parliament saw need to agree constitutional status for monarchy.

The role of Parliament

- Parliament resented James II's abuses of power but took comfort from thought that he would be succeeded by his Protestant daughter Mary.
- However, the king married again and had son, to be raised as Roman Catholic.
- June 1688, Parliament wrote to Mary, by now married to Dutch Prince William of Orange, offering the Crown.
- They arrived in November with an army and on Christmas Day James II fled to France after his younger daughter Anne as well as leading generals declared support for Mary.
- William and Mary became joint sovereigns on February 13th 1689.
- With no Bill of Rights, any future monarchs, including William and Mary, could preach notions of Divine Right, absolutism and passive obedience.
- Future limitations on power of monarchy would have to be written into law.

- In 1689 Parliament drew up the Bill of Rights, which legalised the new relationship between Crown and Parliament.
- This would ensure no future king or queen could attempt absolutism.
- Bill of Rights would be part of a wider set of legal provisions for new order in the country.
- Settlement established that kings and queens should depend upon Parliament for finance, succession would be determined by Parliament and not the sitting monarch, judicial system would be controlled by Parliament, and no future monarch could rule without Parliament.

James II
- Ascended throne in 1685 upon death of older brother.
- James II, who practised Roman Catholicism, attempted to rule absolutely.
- Dismissed Parliament in 1685.
- Replaced Anglican advisors with Roman Catholic ones; placed Roman Catholics in important posts at Oxford and Cambridge Universities.
- Stationed 13,000-strong army outside London.
- Re-established Prerogative Courts in 1686.
- In 1687 used Suspending Powers to suspend laws against Roman Catholics.
- Used Dispensing Powers to dismiss these laws from statute books.

Legacy of Charles II
- Charles II, who had been exiled in France during Interregnum, had accepted limitations on his power when monarchy was restored in 1660.
- Prerogative law courts were abolished, non-parliamentary taxation was prohibited, and Triennial Act remained in place.
- Loopholes, however, meant the king could still make policy.
- Puritans lost power in House of Commons.
- Towards the end of his reign Charles II ruled without Parliament for 4 years.
- Divine Right preached from pulpits

Any other relevant factors
Candidates can be credited up to a maximum of 20 marks.

21. **'Financial reform was the most significant change brought about by the Revolution Settlement.' How valid is this view?**

Context
The Revolution Settlement brought a succession of profound changes to the countries of Britain. Parliament gained power in England and there was a huge expansion of state power, but loopholes remained. The legacy of the settlement in Scotland and Ireland was more violent and divisive however.

Finance
- In the times of James I and Charles I, monarchy could exist financially independently of Parliament. This was now impossible.
- The king and queen were granted £700,000 for court expenses in 1689.
- From then on, Parliament voted to give the Crown money annually as part of Civil List system.
- Procedure of audit established for MPs to check expenditure of the monarch.
- Fiscal power now in the hands of the House of Commons.
- However, the monarch would not have to make unpopular moves of raising taxes himself from now on.

Religion
- Before 1688, the Crown dictated religious development of country.
- After Settlement, hundreds of High Anglicans were expelled from their posts because they refused to recognise the authority of William III.
- Toleration Act of 1689 passed which provided for free public worship for all except Roman Catholics and Unitarians.
- Roman Catholics still ineligible for elected posts in towns or Parliament.
- Parliament now held more sway in religious matters.
- However, the monarch still enjoyed political advantages of being head of church.

Legislation
- Stuart monarchs had abused the legal system and courts.
- Legal settlement established Parliamentary control over these areas.
- Later, the Act of Settlement of 1701 stated judges could only be removed from their positions if Parliament demanded this.
- From now on, ministers impeached by the House of Commons could not be pardoned by the Crown.
- In 1695, the Law of Treason was altered to give defendants the right to be given a copy of the indictment against them, the right to be defended by Counsel and call witnesses in their defence.
- An act of treason needed two witnesses against the defendant instead of the one needed previously.
- Parliament now enforcing own control over judicial procedure.
- However, monarchs could still appoint judges who might be favourable to them.

Political
- In the days before Civil War, Stuart monarchs had been able to rule without Parliament and curtail Parliamentary freedom of speech.
- Revolution Settlement provided for another Triennial Act in 1694, which was intended to keep MPs more closely in touch with public opinion.
- Licensing Act was repealed in 1695, removing restrictions on freedom of press to report Parliamentary criticism of the Crown.
- William and Mary had to agree to the Bill of Rights before they were given throne, legalising the new relationship between the Crown and Parliament.
- This ensured no future king or queen could attempt absolutism.
- Members of Parliament could now speak freely when voicing their opinion of the monarch.
- However, monarch could still dismiss Parliament at will.

The succession
- Before Settlement, monarchs approved their own successors.
- Bill of Rights declared no Roman Catholic could become king or queen.
- Later, Act of Settlement of 1701 stated if William and Mary had no heirs the throne would pass to Sophia of Hanover, Protestant daughter of Elizabeth of Bohemia, sister of Charles I.
- The Act said all future monarchs should be members of the Church of England.
- Parliament now governed the question of who ascended throne.

Differences between England and Scotland

- Settlement now allowed Scotland to have its own church, the Presbyterian Kirk.
- Scottish Parliament had a greater share in government of Scotland.

The status of the army

- Charles I had been able to raise an army in 1642.
- Revolution Settlement meant Parliament gained partial control of army.
- The monarch was not given enough money to maintain a standing army.
- The Mutiny Act of 1689 legalised army, this act had to be passed annually by Parliament, which forced the king to summon Parliament in order to do so.
- Implications for implementation of foreign policy.
- Royal authority over military matters now passed to the House of Commons.

Loopholes in the Settlement

- Although the Revolution Settlement handed a lot of power from the Crown to Parliament, loopholes in the agreement meant the monarch still held executive power and controlled foreign policy, declaring war and signing treaties.
- The monarch was still the source of patronage in the army and navy.
- The monarch still created peers, and could therefore control the House of Lords.
- The Revolution Settlement, therefore, did not completely hand over power to Parliament.
- It was a compromise which acted as a halfway-house between the Crown and Parliament, and government business was negotiated and conducted between the two.

Any other relevant factors.

Part C: The Atlantic Slave Trade

Candidates can be credited up to a maximum of 20 marks.

22. **To what extent was the slave trade the major factor in the development of the British economy in the eighteenth century?**

Context

The British economy developed due to mercantile activity, including the slave trade, coupled to colonial development early in the century. However, industrial innovation within Britain through the Agricultural and Industrial revolutions also generated change. At times this was complementary, at others it rivalled the mercantile economy.

Evidence that the slave trade was important

- Importance of the slave trade to the development of the economy: profits accruing from tropical crops; financial, commercial, legal and insurance institutions emerged to support the activities of the slave traders. Slave traders became bankers and many new businesses were financed by profits made from slave trading.
- The slave trade played an important role in providing British industry with access to raw materials and this contributed to the increased production of manufactured goods.
- Ports such as London, Bristol and Liverpool prospered as a direct result of involvement in the slave trade; other ports such as Glasgow profited from trade with the colonies. Thousands of jobs were created in Britain supplying goods and services to slave traders.

- Liverpool became a major centre for shipbuilding largely as a result of the trade.
- Manchester exported a large percentage of cotton goods to Africa.
- The slave trade was important to the economic prosperity and well-being of the colonies.
- Investment from the slave trade went into the Welsh slate industry.
- The slave trade was an important training ground for British seamen, providing experienced crews for the merchant marine and the Royal Navy.
- Wealth generated by the slave trade meant that domestic taxes could be kept low.
- Argument that the slave trade was the vital factor in Britain's industrialisation was put forward in Williams' *Capitalism and Slavery* thesis.

Evidence that other factors were important

- Changes in agriculture: these created an agricultural surplus which:
  - fed an expanding population
  - produced a labour force in the towns for use in factories
  - created a financial surplus for investment in industry and infrastructure.
- Technological innovation: development of water and steam power; new machinery; transport changes.
- Mineral and energy resources, particularly iron and coal.
- Political stability.
- Much of the profits of slavery were dissipated in conspicuous consumption, eg landed estates.

Candidates can be credited up to a maximum of 20 marks.

23. **"The slave trade was too important to the British economy to allow it to be abolished." How valid is this view?**

Context

During the 18th century the British economy (industry) prospered. British ports such as Liverpool and Bristol grew into international trading centres and cities such as London grew rich due to the development of financial and insurance institutions.

The importance of the slave trade to the British economy

- It generated finance — West Indian colonies were an important source of valuable exports to European neighbours. Taxes would have to be raised to compensate for the loss of trade and revenue. Abolition would help foreign rivals such as France as other nations would fill the gap left by Britain.
- British cotton mills depended on cheap slave-produced cotton.
- Africa provided an additional market for British manufactured goods.
- Individuals, businesses and ports in Britain prospered on the back of the slave trade.
- Shipbuilding benefited as did maritime employment.

Other factors

Pressure exerted by vested interests

- Successive British governments were influenced by powerful vested interests such as MPs and merchants from London, Liverpool and Bristol.
- Slave owners and their supporters argued that millions of pounds worth of property would be threatened by the abolition of the slave trade. The slave trade was necessary to provide essential labour on the plantations. Abolition of the slave trade would ruin the colonies.

The events of the French Revolution
- These encouraged the belief among many MPs that the abolitionist cause was associated with revolutionary ideas, eg Clarkson openly supported the French Revolution.
- Radicals used the same tactics as abolitionists to win public support — associations, petitions, cheap publications, public lectures, public meetings, pressure on Parliament. Some abolitionists were linked to radicals and therefore they had to be resisted because of fear that events in France may be repeated in Britain.

Slave rebellion in Saint-Domingue
- Abolition was associated with this symbol of brutal violence and in turn led to an exaggerated, general fear of slave revolts. Toussaint l'Ouverture was denounced. This was linked to fears of Jacobinism.
- Slave violence played into the hands of the slave lobby, confirming their warnings of anarchy.
- Britain suffered humiliation when it attempted to take the rebel French Colony beaten by disease and the ex-slave army.

Propaganda against abolition
- Supporters of slavery and the slave trade could try to claim that the enslaved on plantations were treated at least as well as the working classes in Britain.

Fears over national security
- Abolition could destroy an important source of experienced seamen it was argued, thus there was a possibility that Britain would lose its advantage over its maritime rivals. On the other hand, the Triangular Trade was arguably a graveyard for British seamen.

Any other relevant factors.

Candidates can be credited up to a maximum of 20 marks.

24. **How important was the campaign organised by the Anti-Slavery Society in bringing about the abolition of the slave trade?**

Context
Opposition to the slave trade within Britain came from a variety of sources. Much of it originated from a Christian moral point of view, while later more pragmatic reasons such as the war with France and the use of abolition as a tool of war.

The campaign of the abolitionist movement
- Thomas Clarkson obtained witnesses for the Parliamentary investigations of the slave trade which provided Wilberforce with convincing evidence for his speeches.
- Books and pamphlets were published, eg eyewitness accounts from former slaves such as Olaudah Equiano.
- Campaigns to boycott goods produced by slaves in the West Indies such as sugar and rum.
- Petitions and subscription lists, public meetings and lecture tours involving those with experience of slave trade, eg Olaudah Equiano, churches and theatres used for abolitionist propaganda, artefacts and illustrations, eg Wedgwood pottery.
- Lobbying of Parliament by abolitionists to extract promises from MPs that they would oppose the slave trade.
- Effective moderate political and religious leadership among the abolitionists influenced major figures such as Pitt and Fox; abolitionists gave evidence to Parliamentary Commissions.

- **Other factors**

The role of Wilberforce
- Wilberforce put forward the arguments of the Society for the Abolition of the Slave Trade in Parliament for eighteen years.
- Wilberforce's speeches in Parliament were graphic and appealing.
- Wilberforce's Christian faith had led him to become interested in social reform and link the issues of factory reform in Britain and the need to abolish slavery and the slave trade within the British Empire.
- Wilberforce was prepared to work with other abolitionists to achieve his aims, eg Thomas Clarkson.

The effects of slave resistance
- Successful slave rebellion in Saint-Domingue led to an exaggerated, general fear of slave revolts.

Economic factors
- Effects of wars with France — slave trade declined by two-thirds as it was seen as harming the national interest in time of war. The slave trade had become less important in economic terms — there was no longer a need for large numbers of slaves to be imported to the British colonies. There was a world over-supply of sugar and British merchants had difficulties re-exporting it.

Military factors
- Napoleon's efforts to restore slavery in the French islands meant that the abolitionist campaign would help to undermine Napoleon's plans for the Caribbean. The Act banning any slave trade between British merchants and foreign colonies in 1806 was intended to attack French interests.

The religious revival
- Role of the Quakers and other non-conformists.
- Role of people like John Newton: ex slave-ship captain and now clergyman.
- Religious arguments against slavery.

Any other relevant factors.

Part D: Britain, 1851–1951

Candidates can be credited up to a maximum of 20 marks.

25. **'Britain was still far from being a democratic country by 1928.' How valid is this view?**

Context
Changes to the British political system occurred throughout the 19th and early 20th century. These developments ranged from extensions to the franchise to dealing with corruption and privilege.

The vote
- In 1867 most skilled working-class men in towns got the vote.
- In 1884 many more men in the countryside were given the vote.
- In 1918 most men over 21 and some women over 30 gained the vote.
- Finally, in 1928 all men and women over 21 were given the vote.

Fairness
- The Secret Ballot 1872 freed voters from intimidation.
- The Corrupt and Illegal Practices Act 1883 limited the amount spent campaigning.
- The re-distribution of seats in 1867, 1885 and 1918 all helped create a fairer system of voting.

- The effectiveness of these varied; they were less effective in areas where the electorate was small, or where a landowner or employer was dominant in an area, eg Norwich.

Choice

- Although the working class electorate increased by 1880s, there was no national party to express their interests. The Liberals and Conservatives promoted middle-, even upper-class, capitalist values.
- The spread of socialist ideas and trade unionism led to the creation of the prototype Labour Party — the LRC — by 1900, thereby offering a wider choice to the electorate.

Access to information

- Education — in the later 19th Century there was a great increase in literacy and, hence, access to information on which to base choice. Also, railways spread information nationally and were important to the growth of democracy.

National party organisation

- As the size of the electorate grew, individual political parties had to make sure their 'message' got across to the electorate, eg development of National Liberal Federation, Conservative Central Office, Primrose League.

Power of Lords

- From 1911, Lords could only delay bills from the House of Commons for two years rather than veto them. They had no control over money bills.

Widening opportunity to become an MP

- The property qualification to be an MP was abolished in 1858. Payment for MPs began in 1911, enabling working class men to sit.
- By 1928 Parliament was much more representative of the British people.

Points still to be resolved included

- Undemocratic anomalies — plural votes and the university constituencies — were not abolished until 1948.
- In 1949 the two-year delaying power of the House of Lords was reduced to only one year, but the power of the House of Lords in law making still continues.
- The Voting system is still 'first past the post' in UK.

Any other relevant factors.

Candidates can be credited up to a maximum of 20 marks.

26. To what extent did the Liberal reforms of 1906 to 1914 make a significant improvement to the lives of the British people?

Context

Although not the first example of government intervention to help those who found themselves out of work and in poverty, the Liberal Reform programme of 1906–14 saw a comprehensive series of reforms passed for a range of social groups. Each reform had both positive and negative aspects.

The young

- Children were thought to be the victims of poverty and unable to escape through their own efforts. In this way they were seen as 'the deserving poor'. Child neglect and abuse were seen as problems associated with poverty.
- The Provision of School Meals Act allowed local authorities to raise money to pay for school meals but the law did not force local authorities to provide school meals.
- Medical inspections after 1907 for children were made compulsory but no treatment of illnesses or infections found was provided until 1911.

- The Children's Charter of 1908 banned children under 16 from smoking, drinking alcohol, or begging. New juvenile courts were set up for children accused of committing crimes, as were borstals for children convicted of breaking the law. Probation officers were employed to help former offenders in an attempt to avoid re-offending.
- The time taken to enforce all the legislation meant the Children's Charter only helped improve conditions for some children during the period.

The old

- Rowntree had identified old age as the time when most people dropped below his poverty line. Old age was inescapable so was clearly associated with the problem of poverty.
- The Old Age Pensions Act (1908) gave people over 70 up to 5 shillings a week. Once a person over 70 had income above 12 shillings a week, their entitlement to a pension stopped. Married couples were given 7 shillings and 6 pence.
- The level of benefits was low. Few of the elderly poor would live till their 70th birthday. Many of the old were excluded from claiming pensions because they failed to meet the qualification rules.

The sick

- Illness can be seen as both a cause and consequence of poverty.
- The National Insurance Scheme of 1911 applied to workers earning less than £160 a year. Each insured worker got 9 pence in benefits from an outlay of 4 pence — 'ninepence for fourpence'.
- Only the insured worker got free medical treatment from a doctor. Other family members did not benefit from the scheme. The weekly contribution was in effect a wage cut which might simply have made poverty worse in many families.

The unemployed

- Unemployment was certainly a cause of poverty.
- The National Insurance Act (Part 2) only covered unemployment for some workers in some industries and like (Part 1) of the Act, required contributions from workers, employers and the government. For most workers, no unemployment insurance scheme existed.
- There were other reforms which could be argued helped address problems associated with poverty.
- In 1906 a Workman's Compensation Act covered a further six million workers who could now claim compensation for injuries and diseases which were the result of working conditions.
- In 1909 the Trade Boards Act tried to protect workers in the sweated trades like tailoring and lace-making by setting up trade boards to fix minimum wages.
- The Mines Act and the Shop Act improved conditions.

Any other relevant factors.

Candidates can be credited up to a maximum of 20 marks.

27. 'The Labour government of 1945 to 1951 met the needs of the people "from the cradle to the grave".' How valid is this view?

Context

The Beveridge Report of 1942 promised a comprehensive answer to the social problems Britain experienced. The Labour Government of 1945-51 was elected by a landslide on a promise to implement these reforms.

The Beveridge Report in 1942 identified 5 giants of poverty: Want, Disease, Ignorance, Squalor and Idleness.

Want

- In 1946 the first step was made: the National Insurance Act consisted of comprehensive insurance sickness and unemployment benefits and cover for most eventualities.
- It was said to support people from the ' cradle to the grave' which was significant as it meant people had protection against falling into poverty throughout their lives.
- This was very effective as it meant that if the breadwinner of the family was injured then the family was less likely to fall further into the poverty trap, as was common before. However, this act can be criticised for its failure to go far enough.
- Benefits were only granted to those who made 156 weekly contributions.
- in 1948 the National Assistance Board was set up in order to cover those for whom insurance did not do enough.
- This was important as it acted as a safety net to protect these people.
- This was vital as the problem of people not being aided by the insurance benefits was becoming a severe issue as time passed. Yet, some criticised this as many citizens still remained below subsistence level, showing the problem of want had not completely been addressed.

Disease

- The establishment of the NHS in 1948 dealt effectively with the spread of disease.
- The NHS was the first comprehensive universal system of health in Britain.
- It offered vaccination and immunisation against disease, almost totally eradicating some of Britain's most deadly illnesses.
- It also offered helpful services to Britain's public such as childcare, the introduction of prescriptions, health visiting and provision for the elderly, providing a safety net across the whole country: the fact that the public did not have to pay for their health meant that everyone, regardless of their financial situation, was entitled to equal opportunities of health care they had previously not experienced.
- The NHS could be regarded as almost too successful. The demand from the public was overwhelming, as the estimated amount of patients treated by them almost doubled. Introduction of charges for prescriptions, etc.

Ignorance

- Reform started by the wartime government: The 1944 Education Act raised the age at which people could leave school to 15 as part of a drive to create more skilled workers which Britain lacked at the time. Introduction of school milk, etc.
- Labour introduced a two-tiered secondary schooling whereby pupils were split at the age of 11(12 in Scotland) depending on their ability. The smarter pupils who passed the '11+ exam' went to grammar and the rest to secondary moderns.
- Those who went to grammar schools were expected to stay on past the age of 15 and this created a group of people who would take senior jobs in the country thus solving the skills shortages. Whilst this separation of ability in theory meant that children of even poor background could get equal opportunities in life, in practice the system actually created a bigger division between the poor and the rich.
- Labour expanded university education: introduction of grants so all could attend in theory.

Squalor

- After the war there was a great shortage of housing as the war had destroyed and damaged thousands of homes; and the slum cleaning programmes of the 1930s had done little to rectify the situation which was leading to a number of other problems for the government.
- Labour's target for housing was to build 200,000 new homes a year. 157,000 pre-fabricated homes were built to a good standard, however, this number would not suffice and the target was never met.
- Bevan encouraged the building of council houses rather than privately funded construction.
- The New Towns Act of 1946 aimed to target overcrowding in the increasingly built-up older cities. By 1950, the government had designed 12 new communities.
- In an attempt to eradicate slums, the Town and Country Planning Act provided local communities more power in regards to building developments and new housing.
- By the time Labour left government office in 1951 there was still a huge shortfall in British housing.

Idleness

- Unemployment was basically nonexistent so the government had little to do to tackle idleness.
- The few changes they did make were effective in increasing the likelihood of being able to find work, because they increased direct government funding for the universities which led to a 60% increase in student numbers between 1945–46 and 1950–51,which helped to meet the manpower requirements of post-war society. This provided more skilled workers and allowed people from less advantaged backgrounds to pursue a higher education, aiming to keep unemployment rates down.
- The Labour government also nationalised 20 percent of industry – the railways, mines, gas and electricity. This therefore meant that the government was directly involved with people employed in these huge industries which were increasing in size dramatically.
- This tackled idleness by the government having control which meant that employees were less likely to lose their job through industries going bankrupt and people were working directly to benefit society.

Any other relevant factors.

Part E: Britain and Ireland, 1900–1985

Candidates can be credited up to a maximum of 20 marks.

28. To what extent did World War One change political attitudes towards British rule in Ireland?

Context

Initially war brought prosperity to Ireland. The demands on manufacturing and farming brought low unemployment thus improving relations between Great Britain and Ireland. However, Sinn Fein, the Easter Rising and Protestant reaction were to change this along increasingly sectarian lines.

Irish Attitudes to World War I

- Propaganda – powerful Germany invading helpless and small Catholic Belgium so Ireland supported Great Britain.
- Ulster was very supportive of Britain to ensure favourable treatment at the end of the war.
- Nationalists and Redmond backed war to get Home Rule, urging Irish men to enlist.
- Press gave support to the war effort.
- Irish Volunteers gave support to help Home Rule be passed after the war.

- Recruitment was successful in the south as almost a quarter of a million men join up.

The Nationalist Movement

- Opposition to war was very much a minority in 1914 but supported by Sinn Fein and Arthur Griffith (not powerful at this time), as well as Pearse, Connolly and their supporters and also a section of the Irish Volunteers. This damaged relations with Britain.

Easter Rising

- Rebels saw war as chance to rid Ireland of the British by force.
- Felt it was an opportunity to gain independence by force as Britain had their troops away fighting the Germans in World War I. This greatly strained relations between Britain and Ireland.
- Britain had to use force to suppress rebellion, such as using the Gunboat, 'Helga' to sail up the River Liffey and fire on the rebels in the GPO, thus distracting Great Britain's attention and resources away from the War effort, thus straining relations.
- Strong criticism of the Rising initially from the public, politicians, churchmen, as well as press for unnecessary death and destruction. 450 dead, 2,500 wounded, cost £2½ million, showing that majority still sided with Great Britain therefore indicating that there was not too much damage to relations between the two countries.
- Initial hostility by the majority of Irish people to the Rising by a small group of rebels; the majority of people supported Redmond and the Nationalists Party.
- Strong hostility and criticism by Dubliners of the rebels for destruction of the city centre.

Changing attitudes towards British rule after 1916

- The secret court martial, the execution of leaders over 10 days, as well as imprisonment without trial and at least one execution without a trial, saw the rebels gain a lot of sympathy from the Irish public, turning them against British rule.
- These political developments meant a growth of sympathy and compassion for the rebels who were seen as martyrs and replaced the initial condemnation of the Rising.
- Sinn Fein, initially blamed for the Rising, saw a subsequent rise in support for them.
- The Catholic Church and the business community became more sympathetic to the cause of independence.

Anti-conscription campaign

- Irish opposed conscription so the people were pushed to Sinn Fein who openly opposed it.
- Caused the Nationalists to withdraw from Westminster.
- Sinn Fein and Nationalists organised campaign, eg general strike April 23rd.
- Catholic Church, Mayor of Dublin drew up the National Pledge opposing conscription.
- Conscription was not extended to Ireland which Sinn Fein was given credit for.
- Conscription campaign drove Sinn Fein underground which improved their organisation.

Decline of Nationalist Party

- Irish Convention failed to reach agreement, which weakened position of Nationalists.
- Led to feeling British could not be trusted and Nationalists could not deliver.
- Three by-elections wins for Sinn Fein gave impression they spoke for people not Nationalists which increased tension between Ireland and Britain politically.

- In March 1918 Redmond died which accelerated the decline of the Nationalists. Sinn Fein gained influence and popularity as a result.
- Many moved from the Nationalist Party as they felt Sinn Fein was doing more for Ireland.

Rise of Sinn Fein

- Release of rebel prisoners from Frongoch meant Sinn Fein's struggle against British Rule in Ireland gained momentum.
- Michael Collins was building up IRB and Irish Volunteers when in prison.
- Collins ready to encourage anti-British activity in Ireland on release.
- Collins and De Valera improved Sinn Fein's leadership.
- Opposition to Britain due to martial law, house searches, raids, control of press, arrest of 'suspects' without trial, and vigorous implementation of the Defence of the Realm Act.
- Hunger striker Thomas Ashe died in 1917. His funeral became a propaganda tool for Sinn Fein.

Any other relevant factors.

Candidates can be credited up to a maximum of 20 marks.

29. How important were economic issues in contributing to the developing crisis in Northern Ireland up to 1968?

Context

By the early 1960s, Northern Ireland was relatively stable. However, there was a toxic legacy dating from the 1920s. Both the Northern Ireland Nationalist and Protestant communities saw each other in negative ways. In 1964 a peaceful civil rights campaign started to end the discrimination against Catholics in Northern Ireland.

Economic issues

- Northern Ireland was left relatively prosperous by World War Two, with the boom continuing into the 1950s. But by the 1960s, as elsewhere in Britain, these industries were in decline. Eg Harland and Wolff profitable 'til early'60s, but government help in 1966. Largely Protestant workforce protected as a result.
- Catholic areas received less government investment than their Protestant neighbours. Catholics were more likely to be unemployed or in low-paid jobs than Protestants in Northern Ireland. Catholic applicants also routinely excluded from public service appointments.
- The incomes of mainly Protestant landowners were supported by the British system of 'deficiency payments' which gave Northern Ireland's farmers an advantage over farmers from the Irish Republic.
- Brookeborough's failure to address the worsening economic situation saw him forced to resign as Prime Minister. His successor, Terence O'Neill, set out to reform the economy. His social and economic policies saw growing discontent and divisions within his unionist party.

Other factors

The Unionist ascendancy in Northern Ireland and challenges to it

- Population of Northern Ireland divided: two-thirds Protestant and one-third Catholic; it was the minority who were discriminated against in employment and housing.
- In 1963 the Prime Minister of Northern Ireland, Viscount Brookeborough, stepped down after 20 years in office. His long tenure was a product of the Ulster Unionist domination of politics in Northern Ireland since partition in 1921.

- Before 1969 elections not held on a 'one person, one vote' basis: gerrymandering used to secure unionist majorities on local councils. Local government electoral boundaries favoured unionist candidates, even in mainly Catholic areas like Derry/Londonderry. Also, the right to vote in local elections restricted to ratepayers, favouring Protestants, with those holding or renting properties in more than one ward receiving more than one vote, up to a maximum of six. This bias was preserved by unequal allocation of council houses to Protestant families.
- Challenges as Prime Minister O'Neill expressed desire to improve community relations in Northern Ireland and create a better relationship with the government in Dublin, hoping that this would address the sense of alienation felt by Catholics towards the political system in Northern Ireland.
- Post-war Britain's Labour government introduced the welfare state to Northern Ireland, and it was implemented with few concessions to traditional sectarian divisions. Catholic children in the 1950s and 1960s shared in the benefits of further and higher education for the first time. This exposed them to a world of new ideas and created a generation unwilling to tolerate the status quo.
- Many Catholics impatient with pace of reform and remained unconvinced of Prime Minister O'Neill's sincerity. Founding of the Northern Ireland Civil Rights Association (NICRA) in 1967. NICRA did not challenge partition, though membership was mainly Catholic. Instead, it called for the end to seven 'injustices', ranging from council house allocations to the 'weighted' voting system.

Role of the IRA
- Rioting and disorder in 1966 was followed by the murders of two Catholics and a Protestant by a 'loyalist' terror group called the Ulster Volunteer Force, who were immediately banned by O'Neill.
- Peaceful civil rights marches descended into violence in October 1968 when marchers in Derry defied the Royal Ulster Constabulary and were dispersed with heavy-handed tactics. The RUC response only served to inflame further the Catholic community and foster the establishment of the Provisional IRA by 1970 as the IRA split into Official and Provisional factions.
- The Provisional IRA's strategy was to use force to cause the collapse of the Northern Ireland administration and to inflict casualties on the British forces such that the British government be forced by public opinion to withdraw from Ireland.
- PIRA were seen to defend Catholic areas from Loyalist attacks in the summer of 1970.

Cultural and political differences
- The Catholic minority was politically marginalised since the 1920s, but retained its distinct identity through its own institutions such as the Catholic Church, separate Catholic schools, and various cultural associations, as well as the hostility of the Protestant majority.
- Catholic political representatives in parliament refused to recognise partition and this only increased the community's sense of alienation and difference from the Unionist majority in Northern Ireland.
- Nationalists had an average of 10—12 in the NI Parliament compared to an average of 40 Unionists. In Westminster there were 10—12 Unionists to 2 Nationalists.
- As the Republic's constitution laid claim to the whole island of Ireland, O'Neill's meeting with his Dublin counterpart, Seán Lemass, in 1965, provoked attacks from within unionism, eg the Rev. Ian Paisley.

- Violence erupted between the two communities in 1966 following the twin 50th anniversaries of the Battle of the Somme and the Easter Rising. Both events were key cultural touchstones for the Protestant and Catholic communities.

The issue of civil rights
- From the autumn of 1968 onwards, a wide range of activists marched behind the civil rights banner, adopting civil disobedience in an attempt to secure their goals. Housing activists, socialists, nationalists, unionists, republicans, students, trade unionists and political representatives came together across Northern Ireland to demand civil rights for Catholics in Northern Ireland.
- The demand for basic civil rights from the Northern Ireland government was an effort to move the traditional fault-lines away from the familiar Catholic—Protestant, nationalist—unionist divides by demanding basic rights for all citizens of Britain.
- Civil rights encouraged by television coverage of civil rights protest in the USA and student protests in Europe. Also by widening TV ownership: 1954 there were 10,000 licences, by 1962 there were 200,000 leading to increased Catholic awareness of the issues that affected them.
- As the civil rights campaign gained momentum, so too did unionist opposition. Sectarian tension rose: was difficult to control, and civil disobedience descended into occasions of civil disorder.

Any other relevant factors.

Candidates can be credited up to a maximum of 20 marks.

30. How important were the religious and communal differences between both communities in preventing peace in Ireland between 1968 and 1985?

Context
The civil rights movement of the mid to late 1960s saw a backlash against it from elements of the unionist community, including the largely Protestant RUC. The two sides: Nationalist and unionist were increasingly polarised through the period with communities dividing, socially and politically, along sectarian lines. The deployment of British troops in Northern Ireland and imposition of Direct Rule saw the conflict widen.

Religious and communal differences
- The Protestant majority in Northern Ireland belonged to churches that represented the full range of reformed Christianity, while the Catholic minority was united in its membership of a Church that dominated life in the Republic and much of Europe. These religious divisions made it very difficult for both communities to come together.
- These divisions were further enhanced by traditions embraced by both communities, such as the 'marching season', which became a flashpoint for sectarian violence. Also differences in sport, language.
- Many Catholic political representatives refused to recognise partition and their views only heightened the nationalist community's sense of alienation and fostered unionist hostility towards the Catholic minority.
- The speeches and actions of unionist and nationalist leaders such as Reverend Ian Paisley and Gerry Adams polarised views in the province, and emphasised the divisions between both communities.

- **Other factors**

Economic differences

- From 1973, the Common Agricultural Policy changed the decision making environment for food prices and farm economics, and employment in the farming sector continued to decline. Traditionally this sector had been dominated by the unionist community.
- Discrimination against Catholic applicants for employment declined steadily during this period as Catholics in the province began to enjoy the same civil rights enjoyed by the population of the rest of the UK.

Hardening attitudes — the role of terrorism

- Paramilitary groups began to operate on both sides of the sectarian divide, while civil rights marches became increasingly prone to confrontation.
- In late 1969, the more militant 'Provisional' IRA (PIRA) broke away from the so-called 'Official' IRA. PIRA was prepared to pursue unification in defiance of Britain and would use violence to achieve its aims.
- Unionist paramilitaries also organised. The UVF was joined by the Ulster Defence Association, created in 1971.
- Examples of terrorist activity: by the end of 1972 sectarian violence had escalated to such an extent that nearly 500 lives were lost in a single year.
- PIRA prisoners protest at loss of special status prisoners leading to hunger strikes. Second hunger strike in 1981, led by Bobby Sands. Sands was put forward for a vacant Westminster seat and won. Sands and nine other hunger strikers died before the hunger strikes were called off in October 1981.
- Sinn Fein won the by-election following Sands' death in June 1983. These electoral successes raised the possibility that Sinn Fein could replace the more moderate SDLP as the political voice of the Catholic minority in Northern Ireland.
- Indiscriminate terrorism meant Eire public opinion turned against PIRA.
- In 1985 the violence of Northern Ireland's paramilitary groups still had more than a decade to run and the sectarian divide remained as wide as it had ever been.

British government policies — internment

- New Prime Minister Brian Faulkner reintroduced internment, ie detention of suspects without trial, in 1971 in response to unrest. Policy was a disaster, both in its failure to capture any significant members of the PIRA and in its sectarian focus on nationalist rather than loyalist suspects. The reaction was predictable, even if the ferocity of the violence wasn't. Deaths in the final months of 1971 numbered over 150.

Direct Rule

- A number of reforms had followed on from the Downing Street Declaration, ie on allocation of council housing, investigate the recent cycle of violence and review policing, such as the disbanding of the hated 'B Specials' auxiliaries.
- The British government, now led by Prime Minister Edward Heath, decided to remove control of security from the government of Northern Ireland and appointing a secretary of state for the province leading to resignation of Stormont government. Direct Rule imposed.
- Despite attempts to introduce some sort of self-rule, such as the Sunningdale agreement of 1973, which failed in the face of implacable unionist opposition and led to the reintroduction of Direct Rule. It would last for another 25 years.

The role of the British Army

- The so-called 'Battle of Bogside' in 1969 only ended with the arrival of a small force of British troops at the request of Chichester Clark. An acknowledgement that the government of Northern Ireland had lost its grip on the province's security.
- By 1971 policing the province was fast becoming an impossible task, and the British Army adopted increasingly aggressive policies on the ground.
- On 30 January 1972, the army deployed the Parachute Regiment to suppress rioting at a civil rights march in Derry. Thirteen demonstrators were shot and killed by troops, with another victim dying later of wounds. Appalling images of 'Bloody Sunday' led to increased recruitment by Provisional IRA.
- The British Army's various attempts to control the PIRA, such as house-to-house searches and the imposition of a limited curfew, only served to drive more recruits into the ranks of the paramilitaries.

The role of the Irish government

- Irish government's role in The Anglo—Irish Agreement, signed in November 1985, confirmed that Northern Ireland would remain independent of the Republic as long as that was the will of the majority in the north. Also gave the Republic a say in the running of the province for the first time.
- The agreement also stated that power could not be devolved back to Northern Ireland unless it enshrined the principle of power sharing.

Any other relevant factors.

MODEL PAPER 2
SECTION 3: EUROPEAN AND WORLD

Part A: The Crusades, 1071–1204

Candidates can be credited up to a maximum of 20 marks.

31. How important were religious factors in the decision of Europeans to go on crusade?

Context
When Urban II called for a crusade in response to a call from help from Byzantium, he appealed to largely religious motives in people. However, the reality was that a variety of motives influenced a range of people.

Religious motives
- It was generally believed that the Remission of Sins offered by Pope Urban was an attractive solution to the dilemma of knights. Salvation was a constant worry for those trained to kill. Urban successfully resolved the need to protect Christianity from the Muslim threat and the general desire to re-establish the pilgrimage routes to the holy lands.
- The promise of remission of current sins was also a great relief to those knights worried about their eternal soul. Tancred's biographer wrote about both his worry over this dilemma and his relief at Urban's suggestion.
- The appeal of the People's Crusade shows the power of the belief that they were doing good and helping God.
- Of the leaders of the Princes' Crusade, Raymond of Toulouse is often held up as an example of a knight riding to the defence of the Holy Lands. His decision to take Tripoli in 1100 casts a shadow over this interpretation of his motives.
- In later crusades many of the religious aspects of the crusade are adopted and modified by the growing idea of chivalric codes.

Other factors
The desire to acquire territory in the Holy Land
- Many of the great magnates on this expedition had intentions to acquire new estates for themselves. The motives of many of the leaders of the Princes' Crusade have been put down to this.
- Bohomend and Baldwin in particular showed little zeal in carrying on with the Crusade once they had acquired Antioch and Edessa respectively.

Peer pressure
- The pressure put on knights by their families to take the cross was at times severe. Noblemen's wives tended to be keenly aware of the politics at court and had a role in influencing the decisions of some.
- Stephen of Blois had married Adela, daughter of William I of England. It would have been unthinkable for such a notable knight not to go on the Crusade.

Seeking of fame and riches
- Some knights did go seeking glory. The Crusade had provided the solution to the problem of knights and their need for salvation. Killing was only wrong if you killed Christians. Urban indicated that the killing of a Muslim was a just act, and the equivalent to prayer or penance.
- Seeking of riches per se was uncommon; land was the real source of wealth and power.

The sense of adventure
- Going on crusade was exciting and engendered a sense of adventure.

- Pilgrimages had always been seen as important, and the idea of this as an armed pilgrimage was very appealing. It offered a way out for many serfs from their lives in bondage, or perhaps a chance to see the Holy Land.

Overpopulation and famine
- Many were forced to leave because of the lack of available farmland in an already overcrowded Europe.
- Several famines have also been suggested as a possible motive. It was popularly believed that the Holy Land was a land of plenty.

Any other relevant factors.

Candidates can be credited up to a maximum of 20 marks.

32. 'While Richard was a greater military leader, Saladin was a better diplomat.' How valid is this view?

Context
The Third Crusade did not see the recovery of Jerusalem by the Crusaders, but it did enhance Richard of England's reputation as a military leader. Saladin had not been as militarily successful, but the Crusade had left his lands.

Saladin's strengths and weaknesses
- Saladin had unified Muslim forces in the Middle-East and enjoyed a considerable reputation after the defeat of Crusader forces at Hattin and the subsequent recapture of Jerusalem.
- Saladin negotiated that Jerusalem remain in Muslim hands after Christian military success.
- Saladin negotiated for the destruction of the Crusader fort at Ascalon.
- Saladin managed to take Jaffa and threaten Crusader forces, but lost control of his forces and subsequent battle with Richard's forces.
- The negotiated settlement allowed for considerable economic activity in the area.
- Richard's victory over Saladin's forces at Arsuf severely dented Saladin's reputation as an invincible military leader.
- Not all of Saladin's supporters were happy with the Treaty of Ramla in 1192, as it allowed Christian pilgrims and merchants to enter the city if unarmed, but the surviving Crusader states were forced onto a coastal strip of land.
- Saladin was panicked into peace with Richard. Saladin was worried over the close relationship between Al-Adil and Richard. If he had held out it was probable that Richard would have had to return to England anyway without the peace treaty.

Richard's strengths and weaknesses
- Richard's temper did result in the loss of potential allies. His treatment of Leopold of Austria, the leader of the much-reduced German contingent, resulted in an injury to the pride of Leopold and the loss of his German knights to the cause.
- Richard's inability to share the spoils taken during this attack on Cyprus with Philip Augustus helped persuade the ill king of France that he was needed at home.
- Against advice Richard backed Guy de Lusignan to become King of Jerusalem, rather than the popular Conrad of Montferrat, perhaps because he was the favourite of Philip. This continued support of Guy resulted in a compromise that no one liked. The assassination of Conrad was whispered by some to be Richard's fault. The end result was the withdrawal of the support of Conrad's forces and those of the Duke of Burgundy's remaining French knights.

- Richard proved himself in the art of diplomacy during the Crusade, when he successfully negotiated with Al-Adill, Saladin's brother. Saladin was increasingly concerned when Richard knighted one of Al-Adill's sons and even offered his sister in marriage. Al-Adill's connection to Richard was enough of an incentive for Saladin to agree to a truce with Richard.
- However, Richard was forced into a negotiated settlement with Saladin in 1192 instead of pressing on and taking Jerusalem. Affairs at home in the Angevin Empire, and particularly the growing threat from his brother meant Richard had to return to Europe.
- Richard was good at motivating troops, and his arrival at the siege of Acre galvanised the troops in a way that Philip had been unable to do. Even when confined to his bed due to illness he was still able to direct the operations
- While journeying to the Holy Lands Richard captured Cyprus.
- Richard, despite being lured into a trap, won the Battle of Arsuf with an impressive charge of knights that routed Saladin's men. Saladin was defeated in battle and it helped raise morale; the great defeat of Hattin had been erased from the minds of the crusaders
- Richard won the Battle of Jaffa against overwhelming odds. Saladin had failed to defeat Richard in battle, and he lost control of his men at Jaffa; they refused to obey his orders.

Any other relevant factors.

Candidates can be credited up to a maximum of 20 marks.

33. To what extent had the crusading ideal declined by the Fourth Crusade in 1204?

Context
The continuing Muslim control of Jerusalem after the Third Crusade was the main motivation for the calling of the Fourth Crusade by Innocent III. However, latent Latin resentment towards Byzantium and its wealth meant that the original plan to invade Egypt was changed.

The Fourth Crusade
- The initial inspiration of the Forth Crusade had a strong crusading ideology behind it. Pope Innocent III was a highly effective pope. He had managed to settle the problem of the investiture contest with Germany, and hoped to sort out the issue of the Holy Lands as well. Innocent believed that the inclusion of medieval monarchs had caused the previous two crusades to fail, unlike the first Crusade that was nominally under the command of Bishop Adhemar. This crusade would fall under the command of six papal legates. These men would hold true to the ideal of the Crusade and not be bound by earthy greed of politics.
- However, The Fourth Crusade has also been described as the low point of the crusading ideal. Hijacked by the Venetians, the Crusade instead became a tool for their growing political and economic ambitions.
- While attacking Zara, Alexius, son of the deposed emperor of Byzantium, arrived with a new proposal for the Crusaders. He asked them to reinstate his father, who had been imprisoned by his brother, and if they agreed they would be handsomely rewarded. He also promised to return control of the Byzantine Church to Rome. The church was against such an attack on another Christian city, but the prospect of wealth and fame led the Crusade to Constantinople.
- When the crusaders discovered that Alexius and his father could not, or would not, meet the payment as agreed, the Crusaders stormed the city. The murder, looting and rape continued for three days, after which the crusading army had a great thanksgiving ceremony.

- The amount of booty taken from Constantinople was huge: gold, silver, works of art and holy relics were taken back to Europe, mostly to Venice. Most crusaders returned home with their newly acquired wealth. Those that stayed divided up the land amongst themselves, effectively creating several Latin Crusader States where Byzantium had once stood.

Role of Venice
- By 1123 the city of Venice had come to dominate maritime trade in the Middle East. They made several secret trade agreements with Egypt and North African emirs, as well as enjoying concessions and trade agreements within the Kingdom of Jerusalem. Byzantium, however, remained a constant rival for this dominance of trade and in 1183 Venice was cut off from the lucrative trading centres of the empire.
- Venice's participation in the Crusade was only secured when the Pope agreed to pay huge sums of money to Venice for the use of its ships, and supplies as well as half of everything captured during the Crusade on land and sea.
- Venice's leader, the Doge Enrico Dandolo, had sold the crusaders three times as much supplies and equipment as required for the Crusade. The crusading leader, Boniface of Montferrat, found that he was unable to raise enough money to pay, and the Crusaders were all but imprisoned on an island near Venice. Dandolo's proposal to pay off the crusaders' debt involved attacking Zara, a Christian city that had once belonged to Venice but was now under the control of the King of Hungary, a Christian monarch. Thus the Crusade had become a tool of the Venetians.
- The Fourth Crusade's intended target, Egypt, was totally unsuitable from a Venetian perspective. Thus when the Pope's representative approached the Venetians in 1201 they agreed to help transport the Crusaders, hoping to divert the Crusade to a less friendly target. The final target for the Fourth Crusade was therefore determined by politics and economics.

Coexistence of Muslim and crusading states
- Attempts at peace between Muslim and the Crusading states during the reign of Baldwin IV, before his death and the fall of Jerusalem.
- Also other examples, such as the treaty of mutual protection signed between King Alric of Jerusalem and the Emir of Damascus prior to the second crusade.

The corruption of the crusading movement by the Church and nobles
- Popes were willing to use crusades against Christians, such as the Albegensian crusade against the Cathar heretics of Languedoc (Toulouse and southern France) in 1209–1229. The Cathars did not believe in the hierarchy of Rome, all you needed was to be able to read the bible. This is only the first of many such crusades in Europe, seen as diluting the crusading ideal, ie killing Muslims.
- Examples of nobles using the crusade for their own ends are all over the place, from Bohemond and Baldwin in the First Crusade, to arguably Richard in the third. The Fourth Crusade is littered with examples.

Effects of trade
- Trade links directly into the Fourth Crusade and the influence of Venice.
- Pisa and Genoa both had a lot of influence in events during the Third Crusade, they both had favoured candidates for the vacant throne of Jerusalem for example and used trade rights as a bargaining chip to get what they wanted.

Any other relevant factors.

Part B: The American Revolution, 1763—1787

Candidates can be credited up to a maximum of 20 marks.

34. How important was the rejection of the Olive Branch petition in the colonists' declaration of independence in 1776?

Context

In 1765 the American colonies rejected the ability of the British Parliament to tax them without representation. This was the start of a series of social, political and economic events that led to the Declaration of Independence in 1776.

Rejection of the Olive Branch Petition

- George III rejected the colonists' last attempt at compromise.
- 2nd Continental Congress had written an appeal to the king pledging its allegiance to crown and bitterness towards Parliament, yet appeal fell on deaf ears as George III declared colonists to be in rebellion.
- Many colonists started to consider independence as the only means of changing their relationship with Britain.
- However, petition was expression of loyalty to George III which masked many colonists' intentions to declare greater autonomy for themselves, regardless of the king's reaction.
- George III rejected the Olive Branch petition, possibly as a consequence of increased colonist military activity, eg Lexington and Bunker Hill.

Other factors

Disputes over taxation

Stamp Act

- This first form of taxation on colonies, in 1765, was objected to by colonists because they were not represented in the British Parliament which imposed these taxes.
- 'No taxation without representation' became a familiar protest during this time.
- The Act stated that an official stamp had to be bought to go on any printed matter, and colonists subsequently refused to pay for this.
- Colonists stated that they already paid financial dues to British through Navigation Acts and other restrictions, and that they had their own militia and did not need to pay for the British Army to protect them.
- However, the British said taxation would contribute to costs of the Seven Years' War and also pay for continued presence of the British Army in America to protect colonies.

Townshend Duties

- After Stamp Act was repealed in 1766, these Duties, which were on glass, tea, paper and lead, were imposed in 1767.
- Colonists challenged right of Parliament to impose duties that seemed designed purely to raise revenue.
- However, the British insisted that duties be paid in order to maintain costs of acting as the Mother Country to protect colonies.

Boston Massacre

- Massacre occurred in 1770.
- Although 5 working-class men died, including one black man, reports of 5 middle-class white men dying caused outrage amongst politically-minded colonists.
- Committees of Correspondence meant that news of the Massacre spread quickly around 13 colonies.
- Acquittal of British soldiers led many colonists to fear for their personal liberty and believe that they would one day be enslaved by the British.
- However, the Massacre was an incident which animated people mainly in the New England area, something which later caused George III to voice his belief that problems in America were 'localised'.

Punishment of Massachusetts

- Tax remained on tea from 1770 in order to maintain British right to tax colonists.
- Boston Tea Party in December 1773 was an expression of some colonists' frustrations at British policy towards them.
- The British response to the Boston Tea Party, in a series of acts starting in March 1774, known to colonists as Intolerable Acts — closing port of Boston, altering constitution of legislature of Massachusetts, billeting British troops in colonial homes, and suspending trial by jury in colony.
- Other colonists acted in sympathy with Massachusetts and showed unity at First Continental Congress in September 1774.
- However, the British spoke of punishments as Coercive Acts, which were an attempt to get colonists to see that acts of hostility towards Britain would not be tolerated.

British intransigence

- Britain retained an uncompromising attitude in the face of continued colonist protest and pleas for compromise.

Influence of Thomas Paine

- Republican pamphlet 'Common Sense' was published in January 1776 and sold 100,000 copies.

Any other relevant factors.

Candidates can be credited up to a maximum of 20 marks.

35. How important was the colonists' advantage of fighting on home ground in their eventual victory in the American Revolution?

Context

Although a global power, Britain lost the American War of Independence. Ultimately, the 8-year conflict rested on the fact that there were too few loyalists, the British Army made errors and had no international allies. The American revolutionaries on the other hand had a wealth of local knowledge and support as well as important help from countries like France.

Colonists' advantage of fighting on home ground

- Land war fought on American soil: this gave the Continental Army an advantage, as the colonists' knowledge of the theatre of war meant they handled the terrain better than the British.
- Local people burned their crops rather than let them fall into British hands, reducing potential supplies for the British.

Other factors

George Washington

- Washington was an inspirational leader, a self-made Virginian whose choice as Commander of the Continental Army gave heart to many.
- Washington fought guerrilla warfare effectively. He taught his troops to fire accurately from distance in open battle. He had experience of the British Army during the Seven Years' War.
- Washington's speeches to troops offered them the incentive of independence if they won the war.
- Washington benefited from luck on several occasions, such as when inefficiency led the British into traps or when the French arrived at Yorktown.

French entry into the war

- Franco–American Treaty of Alliance in February 1778 was a turning point in the war.
- France contributed troops, ammunition, expertise and supplies to the colonists.
- Strength of the French navy meant Britain had to spread its forces worldwide, thus reducing its effort in the colonies.
- French intervention on the part of Admiral de Grasse preceded the final British surrender at Yorktown.
- Entry of France into the war may have encouraged Spain and Holland to follow suit within the next two years.
- However, the war had been taking place for over eighteen months by the time France entered. France's main contribution was at sea rather than on land.

British military inefficiency

- On several occasions British generals did not act appropriately to orders received. Orders from London were misinterpreted; eg Howe marching south to Brandywine instead of north into New England, thus isolating Burgoyne who subsequently surrendered his forces at Saratoga.
- Petty jealousies obstructed co-operation amongst British military leaders.
- Changes in personnel holding high office hindered progress.
- However, in many instances the British were forced into bad decisions by the tactics of Washington's army.
- Distance between Britain and the colonies caused a delay in communications between London and the generals, with orders from Britain often overtaken by events by the time they reached America.

British political mistakes

- The government ignored pleas by those such as Chatham (Pitt the Elder) to reconcile with America.
- Burke's attempts in the House of Commons to persuade the government to make peace were also dismissed.
- George III and British ministers treated Americans as rebels and therefore ignored arguments for the colonies' rights to autonomy, self-legislation and self-taxation.
- George III and British ministers' dismissal of Olive Branch Petition in 1775 led colonists to believe the war must be won.
- Inefficiencies at the Admiralty under Lord Sandwich's tenure as First Lord meant Royal Navy was ill-prepared for attacks on Britain by French and Spanish which diverted British efforts in America.
- Lord North's attempts to conciliate the colonists later in the war were too little too late; the colonists were motivated by independence.

Control of the seas

- **Spanish and Dutch entry into the war** — they stretched British resources even further and made the British less effective in the colonies.
- **Armed League of Neutrality** — Russian, Danish and Swedish willingness to fire on the Royal Navy placed extra pressure on Britain.

Any other relevant factors.

*Candidates can be credited **up to a maximum of 20 marks***

36. To what extent was the American Constitution of 1787 an answer to the problems highlighted by the experience of British rule?

Context

The Constitution of 1787 is the supreme law in America. It was designed to ensure a separation of powers between the executive, judiciary and legislature. The experience of rule by Britain undoubtedly influenced the Constitution.

The experience of rule by Britain

- As part of the British Empire, colonists had been ruled by the king and the British Parliament, who together made key policy decisions, set laws and taxes, and enforced the law; there were no checks and balances.
- Colonists feared the potentially tyrannical power of a monarch, and designed the Constitution to prevent any such future threat.
- Branches of government were to be predominantly elective, to ensure the participation of the people.

Significance of the Constitution

- When the colonists drew up their Constitution, they built in a separation of powers providing checks and balances within the political system. The Bill of Rights established liberty for individuals in states within a federal union of all states, and set out clear lines of authority between federal government and individual states. This would avoid central government exerting a controlling power over people's lives.
- The hierarchy which existed under rule by Britain was altered by the Constitution, which stated that 'all men are created equal' and that everyone was entitled to 'life, liberty and the pursuit of happiness'. Now people would be asked to ratify many of the stages within the democratic processes at state and national level. However, women and blacks were excluded from the franchise, and in reality only one-fifth of eligible voters turned out for national elections.

Executive: role of President

- Executive power was vested in the elected President, and his Vice-President and Cabinet. The President acted as head of state and Commander-in-Chief but would have no vote in the law-making process, although he could veto legislation.
- The President would make all key decisions and establish policy.
- Members of the Executive could be removed from office by the electorate or the other branches of government if it was felt they were not doing their job properly.

Legislature: Congress

- Legislative power lay in the hands of an elected Congress which was divided into two Houses, the Senate and Representatives.
- Congress passed laws and raised taxes, as well as having responsibility for international trade, war and foreign relations.
- No one in the legislature could serve in the judiciary or executive without first resigning from the legislature.
- Congressional elections were held regularly to ensure that Congressmen remained in touch with the people they served.

Judiciary: Supreme Court

- Judicial power was granted to the Supreme Court of the United States.
- The Supreme Court acted as the highest court of appeal in the country. It also debated the legality of new laws passed by Congress.
- Supreme Court judges were nominated by the President and their appointment was ratified by Congress after a rigorous checking process.
- Appointees to the Supreme Court could be removed from their position if they acted improperly.

Any other relevant factors.

Part C: The French Revolution, to 1799

Candidates can be credited up to a maximum of 20 marks.

37. To what extent did revolution break out in France in 1789 as a result of the economic crisis of 1788—9?

Context

By 1789 the problems of the Ancien Regime were coming to a head. A series of foreign wars had led the state into debt. The need for more cash, attempts to reform the taxation system, demands for political change and an ineffectual monarch all led to pressures on the Ancien Regime, which was put into stark relief by the economic crisis of 1788/9.

The economic crisis of 1788/9

- Bad harvests and grain shortages inspired unrest among the peasantry and the urban workers in Paris and in provincial cities throughout France, exerting critical pressures on the Ancien Regime.
- There was less demand for manufactured goods, which led to unemployment increasing amongst the urban workers.
- The nobility were increasingly blamed as peasants started to take political action.
- The economic crisis clearly created an environment in which the Ancien Regime was struggling to survive.

Other Factors

Financial problems of the Ancien Regime

- Because of exemptions the crown was denied adequate income. The privileged orders were an untapped source of revenue but it would require reforms to access it.
- This created resentment amongst the Third Estate.
- Exacerbated divisions that already existed between the estates.
- Tax-farming meant not all revenues were reaching the government.
- By the 1780s France faced bankruptcy due to heavy expenditure and borrowing to pay for wars.
- Government failed to gain agreement on tax reform.
- This was arguably the biggest threat facing the Ancien Regime. The opposition which this generated not only led to Calonne's dismissal in 1787 but more importantly to the convocation of the Estates General in 1788. When it met in May 1789 the long-standing divisions between the three estates unleashed forces which culminated in the overthrow of the Ancien Regime.

Influence of the Enlightenment

- The Enlightenment encouraged criticism and freedom of thought, speech and religion, and was seen as the end of man's self-imposed irrationality at the hands of the Church in particular.
- Ideas of philosophs like Voltaire who attacked God, Montesquieu who favoured a British system of government and Rousseau who put forward the idea of direct democracy.
- Very much appealed to the middle-classes, who led the revolution.

The American Revolution

- This war contributed to the financial crisis which came to a head in France post-1786 but for many in France at the time they also represented the practical expression of the enlightened views of the Philosophes in terms of the rights of the individual, no taxation without representation and freedom from tyrannical government. The wars inspired many of the lesser nobility and the bourgeoisie to seek the same freedoms.

The political crisis of 1788/9

- The convocation of the Estates General in August 1788 sharpened divisions between the three estates which came to a head between May and August 1789. The Cahiers des Doleances revealed the depth of dissatisfaction with the existing order, especially among the bourgeoisie and the peasantry. The creation of the National Assembly, the abolition of feudalism and the Declaration of the Rights of Man and the Citizen all contributed to a revolutionary change in French government, society and economy.

Actions of Louis XVI

- Louis was largely under the influence of his wife, Marie Antoinette who, although strong minded, failed to grasp the serious nature of situation and was also unpopular as she was Austrian.
- Louis XVI's handling of the Estates-General contributed towards the start of the Revolution. He wanted to make reform difficult by making the three estates meet separately, in the hope that the first and second estates would vote the third down.
- This backfired: opposition to the king grew, the third estate refused to act separately, and many of the clergy changed sides, changing the balance of power.
- Louis allegedly closed the meeting halls, which led to the Tennis Court Oath from members of the Third Estate. He later agreed to a constitution when the Third Estate representatives occupied the royal tennis courts.
- The king had lost more political ground than if he had just listened to the grievances of the middle classes and the third estate from the start.

Role of bourgeoisie

- As part of the Third Estate, resented paying the taxation.
- Dominated the Third Estate representatives in the Estates-General.
- Were outside the political process unless they bought a noble title: wanted access to power.
- Very attracted to ideas of a constitutional monarchy as advocated by people like Montesquieu.
- Provided the leadership for the revolution.

Any other relevant factors.

Candidates can be credited up to a maximum of 20 marks.

38. To what extent did the increasing intervention of the army in politics bring about Napoleon's coup of 1799, which created the Consulate?

Context

French military performance in 1798 and 1799 led to the eventual collapse of the Directory. A British encouraged Royalist insurrection in the south of France further complicated matters. Subsequent political intrigue by Sieyes backed by the military reputation of Bonaparte led to the coup that ended the Directory.

Increasing intervention of the army in politics

- Even before the 1795 constitution was ratified the army had been used to quell sans-culottes insurgents who sought to invade the Convention and to repel an émigré invasion at Quiberon.
- Napoleon's use of a 'whiff of grapeshot' to put down the disturbances in October merely underlined the parlous nature of politics at the time.
- The deployment of the army in May 1796 to put down the left-wing Babcuf Conspiracy was followed by the Coup of Fructidor in September 1797 when the first 'free' Convention elections returned a royalist majority.

Other factors

Role of Sieyes

- Afraid that France would descend into anarchy as a result of the on-going political conflict and deeming the 1795 constitution unworkable, Sieyes enlisted the aid of Bonaparte in mounting a coup against it.
- The Convention, the Directory and the legislative councils had run their course and few, if any, mourned their passing.

Political instability

- In the late summer of 1794 France was emerging from two years of increasing radicalisation and resulting bitterness between opposing factions.
- The Jacobins under Robespierre had been overthrown and a 'White Terror' was soon to sweep the country in revenge for the excesses of the radical left during the Terror.
- France had been torn apart by civil war, threatened by foreign armies egged on by émigré nobles seeking to overthrow the Revolution and riven by religious conflict occasioned by the State's opposition to the primacy of the Catholic Church.

The Constitution of 1795

- Policy-makers framed a new constitution which sought to reconcile the bitterness of the preceding years by imposing checks and balances against the emergence of one dominant individual, group or faction. In so doing, many historians argue that the new constitution was a recipe for instability in the years which followed.
- A bi-cameral legislature was established wherein each chamber counter-balanced the power of the other. By doing so it inhibited strong and decisive government.
- To ensure continuity, the new Convention was to include two-thirds of the outgoing deputies from the old. This enraged sections of the right who felt that the forces of left-wing radicalism still prevailed in government.
- The resulting mass protests in October 1795 were put down by the army under Bonaparte. The principle of using extra-parliamentary forces to control the State had been established with Bonaparte right at the heart of it. It was to prove a dangerous precedent.
- Annual elections worked against consistent and continuous policy-making
- So did the appointment of an Executive — the Directory — one of whose members rotated on an annual basis.
- Again, the counter-balance between the legislature and the executive may have been commendable but it was to prove inherently unstable in practice.

Role of Bonaparte

- A supreme self-propagandist, he seemed to offer the strength and charisma which the Directory and the legislative councils singularly lacked.
- Afraid that his spectacular victories in Italy during 1795 might be jeopardised by the election of a right-wing government less sympathetic to conducting a war against monarchical states, Bonaparte threw his support behind the Directory who effectively annulled the election results by purging right-wing deputies.
- The 1788 and 1799 elections were similarly 'adjusted'.
- The Consulate — with Bonaparte as First Consul — came into being. A notably more authoritarian constitution was promulgated by referendum, supported by a populace tired of weak and ineffectual government and the instability it had brought between 1795 and 1799.

Any other relevant factors.

Candidates can be credited up to a maximum of 20 marks.

39. **'The bourgeoisie gained most from the French Revolution.' How valid is this view?**

Context

The French Revolution is widely considered to be one of the most important historical events in human history. The impact on the French Aristocracy and Clergy was long lasting as was the enduring French liking for Republicanism.

The impact of the Revolution on the bourgeoisie

- The Revolution instigated a fundamental shift in political and economic power from the First and Second Estates to the bourgeoisie.
- The ending of feudalism in August 1789 heralded profound social and economic change (eg facilitating the development of capitalism) whilst the Declaration of the Rights of Man and the Citizen later in the month did the same for political life. In both cases the main beneficiaries were the bourgeoisie.
- Successive constitutions and legislative reforms throughout the1790s favoured the bourgeoisie above all other social groups by emphasising the notion of a property-owning democracy with voting rights framed within property qualifications, whilst the ending of trade restrictions and monopolies favoured an expanding business and merchant class.
- France had moved from a position of privileged estates to one where increasingly merit was what counted. It was the educated Bourgeoisie who were best placed to benefit from this profound change in French society.

The impact on other sections of society

The peasantry

- In contrast to the Catholic Church and the nobility, the position of the peasantry was in many ways strengthened by the Revolution. The ending of feudalism in August 1789 removed many of the legal and financial burdens which had formed the basis of peasant grievances in the Cahiers des Doleances presented to the Estates-General in 1789.
- The revolutionary land settlement, instigated by the nationalisation of church lands in November 1789, had transferred land from the nobility and the clergy to the peasantry to their obvious advantage. It should be noted, however, that not all peasants benefited equally from this. Only the well-off peasants could afford to purchase the Church lands which had been seized by the National Assembly.

The urban workers

- At key points throughout the Revolution overt demonstrations of discontent by the urban masses — particularly in Paris — impacted on key events as successive regimes framed policy with an eye to appeasing the mob. However, any modest gains by the urban poor were short-lived. A decade of almost continuous wars in the 1790s had created shortages and inflation which hit the urban poor particularly hard.
- The passing of the Chapelier Law in May 1791, by a bourgeois-dominated National Assembly protecting the interests of industrialists, effectively banned the formation of trade unions and thereafter the Revolution brought few tangible economic or political gains for urban workers.

The impact of the Revolution on the First Estate

- The Catholic Church was a key pillar of the Ancien Regime. The Upper Clergy (usually drawn from the ranks of the traditional nobility) enjoyed considerable wealth and status based on a raft of privileges and tax exemptions. These privileges and exemptions were swept away by the Revolution and the position of the Catholic Church within France by 1799 was far less assured than it had been under the Ancien Regime.

- The Civil Constitution of the Clergy (July 1790) polarised attitudes towards the place of the Catholic Church within French society and promoted conflict between opposing factions through the rest of the period to 1799. In November 1789 Church lands were nationalised, stripping the Church of much of its wealth. The net result of all of this was that the Church never regained its primacy within the French state and can be seen to have lost far more than it gained.

The impact of the Revolution on the Second Estate

- The aristocracy had enjoyed similar privileges and tax exemptions to those of the Catholic Church under the Ancien Regime. Advancement in the key positions of the State, the Army, and indeed the Church, depended more often on birth than merit. The traditional nobility monopolised these key positions and sought at all times to defend its favoured position. Again, the Revolution swept away aristocratic privilege even more completely than that of the clergy.
- The ending of feudalism in August 1789 marked the prelude to a decade when the status of the nobility in France effectively collapsed. In 1790 outward displays of 'nobility' such as titles and coats of arms were forbidden by law and in 1797, after election results suggested a pro-royalist resurgence, the Convention imposed alien status on nobles and stripped them of French citizenship.
- The Revolution brought in a regime where careers were open to talent regardless of birth or inheritance and the traditional aristocracy simply ceased to exist. Having said that, some nobles simply transformed themselves into untitled landlords in the countryside and continued to exercise significant economic and political power.

Any other relevant factors.

Part D: Germany, 1815—1939

Candidates can be credited up to a maximum of 20 marks.

40. To what extent had nationalism grown in Germany by 1850?

Context
The belief that the disparate Germanic states should join together developed strongly in the years after the French Revolution of 1789. The strength of Austria and powerful forces that opposed the growth of nationalism meant that by 1850 there was no united German state.

Supporters of nationalism
- Liberal nationalists — a united Germany should have a Liberal constitution that would guarantee the rights of citizens.
- Cultural nationalists — unity was more important than individual rights and that what mattered was the preservation of German identity and culture.
- Economic nationalists — unity would remove the trade barriers between states and this would allow economic growth and prosperity.
- To encourage trade, Prussia formed a customs union in 1818 that by the 1830s was called the Zollverein; the Zollverein helped nationalist ideas to spread.
- Nationalist ideas were spread by philosophers, historians, poets and dramatists who influenced the literate middle classes and especially the students: Jahn and the burschenschaten movement; Wartburg in 1817; Hamburg in 1832; Young Germany in 1833; the Rhine Movement in 1840.

- Fichte described 'Germany' as the Fatherland where all people spoke the same language and sang the same songs.
- German poets and authors such as the Grimm brothers, and composers such as Beethoven, encouraged feelings of national pride in the German states.
- In 1830 anti-French feelings promoted 'the watch on the Rhine' and nationalist festivals such as Hambach (1832) also encouraged nationalist feelings.

Opponents of nationalism
- One-fifth of the population of the Austrian empire were German; the Austrian Emperor feared nationalism would encourage them to break away and join Germany; this would leave Austria weaker and cause other national groups in the Empire to demand their independence.
- In 1815 Metternich became worried about the growth of liberal and nationalist student societies.
- In 1819 Carlsbad Decrees banned student societies and censored newspapers.
- The following year the power of the Diet was increased so that soldiers could be ordered to stop the spread of new ideas in any of the German States.
- The particularism of the various German states — autonomous and parochial in many ways.
- Popular apathy — most Germans had little desire to see a united Germany.
- France and Russia feared that a strong, united Germany would be a political, economic and military rival to them.

Attitudes of peasants
- Golo Mann wrote that most Germans 'seldom looked up from the plough'. He doubted the influence of artists and intellectuals whom most Germans knew little or nothing about; nationalism attracted mainly the educated/ business/middle classes.
- But by the late 1840s peasants were demanding that remaining feudal dues should be cancelled by their German princes.

Political turmoil in the 1840s
- Trade depression, unemployment and high food prices because of bad harvests led to revolutions throughout Europe.
- In the German Confederation nationalists and liberals saw their chance; the rulers of the small states fled; elections were held to local assemblies and then to a national convention to create a united Germany; this convention or parliament met at Frankfurt.

The Frankfurt Parliament, divisions
- This was the first serious attempt to challenge Austria's political power in Germany and Austrian opposition to the liberals and nationalists.
- Failure of the Frankfurt Parliament — lack of clear aims and no armed force to enforce its decisions.
- Nationalists could not agree on the size of a new Germany — should it include Austria and the Hapsburg lands and Prussia's Polish possessions?
- Should it be governed by a king or be a republic or a mixture of both?
- The Protestants of the North distrusted the Southern Catholics.

The collapse of the revolution in Germany, 1848—1849
- Frankfurt Parliament failed to satisfy the needs of the starving workers who had helped create the revolution.
- Parliament had to rely on the Prussian army to put down a workers revolt.

- Self-interest of German rulers led to opposition to the actions at Frankfurt.
- Frederick William, King of Prussia, tried to take advantage of the defeat of the 1848 revolution to increase Prussian power to exclude Austria from the Confederation – the Erfurt Parliament.
- Austria was still too strong in 1850 and was able to force Prussia to back down; at Olmutz it was agreed to return to the Constitution of 1815.

Any other relevant factors.

Candidates can be credited up to a maximum of 20 marks.

41. To what extent were the weaknesses of the Weimar Republic the major reason for the rise of the Nazi Party between 1920 and 1933?

Context
The origins of the Nazi achievement of power lie in the Peace Treaty of 1919, which the new Weimar Republic had to accept. Economic and political problems further weakened the democracy. However, the strengths of the Nazis in unifying extreme right wing opinion, plus a willingness to use democracy and ruthlessness to use opportunity should also be taken in to account.

Weaknesses of the Weimar Republic
- 'A Republic without Republicans'/'a Republic nobody wanted' – lack of popular support for the new form of government after 1918.
- 'Peasants in a palace' – commentary on Weimar politicians.
- Divisions among those groups/individuals who purported to be supporters of the new form of government, eg the socialists.
- Alliance of the new government and the old imperial army against the Spartacists – lack of cooperation between socialist groups – petty squabbling rife.
- The Constitution/Article 48 ('suicide clause') – arguably Germany too was democratic. 'The world's most perfect democracy – on paper.'
- Lack of real, outstanding Weimar politicians who could strengthen the Republic, Stresemann excepted.
- Inability (or unwillingness) of the Republic to deal effectively with problems in German society.
- Lukewarm support from the German Army and the Civil Service.

Other factors
Resentment towards the Treaty of Versailles
- The Treaty of Versailles: acceptance by Republic of hated terms.
- Land loss and accepting blame for the War especially hated.
- Led to growth of criticism; 'November Criminals', 'Stab in the back' myth.
- Social and economic difficulties
- Over-reliance on foreign investment left the Weimar economy subject to the fluctuations of the international economy.
- 1922/23 (hyperinflation) – severe effects on the middle classes, the natural supporters of the Republic; outrage and despair at their ruination.
- The Great Depression of 1929 – arguably without this the Republic might have survived. Germany's dependence on American loans showed how fragile the recovery of the late 1920s was. The pauperisation of millions again reduced Germans to despair.
- Propaganda posters with legends such as 'Hitler – our only hope' struck a chord with many.

- The Depression also polarised politics in Germany – the drift to extremes led to a fear of Communism, which grew apace with the growth of support for the Nazis.

Appeal of the Nazis after 1928
- Nazi Party had attractive qualities for the increasingly disillusioned voting population: They were anti-Versailles, anti-Communist (the SA took on the Red Front in the streets), promised to restore German pride, give the people jobs.
- The Nazis put their message across well with the skilful use of propaganda under the leadership of Josef Goebbels.
- The SA was used to break up opponents meetings and give the appearance of discipline and order.
- Gave scapegoats for the population to blame from the Jews to the Communists.

The role of Hitler
- Hitler was perceived as a young, dynamic leader, who campaigned using modern methods and was a charismatic speaker.
- He offered attractive policies which gave simple targets for blame and tapped into popular prejudice.

Weaknesses and mistakes of others
- Splits in the left after suppression of Spartacist revolt made joint action in the 1930s very unlikely.
- Roles of von Schleicher and von Papen. Underestimation of Hitler.
- Weakness/indecision of Hindenburg.

Any other relevant factors.

Candidates can be credited up to a maximum of 20 marks.

42. 'Through their economic policies the Nazis gave the people what they wanted.' How valid is this as a reason for the Nazis maintaining power between 1933 and 1939?

Context
The Nazi maintenance of power relied on a mixture of propaganda, genuine popularity and fear. The development of a powerful Nazi state meant that control of the German states was total. However, the Nazis did many popular things such as their foreign policy.

Success of economic policies
- Nazi economic policy – attempted to deal with economic ills affecting Germany, especially unemployment.
- Nazis began a massive programme of public works; work of Hjalmar Schacht.
- Nazi policy towards farming, eg Reich Food Estate – details of various policies.
- Goring's policy of 'guns before butter'. Popular once foreign policy triumphs appeared to justify it.

Other factors
Social policies
- Creation of the volksgemeinschaft (national community).
- Nazi youth policy.
- Nazi education policy .
- Nazi policy towards the Jews – first isolate, then persecute and finally destroy.
- Nazi family policy – Kinder, Kirche, Kuche.
- Kraft durch Freude programme.
- A Concordat with the Catholic Church was reached; a Reichsbishop was appointed as head of the Protestant churches.

Success of foreign policy
- Nazi success in foreign policy attracted support among Germans; Rearmament, Rhineland, Anschluss.
- *'Much of Hitler's popularity after he came to power rested on his achievements in foreign policy'.* (Welch)

Establishment of a totalitarian state
- Political parties outlawed; non-Nazi members of the civil service were dismissed.
- Nazis never quite able to silence opposition to the regime.
- Speed of takeover of power, and ruthlessness of the regime made opposition largely ineffective.
- Anti-Nazi judges were dismissed and replaced with those favourable to the Nazis.
- Acts Hostile to the National Community (1935) — all-embracing law which allowed the Nazis to persecute opponents in a 'legal' way.

Fear and state terrorism
- The use of fear/terror through the Nazi police state; role of the Gestapo.
- Concentration camps set up; the use of the SS.

Crushing of opposition
- Opponents liable to severe penalties, as were their families.
- Opponents never able to establish a single organisation to channel their resistance — role of the Gestapo, paid informers.
- Opposition lacked cohesion and a national leader; also lacked armed supporters.
- Lack of cooperation between socialists and communists — role of Stalin considered.

Propaganda
- Use of Nuremburg Rallies.
- Use of radio.
- Cult of the leader: the Hitler myth.
- Use of the cinema: Triumph of the Will, the Eternal Jew, etc.
- Role of Goebbels.

Any other relevant factors.

Part E: Italy, 1815—1939

Candidates can be credited up to a maximum of 20 marks.

43. To what extent had nationalism grown in Italy by 1850?

Context
Support for Italian nationalism grew in the years before 1850. This was largely within the educated classes, although there was some general popular support as well. However, the forces that opposed nationalism, such as the Austrians, meant that a unified Italian state had not emerged by 1850.

Supporters of nationalism
Educated middle class
- Risorgimento saw 'patriotic literature' from novelists and poets including Pellico, and Leopardi. These inspired the educated middle class.
- Gioberti, Balbo and Mazzini promoted their ideas for a national state, this inspired nationalism amongst the middle classes.

Liberals
- Some liberals and business classes were keen to develop an economic state. Napoleon Bonaparte had built roads and encouraged closer trading. One system of weights, measures and currency appealed.

Popular sentiment
- French revolutionary ideals had inspired popular sentiment for a national Italian state.
- There was a growing desire for the creation of a national state amongst students; many joined Mazzini's 'Young Italy'.
- Operas by Verdi and Rossini inspired growing feelings of patriotism.
- The use of Tuscan as a 'national' language by Alfieri and Manzoni spread ideas of nationalism.
- Membership of secret societies such as the Carbonari grew. Members were willing to revolt and die for their beliefs which included desire for a national state.

Opponents of nationalism
- **Austria**
  Resentment against Austria and its restoration of influence in the Italian peninsula and their use of spies and censorship, helped increase support for the nationalist cause. However, any progress made by nationalists was firmly crushed by the Austrian army. Strength of the Quadrilateral. Austrians never left Italian soil. Carbonari revolts in Kingdom of Naples 1820 – 1821, Piedmont 1821, Modena and the Papal States 1831 all crushed by Austrian army. During 1848 – 1849 revolutions, Austrian army defeated Charles Albert twice — Custoza and Modena, retook Lombardy and destroyed the Republic of St Mark.
- **Italian princes and rulers**
  Individual rulers were opposed to nationalism and used censorship, police and spies as well as the Austrian army, to crush revolts in 1820–1821, 1830 and 1848–1849.
- **Attitude of the peasants**
  The mass of the population were illiterate and indifferent to politics and nationalist ideas. They did revolt during bad times as can be seen in 1848 — but their revolts were due to bad harvests and bad economic times and were not inspired by feelings of nationalism.
- **Position of the Papacy**
  Pope Pius IX. Nationalist movement had high hopes of New Pope Pius IX, initially thought of as a liberal and sympathetic to nationalist cause. Hopes, dashed when Pope Pius IX denounced the nationalist movement during 1848–49 revolutions.
- **Failures of 1848–1849 revolutions**
  These showed that nationalist leaders would not work together, nor did they seek foreign help thus hindering progress. Charles Albert's 'Italia farad a se' declared that Italy would do it alone — she did not. Lombardy and Venetia suspected Charles Albert's motives and were reluctant to work with him. Venetians put more faith in Manin.
  All progress was hampered when Pope Pius IX denounced nationalism.
  Charles Albert hated Mazzini and would not support the Roman Republic.
  Austrian military might based on the Quadrilateral defeated Charles Albert twice — at Custoza and Modena, retook Lombardy and destroyed the Republic of St Mark. The French crushed the Roman Republic.

Any other relevant factors.

Candidates can be credited up to a maximum of 20 marks.

44. How important was the appeal of fascism in Mussolini's achievement of power in Italy by 1925?

Context
Dissatisfaction with the post-war settlement meant that the weak democracy in Italy did not survive the rise of Mussolini's fascists. The weakness and divisions among the

democratic parties, allied with the strengths of the fascist movement led to its eventual achievement of power.

Appeal of the fascists

- They exploited weaknesses of other groups by excellent use of Mussolini's newspaper 'Il Popolo D'Italia'.
- The Fascio Italiano di Combattimento began as a movement not a political party and thus attracted a wide variety of support giving them an advantage over narrower rivals.
- By 1921 fascism was anti-communist, anti-trade union, anti-socialist and pro nationalism and thus became attractive to the middle and upper classes.
- Fascism became pro-conservative, appealed to family values, supported church and monarchy; promised to work within the accepted political system. This made fascism more respectable and appealing to both the monarchy and the papacy.
- Squadristi violence was directed against socialism so it gained the support of elites and middle classes.
- Violence showed fascism was strong and ruthless. It appealed to many ex-soldiers.
- Fascists promised strong government. This was attractive after a period of extreme instability.
- Fascists promised to make Italy respected as a nation and thus appealed to nationalists.
- Fascist policies were kept deliberately vague to attract support from different groups.

Other factors

Role of Mussolini

- Key role in selling the fascist message: Powerful orator—piazza politics
- He seized his opportunities. He changed political direction and copied D'Annunzio.
- He used propaganda and his newspaper effectively and had an ear for effective slogans.
- He dominated the fascist movement and kept the support of fascist extremists (Ras).
- He relied on strong nerves to seize power and to survive the Matteotti crisis.
- Mussolini manipulated his image, kept out of violence himself but exploited the violence of others.

Weaknesses of Italian governments

- Parliamentary government was weak — informal 'liberal' coalitions. Corruption was commonplace (trasformismo). Liberals were not a structured party. New parties formed: PSI (socialists), PPI (Catholic Popular Party) with wider support base threatening existing political system.
- WWI worsened the situation; wartime coalitions were very weak. 1918; universal male suffrage and 1919 Proportional Representation; relied on 'liberals' — unstable coalitions. Giolitti made an electoral pact with Mussolini (1921); fascists gained 35 seats then refused to support the government. Over the next 16 months, three ineffective coalition governments.
- Fascists threatened a 'March on Rome' — King refused to agree to martial law; Facta resigned; Mussolini was invited to form coalition. 1924 Acerbo Law.

Resentment against the Peace Settlement

- Large loss of life in frustrating campaigns in the Alps and the Carso led to expectation that these would be recognised in the peace settlement; Wilson's commitment to nationalist aims led to the creation of Yugoslavia and a frustration of Italian hopes of dominating the Adriatic.
- 'Mutilated victory' — Italian nationalists fuelled ideas that Italy had been betrayed by her government.

Role of the king

- The king gave into fascist pressure during the March on Rome. He failed to call Mussolini's bluff.
- After the Aventine Secession, the king was unwilling to dismiss Mussolini.

Economic difficulties

- WWI imposed serious strain on the Italian economy. The government took huge foreign loans and the National Debt was 85 billion lira by 1918. The Lira lost half of its value, devastating middle class savers. Inflation was rising; prices in 1918 were four times higher than 1914. This led to further major consequences:
  - no wage rises
  - food shortages
  - two million unemployed in 1919
  - firms collapsed as military orders ceased.

Social and economic divisions

- Membership of Trade unions and PSI rose — strikes, demonstrations, violence. 1919/20 'Biennio Rosso' in towns — general strike 1920; army mutiny; occupation of factories.
- Industrialists/middle classes were fearful of revolution.
- Governments failed to back the police so law and order broke down.
- In the countryside, there was seizure of common land — peasant ownership increased.

Weaknesses and mistakes of opponents

- D'Annunzio's seizure of Fiume was not stopped by the government.
- Government failed to get martial law to stop fascist threat. Some liberals supported the Acerbo Law.
- Socialist General Strike July 1922 – failed. Socialists' split weakened them; refused to join together to oppose fascism.
- Liberals fragmented into four factions grouped around former PMs. They were too weak to effectively resist. Hoped to tame fascists.
- PPI were divided over attitude to fascism — right wing supported fascism. Aventine Secession backfired; destroyed chance to remove Mussolini.

Any other relevant factors.

Candidates can be credited up to a maximum of 20 marks.

45. How important was the use of fear and intimidation in maintaining Fascist control over Italy between 1922 and 1939?

Context

Fascist government in Italy relied on a mixture of fear and general support. The fascist party developed a popular foreign policy and some domestic policies. However, this is balanced by the development of a police state and the banning of political opposition.

Fear and intimidation

- Mussolini favoured complete State authority with everything under his direct control. All Italians were expected to obey Mussolini and his Fascist Party.
- The squadristi were organised into the MVSN Milizia Voluntaria per la Sicurezza Nazionale, the armed local Fascist militia (Blackshirts). They terrorised the cities and provinces causing fear with tactics such as force-feeding with toads and castor oil.
- After 1925–6 around 10,000 non-fascists/opposition leaders were jailed by special tribunals.

- The Secret police, OVRA was established in 1927 and was led by Arturo Bocchini. Tactics included abduction and torture of opponents. 4,000 people were arrested by the OVRA and sent to prison.
- Penal colonies were established on remote Mediterranean islands such as Ponza and Lipari. Conditions for those sentenced to these prisons were primitive with little chance of escape.
- Opponents were exiled internally or driven into exile abroad.
- The death penalty was restored under Mussolini for serious offences, but by 1940 only ten people had been sentenced to death.

Other relevant factors
Establishment of the fascist state
- Nov/Dec 1922 — Mussolini was given emergency powers. Nationalists merged with PNF 1923. Mussolini created MSVN (fascist militia) — gave him support if the army turned against him — and Fascist Grand Council — a rival Cabinet. These two bodies made Mussolini's position stronger and opposition within PNF weaker. The establishment of a dictatorship began.
- 1926 — opposition parties were banned. A one party state was created.
- 1928 — universal suffrage abolished.
- 1929 — all Fascist Parliament elected.

Crushing of opposition
- Liberals had divided into four factions so were weakened.
- The Left had divided into three — original PSI, reformist PSU and Communists — they failed to work together against fascists.
- Pope forced Sturzo to resign and so PPI (Catholic Popular Party) was weakened and it split.
- Acerbo Law passed. 1924 elections — fascists won 66% of the vote.
- Opposition parties failed to take advantage of the Matteotti crisis. By walking out of the Chamber of Deputies (Aventine Secession) they gave up the chance to overthrow Mussolini; they remained divided - the Pope refused to sanction an alliance between PPI and the socialists. The king chose not to dismiss Mussolini.
- Communists and socialists did set up organisations in exile but did not work together. Communist cells in northern cities did produce some anti-fascist leaflets but they suffered frequent raids by OVRA.
- PPI opposition floundered with the closer relationship between Church and State (Lateran Pacts).

Social controls
- Workers were controlled through 22 corporations, set up in 1934; overseen by National Council of Corporations, chaired by Mussolini.
- Corporations provided accident, health and unemployment insurance for workers, but forbade strikes and lock-outs.
- There were some illegal strikes in 1930s and anti-fascist demonstrations in 1933 but these were limited.
- The majority of Italians got on with their own lives conforming as long as all was going well. Middle classes/elites supported fascism as it protected them from communism.
- Youth knew no alternative to fascism, were educated as fascists and this strengthened the regime. Youth movements provided sporting opportunities, competitions, rallies, camps, parades and propaganda lectures — 60% membership in the north.

Propaganda
- Press, radio and cinema were all controlled.
- Mussolini was highly promoted as a 'saviour' sent by God to help Italy — heir to Caesar, world statesman, supreme patriot, a great thinker who worked 20 hours a day, a man of action, incorruptible.

Foreign policy
- Mussolini was initially extremely popular, as evidenced by huge crowds who turned out to hear him speak.
- Foreign policy successes in the 1920s, such as the Corfu Incident, made him extremely popular. He was also able to mobilise public opinion very successfully for the invasion of Abyssinia.
- Mussolini's role in the Munich Conference of 1938 was his last great foreign policy triumph.
- As Mussolini got more closely involved with Hitler his popularity lessened. His intervention in Spain proved a huge drain on Italy's resources. The invasion of Albania was a fiasco. The Fascist Grand Council removed him in 1943.

Relations with the Papacy
- Lateran treaties/Concordat with Papacy enabled acceptance of regime by the Catholic majority.
- Many Catholics supported Mussolini's promotion of 'family values'.

Economic and social policies.
- Fascists tried to develop the Italian economy in a series of propaganda-backed initiatives, eg the 'Battle for Grain'. While superficially successful, they did tend to divert resources from other areas.
- Development of transport infrastructure, with building of autotrade and redevelopment of major railway terminals, eg Milan
- One major success was the crushing of organized crime. Most Mafia leaders were in prison by 1939.
- Dopolavoro had 3.8 million members by 1939. Gave education and skills training; sports provision, day-trips, holidays, financial assistance and cheap rail fares. This diverted attention from social/economic problems and was the fascist state's most popular institution.

Any other relevant factors.

Part F: Russia, 1881—1921

Candidates can be credited up to a maximum of 20 marks.

46. How important was working class discontent in causing the 1905 revolution in Russia?

Context
By 1905, Russia's problems had led to open opposition to the tsarist state. Poor military performance in the war with Japan exposed the social, economic and political weaknesses of the state.

Discontent of working class
- At the start of the 1900s there was industrial recession which caused a lot of hardship for the working class.
- The working class's complaints were long hours, low pay, poor conditions, the desire for a constitutional government and an end to the war with Japan.
- There was a wave of strikes in January 1905 with nearly half a million people on strike (10 times the number in the previous decade).
- In October there were two and half million people on strike as well as demonstrations carried out.
- Soviets were speaking for the workers and expressing political demands.

Other Factors

Discontent with repressive government and its policies

- There was discontent amongst various factions in Russian society.
- The middle class and some of the gentry were unhappy with the government at the time.
- The middle class were aggrieved at having no participation in government, and angry at the incompetence of the government during the war with Japan.
- There was propaganda from middle class groups, Zemstva called for change, the Radical Union of Unions was formed to combine professional groups.
- Students rioted, and carried out assassinations.
- The gentry tried to convince the Tsar to make minor concessions.
- Political groups did not really play a role although they encouraged peasant unrest, and strikes in the urban areas.
- The Mensheviks had influence in the soviets and the Bolsheviks were involved in the Moscow Rising.
- Russification: The national minorities were aggrieved at the lack of respect for their culture language and religion, and the imposition of the Russian language.
- The national minorities harboured a great desire for independence or at least greater autonomy and began to assert themselves, such as Georgia which declared its independence.

Economic problems

- Worsening economic conditions such as famines in 1897, 1898 and 1901 had led to shortage and distress in the countryside. Urban workers' conditions and pay also dreadful.
- Economic recession between 1899 and 1903 had also led to growing unemployment throughout the Empire.

Discontent amongst the peasants

- The peasants had several grievances such as redemption payments, high taxes, land hunger and poverty.
- There was a wave of unrest in 1902 and 1903, which had gradually increased by 1905. There were various protests like timber cutting, seizure of lords' lands, labour and rent strikes, attacks on landlords grain stocks, landlords' estates seized and divided up.
- There were claims that peasants should boycott paying taxes, redemption payments and refuse to be conscripted to the army.

War with Japan

- The war with Japan was a failure and humiliation for the country and moreover this was compounded by the heavy losses suffered by the Russian army.
- The war was initially to distract the public from domestic troubles by rallying patriotism.
- The incompetence of the government during the war made social unrest worse rather than dampening it.
- Troops suffered from low morale after the defeat and complained about poor pay and conditions.
- There were some sporadic but uncoordinated revolts although nothing too major.
- There were mutinies by troops waiting to return from the war and on the Trans Siberian Railway.
- In June there was the Potemkin mutiny although the planned general mutiny did not follow.
- Generally though most of the troops remained loyal (unlike 1917).

Bloody Sunday

- On 22nd Jan 1905 Father Gapon, an Orthodox priest, attempted to lead a peaceful march of workers and their families to the Winter Palace to deliver an petition asking the Tsar to improve the conditions of the workers.
- Marchers were fired on and killed by troops.
- Many of the people saw this as a brutal massacre by the Tsar and his troops.
- Bloody Sunday greatly damaged the traditional image of the Tsar as the 'Little Father', the Guardian of the Russian people.
- Reaction to Bloody Sunday was strong and was nationwide with disorder strikes in urban areas, terrorism against government officials and landlords, much of which was organised by the SRs.
- The situation was made worse by the defeat to Japan in 1905.
- There was the assassination of government minister Plehve.

Any other relevant factors.

Candidates can be credited up to a maximum of 20 marks.

47. To what extent did the Bolsheviks gain power due to the weaknesses of the Provisional Government?

Context

The Provisional Government made a serious error in keeping Russia in the First World War. Its lack of popular support led to a power vacuum which the Bolsheviks exploited.

Weaknesses of the Provisional Government

- The Provisional Government was an unelected government; it was a self-appointed body and had no right to exercise authority, which led it into conflict with those bodies that emerged with perceived popular legitimacy.
- The Provisional Government gave in to the pressure of the army and from the Allies to keep Russia in the war.
- Remaining in the war helped cause the October Revolution and helped destroy the Provisional Government as the misery it caused continued for people in Russia.
- General Kornilov, a right wing general, proposed to replace the Provisional Government with a military dictatorship and sent troops to Petrograd.
- Kerensky appealed to the Petrograd Soviet for help and the Bolsheviks were amongst those who were helped.
- Some Bolsheviks were armed and released from prison to help put down the attempted coup.

Other Factors

Appeal of the Bolsheviks

- Lenin returned to Russia announcing of the April Theses, with slogans such as 'Peace, Land and Bread' and 'All Power to the Soviets' which were persuasive.
- Lenin talked of further revolution to overthrow the Provisional Government and his slogans identified the key weaknesses of the Provisional Government.
- The Bolsheviks kept attending the Petrograd Soviet when most of the others stopped doing so and this gave them control of the Soviet, which they could then use against the Provisional Government.
- The Bolsheviks did not return their weapons to the Provisional Government after they defeated Kornilov.
- Bolsheviks were able to act as protectors of Petrograd.
- Dual power — the role of the Petrograd Soviet.
- The old Petrograd Soviet re-emerged and ran Petrograd.
- The Petrograd Soviet undermined the authority of the Provisional Government especially when relations between the two worsened.

- Order No. 1 of the Petrograd Soviet weakened the authority of the Provisional Government as soldiers were not to obey orders of the Provisional Government that contradicted those of the Petrograd Soviet.

Economic problems

- The workers were restless as they were starving due to food shortages caused by the war.
- The shortage of fuel caused lack of heating for the workers in their living conditions.
- The shortage of food and supplies made the workers unhappy and restless.
- The Bolsheviks' slogans appealed to them such as the workers' control of industry.

The Land Issue

- All over Russia peasants were seizing nobles' land and wanted the Provisional Government to legitimise this.
- The failure of the Provisional Government to recognise the peasants' claims eroded the confidence in the Provisional Government.
- Food shortages caused discontent, and they were caught up by revolutionary slogans such as 'Peace, Land And Bread'.

The July Days

- The Bolsheviks staged an attempt to seize power, rising in support of the Kronstadt sailors who were in revolt. The revolt was easily crushed by the Provisional Government but showed increasing opposition to the Provisional Government, especially from the forces.
- The revolt also showed that the Provisional Government was still reasonably strong and able to crush opposition such as the Bolsheviks who now appeared to be weakened.

Any other relevant factors.

Candidates can be credited up to a maximum of 20 marks

48. How important was the use of terror by the Reds in allowing them to win the Civil War?

Context

The numerous groups who opposed the Reds tried to defeat them militarily. However, a lack of unified purpose, plus geographic and logistical advantages for the Reds led to a Civil War.

Terror (Cheka)

- The Cheka was set up to eradicate any opposition to the Reds.
- There was no need for proof of guilt for punishment to be exacted.
- There was persecution of individual people who opposed the Reds as well as whole groups of people, which helped to reduce opposition due to fear, or simply eradicate opposition.
- The Cheka group carried out severe repression.
- Some of the first victims of the Cheka were leaders of other political parties.
- 140,000 were executed by 1922 when Lenin was happy that all opposition had been suppressed.

Other Factors

Organisation of the Red Army

- The Red Army was better organized than the White Army and better equipped, and therefore able to crush any opposition from the White forces.
- Use of ex-officers from the old Imperial Army.
- Reintroduction of rank and discipline.
- Role of Commissars.

Role of Trotsky

- Trotsky had a completely free hand in military matters.
- HQ was a heavily armed train, which he used to travel around the country.
- He supervised the formation of the Red Army, which became a formidable fighting force of three million men.
- He recruited ex Tsar army officers and used political commissars to watch over them, thus ensuring experienced officers but no political recalcitrance.
- He used conscription to gain troops and would shoot any deserters.
- Trotsky helped provide an army with great belief in what it was fighting for, which the Whites did not have.

Disunity among the Whites

- The Whites were an uncoordinated series of groups whose morale was low.
- The Whites were a collection of socialists, liberals, moderates etc. who all wanted different things and often fought amongst themselves due to their political differences. All of the Whites shared a hatred of communism but other than this they lacked a common purpose.
- No White leader of any measure emerged to unite and lead the White forces whereas the Reds had Trotsky and Lenin.

Superior Red resources

- Once the Reds had established defence of their lines they were able to repel and exhaust the attacks by the Whites until they scattered or surrendered.
- By having all of their land together it was easier for the Reds to defend.
- With the major industrial centres in their land (Moscow and Petrograd) the Reds had access to factories to supply weapons etc. and swiftly due to their control of the railways. Control of the railways meant they could transport troop supplies quickly and efficiently and in large numbers to the critical areas of defence or attack.
- The decisive battles between the Reds and Whites were near railheads.
- The Reds were in control of a concentrated area of western Russia, which they could successfully defend due to the maintenance of their communication and supply lines.
- Having the two major cities of Moscow and Petrograd in their possession meant that the Reds had hold of the industrial centres of Russia as well as the administrative centres.
- Having the two major cities gave the Reds munitions and supplies that the Whites were unable therefore to obtain.

Foreign intervention

- The Bolsheviks were able to claim that the foreign 'invaders' were imperialists who were trying to overthrow the revolution and invade Russia.
- The Reds were able to stand as champions of the Russian nation from foreign invasion.
- The help received by the Whites from foreign powers was not as great as was hoped for.
- The Foreign Powers did not provide many men due to the First World War just finishing and their help was restricted to money and arms.

Propaganda

- The Whites were unable to take advantage of the brutality of the Reds to win support as they often carried out similar atrocities.
- The Whites were unable to present themselves as a better alternative to the Reds due to their brutality.

- The Reds kept pointing out that all of the land that the peasants had seized in the 1917 Revolution would be lost if the Whites won. This fear prevented the peasants from supporting the Whites.

Leadership of Lenin

- Introduction of War Communism.
- By forcing the peasants to sell their grain to the Reds for a fixed price, the Reds were able to ensure that their troops were well supplied and well fed.
- The White troops were not as well supplied and fed as the Red troops.
- Skilled delegation and ruthlessness.

Any other relevant factors.

Part G: USA, 1918—1968

Candidates can be credited up to a maximum of 20 marks.

49. **How important were the activities of the Ku Klux Klan as an obstacle to the achievement of civil rights for black people before 1941?**

Context

Within the USA, changing attitudes towards immigration had been growing during the 19th and early 20th centuries. Many Americans felt their way of life was being challenged by immigrants from Southern and Eastern Europe.

Activities of the Ku Klux Klan

- Founded in 1860s to prevent former slaves achieving equal rights.
- Suppressed by 1872, but in the 1920s there was a resurgence.
- Black population in the South were terrified to campaign for civil rights by actions of the KKK
- By 1925 it had three million members, including the police, judges and politicians.
- Secret organisation with powerful members.
- 1923 — Hiram Wesley Evans became the Klan's leader.
- Horrific methods: included beatings, torture and lynching.
- Roosevelt refused to support a federal bill to outlaw lynching in his New Deal in 1930s — feared loss of Democrat support in South.
- Activities took place at night — men in white robes, guns, torches, burning crosses.
- The 'second' Klan grew most rapidly in urbanizing cities which had high growth rates between 1910 and 1930, such as Detroit, Memphis, Dayton, Atlanta, Dallas, and Houston.
- Klan membership in Alabama dropped to less than 6,000 by 1930. Small independent units continued to be active in places like Birmingham, where in the late 1940s, members launched a reign of terror by bombing the homes of upwardly mobile African Americans.
- However, their activities in the 1940s led to continued migration of black Americans from the South to the North.

Other Factors

Legal impediments

- 'Jim Crow laws' — separate education, transport, toilets etc. — passed in Southern states after the Civil War.
- 'Separate but Equal' Supreme Court Decision in 1896, when Homer Plessey tested their legality.
- Attitudes of Presidents, eg Wilson — 'Segregation is not humiliating and is a benefit for you black gentlemen'.

Lack of political influence

- 1890s: loopholes in the interpretation of the 15th Amendment were exploited so that states could impose voting qualifications.
- 1898 case of Mississippi v Williams — voters must understand the American Constitution.
- Grandfather Clause: impediment to black people voting.
- Most black people in the South were sharecroppers; they did not own land and some states identified ownership of property as a voting qualification.
- Therefore black people could not vote, particularly in the South, and could not elect anyone who would oppose the Jim Crow laws.

Divisions in the black community

- Booker T Washington, accomodationist philosophy, regarded as an 'Uncle Tom' by many.
- In contrast, W. E. B. De Bois founded the NAACP — a national organization whose main aim was to oppose discrimination through legal action. In 1919 he launched a campaign against lynching, but it failed to attract most black people and was dominated by white people and well-off black people.
- Marcus Garvey and Black Pride — he founded the UNIA (Universal Negro Improvement Association) which aimed to get blacks to 'take Africa, organise it, develop it, arm it, and make it the defender of Negroes the world over'.

Popular prejudice

- After the institution of slavery the status of Africans was stigmatised, and this stigma was the basis for the anti-African racism that persisted.
- The relocation of millions of African Americans from their roots in the Southern states to the industrial centres of the North after World War I, particularly in cities such as Boston, Chicago, and New York (Harlem). In Northern cities, racial tensions exploded, most violently in Chicago, and lynching, usually racially motivated, increased dramatically in the 1920s.

Any other relevant factors.

Candidates can be credited up to a maximum of 20 marks

50. **How important was the emergence of effective black leaders in the growing demand for civil rights between 1945 and 1968?**

Context

Continuing social and economic inequalities and racism led to growing demands for change from the black community. Growing demands for civil rights were furthered by the development of effective political organisations and leadership.

The emergence of effective black leaders

- Martin Luther King — inspirational. Linked with the SCLC. Peaceful non-violence and effective use of the media.
- Malcolm X — inspirational, but more confrontational. Articulate voice of the Nation of Islam.
- Stokely Carmichael — Black power and rejection of much on MLK's non-violent approach. A direct ideas descendant of Marcus Garvey.
- All leaders attracted media coverage, large followings and divided opinion across the USA.
- Black Panthers attracted attention but lost support because of their confrontational tactics.
- Other leaders and organisations were eclipsed by media focus on main personalities.

Other factors
Effective black organisations formed
- 1957 — Martin Luther King and other black clergy formed the Southern Christian Leadership Conference (SCLC) to coordinate the work of civil rights groups.
- King urged African Americans to use peaceful methods.
- 1960 — a group of black and white college students organised the Non-violent Coordinating Committee (SNCC) to help the civil rights movement.
- They joined with young people from the SCLC, CORE and NAACP in staging sit-ins, boycotts, marches and freedom rides.
- Combined efforts of the civil rights groups ended discrimination in many public places including restaurants, hotels, and theatres.

Continuing racial discrimination pushed many black Americans to demand civil rights
- The experience of war emphasised freedom, democracy and human rights, yet in the USA Jim Crow laws still existed and lynching went unpunished.
- The Emmet Till murder trial and its publicity.
- Education: 1954 — Brown v Board of Education of Topeka; 1957 — Little Rock Central High School.
- Transport: 1955 Rosa Parks and the Montgomery Bus Boycott.

Influence of the Second World War
- Black soldiers talked about 'the Double-V-Campaign': Victory in the war and victory for civil rights at home.
- A. Philip Randolph is credited with highlighting the problems faced by black Americans during World War Two.
- Planned March on Washington in 1941 to protest against racial discrimination.
- Roosevelt's response — Executive order 8802.
- Roosevelt also established the Fair Employment Practices Committee to investigate incidents of discrimination.
- Creation of the Congress of Racial Equality (CORE) in 1942.
- Beginning of a mass movement for civil rights.

Any other relevant factors.

*Candidates can be credited **up to a maximum of 20 marks**.*

51. To what extent did the civil rights campaigns of the 1950s and 1960s result in significant improvements in the lives of black Americans?

Context
The civil rights campaigns led to many developments that seemed to offer greater equality for the Black American community. However, social, political and economic inequalities remained.

Aims of Civil Rights Movement
- Were mainly pacifist and intended to bring civil rights and equality in law to all non-white Americans.
- More radical segregationist aims of black radical movements.

Role of NAACP
- Work of NAACP in the Brown v Topeka Board of Education, 1954.
- Work of NAACP in the Montgomery Bus Boycott, 1955.

Role of Congress of Racial Equality (CORE)
- Organised sit-ins during 1961 and freedom rides.
- Helped organise march on Washington.
- Instrumental in setting up Freedom Schools in Mississippi.

Role of SCLC and Martin Luther King
- Emergence of Martin Luther King and the SCLC.
- Little Rock, Arkansas — desegregation following national publicity.
- Non-violent protest as exemplified by sit-ins and freedom rides.
- Birmingham, Alabama 1963: use of water cannon: Reaction of Kennedy.
- March on Washington, August 1963 — massive publicity.
- Martin Luther King believed that the Civil Rights Act of 1964 'gave Negroes some part of their rightful dignity, but without the vote it was dignity without strength'.
- March 1965, King led a march from Selma to Birmingham, Alabama, to publicise the way in which the authorities made it difficult for black Americans to vote easily.

Changes in federal policy
- Use of executive orders: Truman used them to make black appointments, order equality of treatment in the armed services: Kennedy signed 1962 executive order outlawing racial discrimination in public housing, etc.
- Eisenhower sent in army troops and National Guardsmen to protect nine African-American students enrolled in Central High School: Kennedy sent troops to Oxford, Mississippi to protect black student: James Meredith.
- Johnson and the 1964 Civil Rights Act banning racial discrimination in any public place, Voting Rights Act of 1965: by end of 1965 over 250,000 blacks were newly registered to vote, Affirmative Action, etc.

Social, economic and political changes
- Civil Rights Acts of 1964 and 1965 irrelevant to the cities of the North.
- Economic issues more important in the North.
- Watts riots and the split in the Civil Rights Movement.
- King and the failure in Chicago.
- Urban poverty and de facto segregation was still common in urban centres — failure of King's campaign to attack poverty.

Rise of black radical movements
- Stokely Carmichael and Black Power.
- Malcolm X publicised the increasing urban problems within the ghettos of America.
- The Black Panthers were involved in self-help schemes throughout poor cities.
- Kerner commission in 1968 recognised US society was still divided.

Any other relevant factors.

Part H: Appeasement and the Road to War, to 1939

*Candidates can be credited **up to a maximum of 20 marks**.*

52. To what extent did fascist powers use diplomacy to achieve their aims?

Context
By its nature, the fascism of Hitler and Mussolini was expansionist. However, the methods used to fulfil their aims varied owing to the circumstances faced by the fascist powers.

Fascist diplomacy as a means of achieving aims
- Aims can be generally accepted as the destruction of Versailles, the weakening of democracies, the expansion of fascist powers and countering communism.

- Diplomacy and the protestation of 'peaceful' intentions and 'reasonable' demands.
- Appeals to sense of international equality and fairness and the righting of past wrongs, eg Versailles.
- Withdrawal from League and Disarmament Conference.
- Anglo-German Naval Treaty 1935 — Germany allowed to expand its navy. Versailles ignored in favour of bi-lateral agreements. A gain for Germany.
- Prior to the Remilitarisation of the Rhineland Hitler made an offer of a 25-year peace promise. Diplomacy used to distract and delay reaction to Nazi action.

Other reasons

Economic reasons

- Use of economic influence and pressure, eg on south-eastern European states.
- Aid supplied to Franco (Spain) was tactically important to Hitler. Not only for testing weapons but also for access to Spanish minerals.

Pacts and alliances

- The German—Polish Non-Aggression Pact between Nazi Germany and Poland signed on January 26, 1934 — normalised relations between Poland and Germany, and promised peace for 10 years. Germany gained respectability and calmed international fears.
- Rome—Berlin axis — treaty of friendship signed between Italy and Germany on 25 October 1936.
- Pact of Steel — an agreement between Italy and Germany signed on May 22, 1939 for immediate aid and military support in the event of war.
- Anti-Comintern Pact between Nazi-Germany and Japan on November 25th, 1936. The pact directed against the Communist International (Comintern) but was specifically directed against the Soviet Union. In 1937 Italy joined the Pact Munich Agreement — negotiations led to Hitler gaining Sudetenland and weakening Czechoslovakia.
- Nazi Soviet Non-Aggression Pact in August 1939 — both Hitler and Stalin bought time for themselves. For Hitler it seemed war in Europe over Poland was unlikely. Poland was doomed. Britain had lost the possibility of alliance with Russia.

Rearmament

- Open German rearmament from 1935.
- The speed and scale of rearmament, including conscription.
- The emphasis on air power and the growing threat from the air.
- By 1939, Hitler had an army of nearly 1 million men, over 8,000 aircraft and 95 warships.
- Mussolini embarked on a rearmament program to protect Italy from worldwide depression. His building of a modern navy seriously threatened British domination of the Mediterranean as a result.

Military threat and force

- Italy's naval ambitions in the Mediterranean — 'Mare Nostrum'.
- Italian invasion of Abyssinia — provocation, methods, and relatively poor performance against very poorly equipped enemy.
- German remilitarisation of the Rhineland — Hitler's gamble and timing, his generals' opposition, lack of Allied resistance.
- Spanish Civil War — aid to Nationalists, testing weapons and tactics, aerial bombing of Guernica.

- Anschluss — attempted coup 1934; relations with Schuschnigg; invasion itself relatively botched militarily; popularity of Anschluss in Austria.
- Czechoslovakia — threats of 1938; invasion of March 1939.
- Italian invasion of Albania — relatively easy annexation of a client state.
- Poland — escalating demands; provocation, invasion.
- The extent to which it was the threat of military force which was used rather than military force itself – e.g. Czechoslovakia in 1938; and the extent to which military force itself was effective and/or relied on an element of bluff — eg Rhineland.

Any other relevant factors

Candidates can be credited up to a maximum of 20 marks.

53. 'The Munich Agreement of 1938 was a reasonable settlement under the circumstances.' How valid is this view?

Context

In 1938 Hitler threatened invasion to 'protect' the 'persecuted' German minority of Czechoslovakia from Czech aggression. Neville Chamberlain flew out three times to meet Hitler to discuss the crisis, finally at a four-power conference in Munich, conceding the Sudetenland for 'peace in our time'.

Munich reasonable under circumstances

- Czechoslovakian defences were effectively outflanked anyway following the Anschluss.
- Britain and France were not in a position to prevent German attack on Czechoslovakia in terms of difficulties of getting assistance to Czechoslovakia.
- British public opinion was reluctant to risk war over mainly German-speaking Sudetenland.
- Military unpreparedness for wider war — especially Britain's air defences.
- Lack of alternative, unified international response to Hitler's threats: failure of League of Nations in earlier crises
- French doubts over commitments to Czechoslovakia.
- US isolationism.
- British suspicion of Soviet Russia.
- Strong reservations of rest of the British Empire and Dominions concerning support for Britain in event of war.
- Attitudes of Poland and Hungary who were willing to benefit from the dismemberment of Czechoslovakia.
- Munich bought another year for rearmament which Britain put to good use.
- Views of individuals, politicians and media at this time.

Munich not reasonable

- A humiliating surrender to Hitler's threats.
- Another breach in the post-WW1 settlement.
- A betrayal of Czechoslovakia and democracy.
- Czechoslovakia wide open to further German aggression as happened in March 1939.
- Further augmentation of German manpower and resources.
- Furtherance of Hitler's influence and ambitions in Eastern Europe.
- Further alienation of Soviet Union.
- Poland left further exposed.
- A British, French, Soviet agreement could have been a more effective alternative.
- Views of individuals, politicians and media at this time.

Any other relevant factors.

*Candidates can be credited **up to a maximum of 20 marks.***

54. To what extent did the occupation of Czechoslovakia in March 1939 lead to the outbreak of World War Two six months later?

Context

The Nazi occupation of the Sudentenland could be justified in the eyes of Appeasers as Hitler was absorbing fellow Germans into Greater Germany. However, subsequent actions by the Nazis could not be supported in this way and any illusion of justified grievances evaporated at Hitler made demands on powers such as Poland.

The occupation of Bohemia and the collapse of Czechoslovakia

- British and French realisation, after Hitler's breaking of Munich Agreement and invasion of Czechoslovakia in March 1939, that Hitler's word was worthless and that his aims went beyond the incorporation of ex-German territories and ethnic Germans within the Reich.
- Promises of support to Poland and Rumania.
- British public acceptance that all attempts to maintain peace had been exhausted.
- Prime Minister Chamberlain felt betrayed by the Nazi seizure of Czechoslovakia, realised his policy of appeasement towards Hitler had failed, and began to take a much harder line against the Nazis.

Other factors

British abandonment of the policy of appeasement

- Events in Bohemia and Moravia consolidated growing concerns in Britain.
- Czechoslovakia did not concern most people until the middle of September 1938, when they began to object to a small democratic state being bullied. However, most of the press and population went along with it, although the level of popular opposition was often underestimated.
- German annexation of Memel (largely German population, but in Lithuania) further showed Hitler's bad faith.
- Actions convinced British government of growing German threat in south-eastern Europe.
- Guarantees to Poland and promised action in the event of threats to Polish independence.

Importance of Nazi–Soviet Pact

- Pact — diplomatic, economic, military co-operation; division of Poland.
- Unexpected — Hitler and Stalin's motives.
- Put an end to British–French talks with Russia on guarantees to Poland.
- Hitler was freed from the threat of Soviet intervention and war on two fronts.
- Hitler's belief that Britain and France would not go to war over Poland without Russian assistance.
- Hitler now felt free to attack Poland.
- But, given Hitler's consistent long-term foreign policy aims on the destruction of the Versailles settlement and lebensraum in the east, the Nazi–Soviet Pact could be seen more as a factor influencing the timing of the outbreak of war rather than as one of its underlying causes.
- Hitler's long-term aims for destruction of the Soviet state and conquest of Russian resources — lebensraum.
- Hitler's need for new territory and resources to sustain Germany's militarised economy.
- Hitler's belief that British and French were 'worms' who would not turn from previous policy of appeasement and avoidance of war at all costs.

- Hitler's belief that the longer war was delayed the more the balance of military and economic advantage would shift against Germany.

British diplomacy and relations with the Soviet Union

- Stalin knew that Hitler's ultimate aim was to attack Russia.
- Lord Halifax, the British Foreign Secretary, was invited by Stalin to go to Russia to discuss an alliance against Germany.
- Britain refused as they feared Russian Communism, and they believed that the Russian army was too weak to be of any use against Hitler.
- In August 1939, with war in Poland looming, the British and French eventually sent a military mission to discuss an alliance with Russia. Owing to travel difficulties it took five days to reach Leningrad.
- The Russians asked if they could send troops into Poland if Hitler invaded. The British refused, knowing that the Poles would not want this. The talks broke down.
- This merely confirmed Stalin's suspicions regarding the British. He felt they could not be trusted, especially after the Munich agreement, and they would leave Russia to fight Germany alone. This led directly to opening talks with the Nazis who seemed to be taking the Germans seriously by sending Foreign Minister von Ribbentrop and offering peace and land.

The position of France

- France had signed an agreement with Czechoslovakia offering support if the country was attacked. However, Hitler could all but guarantee that in 1938, the French would do nothing as their foreign policy was closely tied to the British.
- French military, and particularly their airforce, had been allowed to decline in years after 1919.
- After Munich, the French were more aggressive towards dictators and in 1939 were keen on a military alliance with the Soviet Union, however, despite different emphasis on tactics they were tied to the British and their actions.

Developing crisis over Poland

- Hitler's long-term aims for the destruction of Versailles, including regaining of Danzig and Polish Corridor.
- British and French decision to stick to their guarantees to Poland.

Invasion of Poland

- On 1 September 1939, Hitler and the Nazis faked a Polish attack on a minor German radio station in order to justify a German invasion of Poland. An hour later Hitler declared war on Poland stating one of his reasons for the invasion was because of 'the attack by regular Polish troops on the Gleiwitz transmitter.'
- France and Britain had a defensive pact with Poland. This forced France and Britain to declare war on Germany, which they did on September 3.

Any other relevant factors.

Part I: The Cold War, 1945–1989

*Candidates can be credited **up to a maximum of 20 marks.***

55. To what extent did the Soviet Union control Eastern Europe up to 1961?

Context

Although Soviet motives in creating a buffer zone of states with sympathetic pro-Stalinist governments made sense to the Russian, many of those in the satellite states did not see it that way. Resentment within the satellite states grew, especially when the standard of living did not rise. The death of Stalin seemed to offer an opportunity for greater freedom.

The international context

- 1955 — emergence of Nikita Khrushchev as leader on death of Stalin. He encouraged criticism of Stalin and seemed to offer hope for greater political and economic freedom across the Eastern European satellite states.
- Speech to 20th Party Congress, February 1956: Khrushchev attacked Stalin for promoting a cult of personality and for his use of purges and persecution to reinforce his dictatorship. Policy of de-Stalinisation.
- Development of policy of peaceful co-existence to appeal to the West.
- Development of policy of different roads to socialism to appeal to satellite states in Eastern Europe who were becoming restless.

Demands for change and reaction: Poland (1956)

- Riots sparked off by economic grievances developed into demands for political change in Poland.
- On the death of Stalinist leader Boleslaw Bierut in 1956 he was replaced by Wladyslaw Gromulka, a former victim of Stalinism which initially worried the Soviets.
- Poles announced their own road to socialism and introduced extensive reforms.
- Release of political prisoners (and Cardinal Wyszynski, Archbishop of Warsaw); collective farms broken up into private holdings; private shops allowed to open, greater freedom to factory managers.
- Relatively free elections held in 1957 which returned a Communist majority of 18.
- No Soviet intervention despite concerns.
- Gromulka pushed change only so far. Poland remained in the Warsaw Pact as a part of the important 'buffer zone'. Political freedoms were very limited indeed. Poland was a loyal supporter of the Soviet Union until the 1980s and the emergence of the Solidarity Movement.

Demands for change and reaction: Hungary (1956)

- Hungarians had similar complaints: lack of political freedom, economic problems and poor standard of living.
- Encouraged by Polish success, criticism of the Stalinist regime of Mátyás Rákosi grew and he was removed by Khrushchev.
- Popular upsurge of support for change in Budapest led to a new Hungarian government led by Imre Nagy, who promised genuine reform and change.
- Nagy government planned multi-party elections, political freedoms, the withdrawal of Hungary from the Warsaw Pact and demands for the withdrawal of Soviet forces.
- Nagy went too far. The Soviet Union could not see this challenge to the political supremacy of the Communist Party and the breakup of their carefully constructed buffer zone. They intervened and crushed the rising brutally.
- Successful intervention, but lingering resentment from mass of Hungarian people, through some economic flexibility allowed the new regime of Janos Kadar to improve economic performance and living standards.

Demands for change and reaction: Berlin (1961)

- Problem of Berlin — a divided city in a divided nation.
- Lack of formal boundaries in Berlin allowed East Berliners and East Germans to freely enter the West which they did owing to the lack of political freedom, economic development and poor living standards in the East.
- Many of those fleeing (2.8 million between 1949 and 1961) were skilled and young, just the people the communist East needed to retain. This was embarrassing for the East as it showed that communism was not the superior system it was claimed to be.

- Concerns of Ulbricht and Khrushchev: attempts to encourage the Western forces to leave Berlin by bluster and threat from 1958 failed.
- Kennedy of America spoke about not letting the Communists drive them out of Berlin. Resultant increase in tension could not be allowed to continue.
- Building of barriers: barbed wire then stone in August 1961 to stem the flood from East to West.
- Success in that it reduced the threat of war and the exodus to the West from the East to a trickle.
- Frustration of many in East Germany. Propaganda gift for the US and allies.

Military and ideological factors

- Buffer zone could not be broken up as provided military defence for Soviet Union.
- Use of force and Red Army to enforce control in late 40s and early 50s.
- Need to ensure success of communism hence policy.

Domestic pressures

- Intention to stop any further suffering of Soviet Union in aftermath of WW2 made leadership very touchy to change.
- Some economic freedoms were allowed, but at the expense of political freedoms.
- Need to stop spread of demands for change.

Any other relevant factors.

Candidates can be credited up to a maximum of 20 marks.

56. To what extent were the superpowers' attempts to manage the Cold War between 1962 and 1985 prompted by the economic cost of the arms race?

Context

Events during the Cuban Missile crisis led to a more conciliatory relationship between the USSR and USA. Each side also had its own reasons for this. The USSR wished to restructure its economic from weapons production and heavy industry to consumer goods. The USA felt that there were other ways to contain communism and wished for more engagement in the context of their involvement in Vietnam.

Economic cost of the arms race

- Developments in technology raised the costs of the arms race.
- The development of Anti-Ballistic Missile technology and costs of war led to SALT 1, and the ABM treaty.
- Limiting MIRV and intermediate missile technology led to SALT 2.
- The cost of 'Star Wars' technology also encouraged the Soviet Union to seek better relations.
- Khrushchev's desire for better relations between the superpowers in the 50s and 60s was, in part, about freeing up resources for economic development in the USSR. He hoped this would show the superiority of the Soviet system.
- Gorbachev wanted to improve the lives of ordinary Russians and part of this was by reducing the huge defence budget, eg Intermediate Nuclear Forces Treaty, December 1987.

Other factors

Mutually Assured Destruction

- The development of vast arsenals of nuclear weapons from 1945 by both superpowers as a deterrent to the other side; a military attack would result in horrific retaliation.
- So many nuclear weapons were built to ensure that not all were destroyed even after a first-strike, and this led to a stalemate known as MAD. Arms race built on fear.

Dangers of military conflict as seen through Cuban Missile Crisis

- The threat of nuclear war seemed very close on the discovery of Soviet nuclear missiles on Cuba in 1962. Before Khrushchev backed down the nuclear war was threatened. It also illustrated the lack of formal contact between the superpowers to defuse potential conflicts.
- Introduction of a 'hot-line' between the Kremlin and White House in order to improve communication between the superpowers. Khrushchev and Kennedy also signed the Limited Nuclear Test Ban Treaty, the first international agreement on nuclear weapons.

Technology: The importance of verification

- American development of surveillance technology (U2 and satellites) meant that nuclear weapons could be identified and agreements verified.
- Example of U2 flight over Cuba where Anderson photographed nuclear sites.
- Also U2 and satellite verification to make sure the Soviets were doing as promised at the negotiating table.
- Some historians think Arms Control would never have taken root, but for the ability of the sides to verify what the other was doing.

Co-existence and Détente

- Policies of co-existence and détente developed to defuse tensions and even encourage trade.
- Role of others like Brandt in West Germany in defusing tension through their policies of Ostpolitik, etc.

Any other relevant factors.

*Candidates can be credited **up to a maximum of 20 marks**.*

57. How important was the role of Gorbachev in ending the Cold War?

Context

When Mikhail Gorbachev became General Secretary in 1985 he sought economic reform and limited political reform in Russia which led to engagement with the West. Gorbachev's attempts to reform Communism, however, unleashed forces that he could not control.

Role of President Mikhail Gorbachev

- Gorbachev saw that the USSR could not afford a new arms race. The Soviet economy was at breaking point. Commitments to the arms race and propping up allied regimes meant consumer goods and other things such as housing that mattered to the Russian people were neglected.
- Gorbachev implemented policies of Perestroika and Glasnost which aimed to reform the Soviet economy and liberalise its political system.
- Gorbachev worked to improve relations with the USA. He took ideology out of his foreign policy, as exemplified by arms agreements to allow the USSR to concentrate on internal matters: Intermediate Nuclear Forces Treaty, December 1987; Nuclear Weapons Reduction Treaty, 1989.
- Gorbachev told leaders of the satellite East European states in March 1989 that the Soviet army would no longer help them to stay in power.

Other factors

Role of President Ronald Reagan

- Unlike many in the US administration Reagan actively sought to challenge Soviet weakness and strengthen the West in order to defeat communism. In 1983 he denounced the Soviet Union as an 'Evil Empire.'
- Programme of improving US armed forces, including nuclear weapons, and he proposed a Star Wars missile shield to challenge the belief in MAD (SDI). He was very charming when he met Gorbachev and visited the Soviet Union.

Western economic strength

- Allowed America to embark on the Star Wars weapons programme.
- Perception of the affluent West through television and consumer goods undermined communist claims of the superiority of their economic system.

Withdrawal of the Soviet Union from Afghanistan

- Symptom of the problems of the Soviet Union.
- Intervention in December 1979: conflict with the Mujaheddin. Russian army morale crumbled when over 20,000 Soviet soldiers died, as did support at home.
- The conflict showed the weaknesses of the Soviet economy. War led to a slump in living standards for ordinary Russians.
- Russians began to question the actions of their own government. Gorbachev withdrew troops in 1988.

Failure of communism in Eastern Europe

- Strong Polish identity and history of hostility with Russia. By 1970s, Poland was in an economic slump. Emergence of opposition around Gdansk in 1980: industrial workers strike led by Lech Walesa, who argued for the creation of an independent trade union. Solidarity grew to nine million members in a matter of months. Movement suppressed in 1981 by General Jaruzelski's government.
- Multiparty elections in Poland, after Soviet troops left, victory for Solidarity.
- Czechoslovakia, political prisoners released in November 1989 and by the end of the month, the communist government had gone. No Soviet intervention.
- Opening of the Berlin Wall: division of Germany finally came to an end.
- Soviet domination ended.
- Perestroika and Glasnost and the end of communist rule in USSR.

Any other relevant factors.

MODEL PAPER 3
SECTION 1: SCOTTISH

Part A: The Wars of Independence, 1249—1329

1. How fully does Source A illustrate the succession problem in Scotland, 1286—1296? (9)

Candidates may be credited in a number of ways up to a maximum of 9 marks.

A maximum of 2 marks may be given for answers which refer only to the source.

Possible points which may be identified in the source include:

- John Balliol's success would both maintain and even increase Comyn power.
- Bruces were determined to stake their claim to power.
- Before the Maid's death in September 1290, Bruce had tried to increase his territorial power.
- Bruce put forward the case that he was the rightful successor to Alexander II.

Possible points of significant omission may include:

- Two rival noble dynasties saw an opportunity to seize power, Robert Bruce (grandfather of the future King Robert I) and John Balliol (ally of the powerful Comyn family).
- The two main claimants were descendants through the daughters of David the Earl of Huntingdon had valid claims as descendant of David I of Scotland.
- The tragic death of Alexander III, 18th March, 1286.
- Alexander's children had all died before him; Alexander, David and Margaret.
- After the Maid's death, the marriage Treaty of Birgham, between Edward (son of King Edward) and Margaret (Maid of Norway) was now null and void.
- There was a real fear of civil war, particularly amongst factions from Bruce.
- The Guardians compromised the Independence of Scotland by inviting Edward's mediation.
- The Guardians negotiated a specific treaty (of Birgham) protecting Margaret's rule as Queen of Scots.
- Edward's aim to establish Feudal Overlordship at Norham, 1291.
- Bishop Fraser was sympathetic to the Balliol claim.
- The Bruce family wrote to make their claim to Edward, known as the 'Appeal of the seven Earls'.
- Edward's decision to make John Balliol King of Scots in November 1292.
- The Bruce family did not accept the decision.
- The Bruce family paid homage to Edward I in 1296.
- **Any other** valid point of explanation that meets the criteria described in the general marking principles for this kind of question.

2. Evaluate the usefulness of Source D as evidence of the growth of Scottish resistance to King Edward, 1296—1297. (6)

Candidates can be credited in a number of ways up to a maximum of 6 marks.

Examples of aspects of the source and relevant comments:

Aspect of the source	Possible comment
Author: Walter of Guisborough	More useful as account based on personal observation and experience. Less useful as author is English so may be biased.
Type of Source: Chronicle	Useful as an informed record of events.
Purpose: To give an account of the Battle of Stirling Bridge	Useful as considered to be a relatively reliable record of events. Possible bias as the priory suffered during the wars so less useful.
Timing: Contemporary	Useful as from the time when the Scottish Wars were taking place.
Content	**Possible comment**
• We are ready for the fight, to free our kingdom.	Useful as shows the Scottish intent throughout the wars.
• There was not a more suitable place to put the English into the hands of the Scots.	Less useful as clearly giving an excuse for the poor English military performance.
• Cressingham was cut down by Scots pikemen and cut into pieces.	Useful as source recognises importance of the loss of Cressingham, the English Treasurer in Scotland.

Possible points of significant omission may include:

- Resistance to the English grew in the South West, and in the North East.
- William Wallace and Andrew Murray brought leadership to Scottish resistance.
- Scottish guerrilla tactics in their early resistance had moved towards a pitched battle at Stirling, under the combined leadership.
- Rebellions began in the spring of 1297.
- The nobles Bruce and Steward started an armed revolt against Edward at Irvine.
- Andrew Murray took castles at Inverness, Elgin and Aberdeen.
- Murray had removed all English garrisons north of Dundee.
- William Wallace present at killing of Sir William Heselrig, the English Sheriff of Lanark.
- Scottish victory at the Battle of Stirling Bridge, 11th September, 1297.
- Wallace and Murray appointed Guardians.
- Wallace invaded the North of England, around Carlisle and Newcastle.
- **Any other** valid point of explanation that meets the criteria described in the general marking principles for this kind of question.

3. Compare the views of Sources B and C about the subjugation of Scotland by Edward I? (5)

Candidates can be credited in a number of ways up to a maximum of 5 marks.

Possible points of comparison may include:

Overall: Source B and **Source C** basically agree that Edward I invaded Scotland with significant forces, attacked the town of Berwick, slaughtering the Scots inside. The English also fought a pitched battle at Dunbar, besieging the Scottish held castle, but the Scots were also defeated by nobles disloyal to King John, such as the Bruce dynasty.

Source B	Source C
The King of England, being strongly stirred up, marched in person on Scotland with a large force.	For Edward the campaign to Scotland was carried out from the outset by using the full force of England's experienced army.
Upon the town of Berwick he put to the sword some 7,500 souls.	He made a swift example of the town of Berwick, slaughtering over 7,000 inhabitants.
On 27 April, was fought the battle of Dunbar, where many Scottish nobles fell wounded in defeat.	In the ensuing battle at Dunbar on 27 April the Scots were defeated resoundingly.
Bruce's party, were generally considered traitors to their king and country.	Scottish nobles who preferred to side with the English King, included the Bruces.

Part B: The Age of the Reformation, 1542—1603

4. How fully does Source A explain the reasons for the Reformation of 1560? (9)

Candidates may be credited in a number of ways up to a maximum of 9 marks.

A maximum of 2 marks may be given for answers which refer only to the source.

Possible points which may be identified in the source include:

- In December 1557 Protestant nobles sent ambitious requests for reform to Mary of Guise.
- Protestant nobles asked to be allowed to host Protestant sermons on their estates; and they also wanted prayers in the vernacular to be used in parish churches.
- The return of John Knox to Scotland and his inflammatory sermon at Perth triggered a full-scale riot.
- Mary of Guise mishandled the situation in 1559, uniting most of the political nation against her.

Possible points of signifcant omission may include:

- The Lords of the Congregation were encouraged by the prospect of support from the English after Elizabeth became Queen in 1558.
- John Knox's return was pivotal in advancing the Protestant cause. In 1545 he was with the Protestant rebels at St Andrew's Castle and, in 1546, involved in the assassination of Cardinal Beaton.
- In Perth religious houses were attacked and religious objects were destroyed and in the early spring of 1559, Perth and Dundee announced they were Protestant.
- Protestant ideas had been coming into Scotland for some time

- English Bibles and books critical of the Catholic Church were distributed in Scotland following the Reformation in England.
- The Catholic Church failed to make sufficient reform to satisfy its critics.
- Increased numbers of the nobility opted for the new faith.
- The Lords of the Congregation had increasing support and took up arms against Mary of Guise.
- The weaknesses of the Catholic Church — decline and corruption; pluralism had not been addressed. Minors being given top positions in church — crown and nobility taking much of churches' revenues; Monarchs placed their offspring in important positions in the Church.
- The 'Beggar's Summons' was nailed to friaries demonstrating anger at the Church's domination and wealth and demanded the flitting of the Friars.
- Mary of Guise's religious attitude and pro-France stance meant she asked the French for help which pushed many Scots into supporting the Lords of the Congregation.
- Mary of Guise's prosecution of reformers was unpopular.
- **Any other** valid point of explanation that meets the criteria described in the general marking principles for this kind of question.

5. Evaluate the usefulness of Source D as evidence of the efforts of the Kirk to maintain its independence. (6)

Candidates can be credited in a number of ways up to a maximum of 6 marks.

Examples of aspects of the source and relevant comments:

Aspect of the source	Possible comment
Author: Committee of around 30 members led by Andrew Melville	Useful as it reflects the views of Protestant reformers.
Type of Source: Book	Useful as its articles were central to the development of Presbyteries in the Kirk and their purpose.
Purpose: To set out views of Presbyterian Kirk	More useful as source shows Kirk's view of the relationship between church and state. Less useful as source inevitably reflects only the views of the Kirk.
Timing: Contemporary	More useful as reflects the views of the Kirk at the time when it was seeking to influence and define its relationship with the state.

Content	Possible comment
• Kings and princes have supreme power over their subjects in civil law.	More useful as shows the Kirk's view of the areas of responsibility that secular rulers have.
• Christ alone is 'Lord and Master' of the Kirk.	More useful as it shows the Kirk's view of who is in charge of the Kirk.
• Christ will 'command and rule in his Kirk, through his Spirit and word' and through the service of 'the ministry of men'.	More useful as defines role of men within the Kirk and the influence of Christ in this.

Possible points of significant omission may include:

- The *Second Book of Discipline* (1578) set out the vision of a Presbyterian Kirk. The views expressed were consistent with Andrew Melville's — in that he protected the rights of the Kirk from the king and government
- The *Second Book of Discipline* led to the development of regular meetings of ministers from 10 to 20 parishes to discuss doctrine which developed into the Presbyteries.
- A Presbyterian system could make the Kirk almost entirely independent of the king and his nobles
- By 1581, plans were in place for 13 Presbyteries with responsibility for Kirk matters such as: visiting parishes; the appointment of ministers; responsibility for disciplinary matters; and the selection of representatives for future General Assemblies.
- At parish level, Kirk Sessions had consisted of elders and deacons who were elected annually until the *Second Book of Discipline* developed the idea of 'once an elder, always an elder'.
- From 1560, Kirk Sessions exercised the right to fine, imprison and excommunicate offenders against their authority in moral matters.
- The *Second Book of Discipline* established a vision of a Presbyterian Kirk but the 'Black Acts' (1584) subsequently stated the supremacy of the monarch in all matters.
- The Golden Act (1592) recognised the recovery of Presbyterian influence within the Kirk but it did not reduce the power of the monarch.
- **Any other** valid point of explanation that meets the criteria described in the general marking principles for this kind of question.

6. Compare the views in Sources B and C about the events which brought Mary's marriage to Darnley to an end. (5)

*Candidates can be credited in a number of ways **up to a maximum of 5 marks**.*

Possible points of comparison may include:

Overall: Sources B and **C** describe the explosion and reaction to Darnley's murder, plus the attendance of the Queen and Bothwell at the masque in Holyrood. However, **Source B** describes the Queen's feeling that she was a target, whereas **Source C** shows that she was accused of the murder.

Source B	Source C
The house in which the King was lodged was in an instant blown in the air ... it must have been done by force of gunpowder and appears to have been a mine.	The Lords of the Council concluded that the Old Provost's Lodging and the Prebedaries Chamber had been blow into the air by the force of the powder.
It is not yet known who carried out this deed and in what manner.	In the aftermath of Darnley's death there was much speculation as to who was implicated in the murder and how exactly it was carried out.
Queen believed that the bomb was intended for her.	The Queen herself was accused of the murder of Darnley.
Mary did not stay the night at Kirk o' Field by chance — 'by reason of some masque in the abbey (of Holyrood)'	Mary returned to Holyrood around midnight, Bothwell was in attendance on her, and conspicuously dressed in a masquing costume.

Part C: The Treaty of Union, 1689—1740

7. How fully does Source A explain the reasons for worsening relations with England after 1690? (9)

*Candidates may be credited in a number of ways **up to a maximum of 9 marks**.*

A maximum of 2 marks may be given for answers which refer only to the source.

Possible points which may be identified in the source include:

- England has ruined Scotland by giving land and pensions as bribes.
- Offices in Scottish government given to those who will comply with English wishes.
- Scotland appears to the rest of the world to be a conquered province.
- English court has bribed Scots so that the English are now masters of us at our own cost.

Possible points of significant omission may include:

- King William and English ministers did seek to gain advantage over Scottish interests, eg over Darien Scheme.
- Successive appointments to posts in Scottish government did go to those who were subservient to English command.
- The 'Ill' Years
- Navigation Acts.
- Effect of English wars.
- English military intervention with Scottish trade.
- Lack of English investment in the Darien scheme.
- Dutch withdrawal from Darien.
- Limits of the Darien scheme.
- William's hand in the Darien failure.
- The cost of Darien.
- Act of Settlement enacting the Hanoverian succession.
- Act of Security proclaiming Scottish independence in terms of trade, law and religion and asserting Scotland's right to choose its monarch.
- Act Anent Peace and War stating future monarchs could not declare war on Scotland's behalf without parliamentary consent.
- Wool Act, Wine Act; Scotland would continue to trade when England was at war.
- Aliens Act; Scots to be treated as Aliens in England if Hanoverian succession not accepted in Scotland.
- Jacobite opposition to William, assassination plot.
- Scottish parliamentary opposition to the Anglican church.
- English Bill of Rights.
- Claim of Right, Articles of Grievance.
- Scots Act of Settlement.
- Opposition to William in the Highlands, Glencoe Massacre.
- Covenanters' objections to monarchical interference in church affairs.
- **Any other** valid point of explanation that meets the criteria described in the general marking principles for this kind of question.

8. **Evaluate the usefulness of Source D as evidence of the passage of the Union through the Scottish parliament.** (5)

Candidates can be credited in a number of ways up to a maximum of 6 marks.

Examples of aspects of the source and relevant comments:

Aspect of the source	Possible comment
Author: Daniel Defoe	More useful as an English spy so gives us an informed account of events. Less useful as possible bias.
Type of Source: Report	More useful as formal report so should be an accurate account of proceedings.
Purpose: To give an account of Scottish Parliamentary proceedings	More useful as shows the influence of the Equivalent on Scottish MPs voting for union.
Timing: Contemporary	More useful as Defoe observed Scottish parliamentary proceedings first-hand.
Content	**Possible comment**
• The Equivalent compensated Darien investors.	Useful as source illustrates the attraction of the Equivalent for those who had lost money in the Darien scheme.
• The Equivalent took the edge off opposition to union.	Useful as illustrates one consequence of Equivalent politically.
• Squadrone Volante could now be persuaded to vote for the Union.	Useful as shows how the money influenced the 25 members of the Squadrone Volante, a political group independent of the Court and Country parties.

Possible points of significant omission may include:

- English spies informed English government of proceedings in parliament.
- Financial payments to Scots were a feature of the debate period.
- The Equivalent was a major factor in swaying many towards union.
- The Equivalent: £398,085.10s to cover the taking on of English debt.
- Bribery of Scottish ministers/politicians through £20,000 issued to Earl of Glasgow by English government to distribute as 'arrears in pay'.
- Promise of favours, pensions, military patronage, high-ranking positions and cash ensured government majorities; threats of loss of civil list pension.
- Act of Security for the Kirk also turned many in favour of union.
- Political management of Court party better than Country party.
- Court members consistently voted through all Articles of the Treaty.
- Role of Hamilton as an erratic and divisive leader of Country party.
- Hamilton may have been bribed by the Court party.
- Hamilton refused to participate in planned walkout of parliament.
- Failed armed rising proved opponents of union were unwilling to engage in violence.

- Hamilton divided opponents of union and obstructed arguments against union.
- Divisions amongst opponents.
- Squadrone Volante's hold on balance of power was crucial.
- Economic assurances, incentive of free trade with England and English colonies.
- Payment made to wool industry as well as payment of Scottish public debt.
- Last minute concessions by Godolphin on tax issues, eg salt, liquor.
- Incentives for Scottish nobles regarding retained privileges, seats in House of Lords.
- Rights of burghs and Royal Burghs to remain.
- Legal protection, Scottish law and courts to remain.
- Future stability within one kingdom secured; peace secured by being in Great Britain.
- Military argument; threat of English invasion as forces moved north in late 1706.
- English and Scottish parliaments in agreement over union for first time.
- Security of liberty and stability under one parliament.
- **Any other** valid point of explanation that meets the criteria described in the general marking principles for this kind of question.

9. **Compare the views in Sources B and C about attitudes towards union in Scotland.** (5)

Candidates can be credited in a number of ways up to a maximum of 5 marks.

Possible points of comparison may include:

Overall: Source B and **Source C** agree that many in Scotland were against union and the nature of this opposition; they differ in their views as to how many people in Scotland understood the issues involved.

Source B	Source C
In November, a flood of addresses to parliament from Royal Burghs, etc.	90-plus addresses streamed into parliament from beginning of November.
Addresses opposed to union, none in favour.	Addresses reveal widespread public opposition to union.
Addresses said union was 'contrary to honour and independence'.	Addresses defended Scotland's honour and independent sovereignty.
Addresses showed widespread literacy and awareness of issues.	Signatures made on behalf of illiterate who were not fully aware of issues.

Part D: Migration and Empire, 1830–1939

10. **How fully does Source A explain the reasons for the migration of Scots?** (9)

Candidates may be credited in a number of ways up to a maximum of 9 marks.

A maximum of 2 marks may be given for answers which refer only to the source.

Possible points which may be identified in the source include:

- Incessant rain had made it impossible for the population of the west coast to harvest the peat on which they depended for domestic fuel.
- The crofts to which the mass of Highlanders had been driven as a result of earlier clearances had long since proved incapable of providing adequately for their occupants.

- Crofting families survived on a diet consisting largely of potatoes and when that crop failed — as it did regularly — hunger became more severe.
- Landlords did not feel a very pressing responsibility for the Highlanders' fate and simply organised more evictions in order to create more sheep farms.

Possible points of significant omission may include:
- Highland Clearances — relevant details about poverty and hardship.
- Harsh employment conditions on the land.
- Pressures on small farmers of poor quality soil and harsh weather conditions.
- The Highland Problem: over-crowding, sub division of land into crofts with each successive generation leading to insufficient land/food to support families.
- Pressure from landlords wishing to 'improve' their land by creating sheep farms.
- Landlords looked to improve their land not only with sheep farms but also deer forests and grouse moors.
- 'Balmoralism' and the tourist income potential of the Highlands became fashionable with Royal approval, also created pressure for change in Highlands.
- Lack of real opportunities encouraged emigration from the Highlands of Scotland.
- Failure of the kelp and herring industries.
- Effects of the Agricultural Revolution on farming and employment.
- Effects of Industrial Revolution on craftsmen.
- Bitterness rarely the sole reason for emigration.
- Better prospects abroad both for self and next generation. Not all were driven out of Scotland — many left willingly.
- Hope, ambition and adventure stronger than despair and resignation.
- Improvement in life expected through emigration.
- Letters from relatives already emigrants.
- Voluntary migrants from a strong, urban economy in Scotland.
- Emigration Agencies actively working to attract emigrants — New Zealand and Australian authorities work was widespread, offering free passages and other inducements.
- Promises of free/cheap land abroad, especially in Canada.
- Discovery of gold in the USA and Australia.
- Use of free and assisted passages by many territories encouraged both agricultural and urban workers to leave Scotland.
- Government schemes to assist emigration, eg Highland and Islands Emigration Society.
- Transport Revolution meant that travel times were greatly reduced by steam ship — an important factor when migrants had to consider loss of wages while en route.
- Migration to Canada seen by many urban industrial workers as a 'back door' to the USA at a time when it was harder to gain direct entry to the USA.
- Attractions of a new life, possibly in a city (including UK cities — employment, better wages, easier work, chances of marriage partner, entertainment.
- **Any other** valid point of explanation that meets the criteria described in the general marking principles for this kind of question.

11. Evaluate the usefulness of Source D as evidence about the contribution of Scots to the economic growth and development of the Empire. (6)

Candidates can be credited in a number of ways up to a maximum of 6 marks.

Examples of aspects of the source and relevant comments:

Aspect of the source	Possible comment
Author: David Laing	More useful as he had personal experience of life in Canada.
Type of Source: Letter	More useful as likely to be an honest and candid account. Less useful as only one account of life in Canada.
Purpose: To inform sister about his life in Canada	More useful as informed comment on the contribution of Scots to the development of the railways in Canada.
Timing: Contemporary	More useful as an eyewitness source from someone working on the railways in Canada thereby contributing towards the economic growth and development of the Empire.
Content	**Possible comment**
• We have 86 locomotive engines to keep in repair and 400 miles of rails to keep in good repair so that the produce of this land can reach the ports and then across the world.	More useful as shows type of work that a skilled Scottish emigrant undertook.
• Our foremen are nearly all Scots.	More useful as shows the number of Scots who emigrated in search of work.
• Without these men there would be no railway, no prosperity and no trade in this part of the world.	More useful as gives a personal view of the importance of Scots workers.

Possible points of significant omission may include:
- Scots were very important to the development of the Transatlantic Canadian Pacific Railway.
- Strong support for the railway came from Sir John A. MacDonald, the first Prime Minister of Canada, born in Glasgow in 1815.
- Scots were important in the financing and engineering of the project. Scots, George Stephen at the Bank of Montreal and John Rose in London, helped finance it. Another Scot, Sandford Fleming, was the railway's main engineer.
- By the 1920s it has been calculated that one quarter of Canada's business leaders were born in Scotland, with another twenty-five percent having Scottish-born fathers.
- The Hudson's Bay Company recruited heavily in the Western and Northern Isles of Scotland.
- Scots brought new ideas on how to farm to Canada such as crop rotation.
- Scots were very important in the development of trade in furs and timber as well as agriculture in Canada.

The impact of Scots on other parts of Empire

Australasia
- Scots were important in the development of farming in Australia.

- Scotland was also a significant investor in developing agriculture in Australia, eg huge sheep runs in New South Wales and Victoria.
- Scots also helped the sugar and wine industries in Australia.
- Samuel McWilliam planted his first vines at Corowa in New South Wales in 1877.
- Scots involved in developing Australian trade, mining, manufacturing, shipping, engineering and finance.
- Robert McCracken from Ayrshire developed brewing in Melbourne.
- Robert Campbell from Greenock played such an important role in developing Australian trade that he was known as 'The father of Australian Commerce'.
- Melbourne Iron works was founded by John Buncle from Edinburgh.
- The Commercial Banking Company of Sydney was founded in 1834 by an Aberdonian.
- Scots dominated many shipping firms in Australia.
- Scottish involvement in the development of education in Australia.
- Schools that were set up and run by Scots were important as they produced many of the political, economic, military and educational leaders of the future.
- Scots founded New Zealand's paper-making industry and were important engineers and shipbuilders.
- Peter and David Duncan, originally from Forfar, developed a successful business in Agricultural implements in Christchurch.
- Scots were skilled farmers and influenced the development of New Zealand through sheep and mixed farming.

India

- Scots had become involved in trading with India before 1830. They were involved with the East India Company.
- After 1830 Scots were of great importance in extending British influence into India, eg James Andrew Broun-Ramsay, 1st Marquess of Dalhousie. Dalhousie was made Governor-General of India in 1848. He served until 1856.
- Dalhousie developed a plan to build railway lines to connect the main regions of India as well as build a telegraph communication system.
- Dalhousie encouraged a national postal service and the development of schools, roads and irrigation.
- **Any other** valid point of explanation that meets the criteria described in the general marking principles for this kind of question.

12. Compare the views in Sources B and C about the experience of Irish immigrants in Scotland. (5)

Candidates can be credited in a number of ways up to a maximum of 5 marks.

Possible points of comparison may include:

Overall: Source B and **Source C** agree that the experience of Irish immigrants in Scotland was negative with both **Source B** and **Source C** complaining about the problems caused by the Irish immigrants in terms of maintaining Scottish identity and limiting numbers of immigrants, pressure on poor rates, competition for jobs and also lowering wages rates and moral standards.

Source B	Source C
Let us redouble our efforts not to keep Scotland for the Scotch, for that is impossible; but to keep Scotland—Scotch!	Irish immigration that washes over us each year should be restricted.
They have swallowed up our rapidly increasing Poor Rates.	Interferes ...in their dependence on adequate funds within the poor rates.
By their great numbers they have ... deprived thousands of the working people of Scotland of that employment which legitimately belonged to them.	We have no doubt that the work of this parish could be done, and the harvest got in, without the competition from Irish labourers.
By their great numbers they have lessened wages.	Irish labourers whose presence forces down the wages to be earned from this work.

Part E: The Impact of the Great War, 1914–1928

13. How fully does Source A describe the involvement of Scots on the Western Front? (9)

Candidates may be credited in a number of ways up to a maximum of 9 marks.

A maximum of 2 marks may be given for answers which refer only to the source.

Possible points which may be identified in the source include:

- His unit was relieved, after holding their own against German counter-attack but their replacements lost one of the trenches that they had taken.
- They got the trench back before coming out of the trenches with only about 70 or 80 men surviving, out of the 1,100 original.
- Sir John French came along just as they were leaving their old billets and praised their efforts.
- French explained that he chose Cameron highlanders as his bodyguard as they never gave up.

Possible points of significant omission may include:

- Detail on Queens Own Cameron Highlanders – recruitment drive led by Colonel D. W. Cameron of Lochiel. Cameron's involvement at Loos, the Somme and Arras.
- Development of detail regarding trench warfare – attacks followed by enemy counter-attacks, gain and loss of trenches with limited movement of trench lines.
- Detail on the battle of Loos which saw the 'blooding' of Kitchener's New Army divisions including Scots.
- Scots units involved in the Loos and Somme offensives with high casualty rates.
- Scots units tended to be seen as 'shock' impact attack formations.
- Controversy regarding role of Commander-in-chief, Sir John French, known to care about the welfare of his troops and failure to co-operate with the French.
- Sir John French replaced by Haig, December 1915.
- Role of Haig at Loos – 'unfavourable ground', use of gas, problem with reserves.
- Details on losses at Loos – 20,598 names on the memorial at Loos – one third are Scottish.

- Details relating to recruitment — volunteering to go to the front.
- Scots in action — 'shock' troops — 'ladies from hell'.
- Conditions facing the Scots.
- 3 Scottish divisions 9th, 15th (Scottish) and 51st (Highland) took part in the Battle of the Somme, as well as numerous Scottish battalions in other units.
- Scottish losses at the Somme — 16th (McCrae's Battalion) Royal Scots lost 12 officers and 573 soldiers, 51st Highland Division suffered 3,500 casualties.
- Somme success — the 51st (Highland) Division launched a successful attack at Beaumont Hamel with relatively few casualties in November 1918.
- Role of Haig at the Somme.
- Attitude of the survivors: losses were replaced and the Scottish units carried on though grousing and criticisms became more common.
- Scots involvement at Arras.
- **Any other** valid point of explanation that meets the criteria described in the general marking principles for this kind of question.

14. Evaluate the usefulness off Source D as evidence of the economic difficulties faced by Scotland after 1918. (6)

*Candidates can be credited in a number of ways **up to a maximum of 6 marks.***

Examples of aspects of the source and relevant comments:

Aspect of the source	Possible comment
Author: Annie and James Watt	More useful as they could speak with knowledge as they worked in the herring industry.
Type of Source: Personal Accounts	More useful as it gives an honest account of events, which is backed up by other sources. Less useful as personal memory can be partial.
Purpose: To explain the adverse changes the war brought to the fishing industry	More useful as an account that reflects what is known about the effect of the war on the fishing industry. Less useful as the source is only about the fishing industry.
Timing: Contemporary	More useful as the source is from the time when there were great changes in the fishing industry in Scotland.

Content	Possible comment
Price of a barrel of herring had been the same throughout the war but, after an initial rise at the end of the war, it began to go down.	More useful as illustrates the immediate impact of the end of the war.
Fuel, gear and wage costs had risen so much that the fishermen could not pay the gutters so they went on strike.	More useful as illustrates industrial relations problems caused by changes to industry.
Those involved in the fishing industry including fish merchants had lost markets in Germany and Russia during the war.	More useful as shows the impact of the loss of foreign markets to the Scottish merchants.

Possible points of significant omission may include:

- The collapse of foreign markets for herring greatly affected the industry — European countries started to compete strongly with Scottish fleets and in 1920 the government removed the guaranteed price for the herring. The price of herring dropped dramatically; it was no longer profitable; and for twenty years the industry went into a steep decline.
- **Agriculture** — competition came after the war from cheap foreign imports of food like refrigerated meat from Argentina, frozen lamb and tinned fruit from Australia and New Zealand.
- **Jute** — During the war Dundee's jute industry boomed as demand for sack cloth rose but after the war the industry faced direct competition from Calcutta in world markets. Price of goods collapsed resulting in mass unemployment, deep social misery and discontent especially in Dundee and several firms went into liquidation.
- **Iron and Steel** — Demand for iron decreased during the war years. Demand for steel increased during the war as it was needed for the shipbuilding industry. But other countries increased their steel making during the war years and Scots manufacturers could not compete. As a result the iron and steel industries were severely affected by the downturn in demand from 1921 onwards.
- **Shipbuilding** — the immediate impact of war on Clydeside shipyards was very positive and profits were good. However, after the war, a return to competitive tendering along with the decline in the demand for steel and for ships, foreign competition, labour disputes and a shortage of manpower and materials all led to problems and shipbuilding went into decline.
- **Any other** valid point of explanation that meets the criteria described in the general marking principles for this kind of question.

15. Compare the views in Sources B and C about recruitment and conscription in Scotland.   (5)

Candidates can be credited in a number of ways up to a maximum of 5 marks.

Possible points of comparison may include:

Overall: Source B and **Source C** agree that Scots volunteered in great numbers at the outbreak of war and that recruitment fell as the war progressed. Both also agree that the National Registration Act did not work. **Source B**, however, shows newspaper support for the introduction of conscription whilst **Source C** mentions the anti-conscription rallies taking place in 1915.

Source B	Source C
Scots responded in great numbers ... indeed by December 1914 25% of the labour force of Western Scotland had signed up.	20,000 recruits in Edinburgh by end of August and in Glasgow over the first weekend of the war six thousand men enlisted.
It was being reported throughout the press from as early as October that the numbers enlisting were falling slightly.	The number of volunteers began to fall off in 1915.
The *Glasgow Herald* reported in December 1914 that if voluntarism did not work then conscription was the only alternative. The *Daily Record* ran similar articles promoting support for conscription.	There were increasing concerns that compulsory military service would be introduced and anti-conscription rallies had been held in Glasgow since the end of 1915, one meeting being addressed by committed anti-war protesters Sylvia Pankhurst and John MacLean.
Despite the National Registration Act recruitment levels fell to around 80,000 per month by January 1916 and conscription became a reality.	The national registration scheme proved to be cumbersome and unworkable and recruitment continued to fall.

MODEL PAPER 3
SECTION 2: BRITISH

Part A: Church, State and Feudal Society, 1066–1406

Candidates can be credited in a number of ways up to a maximum of 20 marks.

16. To what extent was the secular church more important than the regular church in the Middle Ages?

Context
The medieval church came under criticism that it had lost its religious role within society. However, this view would be considered too simplistic. The role of religion within the regular and secular church varied. However, there was more than just religious purpose to the church.

Religious role
- **Belief in Christianity** — this was dominant within society; it provided people with an understanding of the world and how it worked. The church held the key to this understanding and the promise of salvation and eternal life after death. Through the power of the sacrament the church effectively held the keys to heaven.
- **Church services** — the importance of christenings, marriage and funerals which brought people closer to attaining their passage to heaven.
- **Relics and saints** — significance of relics and saints as a means to communicate with God and beg divine favour or protection.
- **Importance of the pilgrimage** — pilgrimage, including the Crusades, to holy centres, eg Jerusalem, was an important part of medieval life.

Political role
- **Investiture contest** — political argument between the Church and State as to who had the right to appoint senior clergy members, eg the Holy Roman Emperor vs the Pope. Such offices came with large grants of land and often held considerable political significance.
- Monarchs did not wish the papacy to choose political undesirables for such an important position, eg William the Lion and the argument over the Bishop of St Andrews in 1180.
- **Position within feudal structure** — within the feudal system bishops and abbots were seen as other large landowners, eg Diocese from St Andrews down to East Lothian. They also had the right to raise troops in time of need, eg Bishop of Durham led the English forces that defeated David I at the Battle of the Standard in 1138.

Administrative role
- The church provided the majority of clerks for the state government. They were needed to keep records, write charters, laws, keep accounts, etc.
- Divine authority — the development of canon law during this period was a direct threat to the growth of the monarchies. The papacy argued that all power of kings was invested in them during their coronation by God through the church. Monarchs argued that the power was given directly to them by God. As such, the papal position was that kings were subservient to popes. The papacy continued to argue its position and used papal sanctions such as excommunication and the interdict to bring monarchs to heel.

Economic role

- The church could be three times as wealthy as the monarchy.
- The church provided employment through its economic role. Employment in the wool industry, wine-making and honey all provided considerable wealth for the church.
- The church could raise taxes, eg the Saladin Tithe (1/10th in tax).
- Additional services provided by the church included education, books, shelter and medicine, but only accessible to the wealthy nobles.

Arguments that the church's role was social

- Hospitals were established, eg leprosy hospitals.
- Education, although usually the preserve of the wealthy for their sons.
- Although superstition and ignorance was crucial to control the peasantry.
- The monasteries provided shelter for travellers.
- Holy days were celebrated regularly throughout the year.

Regular church

- Monasteries were seen as 'prayer factories' and used to intercede with God for the ordinary lay population. Monks were cloistered as part of the First Estate, closest to God, and guided by the papacy.

Secular church

- Priests provided direct contact with the peasantry in villages across Scotland and England. Their preaching was not restricted by the confines of the papal office.

Arguments to suggest the secular church was more important.

Religious importance

- The offer of salvation in the afterlife was the key cornerstone in the power of the church, and many historians have argued that the all the other aspects of the church's power derived from this.
- The church taught everyone of the power of the saints, and how their remains (relics) could have strong spiritual power. Masses believed and travelled far to witness the miracles performed by such relics.
- Even entire kingdoms adopted the help and guidance of saints, and patron saints became popular. This led to the idea of pilgrims and pilgrimages, enforcing the religious power of the church over a wider audience.
- The church performed important religious services, marriage, christenings etc.

Political importance

- The secular church provided an important contact point with ordinary people. This was used by both the kings and clergy to influence the population.
- The church had its own courts; members of the clergy (roughly 1 in 3 in England) couldn't be tried in the king's court.
- The church was an integral part of the feudal system in England, and could even raise troops from their own lands.
- Clerics were used by the government as scribes and accountants.
- Kings believed that the church was so powerful politically that they should have the right to invest vacant church positions; the Investiture Contest between monarchs and the Pope.

Economic importance

- The tithe — people were expected to pay this tax to the church, typically 10% of their income, though it was usually paid in kind.
- After the king, the church was the biggest landholder in England.

Arguments to suggest the regular church as more important

Religious Importance

- Monasteries seen as more religious than other areas of the church, vows of poverty and chastity etc.
- Ideas that the monasteries were 'Prayer Factories' and could help pray for souls.
- Monks were supposed to devote their lives to god and hard work.
- Kings founded monasteries to pray for their souls, ie William the Conqueror and David I.

Political importance

Many monasteries were founded by monarchs

- David I founded monasteries at Dunfermline (1128) and Kelso (1128) to help bring order to less developed areas of Scotland.
- Abbots and monks were strong supporters of law and order; they offered support and advice to nobles and monarchs.

Economic importance

- Monasteries became very wealthy as land was granted in the hope for salvation.
- Cistercian monasteries were usually built in remote areas and they helped to cultivate the land for the first time.
- Monasteries came to dominate local industries, such as Melrose and the Scottish wool trade and Fountains Abbey and metal working.

Any other relevant factors.

*Candidates can be credited in a number of ways **up to a maximum of 20 marks**.*

17. **'The need to develop "Law and Order" was the main factor in the development of centralised monarchy.' How valid is this view on the reign of Henry II?**

Context

Henry inherited a divided kingdom which stretched from the Scottish to the Spanish borders, but which was recovering from civil war. His need to reassert royal authority was paramount as the basis for all other developments.

Law and order

- Throughout England the justice system was liable to change depending on which lord held sway over that part of the land. Money often bought justice, and archaic trial by ordeal or combat was still common.
- Royal justice was usually reserved for more serious crimes. Issues of land, an important aspect of justice, were often poorly judged or unfairly settled. Henry II established the 'curia regis' (royal court) and the exchequer court. Law courts were established throughout England. Juries were introduced in petty assizes. Expanding the role of royal justice and building on Henry I's (Henry II's grandfather) 'good laws'.
- Henry's reforms were the basis for English common law.
- Henry's reforms challenged the baron's role in justice and greatly increased centralised royal power.
- Henry failed to promote state law over church law after the Assize of Clarendon.

Other factors

Desire to develop the economy

- Henry prioritised the restoration of royal finances.
- Henry restored many of his grandfather's financial institutions.
- The development of the treasury and the exchequer, eg the pipe rolls providing economic data. Royal revenue increased during his reign.
- Henry II introduced new forms of shield tax, eg scuttage.

Growing cost of warfare

- Throughout the 12th century, kings found it increasingly more expensive to raise the funds to build castles or raise feudal armies.

Civil war in England

- Constant warfare during the period of civil war in England drained the treasury.
- During the time of upheaval between Stephen and Matilda, barons and sheriffs had become increasingly lax in paying their taxes. Sheriffs kept the taxes collected in their region for themselves, or only a small amount found its way into the royal treasury. Many barons struck their own coinage.

Growth of the nobility

- The power of the monarchy was threatened by the growth in power of the nobility.
- During the time of the Civil War, the barons had increased in stature and political importance due to both sides vying for their support. As a result barons built castles without royal permission, increased the numbers of knights beyond limits agreed by their charters, acquired land illegally and many hired large armies of Flemish mercenaries.
- Henry II took oaths of loyalty from his barons.
- Henry fought the 'Great Revolt' 1173–74 against rebellious barons and his eldest sons.

Administrative efficiency

- The scale of Henry's empire increased the need for an administration which could function largely independent of the king, who would necessarily be absent a great deal of the time, eg Richard the Lionheart (who inherited the throne on Henry's death). This pressure further increased due to Henry's preference for hunting rather than administration. Lawyers and the exchequer needed to find a way to function without constantly looking to Henry for decisions.

Effects of foreign influence

- Having come to the throne following the Civil War, Henry recognised the need to secure a peaceful succession if such circumstances were to be avoided in the future.
- The loss of Northumbria during the reign of David I of Scotland.
- English lands held in France. Inherited through Henry I and Henry II's wife Eleanor of Aquitaine, e.g. Normandy, Aquitaine and Anjou. Increased tension and war with the King of France.

Any other relevant factors.

Candidates can be credited in a number of ways up to a maximum of 20 marks.

18. How important were changing social attitudes in causing the decline of feudal society?

Context

Feudalism was a hierarchical means of organising society based on land ownership. At the top of the social pyramid was the king and at the bottom were serfs. From the top down came benefits and rewards while the power in the social order provided services for their 'feudal superior'.

Changing social attitudes

- Social mobility was increasing for a number of reasons, including the move to an economy based more on cash than service. In England the wars against France had brought riches to some, and enabled them to climb the social ladder.
- Peasants who could afford to purchase or rent extra land could move up the social ladder, e.g. the de la Poles family in Hull rose from traders to become royal bankers, and the Paston family rose out of serfdom to become country gentry.
- It became impossible to tell the difference between 'knave and Knight', because they dressed alike.

Other factors

The Black Death

- The decline in the population meant that the survivors, particularly of the lower classes, could demand and often received better wages for their labour. Wage levels in England roughly doubled. Indeed, the shortage of labourers is often seen as causing the decline of serfdom in Western Europe.
- Landowners for the first time needed to negotiate for their serfs' services, leading to higher wages and better living conditions for those that survived.

The Peasants' Revolt

- In England the attempts of the Statute of Labourers in 1351 to force peasants back into serfdom were widely and strongly resisted. The extent of the revolt and the impressive way in which it was organised shows that the old feudal consensus had broken down.
- There is an argument that the Peasants' Revolt was a reaction to the attempts to force peasants to return to the old ideas of labour services.

The growth of towns

- Many found the freedom of burgh life allowed them to develop trade without the burden of labour services or restrictions in movement.

The growth of trade/mercantilism

- With markets for their goods fluctuating considerably, many nobles came to understand their weak economic position. For some it was better to let their peasants become tenants who rented their land than to continue as their feudal protector.
- Others discovered that sheep were a far more profitable resource than peasants could ever be. The monasteries in particular turned over large areas to sheep pasture to capitalise on the strong demand for wool.
- Peasants who could afford to purchase or rent extra land could propel themselves upwards on the social ladder.

Any other relevant factors

Part B: The Century of Revolutions, 1603–1702

*Candidates can be credited in a number of ways **up to a maximum of 20 marks**.*

19. 'The policies of Charles I led to problems ruling Scotland.' How valid is this view?

Context

Charles I succeeded his father James I in 1625 and ruled over both England and Scotland until 1642. He continued to reign in Scotland until his death in 1649 at the hands of the English Parliament. During this time there were considerable challenges facing the king in his attempts to enforce his policies in Scotland.

Political challenges

- Charles I caused political resentment as a result of his policies which took power and land from Scottish nobles, as well as his decision not to visit Scotland until 1633, when he was crowned there.
- The king appointed bishops rather than nobles to the Scottish Privy Council, including John Spottiswoode as Chancellor, the first non-secular official in this position since the Reformation.
- Charles I gave increasing power to bishops, which undermined the status of the Scottish nobility.
- The Stuart notion of the Divine Right of Kings was chiefly brought to an end by the Scots' opposition to Charles I's attempts to impose his will on the Scottish people.

Religious policy

- Charles I introduced William Laud, the Archbishop of Canterbury, to Scotland in 1633, and Laud proceeded to oversee Anglican practice in Scottish churches, which was resented by many.
- The king approved a unification of the churches without consulting the Privy Council.
- The 1635 Book of Canons declared that the monarch had authority over the Church of Scotland and introduced a new Service Book which was a Scottish bishops' variation of the English Prayer Book; on 23rd July 1637 it was read at St Giles Cathedral by the Dean, John Hanna, who subsequently had a stool thrown at him by a serving woman, Jenny Geddes; in the chaos that ensued, the Bishop of Edinburgh was shouted down by the crowd in support of Geddes.
- Across Scotland people declared their opposition to the Service Book, placing Charles I's Privy Council in a difficult position, caught between the king and his opponents.

The Covenanters

- In Scotland the Covenanting movement challenged Charles I over his religious policies and was also politically active; Covenanters wanted to preserve Presbyterianism in Scotland.
- The National Covenant of 1638 was designed to promote a church free from monarchical meddling.
- Charles I's failure to suppress the Covenanters contributed to the outbreak of the War of the Three Kingdoms, during which the English Parliament's treaty of alliance with the Scottish Covenanters, the Solemn League and Covenant of 1643, was a key feature of the positive change in the fortunes of the king's enemies.

First Bishops' War

- The first Bishops' War took place in 1639; Charles I could not raise enough money to fight the war effectively, and was forced to agree to a truce in June as part of the Pacification of Berwick; as well as conceding military failure, this also gave the Scots religious freedoms.

- Charles I's inability to put down the Scots brought an end to his 'Eleven Years' Tyranny', as he recalled Parliament in 1640 to request revenue to continue his war with Scotland.
- This 'Short Parliament' lasted one month as the king dissolved it rather than debate his role during the Eleven Years' Tyranny as a condition of Parliament's granting of funds.

Second Bishops' War

- The second Bishops' War was a continuation of the first, but ended in equal humiliation for Charles I in the Treaty of Ripon of October 1640, which cost England the price that the Scottish Parliament had to pay for its forces.
- Again, defeat by the Scots forced the king to recall Parliament, this time after being advised to do so by a grouping of peers known as the Magnum Concilium.
- This 'Long Parliament' was to last longer than the previous one, but still represented a downturn in the king's fortunes, as the Civil War shortly followed.

Any other relevant factors.

*Candidates can be credited in a number of ways **up to a maximum of 20 marks**.*

20. How important was the role of the army in the failure to find an alternative form of government between 1649 and 1658?

Context

The English Civil War formally ended in January 1649, with the execution of Charles I. Oliver Cromwell ruled during the Interregnum. He abolished the monarchy and made an attempt at constitutional rule through including the Council of State, the Barebones Parliament, and the First and Second Protectorate Parliaments.

The role of the army

- Army officers formed the Council of State with the Rump Parliament. Extremists in the army opposed Parliament's role in governing the country.
- The creation of a military dictatorship from 1653 drew comparisons with the Stuarts' martial law, as did the formation of the first Protectorate in September 1654 and the drawing up of military districts under major-generals during the second Protectorate from October 1656.
- Parliamentarians resented the influence of the army on constitutional affairs throughout the Interregnum.

Other factors
Cromwell's dominance

- Cromwell dominated politics and was in a unique position to influence the direction of the country; however, he was a contrary character.
- Cromwell espoused democratic principles but acted in a dictatorial manner, as he knew an elected government would contain his enemies.
- Cromwell's roots were in Parliament but his rise to the rank of general during the Civil War meant he favoured the military during the Interregnum.
- Cromwell was conservative but many policies were ahead of his time, such as relief for the poor and insane during the Barebones Parliament.
- Cromwell was a Puritan but passed progressive reforms, such as civil marriages, which horrified many Puritans.

Foreign matters

- Faced with possible invasion, Cromwell was forced to fight several battles to control Scotland.

- He had to put down rebellions in Ireland by Royalists and Catholics brutally, which caused further resentment and hostility.
- War was waged on Holland to enforce the Navigation Acts.
- In the mid-1650s war with Spain caused increased taxes.
- Foreign affairs led to social issues such as coal shortages in winter 1652–3 not being addressed appropriately, and increasing instability in England.

Parliament

- The Rump Parliament consisted of MPs who had failed to avert Civil War in 1642 and who now had to address the same problems in 1649.
- Puritans amongst MPs viewed church reform as their priority.
- Parliament was opposed to the role of the army, and wanted to have a greater say in drawing up the constitution.
- Quarrels between MPs and army officers were a feature of the Interregnum.
- Parliament opposed toleration, thus preventing religious wounds healing.

Absence of monarchy

- After Charles I's execution in 1649, the Council of State abolished the monarchy and declared a Republic, or Commonwealth; now there was no monarchical check on Parliamentary power.
- In Scotland, Charles II was crowned king and some of his supporters wanted him to ascend the throne in England also. Without a king in England, Cromwell ruled on his own during the Interregnum, drawing comparisons with Charles I's 11-year tyranny.

Unpopular legislation

- The Treason Law and Censorship Law were introduced in 1649; in 1650 the Oath of Allegiance was imposed for all men over 18.
- The High Court was abolished in 1654, causing a backlog of 23,000 cases.
- The Barebones Parliament was accused of introducing too many reforms in too short a space of time.
- The constitution was drawn up solely by army Roman Catholics and Anglicans were excluded from voting by the First Protectorate, which also introduced strict moral codes that curtailed popular forms of entertainment and enforced the Sabbath.
- The Commission of Triers and Committee of Ejectors, who appointed clergymen and schoolmasters, were unpopular with the church.
- A 10% land tax was resented by the aristocracy; taxation in general was increased in order to fund wars with Spain.
- Cromwell's approval of his son Richard as his successor led many to feel that Cromwell viewed himself as a monarchical figure.
- Royalists accused Cromwell of regicide.
- Army extremists pushed for greater martial authority.
- Presbyterians impatiently demanded church reforms.

Inexperience

- The Barebones Parliament consisted of many well-intentioned but inexperienced figures who proved incapable of using power effectively.

Doomed from the start

- All the pre-Civil War problems — such as religious, political, legal and economic issues — plus additional foreign policy issues, meant that Cromwell was always going to encounter difficulties.

Any other relevant factors.

Candidates can be credited in a number of ways up to a maximum of 20 marks.

21. How successfully did the Revolution Settlement of 1688–1702 address the key issues between the Crown and Parliament?

Context

William of Orange invaded England on 5 November 1688 and overthrew King James II. Many Protestants supported him and William was able to become king as the majority Protestant population was fearful of a revival of Catholicism under James. William's invasion marked the beginning of a time called the Glorious Revolution.

Parliament

- In the days before the Civil War, Stuart monarchs had been able to rule without Parliament and curtail Parliamentary freedom of speech.
- The Revolution Settlement provided for another Triennial Act in 1694, which was intended to keep MPs more closely in touch with public opinion.
- The Licensing Act was repealed in 1695, removing restrictions on the freedom of the press to report Parliamentary criticism of the Crown.
- William and Mary had to agree to the Bill of Rights before they were given the throne, legalising the new relationship between Crown and Parliament. This ensured that no future king or queen could attempt absolutism.
- Members of Parliament could now speak freely when voicing their opinion of the monarch. However, the monarch could still dismiss Parliament at will.

Religion

- Before 1688, the Crown dictated the religious status of the country.
- Parliament now held more sway in religious matters.
- After the Settlement, hundreds of High Anglicans were expelled from their posts because they refused to recognise the authority of William III. The Toleration Act of 1689 was passed which provided for free public worship for all except Roman Catholics and Unitarians. Roman Catholics were still ineligible for elected posts in towns or Parliament. However the monarch still enjoyed the political advantages of being head of the church.

Finance

- In the time of James I and Charles I, the monarchy could exist financially independently of Parliament. Now this was impossible.
- The king and queen were granted £700,000 for court expenses in 1689, and from then on Parliament voted to give the Crown money annually as part of the Civil List system.
- A procedure of audit was established for MPs to check the expenditure of the monarch. Fiscal power was now in the hands of the House of Commons.
- However, the monarch would not have to make the unpopular moves of raising taxes himself from now on.

Legislation

- Stuart monarchs had abused the legal system and the courts. The legal settlement established Parliamentary control over these areas, and later the Act of Settlement of 1701 stated that judges could only be removed from their positions if Parliament demanded this.
- From now on ministers impeached by the House of Commons could not be pardoned by the Crown.

- In 1695 the Law of Treason was altered to give defendants the right to be given a copy of the indictment against them, the right to be defended by Counsel, and to be able to call witnesses in their defence. An act of treason needed two witnesses against the defendant instead of one as previously.
- Parliament was now enforcing its own control over judicial procedure. However, monarchs could still appoint judges who might be favourable to them.

The succession

- Before the Settlement, monarchs approved their own successors.
- The Bill of Rights declared that no Roman Catholic could become king or queen. Later, the Act of Settlement of 1701 stated that if William and Mary had no heirs the throne would pass to Sophia of Hanover, Protestant daughter of Elizabeth of Bohemia, sister of Charles I. The Act said that all future monarchs should be members of the Church of England.
- Parliament now governed the question of who ascended the throne.

Scotland

- The Claim of Right asserted that James had been deposed; Parliament gave the Crown to William and Mary, ie power flowed upwards from the people.
- The Settlement confirmed the position of the Kirk in Scotland as the Presbyterian Church.
- The abolition of the Committee of the Articles gave the Scottish Parliament a much greater share in the government of Scotland.

Ireland

- Roman Catholics in Ireland had been persecuted by monarchs in the past. The Settlement stated that Roman Catholics would enjoy the same freedoms as they had done under Charles II, although this promise was broken by the Penal Laws of 1693–94 which excluded Roman Catholics from the learned professions and elected positions. Soldiers who had fought for James II against William's troops in 1690 were allowed to flee to France.

The status of the army

- Charles I had been able to raise an army in 1642. The Revolution Settlement meant that Parliament gained partial control of the army. The monarch was not given enough money to maintain a standing army. The Mutiny Act of 1689 legalised the army, and this act had to be passed annually by Parliament, which forced the king to summon Parliament in order to do so. Royal authority over military matters had now passed to the House of Commons.

Loopholes in the Settlement

- Although the Revolution Settlement handed a lot of power from the Crown to Parliament, there were loopholes in the agreement which meant the monarch still held executive power and controlled foreign policy, declaring war and signing treaties.
- The monarch was still the source of patronage in the army and navy.
- The monarch still created peers, and could therefore control the House of Lords.
- The Revolution Settlement, therefore, did not completely hand over power to Parliament.
- It was a compromise which acted as a halfway-house between the Crown and Parliament, and government business was negotiated and conducted between the two.

Any other relevant factors.

Part C: The Atlantic Slave Trade

*Candidates can be credited in a number of ways **up to a maximum of 20 marks.***

22. How important was the slave trade in the development of the British economy in the eighteenth century?

Context
During the 18th century the British economy (industry) prospered. British ports such as Liverpool and Bristol grew into international trading centres and cities such as London grew rich due to the development of financial and insurance institutions.

Evidence that the slave trade was important

- Importance of the slave trade in the development of the economy: financial, commercial, legal and insurance institutions emerged to support the activities of the slave traders; slave traders became bankers and many new businesses were financed by profits made from slave-trading.
- The slave trade played an important role in providing British industry with access to raw materials and this contributed to the increased production of manufactured goods.
- Ports such as London, Bristol and Liverpool prospered as a direct result of involvement in the slave trade; other ports such as Glasgow profited from trade with the colonies; thousands of jobs were created in Britain supplying goods and services to slave traders.
- The slave trade was important to the economic prosperity and wellbeing of the colonies.
- The slave trade was an important training ground for British seamen, providing experienced crews for the merchant marine and the Royal Navy.
- However, the high death rate, particularly from disease, meant that the trade could be considered as a graveyard for seamen.
- Wealth generated by the slave trade meant that domestic taxes could be kept low.
- Argument that the slave trade was the vital factor in Britain's industrialisation was put forward in Williams' Capitalism and Slavery thesis.

Evidence that other factors were important

- Changes in agriculture: these created an agricultural surplus which: fed an expanding population; produced a labour force in the towns for use in factories; created a financial surplus for investment in industry and infrastructure.
- Technological innovation: development of water and steam power; new machinery; transport changes.
- Mineral and energy resources, particularly iron and coal.
- Political stability
- Much of the profits of slavery were dissipated in conspicuous consumption, eg landed estates.

Any other relevant factors.

*Candidates can be credited in a number of ways **up to a maximum of 20 marks.***

23. 'African societies benefited from their involvement in the slave trade.' How valid is this view?

Context
It has been estimated that over 10 million Africans were forcibly transported to the American continent and the Caribbean islands as part of the Atlantic slave trade during the 18th century. However, it is generally agreed that the slave trade also brought about detrimental changes to African societies and led to the long-term impoverishment of West Africa.

Positive effects

- African slave sellers grew wealthy by selling African captives to European traders on the coast; they were able to deal on equal terms with European traders who built 'factories' on the West African coast to house captives before selling them onto the slave-ship captains who in turn transported the captives to the colonies of the New World.
- On the African side, the slave trade was generally the business of rulers or wealthy and powerful merchants, concerned with their own selfish or narrow interests, rather than those of the continent. At that time, there was no concept of being African; identity and loyalty were based on kinship or membership of a specific kingdom or society, rather than to the African continent.
- Growth of states whose basis was the slave trade, notably Dahomey.

Negative effects

- Africans could become slaves as punishment for a crime, as payment for a family debt, or — most commonly of all — by being captured as prisoners of war; with the arrival of European and American ships offering trading goods in exchange for captives, Africans had an added incentive to enslave each other, often by abducting unfortunate victims.
- Rich and powerful Africans were able to demand a variety of consumer goods and in some places even gold for captives, who may have been acquired through warfare or by other means, initially without massive disruption to African societies.
- By the end of the 17th century, European demand for African captives, particularly for the sugar plantations in the Americas, became so great that they could only be acquired through initiating raiding and warfare; large areas of Africa were devastated and societies disintegrated.
- Some societies preyed on others to obtain captives in exchange for European firearms, in the belief that if they did not acquire firearms in this way to protect themselves, they would be attacked and captured by their rivals and enemies who did possess such weapons.
- Europeans seldom ventured inland to capture the millions of people who were transported from Africa as captives; in the areas where slavery was not practised, such as among the Xhosa people of southern Africa, European slave ship captains were unable to buy African captives.
- West Africa was impoverished by its relationship with Europe, while the human and other resources that were taken from Africa contributed to the New World; the trans-Atlantic trade also created the conditions for the subsequent colonial conquest of Africa by the European powers.
- It is estimated that around 10 million people were transported from Africa during the 18th century. This was a huge drain on the most productive and economically active sections of the population and this led to economic dislocation and falls in production of food and other goods.

Any other relevant factors.

Candidates can be credited in a number of ways up to a maximum of 20 marks.

24. To what extent was the decline in the economic importance of slavery the main reason for the abolition of the slave trade?

Context

Between 1787 and 1833, Britain had not only outlawed the slave trade but also abolished slavery throughout its colonies. The debate over the abolition of slavery in the British Empire revolves around the importance of anti-slavery campaigns or the argument that slavery was no longer as profitable to British businessmen.

Decline in the economic importance of slavery

- Effects of wars with France — slave trade declined by two-thirds as it was seen as harming the national interest in time of war.
- The slave trade had become less important in economic terms — there was no longer a need for large numbers of slaves to be imported to the British colonies.
- There was a world over-supply of sugar and British merchants had difficulties re-exporting it.

Other factors
The religious revival

- The religious revival of the late eighteenth century was at the heart of the anti-slavery movement. Many of the early leaders particularly were Quakers. The revival also took on board humanitarian considerations.

The role of Wilberforce

- Wilberforce put forward the arguments of the Society for the Abolition of the Slave Trade in Parliament for eighteen years.
- Wilberforce's speeches in parliament were graphic and appealing.
- Wilberforce's Christian faith had led him to become interested in social reform and link the issues of factory reform in Britain and the need to abolish slavery and the slave trade within the British Empire.
- Wilberforce was prepared to work with other abolitionists to achieve his aims, including the Quakers, Thomas Clarkson and Olaudah Equiano.

The effects of slave resistance and slave revolts

- There was an argument that if conditions were not ameliorated by, for example, the abolition of the slave trade, further revolts would follow. Already on Jamaica a substantial number of runaways lived outside the control of the authorities.

The campaign of the Anti-Slavery Society

- Thomas Clarkson obtained witnesses for the Parliamentary investigations of the slave trade that provided Wilberforce with convincing evidence for his speeches.
- Books and pamphlets were published eg eyewitness accounts from former slaves such as Olaudah Equiano.
- Campaigns to boycott goods produced by slaves in the West Indies such as sugar and rum.
- Petitions and subscription lists, public meetings and lecture tours involving those with experience of slave trade, eg John Newton, churches and theatres used for abolitionist propaganda, artefacts and illustrations, eg Wedgwood pottery.
- Lobbying of Parliament by abolitionists to extract promises from MPs that they would oppose the slave trade.
- Effective moderate political and religious leadership among the abolitionists influenced major figures such as Pitt and Fox; abolitionists gave evidence to Parliamentary Commissions.

Military factors

- Napoleon's efforts to restore slavery in the French islands meant that the abolitionist campaign would help to undermine Napoleon's plans for the Caribbean. The Act banning any slave trade between British merchants and foreign colonies in 1806 was intended to attack French interests.

Any other relevant factors.

Part D: Britain, 1851–1951

Candidates can be credited in a number of ways up to a maximum of 20 marks.

25. To what extent can Britain be described as a fully democratic country by 1918?

Context

Political change in Britain was an evolutionary, rather than revolutionary, process. These slow changes tended to see people given access to the political system in the 19th century because they had proven themselves worthy of the vote. By the 20th century, developments tended to be about the rights of citizens and their equality in the political system.

The vote

- In 1867 most skilled working-class men (also known as artisans) in towns got the vote. In 1884 many more men in the countryside were given the vote. In 1918 most men over 21 and some women over 30 gained the vote. After 1918, in 1928, all men and women over 21 were given the vote.

Fairness

- The Secret Ballot 1872 and the Corrupt and Illegal Practices Act 1883 largely solved the problems of intimidation and corruption.
- The effectiveness of these varied: they were less effective in areas where the electorate was small, or where a landowner or employer was dominant in an area. However, plural voting existed until 1948.
- The Redistribution of Seats Act 1885 equalised electoral districts.

Choice

- Although the working-class electorate increased by the 1880s, there was no national party to express their interests. The Liberals and Conservatives promoted middle-class, even upper-class, capitalist values.
- The spread of socialist ideas and trade unionism led to the creation of the prototype Labour Party — the LRC — by 1900, thereby offering a wider choice to the electorate.

Access to information

- In the later 19th century there was a great increase in literacy and hence access to information on which to base choice. Also, railways spread information nationally and were important to the growth of democracy.
- The development of national newspapers and libraries made information more freely available.

National party organisation

- As the size of the electorate grew, individual political parties had to make sure their message got across to the electorate, eg development of National Liberal Federation, Conservative Central Office, Primrose League.
- Political parties also had to create a coherent identity and a range of policies that would attract voters.

Power of Lords

- From 1911, Lords could only delay bills from the House of Commons for two years rather than veto them. They had no control over money bills.
- House of Lords still exists as a democratic anomaly today. It is a mixture of hereditary and life peers.

Any other relevant factors.

Candidates can be credited in a number of ways up to a maximum of 20 marks.

26. To what extent did the Liberal government of 1906–1914 introduce social reform due to the social surveys of Booth and Rowntree?

Context

Attitudes towards poverty in the 19th century were laissez-faire. Although the Liberals had not been elected on a social reform ticket in 1906, the overwhelming evidence regarding the scale of poverty, as well as developing concerns about the health of the nation (as an Empire Britain could ill afford to let her economic lead slip), led to a series of limited social reforms that were initiated by the Liberal Party.

Concerns over poverty: the social surveys of Booth and Rowntree

- The reports of Charles Booth in London and Seebohm Rowntree in York demonstrated that poverty had causes such as low pay, unemployment, sickness and old age. These were largely outwith the control of the individual.
- They provided the statistical evidence of the scale of poverty.
- The extent of poverty revealed in the surveys was also a shock.
- Booth's initial survey was confined to the east end of London, but his later volumes covering the rest of London revealed that almost one third of the capital's population lived in poverty.
- York was a relatively prosperous small town, but even there poverty was deep-seated. Identified primary and secondary poverty.
- Rowntree identified a cycle of poverty.

Other factors
Municipal socialism

- By the end of the century some Liberal-controlled local authorities had become involved in programmes of social welfare. The shocked reaction to the reports on poverty was a pressure for further reform.
- In Birmingham particularly, but also in other large industrial cities, local authorities had taken the lead in providing social welfare schemes. These served as an example for further reforms.

Foreign examples

- Germany had introduced a much-admired system of social security. Germany was also developing quickly in economic terms. This raised the issue of whether Britain was now no longer a major European nation. It can also be linked to the idea of national efficiency

National efficiency

- By the end of the 19th century, Britain was facing serious competition from new industrial nations such as Germany. It was believed that if the health and educational standards of Britain's workers got worse, then Britain's position as a strong industrial power would be threatened.

Fears over national security

- The government became alarmed when almost 25% of the volunteers to fight in the Boer War were rejected because they were physically unfit to serve in the armed forces. There was concern whether Britain could survive a war or protect its empire against a far stronger enemy in the future if the nation's 'fighting stock' of young men was so unhealthy.

- **The rise of the New Liberalism**
- New Liberals argued that state intervention was necessary to liberate people from social problems over which they had no control. New Liberal ideas were not important issues in the general election of 1905. Only when 'old liberal' Prime Minister Campbell Bannerman died in 1908 was the door opened for new 'interventionist' ideas. Leading New Liberals like Lloyd George and Winston Churchill were important in initiating reform.

Party advantage

- Since 1884 many more working-class men had the vote and the Liberals had tended to attract many of those votes. Social reform was a means of appeasing this constituency.

The rise of Labour

- By 1906 the newly formed Labour Party was competing for the same votes. It can be argued that the reforms happened for the very selfish reason of retaining working class votes.
- The Liberals recognised the electoral threat of the Labour Representation Committee (Labour Party from 1906) and in 1903 negotiated a Liberal–Labour electoral pact which allowed Labour to run unopposed by the Liberals in seats where there was a large working-class vote. By 1910, Labour had 42 seats.

Any other relevant factors.

Candidates can be credited in a number of ways up to a maximum of 20 marks.

27. **'The social reforms of the Labour government of 1945–1951 failed to deal effectively with the needs of the people.' How valid is this view?**

Context

In 1945 Labour won the General Election. Labour had promised to put into operation all the recommendations of the Beveridge Report. After 6 years of war the British people wanted 'post war to be better than pre war' and the Beveridge Report seemed to offer the chance of a better Britain.

Want

- In 1946 the National Insurance Act consisted of comprehensive insurance sickness and unemployment benefits and cover for most eventualities.
- It was said to support people from the 'cradle to the grave' which was significant as it meant people had protection against falling into poverty throughout their lives.
- This was very effective as it meant that if the breadwinner of the family was injured then the family was less likely to fall further into the poverty trap, as was common before. However, this act can be criticised for its failure to go far enough.
- Benefits only granted to those who made 156 weekly contributions.
- In 1948 the National Assistance Board was set up in order to cover those for whom insurance did not do enough. This was important as it acted as a safety net to protect these people.

Disease

- Establishment of the NHS in 1948 dealt effectively with the spread of disease
- The NHS was the first comprehensive universal system of health in Britain.
- It offered vaccination and immunisation against disease, almost totally eradicating some of Britain's most deadly illnesses.
- It also offered helpful services such as childcare, the introduction of prescriptions, health visiting and provision

for the elderly, providing a safety net across the whole country: everyone, regardless of their financial situation, was entitled to equal opportunities of health care they had previously not experienced
- The NHS could be regarded as almost too successful. The demand from the public was overwhelming, as the estimated amount of patients treated by them almost doubled. Introduction of charges for prescriptions, etc.

Education

- Reform started by the wartime government. The 1944 Education Act raised the age at which people could leave school to 15 as part of a drive to create more skilled workers which Britain lacked at the time. Introduction of school milk, etc.
- Labour introduced a two-tiered secondary schooling whereby pupils were split at the age of 11(12 in Scotland) depending on their ability. The pupils who passed the '11+ exam' went to grammar and the rest to secondary moderns.
- Those who went to grammar schools were expected to stay on past the age of 15 and this created a group of people who would take senior jobs in the country thus solving the skills shortages. Whilst this separation of ability in theory meant that children of even poor background could get equal opportunities in life, in practice the system actually created a bigger division between the poor and the rich.
- Labour expanded university education: introduction of grants so all could attend in theory.

Housing

- After the war there was a great shortage of housing as the war had destroyed and damaged thousands of homes; and the slum cleaning programmes of the 1930s had done little to rectify the situation which was leading to a number of other problems for the government.
- Tackling the housing shortage fell upon Bevan's Ministry of Health.
- Labours' target for housing was to build 200,000 new homes a year. 157,000 pre-fabricated homes were built to a good standard, however, this number would not suffice and the target was never met.
- Bevan encouraged the building of council houses rather than privately funded construction.
- The New Towns Act of 1946 aimed to target overcrowding in the increasingly built-up older cities. By 1950, the government had designed 12 new communities.
- In an attempt to eradicate slums, the Town and Country Planning Act provided local communities more power in regards to building developments and new housing.
- By the time Labour left government office in 1951 there was still a huge shortfall in British housing.

Any other relevant factors.

Part E: Britain and Ireland, 1900–1985

Candidates can be credited in a number of ways up to a maximum of 20 marks.

28. **'The decline of the Nationalist Party was the most significant impact of World War One on Ireland.' How valid is this view?**

Context

Initially war brought prosperity to Ireland. The demands on manufacturing and farming brought low unemployment thus improving relations between Great Britain and Ireland. However, Sinn Fein, the Easter Rising and Protestant reaction were to change this along increasingly sectarian lines.

Decline of Nationalist Party

- The Irish Convention failed to reach agreement, which weakened the position of Nationalists.
- This led to the feeling that the British could not be trusted and Nationalists could not deliver.
- Three by-elections wins for Sinn Fein gave impression they spoke for people not Nationalists which increased tension between Ireland and Britain politically.
- In March 1918 Redmond died which accelerated the decline of the Nationalists. Sinn Fein gained influence and popularity as a result.
- Many moved from the Nationalist Party as they felt Sinn Fein was doing more for Ireland.

Other factors

Irish attitudes to World War I

- Initially war brought prosperity to Ireland – manufacturing and farming, low unemployment thus improving relations between Great Britain and Ireland.
- Propaganda — powerful Germany invading helpless and small Catholic Belgium so Ireland supported Great Britain.
- Ulster very supportive of Britain to ensure favourable treatment at the end of the war.
- Nationalists and Redmond backed war to get Home Rule, urging Irish men to enlist.
- Press gave support to the war effort.
- Irish Volunteers gave support to help Home Rule be passed after the war.
- Recruitment was successful in the south as almost a quarter of a million men join up.

Easter Rising

- Rebels saw war as chance to rid Ireland of the British by force.
- Felt it was an opportunity to gain independence by force as Britain had their troops away fighting the Germans in World War I. This greatly strained relations between Britain and Ireland.
- Britain had to use force to suppress rebellion, such as using the Gunboat, 'Helga' to sail up the River Liffey and fire on the rebels in the GPO, thus distracting Great Britain's attention and resources away from the War effort, thus straining relations.
- Strong criticism of the Rising initially from the public, politicians, churchmen, as well as press for unnecessary death and destruction. 450 dead, 2,500 wounded, cost £2½ million, showing that majority still sided with Great Britain therefore indicating that there was not too much damage to relations between the two countries.
- Initial hostility by the majority of Irish people to the Rising by a small group of rebels, the majority of people supported Redmond and the Nationalists Party.
- Strong hostility and criticism by Dubliners of the rebels for destruction of the city centre.

Changing attitudes towards British Rule after 1916

- The secret court martial, the execution of leaders over 10 days, as well as imprisonment without trial and at least one execution without a trial, saw the rebels gain a lot of sympathy from the Irish public, turning them against British rule.
- These political developments meant a growth of sympathy and compassion for the rebels who were seen as martyrs and replaced the initial condemnation of the Rising.
- Sinn Fein, initially blamed for the Rising, saw a subsequent rise in support for them.

- The Catholic Church and the business community became more sympathetic to the cause of independence.

Anti-conscription campaign

- Irish opposed conscription so the people were pushed to Sinn Fein who openly opposed it.
- Caused the Nationalists to withdraw from Westminster.
- Sinn Fein and Nationalists organised campaign, eg general strike April 23rd.
- Catholic Church, Mayor of Dublin drew up the National Pledge opposing conscription.
- Conscription was not extended to Ireland which Sinn Fein was given credit for.
- Conscription campaign drove Sinn Fein underground which improved their organisation.

Rise of Sinn Fein

- Opposition to war was only supported by a minority in 1914 but was supported by Sinn Fein and Arthur Griffith (not powerful at this time), as well as Pearse, Connolly and their supporters and also a section of the Irish Volunteers. This damaged relations with Britain.
- Release of rebel prisoners from Frongoch meant Sinn Fein's struggle against British Rule in Ireland gained momentum. Michael Collins was building up IRB and Irish Volunteers when in prison.
- Collins ready to encourage anti-British activity in Ireland on release.
- Collins and De Valera improved Sinn Fein's leadership.
- Opposition to Britain due to martial law, house searches, raids, control of press, arrest of 'suspects' without trial, and vigorous implementation of the Defence of the Realm Act.
- Hunger striker Thomas Ashe died in 1917. His funeral became a propaganda tool for Sinn Fein.
- Entrenchment of unionism in the North. Unionists' 'blood sacrifice' on the Western Front — expectation that this would be recognised in any post-war settlement.
- The rise of Sinn Fein was viewed with increasing alarm, as was the participation of the Catholic Church in wartime politics, eg the National Pledge.

Any other relevant factors.

Candidates can be credited in a number of ways up to a maximum of 20 marks.

29. How important were divisions in the Republican Movement in causing the outbreak of the Irish Civil War?

Context

The Civil War was a direct consequence of the Anglo—Irish Treaty which was itself the result of the Irish War of Independence. The terms of the treaty were opposed by many Irish Republicans.

Divisions in the Republican Movement

- The treaty was hotly debated in the Dail. Collins and much of the IRA supported the treaty, as Ireland now had an elected government. De Valera opposed it and felt it should be resisted even if it meant civil war. They represented the two wings of the Republican movement.
- Also influential were the widows and other relatives of those who had died; they were vocal in their opposition to the treaty.
- The treaty was particularly disappointing to left-wing Republicans who had hopes of establishing a socialist republic.
- The treaty was accepted by 64 votes to 57 by the Dail Eireann on 7th January 1922.

- Collins and De Valera tried to reach a compromise to avoid war but none was reached. Some of the IRA units supported the treaty, whilst others opposed it. Some of the anti-treaty IRA took over some important buildings in Dublin, eg Four Courts.
- This division, crystallised by the murder of Sir Henry Wilson (security adviser for the Northern Ireland government), forced Michael Collins to call on the official IRA to suppress the 'Irregular IRA'.

The Anglo-Irish Treaty

- Ireland was to be the 'Irish Free State', governing itself, making its own laws but remaining in the Empire. A governor general was to represent the king: Britain was to remove its forces but keep the use of its naval bases. Trade relations were settled. Lloyd George threatened the Irish delegation with war if they did not sign.

Partition

- The Government of Ireland Act split Ireland in two, with six counties in the North and 26 in the South. In Northern Ireland, Unionists won 40 of the 52 seats available. A third of the Ulster population was Catholic and wanted to be united with the South.
- The 26 counties in the South had a separate parliament in Dublin. The Council of Ireland was set up. The IRA refused to recognise the new parliament and kept up its violence. Sectarian violence increased in Ulster; without partition this could have been much worse.
- In the South, the Government of Ireland Act was ignored. Sinn Fein won 124 seats unopposed. Partition was a highly emotive issue, and it alone would have caused discord.

Dominion status

- Under this agreement Ireland became a Dominion of the British Empire, rather than being completely independent of Britain. Under Dominion status the new Irish State had three important things to adhere to: the elected representatives of the people were to take an oath of allegiance to the British Crown; the Crown was to be represented by a Governor General; appeals in certain legal cases could be taken to the Privy Council in London. This aspect of the treaty was repugnant to many Irish people, not just Republicans.

The role of Collins

- Collins negotiated the treaty with Churchill, but was pressured to sign it under a threat of escalation of the conflict. He recognised that the war was unwinnable, both for the IRA and the UK government. Collins claimed Ireland had its own, elected government, so Britain was no longer the enemy. Collins defended the treaty as he claimed it gave Ireland 'freedom to achieve freedom'.

The role of De Valera

- De Valera refused to accept the terms of the treaty as they were in 'violent conflict with the wishes of the majority of the nation'. De Valera claimed that the treaty meant partition of Ireland and abandonment of sovereignty. De Valera felt he should have been consulted before the treaty was signed. De Valera voted against the treaty and resigned as President to be replaced by Griffith and Collins became Head of the Irish Free Government.

Any other relevant factors.

30. To what extent was the British government policy of Direct Rule the main obstacle to peace in Northern Ireland between 1968 and 1985?

Context
Direct Rule

- A number of reforms had followed on from the Downing Street Declaration, ie on allocation of council housing, investigate the recent cycle of violence and review policing, such as the disbanding of the hated 'B Specials' auxiliaries.
- The British government, now led by Prime Minister Edward Heath, decided to remove control of security from the government of Northern Ireland and appointed a secretary of state for the province leading to resignation of Stormont government. Direct rule imposed.
- Despite attempts to introduce some sort of self-rule, such as the Sunningdale agreement of 1973, which failed in the face of implacable unionist opposition and led to the reintroduction of direct rule. It would last for another 25 years.

Other factors
Religious and communal differences

- The Protestant majority in Northern Ireland belonged to churches that represented the full range of reformed Christianity, while the Catholic minority was united in its membership of a Church that dominated life in the Republic and much of Europe. These religious divisions made it very difficult for both communities to come together.
- These divisions further enhanced by traditions embraced by both communities, such as the 'marching season', which became a flashpoint for sectarian violence. Also differences in sport, language.
- Many Catholic political representatives refused to recognise partition and their views only heightened the nationalist community's sense of alienation and fostered unionist hostility towards the Catholic minority.
- The speeches and actions of unionist and nationalist leaders such as Reverend Ian Paisley and Gerry Adams polarised views in the province, and emphasised the divisions between both communities.

Economic differences

- From 1973, the Common Agricultural Policy changed the decision-making environment for food prices and farm economics, and employment in the farming sector continued to decline. Traditionally this sector had been dominated by the unionist community.
- Discrimination against Catholic applicants for employment declined steadily during this period as Catholics in the province began to enjoy the same civil rights enjoyed by the population of the rest of the UK.

Hardening attitudes — the role of terrorism

- Paramilitary groups began to operate on both sides of the sectarian divide, while civil rights marches became increasingly prone to confrontation.
- In late 1969, the more militant 'Provisional' IRA (PIRA) broke away from the so-called 'Official' IRA. PIRA was prepared to pursue unification in defiance of Britain and would use violence to achieve its aims.
- Unionist paramilitaries also organised. The UVF was joined by the Ulster Defence Association, created in 1971.
- Examples of terrorist activity: by the end of 1972 sectarian violence had escalated to such an extent that nearly 500 lives were lost in a single year.

- PIRA prisoners protest at loss of special status prisoners leading to hunger strikes. Second hunger strike in 1981, led by Bobby Sands. Sands was put forward for a vacant Westminster seat and won. Sands and nine other hunger strikers died before the hunger strikes called off in October 1981.
- Sinn Fein won the by-election following Sands' death in June 1983, These electoral successes raised the possibility that Sinn Fein could replace the more moderate SDLP as the political voice of the Catholic minority in Northern Ireland.

Indiscriminate terrorism meant Eire public opinion turned against PIRA

- In 1985 the violence of Northern Ireland's paramilitary groups still had more than a decade to run and the sectarian divide remained as wide as it had ever been.

British government policies — Internment

- New Prime Minister Brian Faulkner reintroduced internment, ie detention of suspects without trial, in 1971 in response to unrest. Policy a disaster, both in its failure to capture any significant members of the PIRA and in its sectarian focus on nationalist rather than loyalist suspects. The reaction was predictable, even if the ferocity of the violence wasn't. Deaths in the final months of 1971 over 150.

The role of the British Army

- The so-called 'Battle of Bogside' in 1969 only ended with the arrival of a small force of British troops at the request of Chichester Clark. An acknowledgement that the government of Northern Ireland had lost its grip on the province's security.
- By 1971 policing the province was fast becoming an impossible task, and the British Army adopted increasingly aggressive policies on the ground.
- On 30 January 1972, the army deployed the Parachute Regiment to suppress rioting at a civil rights march in Derry. Thirteen demonstrators were shot and killed by troops, with another victim dying later of wounds. Appalling images of 'Bloody Sunday; led to increased recruitment by Provisional IRA.
- The British Army's various attempts to control the PIRA, such as house-to-house searches and the imposition of a limited curfew, only served to drive more recruits into the ranks of the paramilitaries.

The role of the Irish government

- Irish government's role in The Anglo—Irish Agreement, signed in November 1985, confirmed that Northern Ireland would remain independent of the Republic as long as that was the will of the majority in the north. Also gave the Republic a say in the running of the province for the first time.
- The agreement also stated that power could not be devolved back to Northern Ireland unless it enshrined the principle of power sharing.

Any other relevant factors.

Part A: The Crusades, 1071—1204

Candidates can be credited in a number of ways up to a maximum of 20 marks.

31. To what extent was peer pressure the main reason for going on crusade?

Context
In 1095 Pope Urban II made his call at Clermont for a crusade to recapture the Holy Land. Pope Urban II's call for crusade was encouraged by Emperor Alexius I of Byzantium. Alexius was facing attacks from Muslims into the Eastern Roman Empire.

Peer pressure

- The pressure put on knights by their families to take the cross was at times severe. Noblemen's wives tended to be keenly aware of the politics at court and had a role in influencing the decisions of some.
- Stephen of Blois had married Adela, daughter of William I of England. It would have been unthinkable for such a notable knight not to go on the Crusade.

Other factors

Religious motives

- It was generally believed that the Remission of Sins offered by Pope Urban was an attractive solution to the dilemma of knights. Salvation was a constant worry for those trained to kill. Urban successfully resolved the need to protect Christianity from the Muslim threat and the general desire to re-establish the pilgrimage routes to the holy lands.
- The promise of remission of current sins was also a great relief to those knights worried about their eternal soul. Tancred's biographer wrote about both his worry over this dilemma and his relief at Urban's suggestion.
- The mass appeal of the People's Crusade shows the power of the belief that they were doing good and helping God.
- Of the leaders of the Princes' Crusade, Raymond of Toulouse, is often held up as an example of a knight riding to the defence of the Holy Lands. His decision to take Tripoli in 1100 casts a shadow over this interpretation of his motives.
- In later crusades many of the religious aspects of the Crusade are adopted and modified by the growing idea of chivalric codes.

The desire to acquire territory in the Holy Land

- Many of the great magnates on this expedition had intentions to acquire new estates for themselves. The motives of many of the leaders of the Princes' Crusade have been put down to this.
- Bohemend and Baldwin in particular showed little zeal in carrying on with the Crusade once they had acquired Antioch and Edessa respectively.

Seeking of fame and riches

- Some knights did go seeking glory. The Crusade had provided the solution to the problem of knights and their need for salvation. Killing was only wrong if you killed Christians. Urban indicated that the killing of a Muslim was a just act, and the equivalent to prayer or penance.
- Seeking of riches per se was uncommon; land was the real source of wealth and power.

The sense of adventure

- For some, the humdrum existence of 11th-century Europe could be replaced by the excitement of the Crusade. Pilgrimages had always been seen as important, and the idea of this as an armed pilgrimage was very appealing. It offered a way out for many serfs from their lives in bondage, or perhaps a chance to see the Holy Lands.

Overpopulation and famine

- Many were forced to leave because of the lack of available farmland in an already overcrowded Europe.
- Several famines have also been suggested as a possible motive. It was popularly believed that the Holy Lands were lands of plenty.

Any other relevant factors.

*Candidates can be credited in a number of ways **up to a maximum of 20 marks.***

32. How important were divisions amongst the crusaders in bringing about the fall of Jerusalem in 1187?

Context

Divisions amongst the crusaders was a key factor in the fall of Jerusalem but so too was the defeat at Hattin. It destroyed the crusader army and the defence of Jerusalem. It allowed Saladin, the Muslim leader, to reassert his authority over the professional Muslim army.

Infighting within Jerusalem

- Two factions struggled for power within Baldwin IV's court, those of Guy de Lusignan and Baldwin's close advisor Raymond III of Tripoli. In 1180 Guy married Sibylla, Baldwin's sister. Guy tended to favour an aggressive policy.
- The activities of Reynald of Chatillon helped to destabilise the fragile peace treaty between Baldwin IV and Saladin.

Death of Baldwin IV

- Baldwin died in March 1185, taking his strategy of non-aggression towards Saladin with him. He was replaced for a short time by his nephew, Baldwin V. However, a short power struggle after the boy's death in August let Guy de Lusignan assume the throne, abetted by Sibylla.

Importance of Hattin

- King Guy led the armies of Jerusalem to save Count Tiberius's wife as Saladin's forces had surrounded her castle. Tiberius himself had a few worries about the safety of his wife. His fortress could have withstood a siege. Saladin's forces lacked the required siege engines to make a successful attack. Additionally, Saladin could not keep his disparate forces in the field for any length of time. Tiberius' advice to Guy was to hold his forces back to protect Jerusalem.
- However, figures such as Reynald persuaded Guy that to leave the Countess of Tripoli besieged would be un-chivalric and that Guy would lose support if he did not ride out.
- The army could find little water to sustain them in the desert. Their only option was to make for Hattin and the oasis there. This was an obvious trap; Saladin surrounded them with burning brushwood and dry grass. Trapped on the Horns of Hattin the Christian army were suffering from the sun and lack of water.
- Eventually they were forced to attack before they lacked the strength to do so. The Christian horses were too weak for a prolonged struggle and their infantry were surrounded by Saladin's horse archers and cut off.

- Saladin ordered the slaughter of all members of the militant orders, but Guy and many of his followers were allowed to surrender and enter captivity.
- Without the army to protect the kingdom even the massive fortifications could not stand against Saladin's forces.

The Knights Templar

- Unlike the Hospitallers, the Knights Templar were firmly in the camp of the 'hawks' (warmongers). They wanted nothing more than to carry on with the crusading ideal and rid the Holy Lands of the Muslims. Treaties and compromise were unacceptable to them.

Lack of resources within the Christian states

- Even the combined armies of the crusader states were not strong enough to successfully win a war, especially in the long run. It is arguable that it was inevitable for the crusader states to fall to a united Islamic state.
- Lack of sufficient forts and castles to provide effective defences. There were not enough knights. Many of those knights saw their role as defending individual crusader states.

Unification of Islamic forces under Saladin

- Saladin had managed to successfully unite the Muslims of Syria and Egypt behind his leadership. This effectively surrounded Jerusalem and left them with a very weak military position.
- Saladin successfully used the idea of a religious war, a jihad, against the Christians to hold the separate Islamic groups together.

Saladin's internal problems

- Saladin himself had his critics within the Muslim ranks, saying he was more interested in maintaining his position than defeating the Christians. It was seen by many that his stance on the Kingdom of Jerusalem was weak. After Guy assumed the throne and Reynald continued his attacks the pressure on Saladin to respond grew. This encouraged him to act aggressively.

Any other relevant factors.

*Candidates can be credited in a number of ways **up to a maximum of 20 marks.***

33. 'By the Fourth Crusade in 1204 the Crusading Ideal was dead.' How valid is this view?

Context

After two centuries, the old crusading enthusiasm died out. The old ideal as 'the way of God' lost its spell. Men had begun to think less of winning future salvation by visiting distant shrines and to think more of their present day-to-day duties,

The Fourth Crusade

- The initial inspiration of the Forth Crusade had a strong crusading ideology behind it.
- Pope Innocent III planned that the Fourth Crusade would be commanded by six papal legates. These men would hold true to the ideal of the Crusade and not be bound by earthly greed or politics.
- However, The Fourth Crusade has also been described as the low point of the crusading ideal. Hijacked by the Venetians, the Crusade instead became a tool for their growing political and economic ambitions.

The distraction of Byzantium

- Alexius, son of the deposed emperor of Byzantium, asked the Crusaders to help him put his father back in control of Constantinople. He promised the crusaders huge wealth. He also promised to return control of the Byzantine Church to Rome.

- When the crusaders discovered that Alexius and his father would not meet the payment as agreed the crusaders stormed the city. The murder, looting and rape continued for three days, after which the crusading army had a great thanksgiving ceremony.
- The amount of booty taken from Constantinople was huge: gold, silver, works of art and holy relics were taken back to Europe, mostly to Venice. Most crusaders returned home with their newly acquired wealth. Those that stayed divided up the land amongst themselves, effectively creating several Latin Crusader States where Byzantium had once stood.

Role of Venice

- By 1123 the city of Venice had come to dominate maritime trade in the Middle East. They made several secret trade agreements with Egypt and North African emirs, as well as enjoying concessions and trade agreements within the Kingdom of Jerusalem. Byzantium however, remained a constant rival for this dominance of trade and in 1183 Venice was cut off from the lucrative trading centres of the empire.
- Venice's participation in the Crusade was only secured when the Pope agreed to pay huge sums of money to Venice for the use of its ships, and supplies as well as half of everything captured during the Crusade on land and sea.
- Venice's leader, the Doge Enrico Dandolo, had sold the crusaders three times as much supplies and equipment as required for the Crusade. The crusading leader, Boniface of Montferrat, found that he was unable to raise enough money to pay, and the crusaders were all but imprisoned on an island near Venice. Dandolo's proposal to pay off the crusaders' debt involved attacking Zara, a Christian city. Thus the Crusade had become a tool of the Venetians.
- The Fourth Crusade's intended target, Egypt, was totally unsuitable from a Venetian perspective. Thus when the Pope's representative approached the Venetians in 1201 they agreed to help transport the Crusaders, hoping to divert the crusade to a less friendly target. The final target for the Fourth Crusade was therefore determined by politics and economics.

Coexistence of Muslim and crusading states

- Attempts at peace between Muslim and the crusading states during the reign of Baldwin IV, before his death and the fall of Jerusalem.
- Also other examples, such as the treaty of mutual protection signed between King Alric of Jerusalem and the Emir of Damascus prior to the second crusade. The corruption of the crusading movement by the Church and nobles.

Popes were willing to use crusades against Christians

- Albegensian crusade against the Cathar heretics of Languedoc (Toulouse and southern France) in 1209–1229. This is only the first of many such crusades in Europe, seen as diluting the crusading ideal, ie killing Muslims.

Examples of nobles using the Crusade for their own ends

- Bohemond and Baldwin in the First Crusade, to arguably Richard in the third. The Fourth Crusade is littered with examples.

Any other relevant factors.

Part B: The American Revolution, 1763–1787

Candidates can be credited in a number of ways up to a maximum of 20 marks.

34. 'Disputes over taxation was the main reason for the outbreak of the American colonists' revolt against British rule in 1776.' How valid is this view?

Context

Since the 1600s, the 13 colonies of North America had been part of the British Empire. However, on 4th July 1776 the Continental Congress met in Freedom Hall, Philadelphia, and issued the Declaration of Independence. This historic event, the turning point in the American Revolution, came after over ten years of opposition by colonists to British rule.

Disputes over taxation

- **The Stamp Act**, the first form of taxation on the colonies, in 1765, was objected to by colonists because they were not represented in the British Parliament; 'No taxation without representation' became a familiar protest during this time; the Act stated that an official stamp had to be bought to go on any printed matter.
- Colonists subsequently refused to pay for this, stating that they already paid financial dues to the British through the Navigation Acts and other restrictions and that they had their own militia and did not need to pay for the British army to protect them.
- **The Declaratory Act** (1766): Britain had the right to tax the colonies.
- After the Stamp Act was repealed in 1766, **the Townshend Duties** on glass, tea, paper and lead were imposed in 1767.
- Colonists challenged Parliament's right to impose duties to raise revenue.
- **Tea duties:** George III insisted that although some taxes had been repealed, a tax should remain on tea from 1770 in order to maintain the British right to tax the colonists.
- Colonists were suspicious that Britain was attempting to get the colonists to buy cheap tea in order to coerce them into accepting British taxation.
- The Boston Tea Party in December 1773 was an expression of frustrations at British policy; however, the British denied that alterations to tea import duties were designed to get the East India Company out of financial trouble.

Other factors

Proclamation of 1763

- This forbade anyone from going beyond the Frontier; adventurers were thus kept within the jurisdiction of Britain; however, Empire Loyalists maintained the Proclamation offered protection to colonists from French hostility.

Re-imposition of the Navigation Acts

- After 1763 these were enforced by the Royal Navy after over 40 years of the colonists disregarding them during the Whig ascendancy.

British intransigence

- Britain retained an uncompromising attitude in the face of continued colonist protest and pleas for compromise.

Rejection of Olive Branch Petition/Role of George III

- George III rejected the colonists' last attempt at compromise; the 2nd Continental Congress had written an appeal to the king expressing allegiance to the crown and bitterness towards Parliament, yet the appeal fell on deaf ears as George III declared the colonists to be in rebellion.

- Many colonists started to consider independence as the only means of changing their relationship with Britain; the petition masked many colonists' intentions to declare greater autonomy.

Parliamentary ignorance

- In America there was a perception that Parliament dismissed the spirit and determination of the colonists to establish constitutional union with Britain.

Influence of Thomas Paine

- The republican pamphlet 'Common Sense' was published in January 1776 and sold 100,000 copies.

Punishment of Massachusetts

- The British response to the Boston Tea Party (the series of acts starting in March 1774, known to the colonists as the Intolerable Acts) — the British closed the port of Boston, altered the constitution of the legislature of Massachusetts, billeted British troops in colonial homes, and suspended trial by jury in the colony.
- Other colonies acted in sympathy with Massachusetts and showed unity at the 1st Continental Congress in September 1774.

Boston Massacre

- This occurred in 1775; although five working-class men died, including one black man, reports of five middle-class white men dying caused outrage amongst politically-minded colonists.
- Committees of Correspondence meant that news of the Massacre spread quickly around the 13 colonies.
- The acquittal of the British soldiers led colonists to fear for their personal liberty and to believe that they would one day be enslaved by the British. However, the Massacre was an incident which animated people mainly in the New England area, something which later caused George III to voice his belief that problems in America were 'localised'.

Any other relevant factors.

Candidates can be credited in a number of ways up to a maximum of 20 marks.

35. 'French intervention changed the whole nature of the American War of Independence.' How valid is this view?

Context

After the Declaration of Independence in 1776, Britain and the 13 American colonies went to war for five years on land and another two at sea. British troops surrendered at Yorktown in 1781, and Britain recognised American independence in 1783.

Franco–American Alliance

- France entered the war and took the conflict to Europe.
- Britain was forced to re-assign its military resources to defend itself and the Empire.
- French contribution to the colonists' cause took many forms — men, ammunition, training, supplies, and uniforms, fighting Britain around the world.
- However, France was not persuaded until February 1778 to make its alliance with America, by which time the Continental Army was already starting to make progress in the war in the colonies.

Dutch and Spanish entry

- When the Dutch and the Spanish entered the war, Britain's navy was stretched even further and it became increasingly difficult to focus on the war in the colonies.

- European nations now competed for parts of Britain's empire around the world. However, the war between Britain and the colonists on land was not directly affected by the Dutch and Spanish involvement.

Armed League of Neutrality

- This grouping of Russia, Sweden and Denmark gave extra cause for concern to Britain, as they were willing to fire on any Royal Navy ships which interfered with their merchant fleets.
- However, the League was not actively involved in the war, merely endeavouring to protect its own shipping.

Control of the sea

- The battle for control of the sea drew massively on the resources of all countries involved and significantly drained Britain's finances. However, the war at sea continued after the surrender at Yorktown, and the British recognised the Treaty of Versailles despite regaining control of the sea, suggesting the war on land was more significant to the outcome for the colonists.

German mercenaries

- Britain used over 7,000 of these in the colonies.

Changing views in Britain

- With the increasing European involvement, some Parliamentarians questioned Britain's ability to win a prolonged war.

Canadian aspect

- The colonists had appealed unsuccessfully for Canadian support, which meant the British were not distracted by concerns about possible rebellion in Canada.

Any other relevant factors.

Candidates can be credited in a number of ways up to a maximum of 20 marks.

36. To what extent did the American Constitution successfully address the issues raised by the experience of rule by Britain?

Context

On July 4, 1776 the Continental Congress announced that the thirteen American colonies, then at war with Britain, regarded themselves as 13 newly independent sovereign states and no longer part of the British Empire. Instead, they formed a new nation — the United States of America.

The experience of rule by Britain

- As part of the British Empire, colonists had been ruled by the king and the British Parliament, who together made key policy decisions, set laws and taxes, and enforced the law; there were no checks and balances.
- Colonists feared the potentially tyrannical power of a monarch, and designed the Constitution to prevent any such future threat.
- Branches of government were to be predominantly elective, to ensure the participation of the people.

Significance of the Constitution

- When the colonists drew up their Constitution, they built in a separation of powers providing checks and balances within the political system.
- The Bill of Rights established liberty for individuals in states within a federal union of all states, and set out clear lines of authority between federal government and individual states. This would avoid central government exerting a controlling power over people's lives.

- The hierarchy which existed under rule by Britain was altered by the Constitution, which stated that 'all men are created equal' and that everyone was entitled to 'life, liberty and the pursuit of happiness'.
- Now people would be asked to ratify many of the stages within the democratic processes at state and national level. However, women and blacks were excluded from the franchise, and in reality only one-fifth of eligible voters turned out for national elections.

Executive: role of President

- Executive power was vested in the elected President, and his Vice-President and Cabinet. The President acted as head of state and Commander-in-Chief but would have no vote in the law-making process, although he could veto legislation.
- The President would make all key decisions and establish policy.
- Members of the Executive could be removed from office by the electorate or the other branches of government if it was felt they were not doing their job properly.

Legislature: Congress

- Legislative power lay in the hands of an elected Congress which was divided into two Houses, the Senate and Representatives.
- Congress passed laws and raised taxes, as well as having responsibility for international trade, war and foreign relations.
- No one in the legislature could serve in the judiciary or executive without first resigning from the legislature.
- Congressional elections were held regularly to ensure that Congressmen remained in touch with the people they served.

Judiciary: Supreme Court

- Judicial power was granted to the Supreme Court of the United States.
- The Supreme Court acted as the highest court of appeal in the country. It also debated the legality of new laws passed by Congress.
- Supreme Court judges were nominated by the President and their appointment was ratified by Congress after a rigorous checking process.
- Appointees to the Supreme Court could be removed from their position if they acted improperly.

Any other relevant factors.

Part C: The French Revolution, to 1799

Candidates can be credited in a number of ways up to a maximum of 20 marks.

37. How important was the role of the bourgeoisie in the collapse of royal authority in France by 1789?

Context
The outbreak of the French Revolution was in part due to the collapse of the Ancien Regime and its financial problems. The cost of financing 18th-century wars added considerably to French debt.

Role of bourgeoisie
- The bourgeoisie had grown considerably in number during the 18th century but had little or no influence on state policy-making; however, they were expected to contribute to taxation whereas the nobility and clergy were not.
- As part of the Third Estate, resented paying the taxation.
- Dominated the Third Estate representatives in the Estates-General.

- Were outside the political process unless they bought a noble title: wanted access to power.
- Very attracted to ideas of a constitutional monarchy as advocated by people like Montesquieu.
- Provided the leadership for the revolution.

Other factors
Social divisions
- There were tensions between traditional nobility (of the sword) and the newly ennobled nobility (of the robe) wherein the 'old' sought to hold onto their control of key positions of the state, the army and the church, much to the annoyance of the 'new'.
- The church hierarchy was resented by the lower clergy; parish priests often sided with the peasants in their locality but the upper clergy viewed peasants with contempt and merely as a source of taxation.
- The peasantry was becoming increasingly discontented with the disproportionate burden of taxation which fell on them.
- The urban workers endured exploitation by bourgeois masters and suffered through restrictions on trade.

The economic crisis of 1788/9
- Bad harvests and grain shortages inspired unrest among the peasantry and the urban workers in Paris and in provincial cities throughout France, exerting critical pressures on the Ancien Regime.
- There was less demand for manufactured goods, which led to unemployment increasing amongst the urban workers.
- The nobility were increasingly blamed as peasants started to take political action.
- The economic crisis clearly created an environment in which the Ancien Regime was struggling to survive.

Financial problems of the Ancien Regime
- Because of exemptions the crown was denied adequate income. The privileged orders were an untapped source of revenue but it would require reforms to access it.
- This created resentment amongst the Third Estate.
- Exacerbated divisions that already existed between the estates.
- Tax-farming meant not all revenues were reaching the government.
- By the 1780s France faced bankruptcy due to heavy expenditure and borrowing to pay for wars.
- The cost of the Seven Years' War and France's financing of the American War of Independence had added considerably to the debt incurred by the wars fought by Louis XIV earlier in the century.
- Much of this was financed by loans so that by the 1780s about half of France's national income was going on payment of debt.
- There were severe problems in servicing this debt

Government failed to gain agreement on tax reform
- This was arguably the biggest threat facing the Ancien Regime.
- The nobility and the clergy were almost wholly exempt from the payment of taxes. Attempts to raise taxation revenue from these social groups were opposed at every turn. When short-term loans to finance the American wars had to be repaid from 1786 onwards there could be no more large-scale borrowing since investors were losing faith in the state's ability to re-pay.
- Anticipated tax revenues were projected to fall, making matters worse. There had to be changes to the system of taxation if the Regime was to survive.

- Attempts to introduce tax reforms in the late 1780s brought matters to a head.
- Taxation had to be extended to the previously exempt nobility and clergy since the rest of society (the Third Estate) could bear no further burden of taxation.

Influence of the Enlightenment

- The Enlightenment encouraged criticism, and freedom of thought, speech and religion, and was seen as the end of man's self-imposed irrationality at the hands of the Church in particular.
- Ideas of philosophers like Voltaire who attacked religion, Montesquieu who favoured a British system of government and Rousseau who put forward the idea of direct democracy.
- Very much appealed to the bourgeoisie, who led the revolution.

The American Revolution

- This war contributed to the financial crisis which came to a head in France post-1786 but for many in France at the time they also represented the practical expression of the enlightened views of the Philosophes in terms of the rights of the individual, no taxation without representation and freedom from tyrannical government. The wars inspired many of the lesser nobility and the bourgeoisie to seek the same freedoms.

The political crisis of 1788/9

- The convocation of the Estates General in August 1788 sharpened divisions between the three estates which came to a head between May and August 1789. The Cahiers des Doleances revealed the depth of dissatisfaction with the existing order, especially among the bourgeoisie and the peasantry. The creation of the National Assembly, the abolition of feudalism and the Declaration of the Rights of Man and the Citizen all contributed to a revolutionary change in French government, society and economy.

Actions of Louis XVI

- Louis was largely under the influence of his wife, Marie Antoinette who, although strong minded, failed to grasp the serious nature of situation and was also unpopular as she was Austrian.
- Louis XVI's handling of the Estates-General contributed towards the start of the Revolution. He wanted to make reform difficult by making the three estates meet separately, in the hope that the First and Second Estates would vote the Third down.
- This backfired. Opposition to the King grew, the Third Estate refused to act separately, and many of the clergy changed sides, changing the balance of power.
- Louis allegedly closed the meeting halls, which led to the Tennis Court Oath from members of the Third Estate. He later agreed to a constitution when the Third Estate representatives occupied the Royal tennis courts.
- The king had lost more political ground than if he had just listened to the grievances of the middle classes and the Third Estate from the start.

Any other relevant factors.

Candidates can be credited in a number of ways up to a maximum of 20 marks.

38. How important was the threat of counter-revolution as a cause of the Terror between 1792 and 1795?

Context

The French Revolution shocked Europe when it began in 1789. By 1792 the threat of the revolution spreading across Europe caused European leaders to raise armies against France. To maintain the revolution in the face of foreign threat and possible counter revolution 'The Reign of Terror' began. The 'Reign of Terror' was a period of bloody violence that took place during the French Revolution, 1793–1794.

The threat of counter-revolution

- One of the Convention's major concerns at the start of 1793 was to eliminate counter-revolutionary activity which intensified particularly in the provinces after Louis' execution. At this point the Convention was still controlled by the relatively moderate Girondins.
- The Convention sanctioned a range of counter-revolutionary legislation such as the creation of the Committee of Public Safety and the Committee of General Security Revolutionary tribunals to try opponents of the Republic and impose the death penalty if required. Surveillance Committees were established in local areas to identify counter-revolutionary activity.
- Most agree that most of the essential institutions of the Terror were actually in place before the Jacobins — and Robespierre — came to power. The moderates in the Convention had set up the structure of the Terror by the spring of 1793.

Other factors

Terror as the 'order of the day' (September 1793)

- It was pressure from mass demonstrations in Paris which intimidated the Convention into adopting terror as 'the order of the day', ie a method of government control. This was more to do with the exigencies of the foreign and civil wars which were threatening the Republic at this point than with Robespierre's philosophising over the nature of the Republic and the role of terror within it.

The outbreak of war

- The war put pressure on the Convention to execute the war against the Republic's émigré and foreign opponents as ruthlessly and as effectively as possible. The nation's resources were mobilised to this end. The early reverses raised alarms about sabotage and possible treason in the new armies.

The threat of invasion

- The initial defeats suffered raised the spectre of invasion.
- External dangers France faced radicalised the revolution. It caused a witch hunt for enemies within. The war led to the concept of the 'nation in crisis. This had to be enforced, violently if necessary.

Political rivalries

- The Jacobins were one of a number of political groupings contending for power. Other groups included the Girondins.
- The struggle became increasingly bitter with time. Similarly a number of other prominent individuals had sought to control the course of the revolution. Some had already died violently. The Terror was a legitimised means of the Jacobins eliminating their political rivals — 'a revolution always consumes its children'.

The role of Robespierre

- Robespierre believed that the 'general will' of the sovereign people both created and sanctioned policy-making within the nation. The will of the people could only prevail within a Republic. Any individual who sought to oppose this was, by implication, guilty of treason against the nation itself. In such circumstances death — the ultimate weapon of Terror — was entirely appropriate. Hence Robespierre's belief that 'terror is virtue' — that to create and maintain a 'virtuous' nation which enshrined the revolutionary principles of liberty and equality, it was necessary to violently expunge any counter-revolutionary activity.

- Robespierre became a member of the Committee of Public Safety in July 1793 and came to control its operations. Until his own execution in July 1794, the Committee became the main instrument for the application of terror in defence of Robespierre's ideal of a 'Republic of Virtue'. During this period Robespierre sanctioned the use of terror against many groups.
- With the imposition of the infamous Law of 22nd Prairial (June 1794), Robespierre was given virtually unlimited powers to eliminate opponents of his Republic of Virtue and during the period of the Great Terror in June and July 1794, over 1500 were executed.
- Had Robespierre lived beyond Thermidor there is no doubt the death toll would have risen even higher. However, while Robespierre must bear responsibility for the intensification of the Terror during 1793-1794, the use of terror as an instrument of state policy was by no means confined to Robespierre.

Religious and regional differences

- The uprising in the Vendee was supported by priests and former nobles. It also secured British support. It was brutally suppressed. Many women and children were drowned in the Loire at Nantes.
- There were also demands in the south for greater autonomy.
- Under the Civil Constitution of the Clergy, priests had to swear an oath of loyalty to the state. Many refused and became leaders of resistance.

Any other relevant factors.

*Candidates can be credited in a number of ways **up to a maximum of 20 marks**.*

39. To what extent did the peasants gain most from the French Revolution by 1799?

Context
The Revolution instigated a fundamental shift in political and economic power from the First and Second Estates to the bourgeoisie but by 1799 how much had the peasants benefited?

The impact of the Revolution on the peasantry

- The position of the peasantry was in many ways strengthened by the Revolution. The ending of feudalism in August 1789 removed many of the legal and financial burdens which had formed the basis of peasant grievances in the Cahiers des Doleances presented to the Estates-General in 1789.
- The revolutionary land settlement, instigated by the nationalisation of church lands in November 1789, had transferred land from the nobility and the clergy to the peasantry to their obvious advantage. It should be noted, however, that not all peasants benefited equally from this. Only the well-off peasants could afford to purchase the Church lands which had been seized by the National Assembly.

The impact of the Revolution on the bourgeoisie

- The ending of feudalism in August 1789 heralded profound social and economic change whilst the Declaration of the Rights of Man and the Citizen later in the month did the same for political life. In both cases the main beneficiaries were the bourgeoisie.
- Successive constitutions and legislative reforms throughout the1790s favoured the bourgeoisie above all other social groups by emphasising the notion of a property-owning democracy with voting rights framed within property qualifications, whilst the ending of

trade restrictions and monopolies favoured an expanding business and merchant class.
- France had moved from a position of privileged estates to one where increasingly merit was what counted. It was the educated bourgeoisie who were best placed to benefit from this profound change in French society.

The urban workers

- At key points throughout the Revolution overt demonstrations of discontent by the urban masses — particularly in Paris — impacted on key events as successive regimes framed policy with an eye to appeasing the mob. However, any modest gains by the urban poor were short-lived. A decade of almost continuous wars in the 1790s had created shortages and inflation which hit the urban poor particularly hard.
- The passing of the Chapelier Law in May 1791, by a bourgeois-dominated National Assembly protecting the interests of industrialists, effectively banned the formation of trade unions and thereafter the Revolution brought few tangible economic or political gains for urban workers.

The impact of the Revolution on the First Estate

- The Catholic Church was a key pillar of the Ancien Regime. The Upper Clergy (usually drawn from the ranks of the traditional nobility) enjoyed considerable wealth and status based on a raft of privileges and tax exemptions. These privileges and exemptions were swept away by the Revolution and the position of the Catholic Church within France by 1799 was far less assured than it had been under the Ancien Regime.
- The Civil Constitution of the Clergy (July 1790) polarised attitudes towards the place of the Catholic Church within French society and promoted conflict between opposing factions through the rest of the period to 1799. In November 1789 Church lands were nationalised, stripping the Church of much of its wealth. The net result of all of this was that the Church never regained its primacy within the French state and can be seen to have lost far more than it gained.

The impact of the Revolution on the Second Estate

- The aristocracy had enjoyed similar privileges and tax exemptions to those of the Catholic Church under the Ancien Regime. Advancement in the key positions of the State, the Army, and indeed the Church, depended more often on birth than merit. The traditional nobility monopolised these key positions and sought at all times to defend its favoured position. Again, the Revolution swept away aristocratic privilege even more completely than that of the clergy.
- The ending of feudalism in August 1789 marked the prelude to a decade when the status of the nobility in France effectively collapsed. In 1790 outward displays of 'nobility' such as titles and coats of arms were forbidden by law and in 1797, after election results suggested a pro-royalist resurgence, the Convention imposed alien status on nobles and stripped them of French citizenship.
- The Revolution brought in a regime where careers were open to talent regardless of birth or inheritance and the traditional aristocracy simply ceased to exist. Having said that, some nobles simply transformed themselves into untitled landlords in the countryside and continued to exercise significant economic and political power.

Any other relevant factors.

Part D: Germany, 1815–1939

Candidates can be credited in a number of ways up to a maximum of 20 marks.

40. 'By 1850 political nationalism had made little progress in Germany.' How valid is this view?

Context

German nationalism, the desire for a united Germany, was already in existence in 1815 as a response to the ideas of the French Revolution and due to resentment of French domination under Napoleon. However, the lack of popular support for nationalism — especially amongst the peasants — and the political repression coordinated by Metternich meant there were still many factors unfavourable to German nationalism.

Evidence that nationalists made significant progress

- Vormarz period — evidence suggests that workers were starting to take a real interest in politics and philosophy, but only in relatively small numbers.
- Cultural nationalism — work of poets, musicians, writers and their effects on Germans. The impact was largely on educated Germans and not everyone was interested in such ideas, which were not considered vital to the everyday lives of the ordinary people.
- 1840 — French scare to German states. Ordinary Germans now roused to the defence of the fatherland. Not confined to educated classes. Spread of nationalist philosophy to large numbers of ordinary Germans. Enhanced reputation of Prussia among German nationalists.
- Economic nationalism — middle-class businessmen pushing the case for a more united Germany in order to be able to compete with foreign countries. Benefits evidenced by the Zollverein to German states. Arguments that 'economic' nationalism was the forerunner to political nationalism.

Evidence that nationalists had not made significant progress

- Growth of the Burschenschaften — dedicated to seeing the French driven from German soil. Nationalist enthusiasm tended to be of the romantic type, with no clear idea of how their aim could be achieved. Much of the debate in these societies was theoretical in nature and probably above the comprehension of the mass of ordinary Germans.
- Political nationalism — virtually non-existent between 1820 and 1848. Suppressed by the Karlsbad Decrees and the Six Acts. Work/success of Metternich in suppressing such a philosophy.
- Work of the German Confederation and the rulers of the autonomous German states to suppress nationalism.
- Troppau Congress — decision taken by the representatives of Austria, Prussia and Russia to suppress any liberal or nationalist uprisings that would threaten the absolute power of monarchs; huge blow to nationalists within the German states.
- German Bund — remained little more than a talking shop. Austrian domination of the Confederation and the Bund stifled political change.
- 1848 Revolutions and the Frankfurt Parliament; no agreement was reached on a gross or a kleindeutsch solution. German rulers regained authority. Divided aims of revolutionaries. Self-interest of the rulers of the German states led to their opposition to Frankfurt Parliament.
- Frederick William of Prussia backed down in the face of Austrian pressure at Olmutz and the humiliation of Prussia: German nationalism was arguably a spent force.

Any other relevant factors.

Candidates can be credited in a number of ways up to a maximum of 20 marks.

41. How important was the attitude of foreign states in the achievement of German unification by 1871?

Context

The growth of nationalism and Prussian dominance among the German states led to pressures for unification of Germany. Otto von Bismarck's policies took advantage of these forces to achieve unification. However, it is possible that unification was more of a natural development due to favourable social and economic circumstances.

Attitude of foreign states

- Role of Napoleon Bonaparte and France pre-1815— stimulated German nationalism.
- Attitude of Denmark towards Schleswig-Holstein.
- Attitude of Russia toward Austria after Austrian failure to intervene over Crimea.
- Attitude of Italian states in Austro-Prussian War of 1866.
- Actions of Napoleon III.
- Meeting at Biarritz secured French border while Prussia fought Austria.
- Napoleon III hoped for long war between Austria and Prussia.
- Napoleon III instrumental in ensuing armistice.
- Napoleon III and role over Hohenzollern candidature.

Other factors
The role of Bismarck

- Bismarck's aim was to increase the power of Prussia by whatever means necessary.
- Bismarck and his 'realpolitik'/diplomacy in the '3 wars' against Denmark, Austria and France.
- Bismarck took the initiative, as opposed to Austria, in the war against Denmark; his 'solution' to the Schleswig-Holstein question.
- Bismarck's skilful manipulation of events leading up to the war with Austria in 1866 plus his establishment of friendships with potential allies of Austria beforehand.
- Bismarck's wisdom in the Treaty of Prague, 1866.
- Bismarck's manipulation of the Ems Telegram to instigate a war with France in 1870.
- Bismarck's exploitation of the weaknesses of European statesmen/rulers, eg Napoleon III; mistakes made by Bismarck's adversaries.
- Bismarck's skill in isolating his intended targets (diplomatically).
- Arguments about the role of Bismarck: '*Bismarck did not fashion German unity alone. He exploited powerful forces which already existed...*' (Williamson) — '*...it was he* (Bismarck) *who created the conditions which rendered possible the creation of a Great Germany.*' (Hitler) — '*Bismarck's admirers often exaggerate the extent of the obstacles in his path.*' (Medlicott)

Other factors
Military factors

- Significance of military reforms of Moltke and Roon — creation of modern powerful army which Bismarck used.
- The decline in Austrian power and influence — economically and militarily — during the 1850s particularly.
- Distraction of Austria to commitments in Italy.

Economic factors

- Growth in Prussian economic power, eg development of railways, transport links, roads; importance of the Rhineland and the Saarland to Prussian economic development. Able to finance and equip Prussian army.
- The Zollverein, the Prussian-dominated free-trade area; its significance to German political unification — the 'mighty lever of German unification'.

Political factors

- Influence of Napoleon Bonaparte — reduction of number of German states; growth of a national consciousness.
- The 1848 revolutions in German states — importance of Frankfurt Parliament/decisions taken regarding a unified Germany; Prus Cultural factors
- Growth of German cultural nationalism/Romantic Movement — Burschenschaften, eg writers, music, leading to an increased German national consciousness among the educated classes.

Any other relevant factors.

Candidates can be credited in a number of ways up to a maximum of 20 marks.

42. 'Propaganda was crucial to the maintenance of power by the Nazis between 1933 and 1939.' How valid is this view?

Context

Hitler became Chancellor of Germany in 1933 and by 1934 had established a totalitarian dictatorship. Nazi rule in Germany was absolute but was that because people were persuaded to support the regime by propaganda, fearful of opposing it or did most Germans accept and even support the regime that gave them work and food?

Propaganda

- Use of Nuremburg Rallies.
- Use of radio.
- Cult of the Leader: the Hitler myth.
- Use of the cinema: Triumph of the Will, The Eternal Jew, etc.
- Role of Goebbels.

Other factors

Success of economic policies

- Nazi economic policy — attempted to deal with economic ills affecting Germany, especially unemployment.
- Nazis began a massive programme of public works; work of Hjalmar Schacht.
- Nazi policy towards farming, eg Reich Food Estate — details of various policies.
- Goring's policy of 'guns before butter'. Popular once foreign policy triumphs appeared to justify it.

Social policies

- Creation of the volksgemeinschaft (national community)
- Nazi youth policy.
- Nazi education policy.
- Nazi policy towards the Jews — first isolate, then persecute and finally destroy.
- Nazi family policy — Kinder, Kirche, Kuche.
- Kraft durch Freude programme.
- A Concordat with the Catholic Church was reached; a Reichsbishop was appointed as head of the Protestant churches.

Success of foreign policy

- Nazi success in foreign policy attracted support among Germans; Rearmament, Rhineland, Anschluss.

- 'Much of Hitler's popularity after he came to power rested on his achievements in foreign policy'. (Welch)

Establishment of totalitarian state

- Political parties outlawed; non-Nazi members of the civil service were dismissed.
- Nazis never quite able to silence opposition to the regime.
- Speed of takeover of power, and ruthlessness of the regime made opposition largely ineffective.
- Anti-Nazi judges were dismissed and replaced with those favourable to the Nazis.
- Acts Hostile to the National Community (1935) — all-embracing law which allowed the Nazis to persecute opponents in a 'legal' way.

Fear and state terrorism

- The use of fear/terror through the Nazi police state; role of the Gestapo.
- Concentration camps set up; the use of the SS.

Crushing of opposition

- Opponents liable to severe penalties, as were their families.
- Opponents never able to establish a single organisation to channel their resistance — role of the Gestapo, paid informers.
- Opposition lacked cohesion and a national leader; also lacked armed supporters.
- Lack of cooperation between socialists and communists — role of Stalin considered.

Any other relevant factors.

Part E: Italy, 1815—1939

Candidates can be credited in a number of ways up to a maximum of 20 marks.

43. To what extent was the idea of nationalism well established in Italy in the years before 1850?

Context

By 1850 the forces of nationalism had grown in Italy. The Revolutions of 1849—9 showed this, but it also illustrated the tensions within the nationalist movement and the continued strength of the Austrians.

Supporters of nationalism

Educated middle class

- Risorgimento saw 'patriotic literature' from novelists and poets including Pellico, and Leopardi. These inspired the educated middle class.
- Gioberti, Balbo and Mazzini promoted their ideas for a national state. This inspired nationalism amongst the middle classes.

Liberals

- Some liberals and business classes were keen to develop an economic state. Napoleon Bonaparte had built roads and encouraged closer trading. One system of weights, measures and currency appealed.

Popular sentiment

- French revolutionary ideals had inspired popular sentiment for a national Italian state.
- There was a growing desire for the creation of a national state amongst students; many joined Mazzini's 'Young Italy'.
- Operas by Verdi and Rossini inspired growing feelings of patriotism.
- The use of Tuscan as a 'national' language by Alfieri and Manzoni spread ideas of nationalism.

- Membership of secret societies such as the Carbonari grew. Members were willing to revolt and die for their beliefs, which included desire for a national state.

Opponents of nationalism

Austria

- Resentment against Austria, its restoration of influence in the Italian peninsula and use of spies and censorship, helped increase support for the nationalist cause. However, any progress made by nationalists was firmly crushed by the Austrian army.
- Strength of the Quadrilateral. Austrians never left Italian soil.
- Carbonari revolts in Kingdom of Naples 1820—1821, Piedmont 1821, Modena and the Papal States 1831 all crushed by Austrian army.
- During the 1848—1849 revolutions, the Austrian army defeated Charles Albert twice — Custoza and Modena — retook Lombardy and destroyed the Republic of St Mark.

Italian princes and rulers

- Individual rulers were opposed to nationalism and used censorship, police and spies as well as the Austrian army to crush revolts in 1820—1821, 1830 and 1848—849.

Attitude of the peasants

- The mass of the population was illiterate and indifferent to politics and nationalist ideas. They did revolt during bad times as can be seen in 1848, but these revolts were due to bad harvests and bad economic times and were not inspired by feelings of nationalism.

Position of the papacy

- The nationalist movement had high hopes of the new Pope, Pius IX, initially thought of as a liberal and sympathetic to the nationalist cause. Hopes were dashed when Pope Pius IX denounced the nationalist movement during the 1848—49 revolutions.

Failures of 1848—1849 revolutions

- These showed that nationalist leaders would not work together, nor did they seek foreign help, thus hindering progress. Charles Albert's 'Italia farad a se' declared that Italy would do it alone — she did not. Lombardy and Venetia suspected Charles Albert's motives and were reluctant to work with him. Venetians put more faith in Manin.

Any other relevant factors.

*Candidates can be credited in a number of ways **up to a maximum of 20 marks**.*

44. To what extent was the unification of Italy by 1870 the result of foreign intervention?

Context

The nationalist reaction to the rule of Napoleon across Europe unleashed forces which eventually led to the unification of Italy, among a number of states. In Italy this process was dominated by the state of Piedmont, although the role of individuals like Garibaldi and the declining power of Austria also need to be taken into account.

Foreign Intervention

Actions of Britain

- Britain was involved in diplomacy over the Duchies. British naval presence helped Garibaldi. Britain refused a joint naval blockade with France to stop Garibaldi crossing Strait of Messina — crucial for Garibaldi's success.
- Britain was the first power to officially recognise the Kingdom of Italy.

Prussia

- The Italians made a secret agreement to help Prussia in the war against Austria in 1866.
- The Prussian war against France gave Italians the chance to take Rome in 1870.

Attitudes and actions of Napoleon III

- Napoleon III met Cavour at Plombieres. The result was a formal treaty, January 1859. Napoleon promised 200,000 men to fight for Piedmont if Austria attacked.
- War of Liberation 1859: French victories gained Lombardy for Piedmont.
- Napoleon accepted Duchies/Romagna uniting with Piedmont.
- Secretly, Napoleon accepted Cavour's invasion of Papal States to stop Garibaldi reaching Rome, allowing the Piedmontese to defeat the Papal Army and take the Marches/Umbria. In 1866 Austria handed Venetia to France who gave it to Italy.
- Crimean War/Paris Peace provided opportunity for Cavour to remind Britain and France of Italy's 'unhappy' state.
- Napoleon did not intervene over Garibaldi's expedition. He made a secret agreement accepting Cavour's proposed invasion of the Papal States to stop Garibaldi reaching Rome. This allowed the Piedmontese to defeat the Papal Army, taking The Marches and Umbria. In 1866, Austria handed Venetia to France who gave it to Italy. The Italians took Rome after the defeat of Napoleon in 1870.

Other factors

Role of Garibaldi

- Garibaldi was a committed nationalist; he fought in the War of Liberation for Victor Emmanuel. His role was crucial in forcing north/south unification — the role of 'thousand'; military success in Sicily and Naples; handing his 'conquests' to Victor Emmanuel at Teano. He tried but failed to take Rome.
- He was a committed nationalist and championed the idea of a united Italy. He led the Garabaldini volunteers in the 1859—60 war against Austria. His military expedition resulted in Sicily and Naples being taken.
- Mazzini wanted to make liberated southern Italy a republic. The populace acclaimed Garibaldi as ruler, but Garibaldi himself remained loyal to Victor Emmanuel. After meeting the king at Teano, near Naples, he relinquished his conquests to Sardinia. Shortly afterward (1861), Victor Emmanuel was proclaimed king of a united Italy.
- In 1862, Garibaldi led a volunteer corps against Rome, but the king, fearing international intervention, sent an Italian army that defeated Garibaldi at Aspromonte. Garibaldi was given a pardon.
- Propaganda earned Garibaldi a considerable reputation in Italy and abroad at the time.

The rise of Piedmont

- Piedmont was the most powerful of the independent Italian states. She was the natural leader of the unification movement.
- Piedmont was also the most economically advanced of the Italian states. Industry developed around Turin and a railway network was built.
- The army of Piedmont was advanced by Italian standards.

Role of Cavour

- He played a vital role — modernisation of Piedmont; diplomacy before the War of Liberation.
- Cavour made a secret agreement to help Prussia in the war against Austria in 1866. The Prussian war against France gave the Italians the chance to take Rome.

- Provocation of Austria; encouragement of National Society, especially in Duchies/Romagna, and his handling of the plebiscites.
- The war of 1859 inspired rebellions in Tuscany, Parma, Modena, Romagna and demands for union with Piedmont. Napoleon was not happy, but was persuaded to accept by British diplomacy and Cavour's renewed offer of Nice and Savoy.
- Cavour's diplomacy and manoeuvring over Garibaldi's expedition; the invasion of Papal States forced unification on Piedmontese terms.

Role of Victor Emmanuel II
- The king was supportive of Cavour. Victor Emmanuel of Piedmont/Cavour realised foreign help was needed to drive Austrians from Italy.
- The king 'managed' Garibaldi very well in 1866, preventing a diplomatic crisis.

Decline of Austria
- Austria's position was in decline in economic and military terms, particularly in regard to Prussia. Italy's relative weakness was redressed by her understanding with Prussia.
- Austria's diplomatic position also declined in the 1850s, and she was increasingly isolated. Partly this was self-inflicted. Russia never forgave Austria for her lack of support during the Crimean War.

Candidates can be credited in a number of ways up to a maximum of 20 marks.

45. How important was the use of propaganda in maintaining Fascist power in Italy between 1922 and 1939?

Context
Between 1922 and 1939 Mussolini was the fascist leader of Italy. Did Italians support Mussolini because of effective propaganda or did most Italians accept and even support the regime that gave them work and food and promises of powerful Italy?

Propaganda
- Press, radio and cinema were all controlled.
- Mussolini was highly promoted as a 'saviour' sent by God to help Italy
- Mussolini was portrayed as the heir to Caesar, world statesman, supreme patriot, a great thinker who worked 20 hours a day, a man of action, incorruptible.

Other factors
Fear and intimidation
- Mussolini favoured complete State authority with everything under his direct control. All Italians were expected to obey Mussolini and his Fascist Party.
- The squadristi were organised into the MVSN Milizia Voluntaria per la Sicurezza Nazionale the armed local Fascist militia (Blackshirts). They terrorised the cities and provinces causing fear with tactics such as force-feeding with toads and castor oil.
- After 1925–6 around 10,000 non-fascists/opposition leaders were jailed by special tribunals.
- The Secret police, OVRA was established in 1927 and was led by Arturo Bocchini. Tactics included abduction and torture of opponents. 4,000 people were arrested by the OVRA and sent to prison.
- Penal colonies were established on remote Mediterranean islands such as Ponza and Lipari. Conditions for those sentenced to these prisons were primitive with little chance of escape.

- Opponents were exiled internally or driven into exile abroad. The death penalty was restored under Mussolini for serious offences but by 1940 only ten people had been sentenced to death.

Establishment of the fascist state
- 1926 — opposition parties were banned. A one-party state was created.
- 1928 — universal suffrage abolished.
- 1929 — all-Fascist Parliament elected.

Crushing of opposition
- Liberals had divided into four factions so were weakened.
- The Left had divided into three — original PSI, reformist PSU and Communists — they failed to work together against fascists.
- Pope forced Sturzo to resign and so PPI (Catholic Popular Party) was weakened and it split.
- Acerbo Law passed. 1924 elections — fascists won 66% of the vote.
- Opposition parties failed to take advantage of the Matteotti crisis. By walking out of the Chamber of Deputies (Aventine Secession) they gave up the chance to overthrow Mussolini; they remained divided – the Pope refused to sanction an alliance between PPI and the socialists. The king chose not to dismiss Mussolini.
- Communists and socialists did set up organisations in exile but did not work together. Communist cells in northern cities did produce some anti-fascist leaflets but they suffered frequent raids by OVRA. PPI opposition floundered with the closer relationship between Church and State (Lateran Pacts).

Social controls
- Workers were controlled through 22 corporations, set up in 1934; overseen by National Council of Corporations, chaired by Mussolini.
- Corporations provided accident, health and unemployment insurance for workers, but forbade strikes and lock-outs.
- The majority of Italians got on with their own lives conforming as long as all was going well. Middle classes/elites supported fascism as it protected them from communism.
- Youth knew no alternative to fascism, were educated as fascists and this strengthened the regime. Youth movements provided sporting opportunities, competitions, rallies, camps, parades and propaganda lectures — 60% membership in the north.

Foreign policy
- Mussolini was initially extremely popular, as evidenced by huge crowds who turned out to hear him speak.
- Foreign policy successes in the 1920s, such as the Corfu Incident, made him extremely popular. He was also able to mobilise public opinion very successfully for the invasion of Abyssinia.
- Mussolini's role in the Munich Conference of 1938 was his last great foreign policy triumph.
- As Mussolini got more closely involved with Hitler his popularity lessened. His intervention in Spain proved a huge drain on Italy's resources. The invasion of Albania was a fiasco. The Fascist Grand Council removed him in 1943.

Relations with the Papacy
- Lateran treaties/Concordat with Papacy enabled acceptance of regime by the Catholic majority.
- Many Catholics supported Mussolini's promotion of 'family values'.

Economic and social policies

- Fascists tried to develop the Italian economy in a series of propaganda-backed initiatives, eg the 'Battle for Grain'. While superficially successful, they did tend to divert resources from other areas.
- Development of transport infrastructure, with building of autostrade and redevelopment of major railway terminals, eg Milan.
- One major success was the crushing of organized crime. Most Mafia leaders were in prison by 1939.
- Dopolavoro had 3.8 million members by 1939. Gave education and skills training; sports provision, day-trips, holidays, financial assistance and cheap rail fares. This diverted attention from social/economic problems and was the fascist state's most popular institution.

Any other relevant factors.

Part F: Russia, 1881–1921

*Candidates can be credited in a number of ways **up to a maximum of 20 marks**.*

46. To what extent was Bloody Sunday responsible for the 1905 Revolution in Russia?

Context
By 1905 Russia's problems had led to open opposition to the Tsarist state. Poor military performance in the war with Japan exposed the social, economic and political weaknesses of the state.

Bloody Sunday

- On 22nd January 1905 Father Gapon, an Orthodox priest, attempted to lead a peaceful march of workers and their families to the Winter Palace to deliver a petition asking the Tsar to improve the conditions of the workers.
- Marchers were fired on and killed by troops.
- Many of the people saw this as a brutal massacre by the Tsar and his troops.
- Bloody Sunday greatly damaged the traditional image of the Tsar as the 'Little Father', the Guardian of the Russian people.
- Reaction to Bloody Sunday was strong and was nationwide with disorder strikes in urban areas, terrorism against government officials and landlords, much of which was organised by the SRs.
- The situation was made worse by the defeat to Japan in 1905.
- There was the assassination of government minister Plehve.

Military defeat

- Land battle: decisive defeat at Mukden.
- Sea battle: defeat at Tsushima Strait. They sailed 18,000 miles before being defeated in under an hour.
- The Russo–Japanese War was disastrous for Russia. Defeats by Japan were humiliating and led to discontent in Russia over the Tsar's leadership, the incompetence of the Tsar's government and the inadequate supplies and equipment of Russia's armed forces.
- Russian soldiers and sailors were unhappy with their poor pay and conditions. The incompetence of their leaders and their defeats led to low morale.
- Naval mutiny in the Black Sea fleet, battleship Potemkin, over poor conditions and incompetent leadership threatened to spread and weakened support for the Tsar.

Other factors
Economic problems
Working-class discontent

- Russia had been experiencing a number of economic problems in the period before 1905. Russia had started the process of industrialisation, however, its cost meant that Russia used foreign loans and increased taxes to fund it.
- The working and living conditions in the cities were very poor and this, along with long working hours and low pay, led to discontent.

Peasantry discontent

- The vast majority of Russians were peasant farmers who lived in poverty and were desperate to own their own land.
- Many peasants were frustrated at paying redemption payments and at the unwillingness of the government to introduce reforms.
- An economic slump in Russia hurt the newly created Russian industries and, coupled with famine in 1902/1903, led to food shortages.
- There was an outcry when Russian grain was still being exported to pay for the foreign loans.

Political problems

- Growing unhappiness with Tsarist autocratic rule.
- The middle class and the industrial workers were calling for a constitutionally elected government as they were so frustrated at the incompetence of the Tsar's government, especially during the war with Japan.
- During 1905, workers set up groups called soviets to demand better pay and conditions. The Russian nobility feared a revolution if moderate reforms were not introduced.
- Tsar Nicholas II was seen as being too weak and unable to make good decisions for Russia in a crisis.
- National minorities hated the policy of Russification as it ignored their language, customs and religion and many felt so isolated that the desire for independence intensified.
- As the war with Japan progressed there were a growing number of protests from different parts of Russian society calling for the war to end and the Tsar to share his power.

Events

- Terrorist acts followed Bloody Sunday towards government officials and landowners.
- Peasant violence in the countryside when peasants took over land and burned landowners' estates started after the government threatened to repossess the land of those behind with their redemption payments.

Any other relevant factors.

*Candidates can be credited in a number of ways **up to a maximum of 20 marks**.*

47. To what extent did working class discontent cause the outbreak of the February Revolution in 1917?

Context

After more than 300 years of Romanov rule, the Russian Tsar came under increasing pressure in early 1917. 'The Little Father' was no longer supported and the royal family became the focus of popular discontent increasing pressure.

Working-class discontent

- The growing working class worked and lived in poor conditions, with long hours and poor wages as well as overcrowded accommodation.
- Due to their poor working and living conditions the industrial working class were receptive to the new socialist ideas that were around.

- The working class began to organize a series of strikes and demonstrations in 1917. Many of the working class were starving as grain was being given to the soldiers and much of it was not reaching the cities as the trains were requisitioned for the use of the army.
- There was a lack of food made worse by the transport problems and the loss of agricultural land to the Germans and as a result in the cities there were long queues and bread riots culminating in International Women's Day protest in Petrograd.

Other Factors
Peasant discontent
- Peasant discontent over the land issue did not abate during the war years. When order began to break down, land seizures by peasants became common.
- The war put extra strains on the peasantry with requisitioning of horses and conscription of men. This hit output.
- The horror of Russia's huge casualties was felt most among the peasants.

Impact of the First World War military defeat
- The war did not go well for the Russian armed forces and they suffered many defeats. Russia also lost control of Poland in 1915, which was a severe blow to Russian pride.
- The Russian army lacked vital resources, including adequate medical care, and this led to high fatality and casualty rates.
- There were claims of defeats caused by incompetent officers who refused to cooperate with each other as well as communication difficulties. This led to low morale and desertions.
- The Tsar began to lose control and support of the armed forces. The generals forced his abdication at Pskov.

Economic problems
- The war was costing 17 million roubles a day and Russia had to get loans from Britain and France. Economic problems such as heavy taxes, high inflation and price rises meant that many were living in poverty.
- The people had expected the war to be won by Christmas 1914 so they were war weary by 1917 and suffering from grief, anxiety and low morale. They wanted the war to end but they knew the Tsar would not agree to that and they became so unhappy and frustrated they protested and went on strike which led to the February Revolution as the army sympathised with them and consequently sided with them against the Tsarist system.
- War exacerbated existing economic problems and showed the frailty of the Russian economy in dealing with a modern, industrial conflict.

Inherent weaknesses of autocracy
- Concentration of power in the hands of one person: their character mattered.
- Great difficulties ruling such a vast empire with its varied nationalities.
- Difficulties in managing change, especially political change demanded by economic developments.

Role of Tsar Nicholas II
- The Tsar was seen as a weak ruler as he was so easily influenced by the Tsarina, Rasputin and his Ministers. At times the Tsar appeared to be more interested in his family than in issues facing Russia.
- He was stubborn as he ignored advice and warnings from Rodzyanko and he failed to understand the severity of events in February 1917.

- In September 1915 the Tsar took personal control of the armed forces, which left him personally responsible for any defeats.
- By February 1917 the Tsar had lost control of the armed forces as well as the support and loyalty of the Russian people, which contributed to the February 1917 revolution.

Role of Tsarina Alexandra
- In September 1915 the Tsar left the Tsarina in charge, which was not welcomed in Russia as she was German.
- Her relationship with Rasputin was viewed with suspicion.
- His disreputable behaviour tainted the royal family.
- His increasing political role led to opposition from within the ruling elite.

Political problems
- The propaganda of the Revolutionary parties helped undermine the loyalty to the regime amongst the soldiers and workers. Not a huge reason, but contributory.
- Revolutionary parties frightened the government in to repressive measures which encouraged revolution in 1917.
- Failure to allow growing middle-class a meaningful political voice and role in decision making.
- Bourgeoisie discontent.
- There was a growth of the middle class and they were becoming increasingly critical of the Tsarist regime: the Duma's had not given them the access to political power that they had wanted. This put into stark relief by the way in which the Tsar and the elite ran the war.
- The development of the professions, commerce and industry resulted in a growing desire for change and modernization of the Russian political system.
- Spread of education meant people were becomingly more politically aware and encouraged the spread of propaganda.

Any other relevant factors.

*Candidates can be credited in a number of ways **up to a maximum of 20 marks**.*

48. **'The role of Trotsky was the main reason why the Reds won the Civil War.' How valid is this statement?**

Context
After the October Revolution the Bolsheviks had to fight for their survival against a combination of forces who wanted the destruction of the new Bolshevik State. Some of the anti Bolshevik forces were international, others where internal opponents. This was the Civil War.

Role of Trotsky
- Trotsky had a completely free hand in military matters.
- HQ was a heavily armed train, which he used to travel around the country.
- He supervised the formation of the Red Army, which became a formidable fighting force of three million men.
- He recruited ex-Tsarist army officers and used political commissars to watch over them, thus ensuring experienced officers but no political recalcitrance.
- He used conscription to gain troops and would shoot any deserters.
- Trotsky helped provide an army with great belief in what it was fighting for, which the Whites did not have.

Other Factors

Organisation of the Red Army

- The Red Army was better organized than the White Army and better equipped, and therefore able to crush any opposition from the White forces.
- Use of ex-officers from the old Imperial Army.
- Reintroduction of rank and discipline.
- Role of Commissars.

Terror (Cheka)

- The Cheka was set up to eradicate any opposition to the Reds.
- There was no need for proof of guilt for punishment to be exacted.
- There was persecution of individual people who opposed the Reds as well as whole groups of people, which helped to reduce opposition due to fear, or simply eradicate opposition.
- The Cheka group carried out severe repression.
- Some of the first victims of the Cheka were leaders of other political parties.
- 140,000 were executed by 1922 when Lenin was happy that all opposition had been suppressed.

Disunity among the Whites

- The Whites were an uncoordinated series of groups whose morale was low.
- The Whites were a collection of socialists, liberals, moderates etc: who all wanted different things and often fought amongst themselves due to their political differences.
- All of the Whites shared a hatred of communism but other than this they lacked a common purpose.
- No White leader of any measure emerged to unite and lead the White forces whereas the Reds had Trotsky and Lenin.

Unity of the Reds

- Unified political leadership.
- Unity of land controlled.
- Co-ordinated military action.

Superior Red resources

- Once the Reds had established defence of their lines they were able to repel and exhaust the attacks by the Whites until they scattered or surrendered.
- By having all of their land together it was easier for the Reds to defend.
- With the major industrial centres in their land (Moscow and Petrograd) the Reds had access to factories to supply weapons etc. and swiftly due to their control of the railways.
- Control of the railways meant they could transport troop supplies quickly and efficiently and in large numbers to the critical areas of defence or attack.
- The decisive battles between the Reds and Whites were near railheads.
- The Reds were in control of a concentrated area of western Russia, which they could successfully defend due to the maintenance of their communication and supply lines.
- Having the two major cities of Moscow and Petrograd in their possession meant that the Reds had hold of the industrial centres of Russia as well as the administrative centres.
- Having the two major cities gave the Reds munitions and supplies that the Whites were unable to therefore obtain.

Foreign intervention

- The Bolsheviks were able to claim that the foreign 'invaders' were imperialists who were trying to overthrow the revolution and invade Russia.
- The Reds were able to stand as Champions of the Russian nation from foreign invasion.

- The help received by the Whites from foreign powers was not as great as was hoped for.
- The Foreign Powers did not provide many men due to the First World War just finishing and their help was restricted to money and arms.

Propaganda

- The Whites were unable to take advantage of the brutality of the Reds to win support as they often carried out similar atrocities.
- The Whites were unable to present themselves as a better alternative to the Reds due to their brutality.
- The Reds kept pointing out that all of the land that the peasants had seized in the 1917 Revolution would be lost if the Whites won. This fear prevented the peasants from supporting the Whites.

Leadership of Lenin

- Introduction of War Communism.
- By forcing the peasants to sell their grain to the Reds for a fixed price the Reds were able to ensure that their troops were well supplied and well fed.
- The White troops were not as well supplied and fed as the Red troops.
- Skilled delegation and ruthlessness.

Any other relevant factors.

Part G: USA, 1918—1968

*Candidates can be credited in a number of ways **up to a maximum of 20 marks**.*

49. To what extent were divisions within the black community the main obstacle to achieving civil rights before 1941?

Context

Between 1918 and 1941 the USA was a racist society to a large extent. Black Americans faced hostility due to racist attitudes. Such racism was underpinned by legal sanction, social attitudes and organisations that persecuted black Americans.

Divisions in the black community

- Booker T. Washington, accomodationist philosophy, regarded as an 'Uncle Tom' by many.
- In contrast, W.E.B. De Bois founded the NAACP, a national organisation whose main aim was to oppose discrimination through legal action. In 1919 he launched a campaign against lynching, but it failed to attract most black people and was dominated by white people and well-off black people.
- Marcus Garvey and Black Pride — he founded the UNIA (Universal Negro Improvement Association) which aimed to get blacks to 'take Africa, organise it, develop it, arm it, and make it the defender of Negroes the world over'.

Separate but equal

- 'Separate but equal' Supreme Court decision 1896, when Homer Plessey tested its legality.
- 'Jim Crow laws' — separate education, transport, toilets, etc. — passed in Southern states after the Civil War.
- Attitudes of Presidents, eg Wilson: 'Segregation is not humiliating and is a benefit for you black gentlemen'.

Other factors

Activities of the Ku Klux Klan

- Racist organisation formed in 1860s to prevent former slaves achieving equal rights. Suppressed by 1872, but in the 1920s there was a resurgence.
- Horrific methods: included beatings, torture and lynching.

- Roosevelt refused to support a federal bill to outlaw lynching in his New Deal in 1930s — feared loss of Democrat support in the South.
- Activities took place at night — men in white robes, guns, torches, burning crosses.
- The 'second' Klan grew most rapidly in urbanising cities which had high growth rates between 1910 and 1930, such as Detroit, Memphis, Dayton, Atlanta, Dallas and Houston.
- Klan membership in Alabama dropped to less than 6,000 by 1930. Small independent units continued to be active in places like Birmingham, where in the late 1940s members launched a reign of terror by bombing the homes of upwardly mobile African Americans.
- However, their activities in the 1940s led to continued migration of black Americans from the South to the North.

Lack of political influence
- 1890s: loopholes in the interpretation of the 15th Amendment were exploited so that states could impose voting qualifications.
- 1898 case of Mississippi v Williams — voters must understand the American Constitution.
- Grandfather Clause: impediment to black people voting.
- Most black people in the South were sharecroppers: they did not own land and some states identified ownership of property as a voting qualification.
- Therefore black people could not vote, particularly in the South, and could not elect anyone who would oppose the Jim Crow laws.

Popular prejudice
- After the institution of slavery the status of Africans was stigmatised, and this stigma was the basis for the anti-African racism that persisted.
- Relocation of millions of African Americans from their roots in the Southern states to the industrial centres of the North after World War I, particularly in cities such as Boston, Chicago, and New York (Harlem).
- In Northern cities, racial tensions exploded, most violently in Chicago, and lynching, usually racially motivated, increased dramatically in the 1920s.

Any other relevant factors.

Candidates can be credited in a number of ways up to a maximum of 20 marks.

50. How effective was the New Deal in solving America's problems in the 1930s?

Context
The New Deal followed Roosevelt's victory in the 1932 presidential election after the inadequate response of Hoover and the Republicans to the Great Depression that followed the Wall Street Crash. The New Deal is associated with Roosevelt and the Democrats who took a more interventionist approach to dealing with the economy than the Republicans.

The First New Deal 1933—34
- Launch of 'Alphabet Agencies' giving relief and recovery in first 100 days of Roosevelt presidency, eg Federal Emergency Relief Administration [FERA], Tennessee Valley Authority [TVA], Public Works Administration [PWA] providing relief and work.
- Economy Act sought to balance the budget.
- Economic prudence by cutting wages of state employees by 15% and spending savings on relief programmes.
- Ending unpopular prohibition to raise revenue and cheer people up!

The Second New Deal 1935—1937
- Reform to improve living and working conditions for many Americans through legislation.
- National Labour Relations Act ('Wagner Act') [1935]; protecting rights of workers to collectively bargain with employers.
- Banking Act (1935) established the Federal Bank Deposit Insurance Corporation that insured deposits up to $5,000, and later, $10,000.
- WPA [Works Progress Administration] (1935) launched programme of public works across America. By 1938 it provided employment for three million men (and some women).
- Rural electrification (1936) provided loans to electrify rural areas of America.
- Social Security Act (1935) providing a state pension scheme for old people and widows, as well as help for the disabled and poor children.

Power of the federal government
- New Deal increased the role of the federal government in American society and, in particular, the economy.
- Role of government in strengthening the power of organised labour.
- Government role as regulator between business, labour and agriculture was confirmed by its increased intervention. Challenges to this in the Supreme Court.
- Opposition from State governments, especially in the South; employers groups forming Liberty League opposed to the New Deal.

Economic effects
- Debate on the economic effects in terms of relief and recovery: they certainly helped in terms of providing basic relief.
- Roosevelt's first term in office saw one of the fastest periods of GDP growth in US history. However, downturn in 1937—38 raised questions about just how successful the policies were.
- Although it never reached the heights of before the Depression, the New Deal did see a couple of positive results economically. From 1933 to 1939, GDP increased by 60% from $55 billion to $85 billion; the amount of consumer products bought increased by 40% while private investment in industry increased five times in just six years.
- However, unemployment continued to be a problem, never running at less than 14% of the working population.
- The importance of re-armament in reducing unemployment and revitalising the American economy was considerable, particularly after the mini-slump of 1937.

Confidence-building
- Confidence-building measures such as checking banks in 1933 to ensure they were well-run and credit-worthy. (Emergency Banking Act), and only allowing 'sound' banks to reopen.
- By the end of 1933, many small banks had closed or were merged.
- Most depositors regained much of their money.
- Role of Roosevelt and his 'fireside chats': over 30 from March 1933.
- Roosevelt declared that 'the only thing we have to fear is fear itself' and his fireside chats on the radio did a great deal to help restore the nation's confidence.

Any other relevant factors.

Candidates can be credited in a number of ways up to a maximum of 20 marks.

51. 'The Civil Rights Movement of the 1950s and 1960s met the needs of black Americans' How valid is this view?

Context

By the 1960s the Civil Rights Movement was winning successes but how far did these successes change the lives of Black Americans across the USA for the better?

Aims of Civil Rights Movement

- Were mainly pacifist and intended to bring civil rights and equality in law to all non-white Americans.
- More radical segregationist aims of black radical movements.

Role of NAACP

- Work of NAACP in the Brown v Topeka Board of Education, 1954.
- Work of NAACP in the Montgomery Bus Boycott, 1955.

Role of Congress of Racial Equality (CORE)

- Organised sit-ins during 1961 and freedom rides.
- Helped organise march on Washington.
- Instrumental in setting up Freedom Schools in Mississippi.

Role of SCLC and Martin Luther King

- Emergence of Martin Luther King and the SCLC.
- Little Rock, Arkansas — desegregation following national publicity.
- Non-violent protest as exemplified by sit-ins and freedom rides.
- Birmingham, Alabama 1963 — use of water cannon.
- Reaction of Kennedy.
- March on Washington, August 1963— massive publicity.
- Martin Luther King believed that the Civil Rights Act of 1964 'gave Negroes some part of their rightful dignity, but without the vote it was dignity without strength'.
- March 1965, King led a march from Selma to Birmingham, Alabama, to publicise the way in which the authorities made it difficult for black Americans to vote easily.

Changes in federal policy

- Use of executive orders: Truman used them to make black appointments, order equality of treatment in the armed services: Kennedy signed 1962 executive order outlawing racial discrimination in public housing, etc.
- Eisenhower sent in army troops and National Guardsmen to protect nine African-American students enrolled in a Central High School: Kennedy sent troops to Oxford, Mississippi to protect black student: James Meredith.
- Johnson and the 1964 Civil Rights Act banning racial discrimination in any public place, Voting Rights Act of 1965: by end of 1965 over 250,000 blacks newly registered to vote, Affirmative Action, etc.

Any other relevant factor.

Part H: Appeasement and the Road to War, to 1939

Candidates can be credited in a number of ways up to a maximum of 20 marks.

52. To what extent did Fascist governments use military threat and force in pursuing their foreign policies from 1933?

Context

German and Italian fascism was expansionist by nature. However, the methods used to fulfil aims varied owing to the circumstances faced by the fascist powers. There was considerable skill on display as well as the ability to use opportunities when they arose.

Fascist strategies: use of military threat and force

- Italy's naval ambitions in the Mediterranean — 'Mare Nostrum'.
- Italian invasion of Abyssinia — provocation, methods, and relatively poor performance against very poorly equipped enemy.
- Open German re-armament from 1935.
- German re-militarisation of Rhineland — Hitler's gamble and timing, his generals' opposition, lack of Allied resistance.
- Spanish Civil War — aid to Nationalists, testing weapons and tactics, aerial bombing of Guernica.
- Anschluss — attempted coup 1934; relations with Schuschnigg; invasion itself relatively botched militarily; popularity of Anschluss in Austria.
- Czechoslovakia — threats of 1938; invasion of March 1939.
- Italian invasion of Albania — relatively easy annexation of a client state.
- Poland — escalating demands, provocation, invasion.
- The extent to which it was the threat of military force which was used rather than military force itself, eg Czechoslovakia in 1938; and the extent to which military force itself was effective and/or relied on an element of bluff, eg Rhineland.

Other factors

Military agreements, pacts and alliances

- The German—Polish Non-Aggression Pact between Nazi Germany and Poland signed on 26th January 1934 normalised relations between Poland and Germany, and promised peace for ten years. Germany gained respectability and calmed international fears.
- Rome—Berlin axis — treaty of friendship signed between Italy and Germany on 25th October 1936.
- Pact of Steel — an agreement between Italy and Germany signed on 22nd May 1939 for immediate aid and military support in the event of war.
- Anti-Comintern Pact between Nazi Germany and Japan on 25th November 1936. The pact directed against the Communist International (Comintern) but was specifically directed against the Soviet Union. In 1937 Italy joined the Pact Munich Agreement — negotiations led to Hitler gaining Sudetenland and weakening Czechoslovakia.
- Nazi Soviet Non-Aggression Pact August 1939 — both Hitler and Stalin bought time for themselves. For Hitler it seemed war in Europe over Poland was unlikely. Poland was doomed. Britain had lost the possibility of alliance with Russia.

Fascist diplomacy as a means of achieving aims:

- Aims can be generally accepted as destruction of Versailles, the weakening of democracies, the expansion of fascist powers and countering communism.
- Diplomacy and the protestation of 'peaceful' intentions and 'reasonable' demands.
- Appeals to sense of international equality and fairness and the righting of past wrongs, eg Versailles.
- Withdrawal from League and Disarmament Conference.
- Anglo German Naval Treaty 1935 — Germany allowed to expand navy.
- Versailles ignored in favour of bilateral agreements. A gain for Germany.

- Prior to re-militarisation of the Rhineland, Hitler made offer of 25-year peace promise. Diplomacy used to distract and delay reaction to Nazi action.

Fascist strategies: economic

- Use of economic influence and pressure, eg on South-Eastern European states.
- Aid supplied to Franco (Spain) was tactically important to Hitler not only for testing weapons but also access to Spanish minerals.

Any other relevant factors.

Candidates can be credited in a number of ways up to a maximum of 20 marks.

53. 'British foreign policy was a complete failure in containing the spread of Fascist aggression up to March 1938.' How valid is this view?

Context

Britain was keenly aware that it was not fully prepared for war. Therefore Britain's foremost aim was the maintenance of peace. Up to March 1938, this was largely achieved. Conflicts that did occur were on the periphery of Europe/the Mediterranean.

Relations with Germany

- Re-armament: Hitler was successful in reintroducing conscription and re-arming but there were significant economic restraints and by the late 1930s Germany's potential enemies were re-arming at a faster rate.
- The growth of the Luftwaffe was a serious reverse for Britain.

Naval Agreement

- The Anglo—German Naval Agreement (1935). This successfully limited German naval strength to 35% of British.
- Britain accepted that Versailles would no longer contain Germany. Britain bowed to inevitable, but Germany had successfully revised Versailles.

Rhineland

- Hitler was successful in re-militarising the Rhineland, more as a result of bluff, clever timing and French/British weakness than German military strength.

Anschluss

- Failure of attempted Nazi coup in 1934 due to Italian opposition, but successful annexation of Austria in 1938 — although invasion itself was chaotic and inefficient from a military point of view. This was another fait accompli, but Britain could have done little to prevent it.

Relations with Italy

- Mussolini's plans for a new Roman Empire in the Adriatic, the Mediterranean and North Africa were a blow to British foreign policy in hoping to convert Mussolini into an ally.
- Stresa Front (1935) initially seemed successful.
- Hoare—Laval Pact — public revulsion to Franco-British connivance at Italian aggression led to Hoare's resignation.
- Imposition of limited sanctions on Italy alienated Mussolini, thereby driving him closer to Hitler, yet failing to save Abyssinia.

The Spanish Civil War

- Britain's main aim was to prevent this becoming an international war, and in this it was successful.
- The policy of non-intervention sponsored by Britain; it also guaranteed that Britain would be on good terms with the victors.

- The policy was openly breached by Germany and Italy, and to a lesser extent the Soviet Union. Resolute action did end attacks on British merchant shipping.

Any other relevant factors.

Candidates can be credited in a number of ways up to a maximum of 20 marks.

54. **To what extent was the outbreak of war in September 1939 brought about by the failure of British diplomacy and relations with the Soviet Union?**

Context

After the Munich agreement Stalin was suspicious of the motives of Britain and France. When Hitler ripped up his promises in March 1939 it seemed clear where Hitler's next moves would be.

Diplomacy and relations with the Soviet Union

- Stalin knew that Hitler's ultimate aim was to attack Russia.
- Lord Halifax, the British Foreign Secretary, was invited by Stalin to go to Russia to discuss an alliance against Germany.
- Britain refused as they feared Russian Communism, and they believed that the Russian army was too weak to be of any use against Hitler.
- In August 1939, with war in Poland looming, the British and French eventually sent a military mission to discuss an alliance with Russia. Owing to travel difficulties it took five days to reach Leningrad.
- The Russians asked if they could send troops into Poland if Hitler invaded. The British refused, knowing that the Poles would not want this. The talks broke down.
- This merely confirmed Stalin's suspicions regarding the British. He felt they could not be trusted, especially after the Munich agreement, and they would leave Russia to fight Germany alone. This led directly to opening talks with the Nazis who seemed to be taking the Russians seriously by sending Foreign Minister von Ribbentrop and offering peace and land.

Importance of Nazi—Soviet Pact

- Pact — diplomatic, economic, military co-operation; division of Poland.
- Unexpected — Hitler and Stalin's motives.
- Put an end to British—French talks with Russia on guarantees to Poland.
- Hitler was freed from the threat of Soviet intervention and war on two fronts.
- But, given Hitler's consistent long-term foreign policy aims on the destruction of the Versailles settlement and lebensraum in the east, the Nazi—Soviet Pact could be seen more as a factor influencing the timing of the outbreak of war rather than as one of its underlying causes.
- Hitler's long-term aims for destruction of the Soviet state and conquest of Russian resources — lebensraum.
- Hitler's need for new territory and resources to sustain Germany's militarised economy.
- Hitler's belief that British and French were 'worms' who would not turn from previous policy of appeasement and avoidance of war at all costs.
- Hitler's belief that the longer war was delayed the more the balance of military and economic advantage would shift against Germany.

Any other relevant factors

Part I: The Cold War, 1945–1989

Candidates can be credited in a number of ways up to a maximum of 20 marks.

55. 'The Soviet Union effectively controlled Eastern Europe in the years up to 1961.' How valid is this view?

Context

The death of Stalin led to the emergence of Nikita Khrushchev as Soviet leader. His policies of de-Stalinisation and different paths to socialism encouraged the East European states to seek greater freedom.

Demands for change and reaction: Poland (1956)

- Riots sparked off by economic grievances developed into demands for political change in Poland.
- On the death of Stalinist leader Boleslaw Bierut in 1956 he was replaced by Wladyslaw Gomulka, a former victim of Stalinism, which initially worried the Soviets.
- Poles announced their own road to socialism and introduced reforms.
- Release of political prisoners (including Cardinal Wyszynski, Archbishop of Warsaw); collective farms broken up into private holdings; private shops allowed to open; greater freedom given to factory managers.
- Relatively free elections held in 1957 which returned a communist majority of 18.
- No Soviet intervention despite concerns.
- Gomulka pushed change only so far. Poland remained in the Warsaw Pact as a part of the important 'buffer zone'. Political freedoms were very limited indeed. Poland was a loyal supporter of the Soviet Union until the 1980s and the emergence of the solidarity movement. Limited challenge to Soviet control.

Demands for change and reaction: Hungary (1956)

- Hungarians had similar complaints: lack of political freedom, economic problems and poor standard of living.
- Popular upsurge of support for change in Budapest led to a new Hungarian government led by Imre Nagy, who promised genuine reform and change.
- Nagy government planned multi-party elections, political freedoms, the withdrawal of Hungary from the Warsaw Pact and demands for the withdrawal of Soviet forces.
- Nagy went too far. The Soviet Union could not see this challenge to the political supremacy of the Communist Party and the break-up of their carefully constructed buffer zone. They intervened and crushed the rising brutally.
- Successful intervention against a direct challenge to Soviet control, but lingering resentment from mass of Hungarian people, though some economic flexibility allowed the new regime of Janos Kadar to improve economic performance and living standards.

Demands for change and reaction: Berlin (1961)

- Problem of Berlin — a divided city in a divided nation.
- Lack of formal boundaries in Berlin allowed East Berliners and East Germans to freely enter the West which they did owing to the lack of political freedom, economic development and poor living standards in the East.
- Many of those fleeing (2.8 million between 1949 and 1961) were skilled and young, just the people the communist East needed to retain. This was embarrassing for the East as it showed that communism was not the superior system it was claimed to be.
- Concerns of Ulbricht and Khrushchev: attempts to encourage the Western forces to leave Berlin by bluster and threat from 1958 failed.

- Kennedy of America spoke about not letting the communists drive them out of Berlin. Resultant increase in tension could not be allowed to continue.
- Building of barriers: barbed wire then stone in August 1961 to stem the flood from East to West.
- Success in that it reduced the threat of war and the exodus to the West from the East to a trickle. To an extent it suited the West as well, as they did not like the obvious threat of potential conflict and escalation that Berlin represented.
- Frustration of many in East Germany. Propaganda gift for the US and allies, though Soviets had controlled the direct challenge.

Military and ideological factors

- Buffer zone could not be broken up as it provided military defence for the Soviet Union.
- Use of force and Red Army to enforce control in late 40s and early 50s.
- Need to ensure success of communism hence policy.

Domestic pressures

- Intention to stop any further suffering of Soviet Union in aftermath of WW2 made leadership very touchy to change.
- Some economic freedoms were allowed, but at the expense of political freedoms.
- Need to stop spread of demands for change.

Any other relevant factors.

Candidates can be credited in a number of ways up to a maximum of 20 marks.

56. To what extent were the difficulties faced by the US military the reason why America lost the war in Vietnam?

Context

The French withdrawal from their Indo-Chinese colonies in 1954 led to America stepping in as the main foreign power in the region. The Domino Theory was used by American presidents, starting with Eisenhower, to justify American intervention to help the South of Vietnam in their struggles against the communist North.

Failure of military methods

- Mass bombing had no real effect according to the Jason Study by MIT in 1966, owing to the agricultural nature of North Vietnam and the widespread jungle cover.
- Tactics on the ground — US technological superiority in heavy weapons was negated by the terrain.
- Widespread use of helicopter gunships inflicted heavy casualties, but were a blunt weapon. Many civilian deaths which did not help win 'hearts and minds'.
- Use of defoliants like Agent Orange: US (and their South Vietnamese allies) lost the battle for hearts and minds, despite inflicting 2,000,000 casualties for the loss of one tenth that number of their own men.
- Difficulty of using superpower force in a Third World country.
- US Soldiers brave, but a minority did not believe in the war.
- Difficulties dealing with the conditions and knowing which Vietnamese were the enemy led to stress and confusion.
- Short commissions for officers and rotation of troops led to loss of expertise in the field.

Other factors

International isolation of the USA

- The media war turned international opinion against the US.
- Major US allies had had misgivings about US military intervention; Harold Wilson's major achievement in keeping UK out of the war, despite dependence on US support for the British economy.

- Feeling that Vietnam was handing huge propaganda bonuses to the enemies and rivals of the US.
- Widespread criticisms of American conduct of war internationally. A propaganda gift for the Soviet Union.
- Although some 'allied' help from nations like Australia, most main US allies, like Britain, pointedly stayed out of the war.

Public protests in the USA

- Public opposition supported by the press was probably the main reason for withdrawal. Vietnam was a media war — images showed the public the brutality of war, e.g. South Viet police chief executing a Viet Cong in Saigon during the Tet Offensive of '68, Mai Lai massacre. Such images damaged American claims to be the 'good guys'.
- Extent of the opposition is debated. Probably a minority in '65, growing by the time of the crucial Tet offensive in '68. October 1969 saw the largest anti-war protest in US history. There were protestors in every major city in America. Opposition of Black Power groups. Protest could be violent: May 1970 protest at Kent State University, Ohio, led to four students being shot.
- Unpopularity of the draft.
- USA was a democracy: public pressure and perception mattered. Nixon noted the extent of opposition: withdrawal of 60,000 troops in 1969, policy of Vietnamisation. Economic cost of the war: US deficit of $1.6 billion in 1965 increased to $25.3 billion in 1968. Tax increases unpopular. Congress only got involved in limiting money and action in the late 60s and early 70s.
- Divisions within administrations: eg Lyndon B Johnson had Rusk advising to continue the struggle in South-East Asia, compared to Senator Fulbright arguing for de-escalation.

Relative strengths of North and South Vietnam

- North Vietnam: a hard peasant life bred determined soldiers. Viet Cong enlisted for years unlike American troops who signed up for a year. Belief in their cause of communism also a factor. Great determination, eg the Ho Chi Minh trail was kept open despite American bombers continually bombing it.
- Viet Cong knew the jungle, survived in atrocious conditions, developed effective tactics and were more effective in winning the 'hearts and minds' of civilians than the Americans. Military objectives were realistic: General Giap aimed to break the will of the American government. Support of Chinese and Soviet aid from 1965 of importance.

South Vietnam weakness

- Corruption and decay of South Vietnamese government, especially in Saigon.
- A Catholic elite controlled a largely Buddhist population. Lack of political and social cohesion in South Vietnam led to divisions and turmoil which filtered through to their armed forces.

Any other relevant factors.

Candidates can be credited in a number of ways up to a maximum of 20 marks.

57. 'The economic weakness of the Soviet Union led to the end of the Cold War.' How valid is this view?

Context
The Cold War lasted from 1945 through until the late 1980s. Over that time, the USSR had raced to spend as much as the USA on its space and arms programmes. By the late 1980s the USSR economy was failing to keep up with the USA and, at the same time, the trouble in the satellites of the USSR stretched its resources.

Economic problems
- The Soviet economy was at breaking point by the late 1980s.
- Commitments to the arms race meant the Soviet economy was hugely unbalanced.
- Propping up allied regimes was also causing a drain on resources.
- Consumer goods and housing were neglected as a result.

Other factors
Role of President Mikhail Gorbachev
- Gorbachev saw that the USSR could not afford a new arms race. Gorbachev implemented policies of Perestroika and Glasnost which aimed to reform the Soviet economy and liberalise its political system. Gorbachev worked to improve relations with the USA.
- He took ideology out of his foreign policy, as exemplified by arms agreements to allow the USSR to concentrate on internal matters: Intermediate Nuclear Forces Treaty, December 1987, Nuclear Weapons Reduction Treaty, 1989.
- Gorbachev told leaders of the satellite East European states in March 1989 that the Soviet army would no longer help them to stay in power.

Role of President Ronald Reagan
- Unlike many in the US administration Reagan actively sought to challenge Soviet weakness and strengthen the West in order to defeat communism. In 1983 he denounced the Soviet Union as an 'Evil Empire.'
- Programme of improving US armed forces, including nuclear weapons, and he proposed a Star Wars missile shield to challenge the belief in MAD (SDI). He was very charming when he met Gorbachev and visited the Soviet Union.

Western economic strength
- Allowed America to embark on the Star Wars weapons programme.
- Perception of the affluent West through television and consumer goods undermined communist claims of the superiority of their economic system.

Withdrawal of the Soviet Union from Afghanistan
- Symptom of the problems of the Soviet Union.
- Intervention in December 1979: conflict with the Mujaheddin. Russian army morale crumbled when over 20,000 Soviet soldiers died, as did support at home.
- The conflict showed the weaknesses of the Soviet economy. War led to a slump in living standards for ordinary Russians.
- Russians began to question the actions of their own government. Gorbachev withdrew troops in 1988

Failure of communism in Eastern Europe
- Strong Polish identity and history of hostility with Russia. By 1970s, Poland was in an economic slump.
- Emergence of opposition around Gdansk in 1980: industrial workers' strike led by Lech Walesa, who argued for the creation of an independent trade union. Solidarity grew to nine million members in a matter of months. Movement suppressed in 1981 by General Jaruzelski's government.
- Multiparty elections in Poland, after Soviet troops left, victory for Solidarity.
- Czechoslovakia, political prisoners released in November 1989 and by the end of the month, the communist government had gone. No Soviet intervention.
- Opening of the Berlin Wall: division of Germany finally came to an end.
- Soviet domination ended.
- Perestroika and Glasnost and the end of the communist rule in USSR.

Any other relevant factors.

2015
SECTION 1: SCOTTISH

Part A: The Wars of Independence, 1249–1328

1. *Candidates can be credited in a number of ways up to a maximum of 9 marks.*

A maximum of 2 marks may be given for answers which refer only to the source.

Possible points which may be identified in the source include:

- Alexander III's sudden death had brought the male line of the royal dynasty to an end.
- A measure of the problems now facing the Scottish leaders was the desire for 'advice and protection' from Edward I which would later lead to demands for recognition of his authority over the Scottish realm.
- Six Guardians were appointed in response to the vital need to carry on the day to day running of the government in the absence of a royal leader.
- The young child Margaret of Norway was now the only descendant of King Alexander.

Possible points of significant omission may include:

- Scotland faced potential difficulties with the succession of a young female, Alexander's three year old granddaughter.
- The seriousness of the situation after the death of Alexander III required the Scottish nobles to carry on the government of the country.
- Alexander's death presented a problem over the succession as there was no male heir.
- The Scottish leaders compromised the independence of Scotland by asking Edward for help and advice.
- Alexander's children had all died before him; Alexander (1284), David (1281) & Margaret (1283).
- There was fear of civil war. Bishop Fraser of St Andrews was afraid of violent disorder when Robert Bruce the elder arrived in Perth with an army. Bishop Fraser asked Edward to come to the Scottish border in order to maintain peace.
- A potential problem was the prospect of war amongst the nobility. In order to avoid civil war, Bishop Fraser asked Edward to help chose the next ruler of Scotland.
- Six Guardians were elected (two bishops, two earls, two barons) in a parliament in Scone.
- There was uncertainty during the winter of 1286–1287 after a rebellion in the South West by the Bruce faction. Robert Bruce seized the Balliol castle of Buittle and the royal castles of Wigtown and Dumfries. Although order was restored by the Guardians, the threat from the Bruce faction created the need to settle securely the question of the succession.
- There were concerns to maintain the independence of Scotland. The Treaty of Birgham, the marriage of Margaret, Maid of Norway and King Edward's son, Edward, Prince of Wales, appeared to solve the potential threat of civil war and to establish a secure relationship with England through marriage. The Guardians however, were concerned to keep Scotland's separate customs and laws.
- Although Edward made concessions to the separate identity of Scotland in the Treaty of Birgham, Edward's actions, such as his seizure of the Isle of Man and the appointment of the Bishop of Durham, suggested that Edward wanted to increase his influence over the kingdom of Scotland.

- A problem arose over the succession after Margaret's death on her way to Scotland in 1290. Her death left no obvious heir to the kingdom of Scotland.
- There was a renewed threat to stability after the death of the Maid of Norway. Tension grew between the two factions, ie Bruce V Balliol/Comyn. Bishop Fraser's letter to Edward favoured Balliol's claim to the throne while Bruce's claim was put forward in the Letter of the Seven Earls.
- Following the invitation to be arbiter in the issue of Scottish succession, Edward showed his authority by inviting the Scottish leaders to meet him at his parliament at Norham rather than Edward travelling over the border into Scotland. Edward also showed his strength by ordering his northern armies to assemble at Norham. In addition, Edward organised his navy for a blockade of Scotland and raised taxes to prepare for a possible war.
- Edward took advantage of Scotland's weakness. When the Scots leaders travelled to Norham, Roger Brabazon gave a speech on behalf of Edward requiring the Scots to recognise Edward as overlord. Pressure was also brought to bear on the competitors at Norham to recognise Edward's overlordship of Scotland in order for him to make a judgement.
- The task of choosing a new king, known as the Great Cause was a long drawn out process, lasting over 15 months from August 1291 until November 1292. Thirteen claimants presented themselves although only three, John Balliol, Robert Bruce and John Hastings, had a strong legal claim.
- Problems arose at the Great Cause at Berwick due to the self-interest of the nobles. For example, John of Hastings' argument that Scotland should be divided showed little regard for the kingdom.
- Edward continued to exercise his overlordship over Scotland even after deciding in favour of John Balliol in November 1292. Balliol had the strongest legal claim, based on primogeniture, being a descendant of the eldest daughter of Earl David. Balliol however had to swear fealty to Edward. Balliol also did homage to Edward in December 1292 at Newcastle. Edward exercised such authority which created problems for King John's reign.

Any other valid point of explanation that meets the criteria described in the general marking instructions for this kind of question.

2. *Candidates can be credited in a number of ways up to a maximum of 5 marks.*

Possible points of comparison may include:

Source B	Source C
Overall: Both sources agree that as overlord of Scotland, Edward intended to interfere fully in Scottish affairs. Both sources agree that Edward used the issue of appeals to test his relationship with John Balliol and to demonstrate that John, although Scotland's ruler, possessed only the shadow of real power.	

Source B	Source C
King John had sworn homage for the kingdom of Scotland for a second time.	King John did homage to the King of England which clearly recognised Edward I's overlordship of the realm of Scotland.

John's reign was overshadowed by Edward I's determination, right from the start, to enforce the widest possible interpretation of his rights as overlord of Scotland.	Edward was not however content with a mere recognition of his overlordship: he was determined to exercise his authority to the full.
King John was left in no doubt that he personally could, and would, be called to answer for the actions of the Scottish courts in the presence of Edward I and the English parliament.	Edward I would even summon King John to appear before him in England to answer legal claims and complaints in person.
Only one week after King John's enthronement, Edward I had heard a court appeal on behalf of a Scottish merchant, Roger Bartholomew who complained against a decision taken by the Scottish courts.	Edward I made it clear that he intended to hear any appeal cases brought to him as overlord of Scotland, when and where he chose.

3. *Candidates can be credited in a number of ways **up to a maximum of 6 marks**.*

Examples of aspects of the source and relevant comments:

Aspect of the source	Possible comment
Author: A chronicler of Lanercost Priory in northern England. An English source.	• The source is useful as the author is a monk, educated and well informed as Lanercost Priory was a favourite stopping place for both King Edward I and King Edward II. The source is less useful as it is biased against the Scots.
Type of source: A Chronicle	• Useful as the chronicle records the key events of the Scottish Wars.
Purpose: To keep a record of local, national and international affairs	• It is useful as it describes the effects of the Scottish invasions of northern England after the Battle of Bannockburn.
Timing: August 1314	• The source is more useful as it dates from the time of the Scottish attacks on the north of England and reflects the viewpoint of the English at the time of the raids and the Priory was attacked during Bruce's campaigns in Northern England.

Content	Possible comment
• In August 1314, Edward Bruce, James Douglas, John Soules and other nobles of Scotland, under the authority of Robert Bruce, invaded England by way of Berwick with cavalry and a large army.	• Useful as it tells us that raids into northern England were part of Bruce's royal policy in maintaining Scotland's independence. Despite victory at Bannockburn, the war between Scotland and England was not over. Bannockburn won Bruce support in Scotland but not recognition from Edward.
• They devastated almost all Northumberland with fire.	• Useful as it provides a detailed insight into the nature of the warfare Robert Bruce unleashed upon the north of England. Bruce's forces burned and devastated villages. Bruce hoped that such destruction would spread terror and force Edward II to negotiate and recognise Bruce's right to the kingship of Scotland.
• The people of Coupland, fearing their return and invasion, sent messengers and paid money to the Scottish king to escape being burned by them in the same way as they had destroyed other towns.	• Useful as it provides a detailed insight into a short term aim of the raids which was economic. That English shires were prepared to pay tribute tells us that Bruce was prepared to be bought off. Deals were struck with terrified inhabitants. Bruce's forces were willing to grant truces which ensured that his war effort became self-financing. If ransoms were not paid however, Bruce's troops returned to burn and loot.

Possible points of significant omission may include:

• Other common features of the raids into northern England were plundering, the stealing of cattle and the taking of prisoners as hostages.

• For Bruce, a short term aim of the raids was to supplement revenue and to reward and enrich loyal and successful lieutenants.

• The source describes one raid shortly after the Battle of Bannockburn in 1314. Raids were made on the north of England after 1311 and Bruce and his lieutenants led regular raids into England after 1314 to force Edward II to the negotiating table. Bruce attacked England in 1315, 1316, 1318, 1322, 1323 and 1328.

• The raids on England did not succeed in bringing Edward II to the negotiating table. The centre of government and the wealth of England lay in the south and were largely unaffected. The raids into England only seriously affected the nobles and inhabitants of the northern counties. An example being the Earl of Carlisle who rebelled against Edward II and entered into a local truce with Bruce in 1323 to prevent his lands being destroyed.

• The raids into northern England did result in war weariness which contributed to a series of truces in the 1320s. Berwick, England's last major outpost in Scotland was captured by the Scots in 1318 and Bruce inflicted a major defeat on the English at Old Byland in 1322 which almost resulted in the capture of Edward II.

• In addition to the wars in the north of England, other reasons for the triumph of Bruce in maintaining Scotland's independence include

• Bruce recovered his power in Scotland by fighting a highly successful campaign of guerrilla warfare between 1307 and 1309 aimed at harassing English occupation forces and defeating his Scottish enemies led by the Comyns.

• The death of King Edward I in 1307 while leading an army against Bruce removed Bruce's main military adversary. Edward's death also weakened English resolve to prosecute the war in Scotland. King Edward II did not lead a major campaign into Scotland for several years which allowed Bruce to concentrate on fighting his Scottish enemies. Edward's failure to commit to a major campaign in Scotland was also crucial in leaving the major English held Scottish castles vulnerable to attack.

- Bruce defeated his enemies in Scotland. Bruce's campaign in the north east of Scotland, the centre of Comyn power, his decisive victory over the Earl of Buchan in the battle of Inverurie and the destruction of Comyn lands in the 'Herschip of Buchan' removed the threat from the powerful Comyn family. In addition, Bruce's control of the north not only provided a refuge from English attacks but provided manpower and essential supplies from the Continent via Aberdeen.
- Bruce reconquered Scotland from 1310–14 by conducting a successful campaign against English held castles in Scotland. Lacking siege equipment, castles were taken by stealth and their defences dismantled or razed to prevent them being recaptured and used against Bruce in the future. By 1314, most of Scotland's major castles had been recovered including Dundee, Perth, Dumfries, Linlithgow, Roxburgh and Edinburgh.
- The support of the Scottish Church was also significant in Bruce's maintaining Scottish independence. Not only did the Church avoid excommunicating Bruce for the sacrilegious murder of John Comyn in a church in 1306 but Bruce had the active support of the bishops of St Andrews and Glasgow. In the Declaration of the Clergy in 1310 Scotland's bishops declared their support for Bruce as the legitimate king of Scotland.
- Bruce's triumph over a huge English army at the Battle of Bannockburn (23-24 June 1314) completed Bruce's military control of Scotland and gains him increased support thereby securing his position as king of Scots.
- Bruce also weakened English power by sending Scottish armies under his brother Edward to campaign in Ireland. Despite the failure of the Scots to conquer Ireland and the defeat and death of Edward Bruce in 1318, the possibility of a Celtic fringe alliance diverted English attention and forces from Scotland. The opening of a second front in Ireland also stopped the English use of Irish troops and resources against Scotland.
- Diplomacy also contributed to Bruce maintaining Scottish independence. Bruce's position was strengthened by King Philip of France's recognition of Bruce in 1310 which helped to raise Scottish morale. A powerful case for Scottish Independence was presented to the pope, in the letter known as the Declaration of Arbroath in 1320 and in the Treaty of Edinburgh Bruce made major concessions to gain recognition of his kingship and of Scotland's independence.
- Bruce's position was also strengthened by his brutal crushing of the 1320 'Soulis Conspiracy'. However Bruce also showed leniency towards former enemies. Bruce gathered support and ensured loyalty by rewarding his followers. At a parliament held at Cambuskenneth Abbey in 1314, Bruce gave the nobles the opportunity to pledge their allegiance and keep their Scottish lands whilst disinheriting those who chose to side with England.
- Bruce triumphed when he finally secured peace between Scotland and England. Bruce exploited the weakness of the English government after the deposition of Edward II by once more launching attacks into northern England and into Ireland which succeeded in forcing the insecure government of Isabella and Mortimer to negotiate. The Treaty of Edinburgh (1328) formally recognised Bruce as king of an independent Scotland.

Any other valid point that meets the criteria described in the general marking instructions for this kind of question.

Part B: The Age of the Reformation, 1542–1603

4. *Candidates can be credited in a number of ways up to a maximum of 9 marks.*

A maximum of 2 marks may be given for answers which refer only to the source.

Possible points which may be identified in the source include:
- The Reformation of 1560 was sparked off by a riot in Perth in which the town's Catholic religious houses were sacked.
- Knox was installed as its first Protestant minister on the seventh of the month in the capital.
- The change of Regent pleased Knox and his followers as they were unhappy with Mary of Guise's heavy taxation and her pro-French policies.
- Support of England and the arrival of an English army in March 1560 which proved to be a decisive factor.

Possible points of significant omission may include:
- Increase in popular support of Protestant sentiment between 1547 and 1559 despite the absence of the figurehead Knox. Displayed in Perth riot 11th May 1559 and stealing of the image of St Giles on the day of the saints celebration (1st September) 1558 in Edinburgh.
- Return of Knox as a figurehead. Hugely influential in gathering support for the movement through his preaching.
- Unhappiness under Mary of Guise due to heavy taxation. Attempts at engineering a war with England and suspicions of her pro-French policies.
- Increase in support of the poor. Shown by Beggars' Summons copies of which were nailed to the doors of many friaries in Scotland on 1st Jan 1559 declaring that the needs of the poor were greater than that of the friars who were rich and ungodly.
- Evolution of the Protestant Congregation.
- Increase of Protestant literature.
- Presence of Protestant martyrs such as George Wishart (1546) and Walter Myln (1558) helped garner popular support.
- Socio-economic reasons relating to standards of living and over taxation.
- Wish for Scots to create their own national cultural identity. Wish for no interference from England or France.
- Lack of strong leadership from the Catholic Church in Scotland. Particularly following the murder of Cardinal Beaton.
- Scotland disliked being ruled by a woman, Mary of Guise, because she was French and a Catholic.
- Protestant religious commitment. Hard-line and unwavering commitment to the cause.
- The Lords of the Congregation were encouraged by the prospect of support from the English after Elizabeth, a fellow Protestant, became Queen in 1558.
- Protestant ideas had been coming into Scotland for some time.
- English Bibles and books critical of the Catholic Church were distributed in Scotland following the Reformation in England.
- The Catholic Church failed to make sufficient reform to satisfy its critics.
- Increased numbers of the nobility opted for the new faith.
- The Lords of the Congregation had increasing support and took up arms against Mary of Guise.

- The weaknesses of the Catholic Church — decline and corruption; pluralism had not been addressed. Minors being given top positions in church — crown and nobility taking much of churches' revenues; Monarchs placed their offspring in important positions in
- the Church.
- Mary of Guise's religious attitude and pro-French stance meant she asked the French for help. It pushed many Scots into supporting the Lords of the Congregation.
- Mary of Guise's prosecution of reformers was unpopular.

Any other valid point of explanation that meets the criteria described in the general marking instructions for this kind of question.

5. *Candidates can be credited in a number of ways up to a maximum of 5 marks.*

Possible points of comparison may include:

Source B	Source C
Overall: Sources B and **C** agree Mary continued to practise her Catholic faith causing concern. They also agree that Mary having French servants caused problems as the Scots did not like this.	
Source B mentions Mary's marriage to Bothwell and how he was suspected of murdering Darnley. Source C places greater emphasis on the problem of marrying Bothwell.	

Source B	Source C
Went back on her word upon arrival attending mass at Holyrood Chapel.	She ignored advice and attended mass at Holyrood on her arrival, to many Protestants' disgust.
Also upset many of the Scots nobility by surrounding herself with French servants.	Mary surrounding herself with French servants did not go down well with the Scottish nobility.
Most notable was her secret marriage to the Earl of Bothwell, who was suspected of murdering her previous husband Lord Darnley.	Choice of husbands also caused shock waves, particularly her marriage to Bothwell.
Knox had five meetings with Mary Queen of Scots, criticising her marriages.	Knox who held five meetings with the queen to show his disapproval of the goings on in her personal and public life.

6. *Candidates can be credited in a number of ways up to a maximum of 6 marks.*

Examples of aspects of the source and relevant comments:

Aspect of the source	Possible comment
Author: The text was produced by a committee of over 30 members.	Useful as the source, articles from The *Second Book of Discipline* was central to the development of Presbyteries through which the Kirk would be virtually independent of secular government.
Type of source: Book on the role of the church in Scottish society.	Useful as it gives a clear explanation of the position of the church in society.
Purpose: To set out views of Presbyterian Kirk.	Useful in helping to establish the relationship between the church and state.

Timing: 1578	Useful as written at a time when the role of the Monarch in the Kirk was being discussed.

Content	Possible comment
• The Kirk belongs to the poor as much as it does everyone else and our duty is to help them.	• Useful as it tells us that the Kirk had a duty to help the poor. Although the reformed church had great intentions to help the poor it faced difficulties.
• We also call for the liberty of the election of persons called to the ministry to be in the hands of the congregation.	• Useful as it tells us that the congregation was given the freedom to pick their own minister.
• Doctors will be appointed in universities, colleges, and schools to open up the meaning of the scriptures in every parish, and teach the basics of religion.	• This is useful as the reformed church believed in education. However, the aim of a school in every parish was not achieved but there was some advancement in central Scotland.

Possible points of significant omission may include:

- Emphasis was placed upon attendance at daily and Sunday services.
- The Second Book of Discipline led indirectly to a regular meeting of ministers from 10 to 20 parishes for discussion of doctrine, which became the presbytery.
- The Kirk removed all organs from places of worship.
- It proved impractical to dispossess the Catholic clergy of their benefices so they were allowed to retain two-thirds of their revenues for life.
- Concessions made to Catholic clergy, on the grounds of old age or ill-health.
- At the beginning of 1560, Scotland was a Catholic country with a Protestant minority. By 1603, it was a Protestant country with a small Catholic minority.
- The Reformation did not lead to a significant transfer of wealth from the Church and much of the lands of the Catholic Church remained in the hands of the nobility.
- The new church still had the problem of not having enough revenue for the parishes.
- James VI was reluctant to enforce anti-Catholic laws.
- Kirk sessions were instruments of moral and religious control.
- The elaborate interiors of Catholic churches were replaced with plain, whitewashed parish kirks.
- Observance of Catholic festivals and saints' days and festivals were discouraged.
- Literary works and Kirk sermons were conducted in English rather than Latin. (The only Protestant Bibles available to lowland Scots were in English).
- Assistance given to the poor from the friaries ended. New plans to help the poor by literacy rates improved during this period.
- Many of the issues prevalent within the Catholic Church prior to the Reformation remained, such as: attendance; poverty of some parishes; and poor quality of preaching.
- Scots merchants continued to trade with England and trading ports across the North Sea.
- Scots focused on trade with the Protestant Dutch.

- Trade with France continued despite the change in religion — although pro-French foreign policy was replaced with pro-English under James.
- The Presbyterian church faced difficulty.

Any other valid point that meets the criteria described in the general marking instructions for this kind of question.

Part C: The Treaty of Union, 1689—1740

7. *Candidates can be credited in a number of ways up to a maximum of 9 marks.*

A maximum of 2 marks may be given for answers which refer only to the source.

Possible points which may be identified in the source include:

- There was English political opposition because of threat to the English-owned East India Company.
- English sabotage was blamed for underfunding and mismanagement of the scheme.
- King William was held responsible for encouraging Spanish opposition in Central America.
- Anglo-Scottish relations were strained and this was shown by anti-English riots in Edinburgh.

Possible points of significant omission may include:

- The "Ill" Years, famine, poor harvests.
- Favour shown by King William to England.
- Navigation Acts protecting English trade.
- Lack of an empire for Scotland to trade with.
- Effect of English wars on Scottish trade.
- English military intervention in Scots trade with mainland Europe.
- Dutch withdrawal from Darien scheme.
- The cost of Darien, c. £400,000.
- Act of Settlement, Scots did not want Hanoverian Succession imposed on Scotland.
- Act of Security asserting Scots' independence.
- Anne's delay in assenting to the Act of Security.
- Act Anent Peace and War.
- Wool Act defying English military strategy.
- Wine Act defying English military strategy.
- Alien Act threatening sanctions against Scots.
- Jacobite opposition to William.
- Scottish parliamentary opposition to the perceived threat of the Anglican church.
- Revolution of 1688—9.
- Failure to unite in the 1690s.
- Scottish parliament acting independently of William and Mary.
- English Bill of Rights asserting monarchical authority.
- Claim of Right in Scotland proclaiming parliamentary authority.
- Opposition to William in the Highlands.
- Glencoe Massacre.
- Jacobite plot to assassinate William.
- William and the Darien scheme.
- Covenanters' objections to monarchical interference in church affairs.
- The Worcester Affair.
- Scottish disaffection with William's governmental advisors.

Any other valid point of explanation that meets the criteria described in the general marking instructions for this kind of question

8. *Candidates can be credited in a number of ways up to a maximum of 5 marks.*

Source B	Source C
Overall: the sources are in total disagreement in their attitude to union, in particular in relation to the potential military, manufacturing, and land benefits. **Source C** lays greater emphasis upon the emotional argument.	

Source B	Source C
Our brave and courageous Scotsmen will join a British fleet and army and we will be secured by their protection.	Our valiant and brave Scottish soldiers at home asking for a small pension, or left to beg, once their old regiments are broken.
Our burgh merchants will take our manufactures to England and return with profits.	The royal burghs losing all the branches of their old commerce and trades in the face of English competition.
We will see our craftsmen's lives improve as a result of union.	I see the honest industrious craftsman loaded with new taxes, drinking water instead of ale.
Our land will be better cultivated and manured.	The backbroken farmer, with his corn wasted upon his hands, because his land is worthless.

9. *Candidates can be credited in a number of ways up to a maximum of 6 marks.*

Examples of aspects of the source and relevant comments:

Aspect of the source	Possible comment
Author: Jacobite	Useful as the Jacobites were leaders of national sentiment after union, and were known to support repeal. Could argue less useful as author could be biased.
Type of source: Leaflet	This is less useful as this is propaganda so the Jacobites would be justifying their views at the time.
Purpose: To explain the reasons for bringing back the Scottish parliament.	Useful as it expresses an opinion to a reverse union.
Timing: 1723	Useful as it is written 16 years after union when its effects, both positive and negative would be felt across Scotland.

Content	Possible comment
Before union taxes raised by the Scots parliament were not high.	Useful as it informs of the Jacobites desire to return to pre-union government.
Taxes on land, salt, malt, windows, leather, candles, soap, starch, and paper.	Useful as it explains why some Scots would be financially worse off under union.
Custom duties now set at English rates, three times what was paid before union.	Useful as it suggests English influence has been negative for Scots merchants and importers.

Possible points of significant omission may include:

Either economic effects of union:

- Textile and paper industries suffered.
- Smuggling increased.
- Scottish linen lost out to English wool.
- Poverty in some parts of Scotland.
- Opposition from poor farmers to enclosures.
- Merchant shipping increased.
- Caribbean trade increased.
- Scots promotions in East India Company.
- Black cattle trade prospered.
- Improvements in agriculture were made.
- Enclosures benefitted wealthier farmers.
- Development of towns on market routes.
- Government investment in Scotland.
- Royal Bank of Scotland founded.
- Improved industrial practice.
- Growing professional classes.
- Scottish tobacco merchants prospered.

Or political effects of union:

- Opposition to union in the Highlands.
- Some Scottish and English politicians quickly adopted an anti-union stance.
- Motion to repeal union failed in 1713.
- British government wary of Scottish feelings so adopted cautious approach.
- Dominance of Whig party in Scotland.
- Abolition of office of Secretary of State.

Or causes of Jacobite rising of 1715:

- Desire for restoration of Stuart dynasty.
- Desire for return of Episcopalianism.
- Failure of French-sponsored 1708 rebellion.
- Resentment towards George I after 1714.

Any other valid point that meets the criteria described in the general marking instructions for this kind of question.

Part D: Migration and Empire, 1830–1939

10. *Candidates can be credited in a number of ways up to a maximum of 9 marks.*

A maximum of 2 marks may be given for answers which refer only to the source.

Possible points which may be identified in the source include:

- Following the collapse of the kelp trade landlords were looking for change.

- Many landlords were of the view, by the 1840s, that it could only be of benefit to them to rid their land and properties of people.
- They attempted to do this following the hardship of the famine period.
- Gordon chartered a fleet of five ships in order to transport 1,700/landlords contributed to the cost of fares to encourage families to emigrate.

Possible points of significant omission may include:

- In the Lowlands farm consolidation (Enclosures) meant that there was less chance of land ownership.
- Agricultural Revolution — changes in farming methods and new technology (eg mechanical reapers/binders and later tractors) meant there were fewer jobs available.
- In the Highlands the population was growing. Sub-division of land into crofts. Precarious nature of subsistence farming.
- Forced evictions during the Highland Clearances.
- There was poor quality housing in the countryside. Young farm labourers may have lived in bothies — shared accommodation.
- Farm work — long hours, low pay, out in all weathers, few days off.
- Highlanders migrated to the Lowlands to earn money to pay their rents/Rents were increasing.
- Decline of herring fishing industries (especially after Russian Revolution of 1917 brought an end to the Eastern European export trade — trawlermen/gutters lost their jobs).
- Attractions of "big city" employment — easier working life (factory work = indoors, set hours, possibly higher wages). Other jobs attractive, eg railway porter/ticket clerk = steady job, steady wage, possibly a uniform. For females — domestic service often better conditions than farmwork. Shop work offered a half day holiday.
- Social attractions of the towns, eg cinemas, theatres, football matches, pubs and dance halls.
- Emigration — Assisted passage schemes, Emigration agents, posters and advertisements.
- Opportunities to own land overseas, better climate, availability of jobs, possibly better wages.
- Friends and family already overseas encouraged emigration with letters home.
- Economic slump at end of WW1, decline in heavy industries.

Any other valid point of explanation that meets the criteria described in the general marking instructions for this kind of question

11. *Candidates can be credited in a number of ways up to a maximum of 5 marks.*

Possible points of comparison may include:

Source B	Source C
Overall: Sources B and **C** agree that Scots miners were concerned because of the lack of experience of coal mining which the Lithuanians had. The Scots workers also worried that the foreign miners presented a safety risk. The sources also both mention that sometimes the Lithuanians spoke little English and finally the sources also agree that the foreign workers were accused of lowering wages. There was a point of disagreement over the translation of mining regulations.	

Source B	Source C
Some of these aliens may never have seen a coal mine before their arrival in Scotland.	They were the focus of considerable concern largely because of their ignorance of coal mining.
Complained about the employment of aliens in the mines on the grounds of safety.	The employers were adamant that the foreigners did not present additional dangers to safety.
Their lack of English language is a hazard to themselves and fellow workers.	There is adequate provision to instruct them in their duties, including translations of mining regulations into their own language.
There is widespread belief that the foreigners are being used to bring wages down.	Until the early 1900s at least there is evidence that Lithuanian labour was used to cut wages.

12. *Candidates can be credited in a number of ways **up to a maximum of 6 marks**.*

Examples of aspects of the source and relevant comments:

Aspect of the source	Possible comment
Author: Scottish politician	Useful as he was a contemporary commentator/eyewitness. As a politician he would have expertise on local and Scottish issues.
Type of source: Letter to newspaper	Useful as a letter to the public articulating a political viewpoint.
Purpose: To comment on emigration to the newspaper's readership.	Less useful as it might be biased. He believes further emigration to the Empire will have a negative impact on Scotland.
Timing: 1938	Useful as from a time when Scotland's links with the Empire were of great importance to Scotland's economy.

Content	Possible comment
• to showcase the industrial might of Glasgow and the west of Scotland created by the Empire.	• Useful as Glasgow's industry supplied markets all over the Empire.
• It is more than time that a firm check was put on the drain from Scotland of her best types.	• Useful as it was felt that there was a "brain drain".
• Scotland's best have been drawn away by the opportunities that the Empire has presented.	• Useful as Scots were attracted to jobs and careers in the Empire.

Possible points of significant omission may include:
- The Empire enabled some firms and individuals to make great commercial fortunes, eg Clyde shipbuilders, Napiers, John Browns and Beardmores.
- Scotland exported to the Empire in great quantities, eg Springburn produced ¼ of the world's locomotives.
- Empire provides raw material,s eg Jute from Indian province of Bengal. The textile manufactures in Dundee from this resource was subsequently exported all over the world.

- Heavy industry in Scotland exported a high proportion of products, eg American grain might be bagged into sacks made in Dundee, carried in locomotives manufactured in Springburn and then loaded onto ships built on the Clyde.
- Glasgow becomes known as the "workshop of the world". Glasgow's businesses grow which creates jobs.
- People from the countryside/Highlands move to Glasgow in search of employment.
- Employment opportunities offered by the Empire, eg Scottish middle-class boys had successful careers, especially in India, as civil servants, doctors and as soldiers.
- Scots who made their money in the Empire often returned to Scotland and built large mansions near the cities, eg Broughty Ferry.
- Scottish investors pioneer the use of "investment trusts". Cities like Edinburgh, Dundee and Aberdeen hold substantial investments abroad.
- Scottish capital was being used to finance projects abroad and not at home in Scotland.
- Scottish reliance on trade and commerce with the Empire left her vulnerable to trade slumps, eg the economic slump following World War 1.
- The low-wage economy in Scotland led to considerable poverty amongst many of the working people.
- Glasgow 2nd city of Empire.

Any other valid point that meets the criteria described in the general marking instructions for this kind of question.

Part E: The Impact of The Great War, 1914–1928

13. *Candidates can be credited in a number of ways **up to a maximum of 9 marks**.*

A maximum of 2 marks may be given for answers which refer only to the source.

Possible points which may be identified in the source include:
- We had given the Germans gas but it came back on us.
- German shells were falling amongst us and time and time again I was knocked off my feet.
- A pal of mine, a fellow Cameron Highlander from Paisley was alongside me.
- A bullet had got him on the arm and blood gulped out/I got out my field dressing to help him.

Possible points of significant omission may include:

Gas:
- First used by the British (Scots) at Loos 1915.
- Gas cylinders were replaced by gas-filled shells — wind could change direction.
- Different types of gas, chlorine, phosgene, mustard and their effects.

Shelling:
- Dangers of trench warfare, eg soldiers suffered from shell shock.
- Many Scots soldiers killed on the Western Front by artillery fire.

Wounded:
- Bloody minded attitude of the survivors who used it to stimulate them for future battles.
- Losses were replaced and the Scottish units carried on though grousing and criticisms became more common.

Western Front:

- Experience of trench warfare, eg rats, lice, trench foot, snipers, boredom, fear of death, lack of sanitation, food rations and shell shock.
- By the end of the first week in September 1914, Glasgow was able to boast that it had recruited more than 22,000 men.
- By December 1914, 25% of the male labour force of western Scotland had already signed up.
- 13% of those who volunteered in 1914–15 were Scots.
- Young Scots urged to join the army through a mixture of peer pressure, feelings of guilt, appeals to patriotism, hopes for escapism and adventure, heroism, self-sacrifice and honour. For the unemployed, the army offered a steady wage.
- Kitchener's campaign was a huge success: examples such as by the end of August 20,000 men from the Glasgow area had joined up.
- In Scotland there were no official 'Pals Battalions' but in reality – the Highland Light Infantry/Tramway Battalion; the 16th Battalion/the Boys Brigade.
- In Edinburgh, Cranston's battalion and McCrae's battalions became part the Royal Scots. McCrae's Battalion was the most famous because of its connection with Hearts football club.
- Loos: for many of Scotland's soldiers in Kitchener's New Army the initial taste of action for the volunteers came at Loos in September 1915.
- The 9th and 15th Scottish Divisions were involved in the attack; 9th lost almost 3,000 men killed and missing from 25 to 28 September; 15th lost over 3,000 in a single day.
- Loos was part of a series of British battles of Neuve Chapelle, Aubers Ridge, Festubert and Loos. Scottish losses were huge and all parts of Scotland were affected; of the 20,598 names of the missing at Loos a third of them are Scottish.
- Bravery and fighting spirit of Scottish units: 5 Victoria Crosses given to Scots after the Battle of Loos in recognition of their extraordinary bravery; The Somme: Three Scottish divisions 9th, 15th [Scottish] and 51st [Highland] took part in the Battle of the Somme, as well as numerous Scottish battalions in other units, ie the Scots Guards in the Household Division. 51 Scottish infantry battalions took part in the Battle of Somme offensive at some time.
- Piper Daniel Laidlaw of the KOSB played the pipes during an attack at Loos to encourage Scottish troops to charge. Laidlaw was awarded the VC for his bravery.
- Huge Scottish sacrifice: 15th (Cranston's) Royal Scots lost 18 officers and 610 soldiers wounded, killed or missing. 16th (McCrae's) Royal Scots lost 12 officers and 573 soldiers; 16th HLI lost 20 officers and 534 men – examples of Scottish losses on the first day. The 9th (Scottish) Division performed well during the five months of fighting. Casualties were high: 314 officers and 7,203 other ranks, yet morale remained high.
- Battle of Arras in 1917, saw concentration of 44 Scottish battalions and seven Scottish named Canadian battalions, attacking on the first day, making it the largest concentration of Scots to have fought together. One third of the 159,000 British casualties were Scottish.
- High numbers of Scottish deaths at Loos, Somme, Arras
- The official figure given at the end of the war calculated that Scotland had suffered 74,000 dead.

- Huge sacrifice of Scots during the war: of 557,000 Scots who enlisted in the services, 26.4% lost their lives. One in five British casualties were Scottish.
- Experience of Scottish women on Western Front.
- Scottish leadership: role of Douglas Haig; strong Presbyterian background; believed in his mission to win; stubborn and stoical; famous for order in 1918 not to give ground and to fight to the end.
- Debate over Haig's role: considered to be one of the soldiers of his generation, he had a reputation as an innovative commander. In a balanced judgment the historian John Terrain calls him 'The Educated Soldier'. He had to deal with a military situation which was unique and no other general had had to deal with.
- That he did so with a vision of what was needed – he embraced the use of tanks for example – is to his great credit. He could be distant and was touchy, but he did visit the front and was aware of the sacrifices made; he was the architect of eventual victory.

Any other valid point of explanation that meets the criteria described in the general marking instructions for this kind of question.

14. *Candidates can be credited in a number of ways up to a maximum of 5 marks.*

Possible points of comparison may include:

Source B	Source C
Overall: Sources B and **C** broadly agree about the events of the Rent Strikes. The sources agree about the carrying of placards and the summoning of tenants to court. Sources also note the involvement of men and the introduction of the Rent Restriction Act. **Source B** highlights the actions as a victory of people power whereas **Source C** highlights the role of the Glasgow Labour Party Housing Committee.	

Source B	Source C
In the streets women carried placards.	Our committee organised demonstrations with banners.
Prosecution of 18 tenants due to appear in court for refusing to pay rent increases.	With the summoning of a number of munitions workers to attend court the most dramatic incident of the struggle happened.
By then the rent strikes had escalated, with men taking their own wildcat strike action at Fairfield's and Beardmore's.	Men engaged in work on the Clyde stopped working and marched in their thousands with those summoned to the court.
The government rushed through the Rent Restriction Act.	A few days after this an Act to limit rent increases was introduced by the Government.

15. *Candidates can be credited in a number of ways up to a maximum of 6 marks.*

Examples of aspects of the source and relevant comments:

Aspect of the source	Possible comment
Author: Editor, Glasgow Herald newspaper	Useful as it is an informed view of the events. Sensationalist language highlighted a genuine fear, although brief, of a potential revolution.
Type of source: Newspaper	Useful as it explains some of the events of the 40 hours a week strike. It is less useful as it is limited to events of the 40 hours a week strike and not the wider impact of the war on Scottish politics.
Purpose: To express shock at the political events of 'Red Clydeside'	Useful as it highlights the view that the ILP and strikers had a negative impact on Glasgow.
Timing: 1st February 1919	Useful as it is a contemporary source written at the time of the 40 hour a week strike.

Content	Possible comment
David Kirkwood, one of the strike leaders, and a member of the ILP.	Useful as it shows the involvement of the important leaders such as Kirkwood.
It has been known from the first that the strike movement is controlled by a small section of the Clyde Workers Committee who are pressing for a 40 hour week.	Useful as it shows the involvement of the ILP in orchestrating and organising the strike.
The revolutionary activities of these Bolshevists has damaged Glasgow's reputation.	Useful as it highlights the fear of a Bolshevist led revolution in Glasgow.

Points from recall which support and develop those from the source:

- ILP members' activities — involved in resisting the Munitions Act of 1915; in opposing the introduction of the dilution of labour; anti-conscription...
- In Scotland the ILP was to the fore, campaigning on major issues. ILP supported workers' grievances over prices and rents.
- Both the ILP and the Labour party campaigned for reforms in housing and health after the war and their focus on local issues was a big reason for Labour's success in the 1920s.
- Clydeside ILP MPs confronted Conservatives and Liberals, even leadership of PLP MPs
- on issues of poverty and unemployment.
- ILP in Scotland had many women prominent in the party such as Mary Barbour, Agnes Dollan and Helen Crawfurd.
- The Clyde Workers' Committee (CWC) was formed to control and organise action for an extension of workers' control over industry.

- Forty Hours Strike and demonstration at George Square, waving of red flag, riot, troops and tanks appeared on streets of Glasgow. Riot Act was read. The Cabinet agreed with the Scottish Secretary Robert Munro, that the confrontation was not strike action but a 'Bolshevist rising.'
- After the war the Labour Party emerged as an important political force with seven seats in Scotland, winning as many votes as the Conservatives.
- In the 1922 election Labour made the breakthrough as the second political party.
- In 1922 Labour won 29 seats in Scotland (10 in Glasgow) and then in 1924 they won 34 seats but saw this fall to 26 seats in the second election in 1924.
- The role of Manny Shinwell, Willie Gallacher, John MacLean.
- Labour sought gradual reform as the leadership of people like Tom Johnstone, Maxton and Kirkwood took precedence over the more radical leaders like John McLean.
- The Conservative Party was strengthened as they worked hard to gain middle class support, helped by Presbyterian churches. Scottish legal system also had strong links with the Conservatives.
- Events in Ireland — growing fears in Scotland of extremism.
- They won 30% of the vote in 1918, increasingly associated with the growing middle-class.
- Conservatives also benefited from being seen as the party of law and order, especially in the aftermath of the George Square riots.
- In the second election of 1924 the Conservatives won 38 seats in Scotland compared to Labour's 26.
- Changes in newspaper ownership led to pro-Union press which was supported by institutions like the universities and legal profession.
- The rise of 'Red Clydeside' prompted a reaction amongst the Scottish elite (industrialists, bankers and politicians like James Lithgow, Eric Geddes and Andrew Bonar Law) to both restore Scotland's industrial and trading pre-eminence and break the power of the shop stewards' movement; this was done by a (near) doubling of the Treasury bill rate, which raised unemployment and led to cuts in public spending.
- Class conflict — breaking of shop stewards, engineers and miners by 1926.
- Splits and decline of the Liberal Party: Coalition Liberals supported Lloyd George and the coalition with the Conservatives at the end of the war. The supporters of Herbert Asquith, the old party leader, stood as Liberals.
- Old Liberal causes died in the aftermath of the war.
- The Liberal Party, which had claimed guardianship of workers' interests on the pre-war era, was increasingly perceived as defending the well-being of employers and capital.
- In the second 1924 election the Liberals won only 9 seats in Scotland.
- Growth of the Labour Party, in alliance with the Catholic Church, made the middle class feel isolated, but attempts to court the working class Protestant/Orange vote foundered on the Conservatives' support for the 1918 Act giving state support to Catholic secondary schools; separate Orange and Protestant party established in 1922, splitting 'Moderate' (Conservative) vote.

- The transformation of the Labour Party reflected a crisis in confidence; at the end of the war the party in Scotland was dominated by the ILP and appeared strong enough to impose its own radical solutions on society, but the defeats of the early 1920s led to the expulsion of the Communists (1925–27) and the defection of the Home Rule wing of the ILP in 1928.
- It was difficult for Home Rule to make progress in Westminster parliament
- Private Members' Home Rule bills failed
- Support for Home Rule waned within the Labour Party
- Glasgow University Scottish National Association formed 1926
- 1927 John MacCormack and Roland Muirhead, formed the National Party of Scotland.
- It distanced itself from the Labour Party. Drew support from intellectuals like Hugh McDiarmid.
- Some Liberals and Conservatives formed the Scottish Party at the end of the 1920s and proposed some form of devolution in an effort to attract Liberal and Unionist supporters.
- The latter formed the National Party of Scotland but it had little electoral impact. (MacCormack and Muirhead each got less than 3,000 votes in the 1929 election.)
- 'Scottish Renaissance' of the 1920s had strong leanings towards Home Rule and Independence – they challenged both the cultural and political relationship between Scotland and England.
- Beginnings of change in Scottish attitudes to the Empire – linked with the 'profound crisis which overwhelmed the nation between the wars' (Devine).
- Scots' faith in their role as the economic power-house of the Empire had been shattered.
- Extension of the franchise to women. Many working class women had become politicised by their war work and the rent strikes. Women, such as Mary Barbour, Agnes Dollan and Helen Crawfurd became role models for women keen to make their voice heard politically for the first time.

Any other valid point that meets the criteria described in the general marking instructions for this kind of question.

2015
SECTION 2: BRITISH

Part A: Church, State and Feudal Society, 1066–1406

16. The Roman Catholic Church emerged after the fall of Rome to play a central role in daily life in medieval Scotland and England. Although the Church was there to ensure people's salvation it served a broader role as well. Through its religious sacraments it marked the important stages of life. It fulfilled a social, economic and even a political role.

Arguments that the Church's role was religious

Belief in Christianity
- This was dominant within society; it provided people with an understanding of the world and how it worked. People were concerned about the fate of their souls after death. The Church taught that salvation, or the saving of a one's soul, would come to those who followed the Church's teachings.
- Those who failed were damned to a life of torment in hell. To many believers hell was a real place. It was depicted in lurid detail by many medieval painters.

Church services and rituals
- The importance of marriage, funerals and christenings brought people closer to attaining their passage to heaven.
- People were taught that the sacred acts of worship, or sacraments, brought special blessing from God.
- Therefore the ceremonies that marked the passage of life had power and importance to people.
- These could include baptism, confirmation, marriage and penance.

Relics and saints
- Significance of relics and saints as a means to communicate with God and beg divine favour or protection.

Importance of the pilgrimage
- Pilgrimage to holy centres was an important part of medieval life.
- People would travel long distances to places of religious importance, such as Jerusalem and Rome as well as places that had important religious relics like Canterbury.
- Pilgrimages would show devotion to God with such acts as travel was dangerous.
- Crusade was also part of this. The motivation of recovery of the Holy Land from Muslim rule for religious reasons was a powerful one for many Crusaders.

The role of the Regular Church
- Monasteries were seen as 'Prayer Factories' and used to intercede with God for the ordinary lay population.
- Monastic life of dedication to God and a simple life following the rule of St Benedict: poverty, chastity and obedience, was considered important.
- Many rulers clearly thought they were important and spent time and money resourcing the founding of monasteries. David I of Scotland is one example. His dedication to supporting different orders, such as the Cistercians, was undoubtedly pious as well as practical.

Arguments that the church's role was not religious

Economic

- Education provided wealth for the Church. The rich would pay to have their eldest son educated.
- Economic wealth was created through wool gathering eg Melrose Abbey. Additionally, wealth was created through iron foundry, wine making etc.
- The Church as landowners provided significant employment within the community.

Political

Investiture contest

- Political argument between the Church and State as to who had the right to appoint senior clergy members. Such offices came with large grants of land in England and often held considerable political and military significance.
- Monarchs did not wish the papacy to choose political undesirables for such an important position eg William the Lion and the argument over the Bishop of St Andrews in 1180.

Position within Feudal Structure

- Within the feudal system bishops and abbots were seen as other large landowners with the rights to raise troops in time of need eg Bishop of Durham led the English forces that defeated David I at the Battle of the Standard in 1138.

Administrative role

- The Church provided the majority of clerks for the state government. They were needed to keep records, write charters, laws, keep accounts etc.

Divine authority

- The development of canon law during this period was a direct threat to the growth of the monarchies. The papacy argued that all power of kings was invested through them during their coronation by God through the church.
- Monarchs argued that the power was given directly to them by God. As such, the papal position was that kings were subservient to monarchs. The papacy continued to argue their position and used papal sanctions such as excommunication and the interdict to bring monarchs to heel.

Social

- Gathering for religious festivals and services provided social function.
- The Church provided leprosy hospitals and inns for travellers.

Any other relevant factors.

17. **King John was the youngest son of Henry II and Eleanor of Aquitaine. On the death of his elder brother Richard, he became King of England despite the claims of his nephew Arthur. He struggled to hold the widespread Angevin Empire together in the face of the challenges of the Capetian monarch of France and his own barons.**

Impact of the loss of Normandy

- Had an impact on the royal finances as it reduced John's income.
- The recovery of the royal lands north of the Loire became the focus of John's foreign policy and led to policies which eventually led to challenges to his authority.
- The need to fund warfare to recover Normandy led to the frequent use of Scutage to raise cash. It was used much more frequently than under Henry II and Richard, (levied 11 times in 17 years).

Royal Finances

- John was more efficient in collecting taxes.
- Used wardships to raise cash.
- Introduced new taxes: eg 1207 tax on income and moveable goods.
- Improved quality of silver coinage.

Administration of government

- John filled many of the roles in the royal household with new men; especially from Poitou. This was not popular with the English barons.

Military Power

- Established the Royal Navy.
- Extensive use of mercenaries rather than feudal service.
- Able to exert his military strength against the nobility and the French.
- John an able military commander ie when conflict started with France and his nephew Arthur, he defeated them and captured Arthur.
- His forces and his allies were decisively beaten at the Battle of Bouvines in 1214.

Law and justice

- Increasingly partial judgements were resented.
- John increased professionalism of local sergeants and bailiffs.
- Extended the system of coroners.

Relations with the Church

- John fell out with Pope Innocent III over the appointment of the Archbishop of Canterbury. Innocent insisted on the appointment of Langton which John opposed.
- Papel interdict laid on England and Wales for 6 years.
- In 1213 John made England a fief of the papacy.
- Noble uprising led by Archbishop of Canterbury.

Relations with the Nobility

- Nobles refused to fight in France. This was especially true of the northern Barons who had little stake in France.
- Nobles felt their status was reduced by use of mercenaries.
- John became increasingly suspicious of the nobles.
- High cost of titles led to nobles becoming overly indebted.
- John took hostages to ensure nobles behaved. He showed he was prepared to execute children if the father opposed him.
- Relations worsened over the course of the reign, ending with Magna Carta and rebellion
- of many Barons.

John's personality

- He could be generous, had a coarse sense of humour and was intelligent.
- However, could also be suspicious and cruel: vicious in his treatment of prisoners and nobles.
- Arthur, his nephew, died in mysterious circumstances.
- Powerful lords like William de Braose fell from favour and were persecuted. William's wife and son were imprisoned and died. He died in exile in France.

Any other relevant factors.

18. The decline of feudalism happened as the previous order of society where land was exchanged for economic or military service was challenged. The Peasants' Revolt played a part in the decline as did economic developments, which changed the relationship between peasants and lord, as well as the development of new ways to trade and pay for labour/ service led to its decline.

The Peasants' Revolt

- In England, the attempts of the Statute of Labourers Act in 1351 to force peasants back into serfdom were widely and strongly resisted. The extent of the revolt and the impressive way in which it was organised shows that the old feudal consensus had broken down.
- There is an argument that the Peasants' Revolt was a reaction to the attempts to force peasants to return to the old ideas of labour services.
- The use of the Poll Tax was a trigger to the revolt by secular leaders, John Ball and Wat Tyler.

Other factors

The Black Death

- The population decreased between 33% and 50% during the Black Death.
- The decline in the population meant that the survivors, particularly of the lower classes, could demand and often received better wages for their labour. Wage levels in England roughly doubled. Indeed, the shortage of labourers is often seen as causing the decline of serfdom.
- Landowners for the first time needed to negotiate for their serfs' services, leading to higher wages and better living conditions for those that survived.

The growth of towns

- Many found the freedom of burgh life allowed them to develop trade without the burden of labour services or restrictions in movement.
- There was a movement from the countryside to towns which saw a growth.
- Economy in towns did not depend on the ownership of land, rather on the production and selling of goods.

The growth of trade/mercantilism

- With markets for their goods fluctuating considerably, many nobles came to understand their weak economic position. For some it was better to let their peasants become tenants who rented their land than to continue as their feudal protector.
- Others discovered that sheep were a far more profitable resource than peasants could ever be. The monasteries in particular turned over large areas to sheep pasture to capitalise on the strong demand for wool.
- Peasants who could afford to purchase or rent extra land could propel themselves upwards on the social ladder.

Changing social attitudes

- Social mobility was increasing for a number of reasons, including the move to an economy based more on cash than service. In England the wars against France had brought riches to some, and enabled them to climb the social ladder.

Any other relevant factors.

Part B: The Century of Revolutions, 1603–1702

19. Charles I succeeded his father James I in 1625 and ruled over both England and Scotland until 1642. He continued to reign in Scotland until his death in 1649 at the hands of the English Parliament. During this time there were considerable challenges facing the king in his attempts to enforce his policies in Scotland.

Religious policy

- 1629 the king issued a Royal Demand that Scottish religious practice should conform to English models, and in 1633 the king's coronation at St. Giles in Edinburgh included many Anglican rituals such as candles and crucifixes. In the same year, Charles I introduced William Laud, the Archbishop of Canterbury, to Scotland, and he proceeded to oversee Anglican practice in Scottish churches. This meant that many Presbyterians resented the influence of Laud, whose position as the king's representative on spiritual matters led to resentment of royal authority.
- Acting on advice from Laud, Charles I agreed to the unification of the Churches of Scotland and England in 1625 without consulting the Privy Council. Despite Presbyterians' refusals to ratify this decision, in 1635 Laud issued the Book of Canons, which declared that the monarch had authority over the Church of Scotland, and he subsequently approved a new Service Book, a variation of the English Prayer Book, drawn up by the Scottish bishops. Scottish Presbyterian opposition grew in response to these developments.
- On 23 July 1637, a Prayer Book for Scotland modelled on the English Prayer Book was read at St. Giles Cathedral by the Bishop of Brechin who had two loaded pistols sitting in front of him in case of unrest. The Dean, John Hanna, subsequently had a stool thrown at him by a serving woman, Jenny Geddes, and in the chaos that ensued, the Bishop of Edinburgh was shouted down by the crowd in support of Geddes. This incident demonstrates the violent opposition to Charles I's policies in Scotland.
- Across Scotland people declared opposition to the new Prayer Book, placing the king's Scottish Privy Council in a difficult position, caught between Charles I and his rivals. A committee called the Tables was formed in Edinburgh in late 1637 by nobles, middle-class lawyers, Privy Councillors and ministers, all pledged to oppose the king's religious tyranny. This development represented a strengthening of the organised opposition to Charles I.

The Covenanters

- The Tables drew up the National Covenant and publically unveiled it at Greyfriars Kirk on 28 February 1638, and in the 3 days which followed many flocked to Edinburgh to sign it. Amongst its many undertakings, the Covenant pledged to preserve Presbyterianism in Scotland and promote a church free from monarchical meddling. The ensuing months when copies of the Covenant were carried by messengers around the country to be signed by thousands of new Covenanters symbolised the rejection in Scotland of the Divine Right of Kings, a significant political as well as religious development.
- In November 1638 the General Assembly met and deposed all bishops and excommunicated some, thereby abolishing Episcopalianism. These proceedings were, however, dismissed as invalid by Charles I because his representative, the Duke of Hamilton, had not been present. This highlights the open breach that was widening between the Kirk and the king.

- The Covenanting movement was growing, with the Campbells of Argyll prominent in promoting committed opposition to the king's influence in the west. Throughout Scotland, Covenanters were being equipped with arms coming into the country from overseas, and General Leslie assumed command of their army. This placed the
- movement at an advantage over Charles I who had no standing army and a floundering government in Edinburgh
- Charles I failed to suppress Covenanters, and this failure contributed to outbreak of the "Wars of the Three Kingdoms" which lasted from 1639 to 1651, were spread across Scotland, England and Ireland, and included the English Civil War. During this war, the English Parliament's treaty of alliance with Scottish Covenanters - called the Solemn League and Covenant of 1643 - was a key feature of positive change in fortunes of king's enemies. Therefore the Covenanters proved to be a major issue in a British context for the king.

First Bishops' War

- Charles I could not raise enough money to fight effectively as the English Parliament had not been called since 1629, so he could only put together a poorly trained force of 20,000 men at Berwick-on-Tweed, 12 miles from General Leslie's 12,000-strong force camped at Duns. Meanwhile there were several minor engagements in the north east of Scotland between Covenanters and Scottish Royalists, but as the king was unwilling to send his troops into open battle he was forced to agree to a truce in June. This demonstrates Charles I's inability to impose his authority on Scotland with military force.
- The king signed the Pacification of Berwick on 18 June 1639, agreeing to the General Assembly being the highest religious authority in Scotland. The treaty also acknowledged the freedom of the Scottish Parliament in legislative matters. It is clear that the Covenanters were, for the moment, succeeding in their action against Anglicanism.
- Charles I's inability to put down the Scots brought an end to his "Eleven Years' Tyranny" in England, as he recalled Parliament in 1640 to request revenue to continue war with Scotland. This "Short Parliament" lasted one month as the king dissolved it again rather than concede powers to Parliament as a condition of their granting him funds. Scotland, therefore, was proving a constant frustration to Charles I.

Second Bishops' War

- General Leslie crossed the English border with his troops and they successfully captured Newcastle and Durham. Charles I, having dismissed the Short Parliament before obtaining funds, was once more unable to wage war. This put the king in the weak position of having to negotiate a peace with Scotland in order to avoid defeat by the Covenanters.
- Charles I was forced to sign the Treaty of Ripon on 26 October 1640, the terms of which were dictated by the Scots. Aside from the Covenanters maintaining a military presence in Northumberland, the treaty cost England the price that the Scottish Parliament had to pay for its forces, which amounted to roughly £850 per day. The Treaty of Ripon meant that the Second Bishops' War ended in humiliation for the king at the hands of the Covenanters.

Political challenge

- In 1625 he introduced the Act of Revocation which restored those lands to the Church which had been transferred to the nobility at the time of the Reformation in 1560. This development also saw the proceeds from the tithe also passed back to the church, and the king continued to give increasing power to bishops. This behaviour undermined the status of the Scottish nobility, which they in turn deeply resented.
- Charles I's policy was to appoint bishops rather than nobles to the Scottish Privy Council, his chief advisory body in Scotland. In 1635 Archbishop John Spottiswoode was appointed as the king's Chancellor for Scotland, the first non-secular official in this position since the Reformation. Spottiswoode's position led to growing fears that the king would impose Anglicanism on the country.
- Charles I did not visit Scotland until 1633 when he was crowned there by Spottiswoode. His ignorance of the country's political customs and traditions led to a lack of understanding of Scottish affairs. Scots opposition to Charles I meant that the Stuart notion of the Divine Right of Kings was brought to an end by the king's own subjects.

Any other relevant factors.

20. After the Interregnum, the monarchy was restored in 1660. Charles II reigned until 1685, although he used loopholes in the Restoration Settlement to rule without Parliament from 1681 onwards. His brother James II ruled from 1685, but his attempts at absolutism led to the Revolution of 1688-9, when his daughter Mary and her husband William of Orange were asked by Parliament to become joint monarchs, under terms known as the Revolution Settlement.

James II

- The king, a Roman Catholic, ruled absolutely by dismissing Parliament in November 1685 before it could condemn Louis XIV's persecution of Huguenots, French Protestants. He then stationed a 16,000-strong army, including Roman Catholic officers, outside London. Parliament opposed absolutism as well as any monarch's control of a standing army.
- James II imposed his will on the judicial system, re-establishing Prerogative Courts in 1686. In 1687, he used the monarch's Suspending Powers to suspend laws against Roman Catholics, and used the Dispensing Powers later that year to dismiss these laws from the statute books. For Parliament, this demonstrated the old Stuart interventionist attitude towards legislation.
- James II replaced Anglican advisors and office-holders with Roman Catholic ones, including making the Earl of Tyrconnel the Lord Lieutenant of Ireland and Sir Roger Strickland the Admiral of the Royal Navy. He appointed Roman Catholics to important posts at Oxford and Cambridge Universities. Parliament resented these abuses of his power.
- In late 1688 as MPs made clear their determination to invite the king's Protestant daughter Mary to become queen, he tried to use the Stuarts' links with Louis XIV to appeal for military and financial assistance. However, the French king offered little more than vocal support. This actually harmed James II's cause more as Parliament had always disapproved of any monarch's attempt to promote an Anglo-French alliance.

Legacy of Charles II

- The king, exiled in France for the Interregnum, had accepted limitations on his power when the monarchy was restored in 1660. However, loopholes in the Restoration Settlement allowed him to make policy without Parliament. This caused indignation among MPs who had felt that one of the results of the Civil War would be monarchical recognition of the rights of the House of Commons.

- The legal terms of the 1660 Restoration had upheld the Triennial Act and the abolition of prerogative law courts, and prohibited non-parliamentary taxation. It also stated that Charles II should live off his own finances and not receive money from Parliament, although in return, Parliament granted the king taxation on alcohol. This was an indication that greater formalisation of the relationship between Crown and Parliament had to take place.
- In 1677 the king's Lord Treasurer, the Earl of Danby, who was anti-French, was persuaded by some MPs to arrange the marriage of the king's niece, Mary, to William of Orange, a Dutch prince. This was a response to Charles II's foreign policy which broke the 1668 Triple Alliance with Holland and Sweden against France, by allying himself with Louis XIV. This did not reduce Parliament's alarm at the king's pro-French and Roman Catholic leanings, which reflected the fear of many in the country.
- Nevertheless, towards end of reign Charles II ruled alone for 4 years after dissolving Parliament in March 1681 and ignoring the Triennial Act in 1684. In 1683 he imposed a new Charter for the City of London which said that all appointments to civil office, including Lord Mayor, should be subject to royal approval. The loss of power experienced by the House of Commons made MPs fear that the old Stuart combative approach to rule was re-asserting itself.

Political issues

- James II's use of the suspending and dispensing powers in 1687, although not illegal, was seen by Parliament as a misuse of royal privilege. Questions had also been raised by MPs over monarchical control of the army after the king called troops to London in 1685, which was perceived as another abuse of power. Therefore, throughout his short reign, James II provoked political controversy.
- As in the pre-Civil War era, both post-Restoration Stuart monarchs advocated Divine Right and practised absolutism. Charles II's dismissal of Parliament in 1681 and James II's dissolution in 1685 resembled Charles I's conduct at the start of his "Eleven Year Tyranny" in 1629. These actions meant that the status of monarchy was questioned by a resentful Parliament.
- Charles II's Lord Chancellor, the Earl of Clarendon, had been unpopular due to his mishandling of the Second Dutch War between 1665 and 1667, and was even blamed for the Great Plague of 1665 and the Fire of London in 1666. MPs opposed his influence at court and impeached him in 1667, forcing him into exile. This demonstrates differences between monarchical and parliamentary power which spanned both Charles II's and James II's reigns.
- So, in June 1688 as crisis approached, James II hastily promised to recall Parliament by November and announced that Roman Catholics would be ineligible to sit in it. He also replaced Roman Catholic advisors, as well as those in the high ranks of the army and navy, with Protestant ones. This suggests that James II was aware of the unpopularity of his political approach up until that point.

Religious issues

- James II issued the First Declaration of Indulgence in April 1687 which suspended the Test Act, which stated that all holders of civil office, both military and political, should be Anglican and should swear an oath against Roman Catholic doctrine. The king also issued the Second Declaration of Indulgence in May 1688, which stated that toleration towards Roman Catholics should be preached in every church in England on two successive Sundays. MPs, unable to meet in Parliament, expressed discontent at this and especially at the imprisonment of seven bishops for refusing to comply with the Declaration.

- Charles II had been an Anglican, but had secretly signed the Treaty of Dover in 1670, a deal agreeing with Louis XIV that he would declare himself Roman Catholic when his relations with Parliament improved. He entered the Third Dutch War in alliance with France in 1673, and eventually declared himself a Roman Catholic on his deathbed. Parliament reacted to the king's pro-French stance by passing the Test Act the same year.
- James II promoted Roman Catholics to key posts in government and the army. The new heir to the throne, born in 1685, was to be raised as a Roman Catholic. This religious crisis thus created in the minds of MPs drove the momentum for Parliamentarians to send for William and Mary.
- The Restoration Settlement in 1660 had stated that the Church of England would carry on using the Prayer Book approved by the Stuarts. There were hostile divisions between Episcopalians and Presbyterians. Many MPs, therefore, continued to be fearful of continued Stuart dominance of Anglican Church policy.

The role of Parliament

- Parliament resented James II's abuses of power but took comfort from the thought that he would be succeeded by his Protestant daughter Mary. However, the king's wife had a son, James Edward, in June 1688; he was to be raised as Roman Catholic. This led to Parliament writing to Mary, by now married to the Dutch Prince William of Orange, offering her the Crown.
- William and Mary arrived at Torbay in November with an army of 15,000, and after many in the House of Lords declared their support for William, on Christmas Day James II fled to France. Parliament had also persuaded the king's younger daughter Anne, as well as leading generals, to declare their support for Mary. Subsequent to these events, William and Mary became joint sovereigns on February 13th 1689.

Absence of a Bill of Rights between Crown and Parliament

- With no document resembling a Bill of Rights that would formalise the powers held by monarch and Parliament, some MPs felt that a settlement involving William and Mary would have to include one. Without one, future monarchs, including William and Mary, could preach notions of Divine Right, absolutism and passive obedience. This meant that Parliament wanted limitations on the power of the monarchy to be written into law.
- In March 1689, therefore, Parliament drew up a Declaration of Right, which legalised a new relationship between Crown and Parliament in matters such as finance, law, the succession and religion. This became the Bill of Rights in December that year, and had to be signed by William and Mary as a condition of their remaining on the throne. The importance of the Bill of Rights confirms the view that the blurred lines between monarchs and Parliament had been a problem in the past.

Any other relevant factors.

21. **After the reign of Charles II, James II ruled between 1685 and 1688. His attempts at absolutism led to the Revolution of 1688-9. Parliament invited the king's daughter Mary and her husband William to become joint monarchs. A series of agreements made between 1689 and 1701, legalising the division of power between Parliament and the Crown, became known as the Revolution Settlement. This included the Bill of Rights, limiting the power of the monarch.**

Finance

- Parliament granted William III and Mary II £1,200,000 for court expenses in 1689, including £700,000 to pay civilians working for the state, and these annual awards became fixed amount in the Civil List Act of 1697. A strict Procedure of Audit was established for MPs to check royal expenditure. This meant that financial independence of the crown was no longer possible.

- The 1689 Bill of Rights stated that the monarch could no longer levy taxes without Parliamentary consent. The House of Commons would now agree an annual Budget as proposed by the Chancellor of the Exchequer, who between 1690 and 1695 was Richard Hampden, son of John Hampden. Fiscal power now lay in the hands of Parliament rather than the Crown.

- It could be argued that the monarch benefited from no longer having to resort to unpopular or anachronistic methods of raising revenue, and from now on it would be Parliament that incurred the wrath of ordinary citizens for increasing taxation. However, financial authority had passed to the House of Commons in 1689, and future kings and queens would not be able to reverse this.

Religion

- Parliament passed the Toleration Act of 1689, which provided for toleration of all Protestants except Unitarians, those who did not acknowledge the Holy Trinity. Roman Catholics were also excluded from toleration in the legislation. This meant that Parliament was ensuring that Roman Catholicism could no longer be accepted as it had been under the Stuart dynasty.

- Although Non-Conformist Protestants could now worship freely, the new law maintained an Exclusion from Public Office clause, so they could not obtain teaching positions at universities or elected posts in towns or the House of Commons. The Toleration Act also insisted that Non-Conformists take the Oath of Allegiance and Supremacy as a condition of their religious freedom. It appeared that MPs were having a greater influence on the issue of toleration than they had been allowed during the rest of the 1600s.

- The Toleration Act stated that William III was the supreme head of the Church of England. In opposition to this, there were over 400 Non-Jurors, who were High Anglican priests and bishops refusing to acknowledge William III, and who maintained loyalty to James II, and who were expelled from their posts by Parliament. Parliament, it seemed, could now use its political power to interfere in religious affairs.

- One compromise in the Religious Settlement for the Crown, however, was that the king, as head of the church, now had the power to appoint bishops and archbishops. Nevertheless, the Revolution of 1688-9 established religion firmly within Parliamentary authority.

Legislation

- The 1689 Bill of Rights stated that monarchs could no longer require excessive bail to be demanded from defendants, nor ask judges to impose cruel and unusual punishments on anyone convicted of crimes against the Crown. In addition, ministers impeached by the House of Commons could not be pardoned by the Crown. William III, therefore, could not have the same sway over the justice system as the Stuart kings had.

- In 1695, the Treason Act was altered to give defendants the rights to be given copy of the indictment against them, to be defended by Counsel, to call witnesses in their defence, and to demand that there be two witnesses against them to prove a case instead of the previous one. The Legal Settlement was, therefore, making it harder for a monarch to use the law to enforce policy.

- Later, the Act of Settlement of 1701 stated that judges could only be removed from their positions if Parliament demanded this. The House of Commons alone would approve of judges' commissions being "quamdiu se bene gesserint" - during good behaviour. For judges now, Parliament was ensuring full judicial independence from the Crown, something which had never existed before in England.

- However, by way a compromise, monarchs could still appoint judges, and could be careful to select those who might be favourable to them, which could be a considerable advantage. Overall though, Parliament now enforced its own control over judicial procedure in England.

Parliament

- William and Mary had to agree to the Bill of Rights in December 1689, which legalised the new relationship between Crown and Parliament, before they were given the throne. The Bill of Rights made it clear that monarchs could no longer use royal prerogative to suspend or dispense with laws passed by Parliament, and also could not interfere in Parliamentary elections. This meant that Parliament could exercise independence in its normal business.

- The Bill of Rights also stated that, from now on, MPs and peers could not be punished for exercising Parliamentary freedom of speech during debates in the House of Commons or House of Lords. In addition, the Licensing Act was later repealed in 1695, which removed restrictions on the freedom of the press to report Parliamentary criticism of Crown. It would, therefore, now be impossible for William and Mary to curtail Parliamentary freedom of speech in the manner of Stuart kings earlier in the century.

- The Revolution Settlement provided for another Triennial Act which was passed in 1694. This was intended to keep MPs more closely in touch with public opinion. Parliament was now more relevant to voters than ever before, although voters were still the landed classes.

- It could be argued that the Revolution Settlement still allowed monarchs executive power, so they could dismiss Parliament at will and also rule alone for up to three years, leaving future kings and queens with a significant amount of constitutional power, and as well as this the monarch could still appoint peers and, therefore, wield considerable influence in the House of Lords. Despite this, Parliament was now in a better position in relation to its own rights than it had been at any time since the reigns of Elizabeth I or Henry VIII.

The succession

- The Bill of Rights of December 1689 had declared that no Roman Catholic could become king or queen in the future. More specifically, it stated that all future monarchs should be members of Church of England. Parliament was, therefore, permanently linking the monarchy with the Religious Settlement.

- Furthermore, the eventual Act of Settlement of 1701 stated that, if William and Mary had no heirs, the throne would pass to Sophia of Hanover, Protestant daughter of Elizabeth of Bohemia, sister of Charles I. MPs wanted to prevent the crown falling back into the hands of the Stuart dynasty. It was now clear that Parliament now held the upper hand in relation to the question of the succession.
- Some historians would argue that the Hanoverian Succession was desired by William anyway, and so the Crown was getting its own way. It cannot be denied, however, that Parliament now governed the subject of who ascended the throne.

Scotland

- In April 1689, the Scottish Parliament, known as the Convention of the Scottish Estate, passed the Claim of Right which was accepted by William and Mary in May. This involved a vote to remove James VII (James II of England) from the throne and approve of William II (William III of England) and Mary II as his successors. The new monarchs' acceptance of the Claim of Right suggests that in Scotland there was now a contractual agreement between the Crown and the people.
- Under the Settlement as it related to Scotland, Scotland was to be allowed to have its own church, the Presbyterian Kirk. In addition, the Scottish Parliament would have a greater share in the government of Scotland and more say in the passing and enforcement of Scots law. These aspects of the Settlement indicate that the Crown had less power in Scotland after 1689 than before.
- There would be disputes in the late 1690s between the English and Scottish Parliaments as the English Parliament said that the monarchy had not approved of the Scots' declarations against Episcopalianism in the Claim of Right. Nevertheless, the Settlement had definitely established Parliamentary authority over the monarchy in Scotland.

Ireland

- The 1691 Treaty of Limerick brought an uprising led by James II's French and Irish volunteers to an end, and was signed by leading generals in James II's and William III's armies. The Treaty stated that, in Ireland, Roman Catholics would enjoy the same freedoms as they had done under Charles II, and the Irish Parliament could allow land confiscated from Roman Catholics by Oliver Cromwell to be given back to its original owners. This suggests that Roman Catholics would be treated with more toleration than they had been before the Revolution of 1688–9.
- The Treaty of Limerick also stated that, in the wake of James II's defeat by William III's troops at the Battle of the Boyne in July 1690, Jacobite soldiers were allowed to flee to France rather than face prosecution. 14,000 soldiers and their families left in a migration which became known as the Flight of the Wild Geese. Again, this freedom awarded by William's government represents an increase in rights for Irish Roman Catholics.
- It is debated by many, however, that promises to treat Roman Catholics better were broken by the Penal Laws of 1693-94, passed by Parliament and excluding Roman Catholics from the learned professions and elected public office. Overall, the Revolution Settlement was not as harsh on Roman Catholics in Ireland as many had feared during a time of cruel and violent persecution of religious minorities across Europe.

The status of the army

- The Bill of Rights in December of 1689 had stated that the monarch could not maintain a standing army during peacetime. The Mutiny Act of 1689 legalised the army, and this act had to be passed annually by Parliament, which forced the king to summon Parliament in order to do so. This meant that Parliament would be sitting on a more permanent basis than ever before.
- However, a significant compromise was the fact that the king still retained control over foreign policy, had the final say on the decision to send the army to war or to sign peace treaties, and used his patronage to appoint officers in both the army and navy. Nevertheless, the Revolution Settlement meant that Parliament had gained at least partial control of the military.

Any other relevant factors.

Part C: The Atlantic Slave Trade

22. **The Atlantic slave trade was important in the development of the British economy in the eighteenth century. British manufacturing and industry was stimulated by the supply of factory made goods in exchange for Africans and profits from the slave trade provided the capital for investment in British industry and agriculture.**

Evidence that the slave trade was important

The importance of tropical crops

- The climate and land in the West Indies were suited to the growing of luxury crops such as sugar, coffee and tobacco. Britain made large profits from the trade in fashionable products such as sugar and tobacco which became very popular with British people.

The role of the trade in terms of navigation

- The slave trade contributed to the growth of the Royal Navy. The slave trade was an important training ground for British seamen, providing experienced crews for the Merchant Marine and the Royal Navy.
- However, the high death rate, particularly from disease, meant that the slave trade could also be considered a graveyard for seamen.

The role of the trade in terms of manufacturing

- Goods manufactured in Britain were used to buy enslaved Africans. These goods included textiles, metals such as iron, copper and brass and metal goods such as pots, pans and cutlery.
- Cloth manufacturing grew. Manchester exported a large percentage of cotton goods to Africa.
- The slave trade was important to the economic prosperity and well-being of the colonies.

The procurement of raw materials and trading patterns

- The slave trade was important in providing British industries with raw materials which were turned into manufactured goods in Britain and then sold for large profits in Europe
- Liverpool grew wealthy from plantation grown cotton while Bristol's wealth was partly based on slave produced sugar.
- Plantation grown goods such as rum, tobacco, coffee, sugar, molasses and cotton was bought from the profits of selling African slaves to the plantation owners and sold for a profit in Britain and Europe.

Industrial development

- There was a growth in industries supplying the slave traders with goods such as guns, alcohol, pots and pans and textiles to exchange for captured Africans on the Outward Passage.

- Profits from the slave trade were invested in the development of British industries.
- Investment from the slave trade went into the Welsh Slate Industry. Canals and railways were also built as a result of investment of profits from the slave trade.
- The argument that the slave trade was the vital factor in Britain's industrialisation was put forward in Williams' Capitalism and Slavery thesis.
- Wealth generated by the slave trade meant that domestic taxes could be kept low which further stimulated investment.
- There was an expansion of the service industries such as banks and insurance companies which offered financial services to slave merchants.
- By the end of the eighteenth century the slave trade had become less important in economic terms. It has been argued that only a small percentage of the profits from the slave trade were directly invested as capital in the Industrial Revolution.

Wealth of ports and merchants

- Ports such as London, Bristol and Liverpool prospered as a direct result of their involvement in the slave trade. In the early eighteenth century London and Bristol dominated the British end of the slave trade. Liverpool also grew into a powerful city, directly through the shipping of slaves. By the end of the eighteenth century Liverpool controlled over 60% of the entire British slave trade. Liverpool's cotton and linen mills and other subsidiary industries such as rope making created thousands of jobs supplying goods to slave traders. Other ports such as Glasgow profited from trade with the colonies.
- Liverpool became a major centre for shipbuilding largely as a result of the slave trade. By the 1780s Liverpool had become the largest slave ship building site in Britain.
- The emergence of financial, commercial, legal and insurance institutions to support the activities of the slave traders also led to the development of the British economy. Huge fortunes were made by slave merchants who bought large country estates or built large town houses. Some merchants used their wealth from the slave trade to invest in banks and new businesses.

Evidence that other factors were important

- Changes in agriculture such as enclosure, mechanisation, four-field crop rotation and selective breeding helped create an agricultural surplus which fed an expanding population, produced a labour force in the towns for use in factories and created a financial surplus for investment in industry and infrastructure.
- The British economy also benefited from technological innovations. New machinery such as the Spinning Jenny in the textile industry played an important part in the growing industrialisation of Britain. Water and steam power were used to power machines for both spinning and weaving and led to the rapid spread of factories and transport changes in the form of the canals allowed heavy goods to be carried easily and cheaply.
- The British economy also benefited from the increased production of coal and iron.
- The relative political stability of the eighteenth century created the conditions through which trade and the British economy could flourish.
- Much of the profits of slavery was spent on individual acquisition and dissipated in conspicuous consumption, for example landed estates and large town houses built as status symbols.

Any other relevant factors.

23. Despite a tireless abolitionist campaign inside and outside Parliament, it took many years before the slave trade was finally abolished in 1807. An important obstacle was the delaying tactics and opposition of well organised and powerful groups who had vested interests in the slave trade.

The power of vested interests

- Successive British Governments were influenced by powerful vested interests in Parliament and industry that had the wealth and power to buy votes and exert pressure on others in support of the slave trade.
- Many absentee plantation owners and merchants involved in the slave trade rose to high office as mayors or served in Parliament. William Beckford, the owner of a 22,000 acre estate in Jamaica, was twice Lord Mayor of London. In the mid to late 1700s over 50 MPs in Parliament represented the slave plantations.
- Many MPs themselves had become wealthy as a result of the slave trade which made it difficult to get a law abolishing the slave trade through Parliament. These MPs were wealthy and powerful enough to bribe other MPs to oppose abolition. Liverpool MPs Banastre Tarleton and Richard Pennant used the House of Commons to protect their families' business interests.
- Members of Parliament who supported the slave trade made speeches in Parliament opposing abolition. They argued that millions of pounds worth of property would be threatened by the abolition of the slave trade. They also argued that the slave trade was necessary to provide essential labour on the plantations and that abolition of the slave trade would ruin the colonies.
- MPs with business interests which made money from the slave trade used delaying tactics to slow down any moves towards abolition or supported compromise solutions. In 1792, in a response to Wilberforce's Bill to end the slave trade, Henry Dundas proposed a compromise of gradual abolition over a number of years. Henry Dundas, termed the 'uncrowned king of Scotland' was Secretary of State for War and First Lord of the Admiralty and as such, protected the interests of Scottish and British merchants in the Caribbean.
- Wealthy merchants from London, Liverpool and Bristol also exerted pressure on governments to oppose the abolition of the slave trade. In 1775 a petition was sent to Parliament by the mayor, merchants and people of Bristol in support of maintaining the slave trade.
- The House of Commons was dominated by various interest groups, of which the West India Lobby was for long the most powerful. Tactics included producing pro-slave trade witnesses to testify in Parliamentary inquiries into the slave trade. The West India Lobby included the Duke of Clarence, one of the sons of George III, and proved tough opposition to the abolitionists. Governments were often coalitions of interests, and often relied on patronage, either through the distribution of posts or the appeasement of such interests.

Other factors

Slave rebellion in St Domingue

- Abolition was associated with this symbol of violence; it exaggerated the general fear of slave revolts. There was high loss of life, perhaps as high as 200,000. Slave violence played into the hands of the slave lobby, confirming their warnings of anarchy.
- Britain suffered humiliation when it attempted to take the rebel French Colony, beaten by disease and the ex-slave army.

- When the revolutionary government of France attempted to regain control, however, support for abolition grew as a means of striking at the French once war was declared.

The events of the French Revolution

- These encouraged the belief among many MPs that the abolitionist cause was associated with revolutionary ideas eg Clarkson openly supported the French Revolution. Radicals used the same tactics as abolitionists to win public support — associations, petitions, cheap publications, public lectures, public meetings, pressure on Parliament. Some abolitionists were linked to radicals and therefore they had to be resisted because of fear that events in France may be repeated in Britain.

The importance of the slave trade to the British economy

- The slave trade generated finance — it was an important source of tax revenue and West Indian colonies were an important source of valuable exports to European neighbours. Taxes would have to be raised to compensate for the loss of trade and revenue. Abolition would help foreign rivals such as France as other nations would fill the gap left by Britain.
- British cotton mills depended on cheap slave produced cotton.
- Africa provided an additional market for British manufactured goods.
- Individuals, businesses and ports in Britain prospered on the back of the slave trade.
- Shipbuilding benefited as did maritime employment.
- It was also argued that the slave trade was vital in Britain being able to sustain an expensive war effort against France.

Fears over national security

- Abolition could destroy an important source of experienced seamen; there was a possibility that Britain would lose its advantage over its maritime rivals. On the other hand, the triangular trade was as much a graveyard as a nursery of seamen.

Anti-abolition propaganda

- Vested interests conducted a powerful propaganda campaign to counter that of the abolitionists, though some of the arguments and evidence were specious.
- Slave owners and their supporters argued that millions of pounds worth of property would be threatened by the abolition of the slave trade. The slave trade was necessary to provide essential labour on the plantations. Abolition of the slave trade would ruin the colonies.

The attitudes of British governments

- Initially British governments were anxious to protect the rights of property, which attacks on slavery seemed to threaten. The tactical decision to concentrate on the abolition of the slave trade circumvented this to an extent.

Any other relevant factors.

24. **By the late eighteenth century, the economic importance of the slave trade had begun to decline. The increased price of slaves and the unpredictability of the triangular slave trade meant that the slave trade was no longer as profitable as it once had been. This was a powerful argument in the case for abolition.**

The decline in the economic importance of slavery

- Effects of wars with France — slave trade declined by two-thirds as it was seen as harming the national interest in time of war.

- The slave trade had become less important in economic terms — there was no longer a need for large numbers of slaves to be imported to the British colonies.
- There was a world over-supply of sugar and British merchants had difficulties re-exporting it.
- Sugar could be sourced at a lower cost and without the use of slavery from Britain's other colonies eg India.
- Industrial Revolution: technological advances and improvements in agriculture were benefiting the British economy.

Other factors
The religious revival

- Many of the first Christian opponents of the slave trade came from non-conformist congregations such as Quakers, Presbyterians, Methodists and Baptists.
- Many of the early leaders were Quakers (the Society of Friends), who opposed slavery on the grounds that Christianity taught that everyone was equal. When the Society for the Abolition of the Slave Trade was formed in 1787, 9 of its 12 original members were Quakers.
- The main thrust of Christian abolitionism emerged from the Evangelical Revival of the eighteenth century based on its beliefs on morality and sin.
- The Methodist founder John Wesley questioned the morality of slavery which influenced many Christian abolitionists including the former slave trader turned clergyman, John Newton.
- Evangelical Christians included Thomas Clarkson, William Wilberforce and Granville Sharp, who fought for the freedom of a young African, Jonathan Strong.
- Clergymen such as James Ramsay who had worked in the Caribbean were influential in exposing the facts of plantation slavery and in pointing out that many Africans died without hearing the Gospel.
- However some Quakers continued to have links with the slave trade eg David and Alexander Barclay set up Barclays Bank, Francis Baring set up Barings Bank.
- The Church of England had links to the slave trade through the United Society for the Propagation of the Gospel (USPG) missionary organisations which owned slave plantations in Barbados.
- Scottish churches were amongst the key drivers in the abolitionist movement, although the Church of Scotland did not petition Parliament to end the slave trade.

The effects of slave resistance

- Successful slave rebellion in Saint-Domingue led to an exaggerated, general fear of slave revolts. There was an argument that if conditions were not ameliorated by, for example, the abolition of the slave trade, further revolts would follow. It was argued that Britain began to plan for an exit from the slave trade as a result of this revolt which shook the whole system to its foundations. Already on Jamaica a substantial number of runaways lived outside the control of the authorities.

Military factors

- Napoleon's efforts to restore slavery in the French islands meant that the abolitionist campaign would help to undermine Napoleon's plans for the Caribbean. The Act banning any slave trade between British merchants and foreign colonies in 1806 was intended to attack French interests.

Campaign of the Society for the Abolition of the Slave Trade

- Thomas Clarkson obtained witnesses for the Parliamentary investigations of the slave trade which provided Wilberforce with convincing evidence for his speeches.
- Books and pamphlets published eg eyewitness accounts from former slaves such as Olaudah Equiano.
- Campaigns to boycott goods produced by slaves in the West Indies such as sugar and rum.
- Petitions and subscription lists, public meetings and lecture tours involving those with experience of slave trade eg John Newton, churches and theatres used for abolitionist propaganda, artefacts and illustrations eg Wedgwood pottery.
- Lobbying of Parliament by abolitionists to extract promises from MPs that they would oppose the slave trade. Effective moderate political and religious leadership among the abolitionists influenced major figures such as Pitt and Fox; abolitionists gave evidence to Parliamentary Commissions.

The role of Wilberforce

- Wilberforce put forward the arguments of the Society for the Abolition of the Slave Trade in Parliament for eighteen years.
- Wilberforce's speeches in Parliament against the slave trade were graphic and appealing and were influential in persuading many others to support the abolitionist cause.
- Wilberforce's Christian faith had led him to become interested in social reform and link the issues of factory reform in Britain and the need to abolish slavery and the slave trade within the British Empire.
- Wilberforce was prepared to work with other abolitionists to achieve his aims, including the Quakers, Thomas Clarkson and Olaudah Equiano.
- Despite campaigning inside Parliament over the course of two decades, his attempts to introduce bills against the slave trade were unsuccessful due to powerful opposition to abolition in Parliament.

Any other relevant factors.

Part D: Britain 1851–1951

25. **Political change in Britain was an evolutionary, rather than revolutionary, process. These slow changes tended to see people given access to the political system in the 19th century because they had proven themselves worthy of the vote. By the 20th century, developments tended to be about rights of citizens and their equality in the political system.**

The widening of the franchise

- In 1867 most skilled working class men in towns got the vote. In 1884 many more men in the countryside were given the vote. In 1918 most men over 21 and some women over 30 gained the vote. It was not until 1928 that all men and women over 21 were given the vote.

Corruption and intimidation

- Secret Ballot 1872, Corrupt and Illegal Practices Act 1883

Distribution of seats

- The re-distribution of seats in 1867, 1885 and 1918 all helped created a fairer system of voting. The effectiveness of these varied; they were less effective in areas where the electorate was small, or where a landowner or employer was dominant in an area eg Norwich.

Choice

- Although the working class electorate increased by 1880s there was no national party to express their interests. The Liberals and Conservatives were perceived as promoting middle, and upper-class capitalist values. The spread of socialist ideas and trade unionism led to the creation of the prototype Labour Party — the LRC — by 1900 thereby offering a wider choice to the electorate.

National Party Organisation

- As the size of the electorate grew individual political parties had to make sure their 'message' got across to electorate eg development of National Liberal Federation, Conservative Central Office, Primrose League.

The role of the House of Lords

- From 1911 Lords could only delay bills from the House of Commons for two years rather than veto them. They had no control over money bills.

Widening opportunity to become an MP

- The property qualification to be an MP was abolished 1858. Payment for MPs began in 1911 enabling working class men to sit.
- However, by 1918 Parliament was more representative of the British people but points still to be resolved included:
  - undemocratic anomalies — plural votes and the university constituencies — were not abolished until 1948
  - in 1949 the two year delaying power of the House of Lords was reduced to only one year but the power of House of Lords (not reformed until 1990s) in law making still continues
  - voting system still first past the post in UK.

Any other relevant factors.

26. **A number of reforms were introduced by the Liberal Government between 1906 and 1914 to help improve the lives of the British people. Although some people benefited, overall they had a limited impact.**

The young

- The Provision of School Meals Act (1906) allowed local authorities to raise money to pay for school meals but the law did not force local authorities to provide school meals.
- Medical inspections after 1907 for children were made compulsory but no treatment of illnesses or infections found was provided until 1911.
- The Children's Charter of 1908 banned children under 16 from smoking, drinking alcohol, or begging. New juvenile courts were set up for children accused of committing crimes, as were borstals for children convicted of breaking the law. Probation officers were employed to help former offenders in an attempt to avoid re-offending.
- The time taken to enforce all the legislation meant the Children's Charter only helped improve conditions for some children during the period.

The old

- Old Age Pensions Act (1908) gave people over 70 up to 5 shillings a week. Once a person over 70 had income above 12 shillings a week, their entitlement to a pension stopped. Married couples were given 7 shillings and 6 pence.
- The level of benefits was low. Few of the elderly poor would live till their 70th birthday. Many of the old were excluded from claiming pensions because they failed to meet the qualification rules.

The sick

- The National Insurance Scheme of 1911 applied to workers earning less than £160 a year. Each insured worker got 9 pence in contributions from an outlay of only 4 pence — 'ninepence for fourpence'.
- Only the insured worker got free medical treatment from a doctor. Other family members did not benefit from the scheme. The weekly contribution was in effect a wage cut which might simply have made poverty worse in many families.

The unemployed

- The National Insurance Act (Part 2) only covered unemployment for some workers in some industries and like Part 1 of the Act, required contributions from workers, employers and the government. For most workers, no unemployment insurance scheme existed.
- Some workers who were covered by the Act benefited, but only for a limited period of time.
- Labour Exchanges were introduced to help people back into work but largely in urban areas.

Other reforms

- In 1906 a Workman's Compensation Act covered a further six million workers who could now claim compensation for injuries and diseases which were the result of working conditions.
- In 1909, the Trade Boards Act tried to protect workers in the sweated trades like tailoring and lace making by setting up trade boards to fix minimum wages.
- The Mines Act and the Shop Act improved conditions.

Any other relevant factors.

27. **Between 1945 and 1951, the Labour Government introduced a number of social welfare reforms aiming to meet the needs of the British people 'from the cradle to the grave'. These reforms dealt with the 5 Giants of Poverty: Want, Disease, Ignorance, Squalor and Idleness as identified in the 1942 Beveridge Report. These reforms dealt successfully with the needs of many but not all of the people.**

Want

- 1946 the first step was made: the National Insurance Act: consisted of comprehensive insurance sickness and unemployment benefits and cover for most eventualities.
- It was said to support people from the 'cradle to the grave' which was significant as it meant people had protection against falling into poverty throughout their lives.
- This was very effective as it meant that if the breadwinner of the family was injured then the family was less likely to fall further into the poverty trap, as was common before. However, this act can be criticised for its failure to go far enough.
- Benefits were only granted to those who made 156 weekly contributions.
- In 1948 the National Assistance Board was set up in order to cover those for whom insurance did not do enough.
- This was important as it acted as a safety net to protect these people.
- This was vital as the problem of people not being aided by the insurance benefits was becoming a severe issue as time passed. Yet, some criticised this as many citizens still remained below subsistence level showing the problem of want had not completely been addressed.

Disease

- Establishment of the NHS in 1948 dealt effectively with the spread of disease.
- The NHS was the first comprehensive universal system of health in Britain.
- Offered vaccination and immunisation against disease, almost totally eradicating some of Britain's most deadly illnesses.
- It also offered helpful services to Britain's public, such as childcare, the introduction of prescriptions, health visiting and provision for the elderly, providing a safety net across the whole country: the fact that the public did not have to pay for their health meant that everyone, regardless of their financial situation, was entitled to equal opportunities of health care they had previously not experienced.
- NHS could be regarded as almost too successful. The demand from the public was overwhelming, as the estimated amount of patients treated by them almost doubled. Introduction of charges for prescriptions, etc.

Education

- Reform started by the wartime government: The 1944 Education Act was implemented by the Labour Government. This act raised the age at which people could leave school to 15 as part of a drive to create more skilled workers which Britain lacked at the time. Introduction of school milk, etc.
- Labour introduced a two-tiered secondary schooling whereby pupils were split at the age of 11 (12 in Scotland) depending on their ability. The smarter pupils who passed the "11+ exam" went to grammar and the rest to secondary moderns.
- Those who went to grammar schools were expected to stay on past the age of 15 and this created a group of people who would take senior jobs in the country thus solving the skills shortages. Whilst this separation of ability in theory meant that children of even poor background could get equal opportunities in life, in practice the system actually created a bigger division between the poor and the rich. In many cases, the already existing inequalities between the classes were exacerbated rather than narrowed.
- Labour expanded university education: introduction of grants so all could attend in theory.

Housing

- After the war there was a great shortage of housing as the war had destroyed and damaged thousands of homes; and the slum cleaning programmes of the 1930's had done little to rectify the situation which was leading to a number of other problems for the government.
- Tackling the housing shortage and amending the disastrous results of the war fell upon Bevan's Ministry of Health.
- Labours' target for housing was to build 200,000 new homes a year. 157,000 pre-fabricated homes were built to a good standard, however this number would not suffice and the target was never met.
- Bevan encouraged the building of council houses rather than privately funded construction.
- The New Towns Act of 1946, aimed to target overcrowding in the increasingly built up older cities. By 1950, the government had designed 12 new communities.
- In an attempt to eradicate slums the Town and Country Planning Act provided local communities more power in regards to building developments and new housing.

- By the time Labour left government office in 1951 there was still a huge shortfall in British housing.

Idleness

- Unemployment was basically non-existent so the government had little to do to tackle idleness.
- The few changes they did make were effective in increasing the likelihood of being able to find work, because they increased direct government funding for the universities which led to a 60% increase in student numbers between 1945—46 and 1950—51, which helped to meet the manpower requirements of post-war society. This provided more skilled workers and allowed people from less advantaged backgrounds to pursue a higher education, aiming to keep unemployment rates down.
- Labour government also nationalised 20 percent of industry — the railways, mines, gas and electricity. This therefore meant that the government were directly involved with people employed in these huge industries which were increasing in size dramatically.
- This tackled idleness by the government having control which meant that employees were less likely to lose their job through industries going bankrupt and people were working directly to benefit society.

Any other relevant factors.

Part E: Britain and Ireland, 1900—1985

28. Initially the First World War brought prosperity to Ireland. The demands on manufacturing and farming brought low unemployment thus improving relations between Britain and Ireland. However, Sinn Fein, the Easter Rising and the Protestant reaction were to change this along increasingly sectarian lines.

Irish Attitudes to World War I

- Propaganda — powerful Germany invading helpless and small Catholic Belgium so Ireland supported Britain.
- Ulster very supportive of Britain to ensure favourable treatment at the end of the war.
- Nationalists and Redmond backed war to get Home Rule, urging Irish men to enlist.
- Press gave support to the war effort.
- Irish Volunteers gave support to help Home Rule be passed after the war.
- Recruitment was successful in the south as almost ¼ million men join up.

The Nationalist Movement

- Opposition to war very much a minority in 1914 but supported by Sinn Fein and Arthur Griffith (not powerful at this time), as well as Pearse, Connolly and their supporters and also a section of the Irish Volunteers. This damaged relations with Britain.

Easter Rising

- Rebels saw war as chance to rid Ireland of British by force.
- Felt it was opportunity to gain independence by force as Britain had their troops away fighting the Germans in World War I. This greatly strained relations between Britain and Ireland.
- Britain had to use force to suppress rebellion, such as using the Gunboat, 'Helga' to sail up the River Liffey and fire on the rebels in the GPO, thus distracting Britain's attention and resources away from War effort, thus straining relations.
- Strong criticism of Rising initially from the public, politicians, churchmen, as well as press for unnecessary death and destruction. 450 dead, 2500 wounded, cost £2½ million, showing that majority still sided with Britain therefore indicating that there was not too much damage to relations between the two countries.
- Initial hostility by majority of Irish people to Rising by small group of rebels, majority of people supported Redmond and the Nationalists Party.
- Strong hostility and criticism by Dubliners to rebels for destruction of city centre.

Changing Attitudes towards British Rule after 1916

- The secret court martial, execution of leaders over 10 days as well as imprisonment without trial and at least one execution without a trial saw the rebels gain a lot of sympathy from the Irish public, turning them against British rule.
- These political developments meant a growth of sympathy and compassion for rebels who were seen as martyrs and replaced the initial condemnation of the Rising.
- Sinn Fein initially blamed for the Rising saw a subsequent rise in support for them.
- Catholic Church and business community became more sympathetic to the cause of independence

Anti-Conscription Campaign

- Irish opposed conscription and pushed people in protest to Sinn Fein who openly opposed it.
- Caused the Nationalists to withdraw from Westminster
- Sinn Fein and Nationalists organised campaign eg general strike April 23rd
- Catholic Church, Mayor of Dublin drew up the National Pledge opposing conscription.
- Conscription was not extended to Ireland which Sinn Fein was given credit for.
- Conscription campaign drove Sinn Fein underground which improved their organization.

Decline of Nationalist Party

- Irish Convention failed to reach agreement, which weakened position of Nationalists.
- Led to feeling British could not be trusted and Nationalists could not deliver.
- Three by-elections wins for Sinn Fein gave impression they spoke for people not Nationalists which increased tension between Ireland and Britain politically.
- March 1918 Redmond died which accelerated the decline of the Nationalists. Sinn Fein gained influence and popularity as a result.
- Many moved from the Nationalist Party as they felt Sinn Fein was doing more for Ireland.

Rise of Sinn Fein

- Release of rebel prisoners from Frongoch meant Sinn Fein's struggle against British Rule in Ireland gained momentum.
- Michael Collins was building up IRB and Irish Volunteers when in prison.
- Collins ready to encourage anti-British activity in Ireland on release.
- Collins and De Valera improved Sinn Fein's leadership.
- Opposition to Britain due to martial law, house searches, raids, control of press, arrest of "suspects" without trial, and vigorous implementation of the Defence of the Realm Act.
- Hunger striker Thomas Ashe died in 1917. His funeral became a propaganda tool for Sinn Fein.

Entrenchment of Unionism in the North

- Unionists' 'blood sacrifice' on the Western Front — expectation that this would be recognised in any post-war settlement. The rise of Sinn Fein was viewed with increasing alarm, as was the participation of the Catholic Church in wartime politics eg the National Pledge.

Any other relevant factors.

29. **In 1964 a peaceful civil rights campaign started to end the discrimination against Catholics in Northern Ireland. This led to a Protestant reaction and the crisis that developed was in part caused by economic issues.**

Economic issues

- Northern Ireland was left relatively prosperous by World War Two, with the boom continuing into the 1950s. But by the 1960s, as elsewhere in Britain, these industries were in decline eg Harland and Wolff profitable until early '60s, but government help in 1966. Largely Protestant workforce protected as a result.
- Catholic areas received less government investment than their Protestant neighbours. Catholics were more likely to be unemployed or in low-paid jobs than Protestants in N. Ireland. Catholic applicants also routinely excluded from public service appointments.
- The incomes of mainly Protestant landowners were supported by the British system of 'deficiency payments' which gave Northern Ireland farmers an advantage over farmers from the Irish Republic.
- Brookeborough's failure to address the worsening economic situation saw him forced to resign as Prime Minister. His successor, Terence O'Neill set out to reform the economy. His social and economic policies saw growing discontent and divisions within his unionist party.

Other factors

The Unionist ascendancy in Northern Ireland and challenges to it

- Population of Northern Ireland divided: two-thirds Protestant and one-third Catholic: it was the minority who were discriminated against in employment and housing.
- In 1963, the Prime Minister of N.Ireland, Viscount Brookeborough, stepped down after 20 years in office. His long tenure was a product of the Ulster Unionist domination of politics in Northern Ireland since partition in 1921.
- Unionist ascendancy: Before 1969 elections not held on a "one person, one vote" basis: gerrymandering used to secure unionist majorities on local councils. Local government electoral boundaries favoured unionist candidates, even in mainly Catholic areas like Derry/Londonderry. Also, right to vote in local elections restricted to ratepayers, favouring Protestants, with those holding or renting properties in more than one ward receiving more than one vote, up to a maximum of six. This bias preserved by unequal allocation of council houses to Protestant families.
- Challenges as Prime Minister O'Neill expressed desire to improve community relations in Northern Ireland and create a better relationship with the government in Dublin, hoping that this would address the sense of alienation felt by Catholics towards the political system in Northern Ireland.
- Post-war Britain's Labour government introduced the welfare state to Northern Ireland, and it was implemented with few concessions to traditional sectarian divisions. Catholic children in the 1950s and 1960s shared in the benefits of further and higher education for the first time. This exposed them to a world of new ideas and created a generation unwilling to tolerate the status quo.
- Many Catholics impatient with pace of reform and remained unconvinced of Prime Minister O'Neill's sincerity. Founding of the Northern Ireland Civil Rights Association (NICRA) in 1967. NICRA did not challenge partition, though membership mainly Catholic. Instead, it called for the end to seven "injustices", ranging from council house allocations to the "weighted" voting system.

Role of the IRA

- Rioting and disorder in 1966 was followed by the murders of two Catholics and a Protestant by a 'loyalist' terror group called the Ulster Volunteer Force, who were immediately banned by O'Neill.
- Peaceful civil rights marches descended into violence in October 1968 when marchers in Derry defied the Royal Ulster Constabulary and were dispersed with heavy-handed tactics. The RUC response only served to inflame further the Catholic community and foster the establishment of the Provisional IRA by 1970 as the IRA split into Official and Provisional factions.
- The Provisional IRA's strategy was to use force to cause the collapse of the Northern Ireland administration and to inflict casualties on the British forces such that the British government be forced by public opinion to withdraw from Ireland.
- PIRA were seen to defend Catholic areas from Loyalist attacks in the summer of 1970.

Cultural and political differences

- The Catholic minority politically marginalised since the 1920s, but retained its distinct identity through its own institutions such as the Catholic Church, separate Catholic schools, and various cultural associations, as well as the hostility of the Protestant majority.
- Catholic political representatives in parliament refused to recognise partition and this only increased the community's sense of alienation and difference from the Unionist majority in Northern Ireland.
- Nationalists on average 10-12 in NI Parliament compared to average 40 Unionists. In Westminster 10-12 Unionists to 2 Nationalists
- As the Republic's constitution laid claim to the whole island of Ireland, O'Neill's meeting with his Dublin counterpart, Seán Lemass, in 1965, provoked attacks from within unionism, eg the Rev. Ian Paisley.
- Violence erupted between the two communities, in 1966 following the twin 50th anniversaries of the Battle of the Somme and the Easter Rising. Both events were key cultural touchstones for the Protestant and Catholic communities.

The issue of Civil Rights

- From the autumn of 1968 onwards, a wide range of activists marched behind the civil rights banner, adopting civil disobedience in an attempt to secure their goals. Housing activists, socialists, nationalists, unionists, republicans, students, trade unionists and political representatives came together across Northern Ireland to demand civil rights for Catholics in Northern Ireland.
- The demand for basic civil rights from the Northern Ireland government was an effort to move the traditional fault-lines away from the familiar Catholic-Protestant, Nationalist-Unionist divides by demanding basic rights for all citizens of Britain.
- Civil rights encouraged by television coverage of civil rights protest in USA and student protests in Europe. Also

by widening TV ownership: 1954, 10,000 licences, by 1962 there were 200,000 leading to increased Catholic awareness of the issues that affected them.

- As the civil rights campaign gained momentum, so too did Unionist opposition. Sectarian tension rose: was difficult to control, and civil disobedience descended into occasions of civil disorder.

Any other relevant factors.

30. **Nationalists and Unionists were polarised throughout the period. The two communities were increasingly divided along sectarian lines and economic differences were in part an obstacle to peace. The deployment of British troops in Northern Ireland and imposition of Direct Rule saw the conflict widen.**

Economic differences

- From 1973, the Common Agricultural Policy changed the decision making environment for food prices and farm economics, and employment in the farming sector continued to decline. Traditionally this sector had been dominated by the Unionist community.
- Discrimination against Catholic applicants for employment declined steadily during this period as Catholics in the province began to enjoy the same civil rights enjoyed by the population of the rest of the UK.

Other factors

Religious and communal differences

- The Protestant majority in Northern Ireland belonged to churches that represented the full range of reformed Christianity, while the Catholic minority was united in its membership of a Church that dominated life in the Republic and much of Europe. These religious divisions made it very difficult for both communities to come together.
- These divisions further enhanced by traditions embraced by both communities, such as the 'marching season', which became a flashpoint for sectarian violence. Also differences in sport, language.
- Many Catholic political representatives refused to recognise partition and their views only heightened the nationalist community's sense of alienation and fostered unionist hostility towards the Catholic minority.
- The speeches and actions of Unionist and Nationalist leaders such as Reverend Ian Paisley and Gerry Adams polarised views in the province, and emphasised the divisions between both communities.

The role of the British Army

- The so-called 'Battle of Bogside' in 1969 only ended with the arrival of a small force of British troops at the request of Chichester Clark. An acknowledgement that the govt. of Northern Ireland had lost its grip on the province's security.
- By 1971 policing the province was fast becoming an impossible task, and the British Army adopted increasingly aggressive policies on the ground.
- On 30 January 1972, the army deployed the Parachute Regiment to suppress rioting at a civil rights march in Derry. Thirteen demonstrators were shot and killed by troops, with another victim dying later of wounds. Appalling images of 'Bloody Sunday' led to increased recruitment by Provisional IRA.
- The British Army's various attempts to control the PIRA, such as house-to-house searches and the imposition of a limited curfew, only served to drive more recruits into the ranks of the paramilitaries.

Hardening attitudes — the role of terrorism

- Paramilitary groups began to operate on both sides of the sectarian divide, while civil rights marches became increasingly prone to confrontation.
- In late 1969, the more militant 'Provisional' IRA (PIRA) broke away from the so-called 'Official' IRA. PIRA was prepared to pursue unification in defiance of Britain and would use violence to achieve its aims.
- Unionist paramilitaries also organised. The UVF was joined by the Ulster Defence Association, created in 1971.
- Examples of terrorist activity: by the end of 1972 sectarian violence had escalated to such an extent that nearly 500 lives were lost in a single year. PIRA prisoners protest at loss of special status prisoners leading to hunger strikes. Second hunger strike in 1981, led by Bobby Sands. Sands was put forward for a vacant Westminster seat and won. Sands and nine other hunger strikers died before the hunger strikes were called off in October 1981.
- Sinn Fein won the by-election following Sands' death in June 1983. These electoral successes raised the possibility that Sinn Fein could replace the more moderate SDLP as the political voice of the Catholic minority in Northern Ireland.
- Indiscriminate terrorism meant Eire public opinion turned against PIRA.
- In 1985 the violence of Northern Ireland's paramilitary groups still had more than a decade to run and the sectarian divide remained as wide as it had ever been.

British government policies — Internment

- New Prime Minister Brian Faulkner reintroduced internment ie detention of suspects without trial, in 1971 in response to unrest. The policy was a disaster, both in its failure to capture any significant members of the PIRA and in its sectarian focus on Nationalist rather than Loyalist suspects.
- Reaction was predictable, even if the ferocity of the violence wasn't. Deaths in the final months of 1971, over 150.

Direct Rule

- A number of reforms had followed on from the Downing Street Declaration, ie on allocation of council housing, investigate the recent cycle of violence and review policing, such as the disbanding of the hated 'B Specials' auxiliaries.
- The British government, now led by Prime Minister Edward Heath, decided to remove control of security from the government of Northern Ireland and appointing a secretary of state for the province leading to resignation of Stormont government. Direct rule imposed.
- Despite attempts to introduce some sort of self-rule, such as the Sunningdale agreement of 1973, which failed in the face of implacable Unionist opposition and led to the reintroduction of direct rule. It would last for another 25 years.

The role of the Irish government.

- Irish government's role in The Anglo-Irish Agreement, signed in November 1985, confirmed that Northern Ireland would remain independent of the Republic as long as that was the will of the majority in the north. Also gave the Republic a say in the running of the province for the first time.
- The agreement also stated that power could not be devolved back to Northern Ireland unless it enshrined the principle of power sharing.

Any other relevant factors.

2015
SECTION 3: EUROPEAN AND WORLD

Part A: The Crusades, 1071-1204

31. It was religious passion which swept across Europe that motivated people first and foremost, overwhelming Pope Urban and the Emperor Alexius. The tradition of pilgrimage, combined with full remissions of sins and entry to Heaven, explains why so many Christians went on Crusade to the Holy Lands.

Religious motives

- A key factor driving the largest range of people to take the cross was spirituality, the belief that the Crusade was a spiritual war which would purify their souls of sin. This was a powerful motive in a world deeply concerned with matters of religion, where everything in life was potentially sinful. Many responded to Urban's promise of spiritual rewards for those who fought for the Church. Urban took an unprecedented step at Clermont and offered entry to heaven to those who pledged their soul to the Crusade.
- All Christians, rich and poor were being promised by God's representative on earth, the Pope that fighting in a war against the enemies of the Church would bring what so many deeply wanted: a full indulgence — the highest of prizes — a direct path to heaven and eternal salvation from the moment of death.
- It was generally believed that the Remission of Sins offered by Pope Urban was an attractive solution to the dilemma of knights. At Clermont, Urban assured nobles and knights that they could slaughter the 'infidel' in the name of Christ and not have to complete penance for such action. The very act of crusading itself would form the penance.
- Urban successfully resolved the need to protect Christianity from the Muslim threat and the general desire to re-establish the pilgrimage routes to the Holy Lands. Many believed it was their Christian duty to help fellow Christians under threat by Muslims. Many felt the Crusade would be a spiritually rewarding pilgrimage. Urban drew on the ancient tradition of pilgrimage. For centuries people had journeyed to Jerusalem and the holy sites as well as Rome as a form of penance and to gain remission for their sins.
- Of the leaders of the Princes' Crusade, Raymond of Toulouse, is often held up as an example of a knight riding to the defence of the Holy Lands. Deeply religious, Raymond was the first Prince to agree to join the Crusade. He sold all his lands and wanted to die in the Holy Land. However, his decision to take Tripoli in 1100 casts a shadow over this interpretation of his motives.
- The appeal of the People's Crusade shows the power of the belief that they were doing good and helping God.
- In the First Crusade recruitment was strongest in areas which had supported Pope Gregory VII's reform movement and among families with a tradition of pilgrimage and from areas of France that Pope Urban had visited in person.
- Such omens as showers of meteorites and heavy rains after years of drought were regarded as prophesies, signs of intervention by the Hand of God. Witnesses to these signs believed they were predestined to join the soldiers of Christ and journey to the Holy City.
- Evidence from the charters reveal Crusaders did indeed want to free Jerusalem and win forgiveness for their sins although it should be noted that most charters were written by clergy who may have recorded the Church's official view.

Other factors
Seeking of fame and riches

- It is recognised that not all Crusaders were motivated purely by religion and that many had mixed motives and agendas which included the prospect of financial gain and glory seeking.
- Some knights did go seeking glory and to prove their bravery. The Crusade had provided the solution to the problem of knights and their need for salvation. Young knights like Tancred may have been partly motivated by the desire to use their military skills in the East.
- The idea of crusading was popular with Norman knights who saw the chance of becoming rich and powerful.
- The lure of unimaginable wealth may have motivated some. It was known that there was a lot of wealth in the East. It was the centre of trade.
- Some were attracted by the prospect of booty and plunder.
- The desire for financial gain motivated the Italian city of Pisa, Genoa and Venice who supported the Crusades in the hope of gaining bases for their trading ships.
- The seeking of riches per se was relatively uncommon. For many lesser knights, going on Crusade meant risking financial ruin. They were more likely to lose money than make money since many had to sell or mortgage their lands on poor terms. In addition, land was the real source of wealth and power.

The desire to acquire territory in the Holy Land

- Urban promised that those who went on Crusade would keep possession of any lands they conquered. The traditional view is that this especially appealed to the younger sons of noble families, because of the system of primogeniture.
- Many of the great magnates on this expedition had intentions to acquire new estates for themselves. The motives of many of the leaders of the Princes' Crusade have been put down to this.
- The prospect of gaining land said to 'flow with milk and honey' was tempting for a younger son who would not inherit his father's lands.
- Territory was important to some of the knights and princes who had nothing in Europe;
- Examples of Crusaders who set off for the Holy Land in search of the 'land of milk and honey' which Urban had offered, were Bohemond and Baldwin who showed little zeal in carrying on with the Crusade once they had acquired Antioch and Edessa respectively. Bohemond of Taranto had not inherited his father's lands in Italy and was eager to gain land elsewhere.
- Some of the leaders of the First Crusade personified the desire for land. Notable examples were Robert Duke of Normandy (son of William the Conqueror) and the Normans from southern Italy, Bohemond of Taranto and his nephew Tancred, one of eleven brothers, a classic example of younger sons of the nobility striving for a living. Robert Guiscard's eldest son, Bohemond saw the Crusade as an opportunity to extend his territory.
- The promise of land was an incentive to some although the traditional historians' view of land hunger being a motivation is questioned by the huge financial cost of going on Crusade. The cost of chain mail, armour, horses and weapons amounted to several years' income for most knights.

Peer pressure

- The pressure put on knights by their families to take the cross was at times severe. Noblemen's wives tended to be keenly aware of the politics at court and had a role in influencing the decisions of some.
- Stephen of Blois had married Adela, daughter of William I of England. It would have been unthinkable for such a notable knight not to go on the Crusade. Stephen of Blois was the son-in-law of William the Conqueror and was devoted to his very religious wife Adela. He may have joined the Crusade to please her but it would have been unthinkable for such a notable knight not to go on the Crusade. Overpopulation and famine
- A motive of many may have been a desire to escape the hardships of life at the time. Northern Europe was experiencing rising population, constant food shortages and petty wars and lawlessness. Many craved a better life, in this world as well as the next.
- Several years of drought and poor harvests in the 1090s led to a widespread outbreak of a deadly disease called ergotism, caused by eating bread made from fungus infected cereal. Against this background, a long and dangerous journey to a distant land in the east from which they might never return must have seemed a risk worth taking.
- Many were forced to leave because of the lack of available farmland in an already overcrowded Europe.
- Several famines have also been suggested as a possible motive. It was popularly believed that the Holy Land was a land of plenty.
- Northern Europe was experiencing rising population and constant food shortages.

The sense of adventure

- Going on Crusade was exciting and engendered a sense of adventure.
- Pilgrimages had always been seen as important, and the idea of this as an armed pilgrimage was very appealing. It offered a way out for many serfs from their lives in bondage, or perhaps a chance to see the Holy Land.

Any other relevant factors.

32. **The military skills and leadership of both Richard the Lionheart and Saladin were much in evidence during the Third Crusade. However away from the battlefield, the relationship between Richard and Saladin demonstrated that both men were also skilled in diplomacy.**

Richard's military strengths

- Despite Muslims and Christians having fought an on and off battle over Acre over two years, Richard's leadership and expertise broke the deadlock and forced the surrender of Acre after 5 weeks of bombardment, mining and repeated assaults.
- Richard's arrival in June 1191 with money and with the cutting edge of western military technology in the form of enormous siege engines struck the fear of God into opponents. This enabled Richard to seize control of the battle and to intensify the bombardment.
- Richard switched tactics at Acre after the destruction of his great war machines. He offered his soldiers four gold coins for every stone they could remove from the base of one of the towers, putting so much effort on the one point that a breach in the wall was created.
- Further evidence of Richard's leadership skills at Acre, were shown when, despite falling ill with 'arnaldia' he ordered himself to be carried to the walls in a silken quilt and there, protected by a screen, fired his crossbow at the city which further inspired his troops.
- The capture of Acre was a major boost for the Crusaders and brought the unimpeded rise of Saladin to a halt.
- Richard demonstrated firm, if brutal, leadership in August 1191 when he took the drastic decision to massacre the 2,700 Muslim prisoners taken at Acre when Saladin failed to meet the ransom payment. Richard knew feeding and guarding the prisoners would be a considerable burden and suspecting that Saladin was deliberately using delaying tactics to pin Richard down, Richard resolved the situation quickly and effectively in order to carry on his momentum and capitalise on his victory at Acre.
- Richard demonstrated that he was a great military strategist on the march from Acre down the coast to Jaffa. Under Richard's leadership, the Crusader army of 12,000 men set out along the coast in immaculate formation. Inland were the foot soldiers with their vital role of protecting the heavy cavalry, the cavalry themselves were lined up with the Templars at the front and the Hospitallers at the back, the strongest men to protect the most vulnerable parts of the march. Between the cavalry and the sea was the baggage train, the weakest, slowest and most difficult part to defend. Finally out to sea was the crusader fleet to provide the well-defended columns with essential supplies.
- Richard's military leadership was crucial to the survival of the Crusaders on the march to Jaffa. Forced to face terrible conditions, Richard allowed the soldiers rest days and prevented fights over the meat of dead horses. Despite the constant attacks, Richard showed enormous discipline as he kept his troops marching even as they were being peppered by arrows. Richard was insistent that no Crusader should respond and break formation denying Saladin an opportunity to inflict a crushing defeat on the Crusader forces. Richard wanted to charge on his own terms. Such discipline showed Richard to be a true military genius.
- At the battle of Arsuf, Richard reacted immediately to the breaking of the Crusader ranks and personally led the attack which eventually swept the Muslims from the battlefield. Richard turned his whole army on the Muslims and fought off two fierce Muslim counter attacks. Led by Richard, the Crusader charge smashed into Saladin's army forcing them to retreat. Richard's planning and meticulous attention to detail created the circumstances in which his personal bravery could shine through. The victory of Richard's army over Saladin's forces at the Battle of Arsuf and the success of the Crusaders in reaching Jaffa were important turning points in the Third Crusade. Saladin's aura of success had been breached.
- Richard displayed inspired military leadership and immense personal bravery at Jaffa. When Richard heard that Saladin had stormed the port of Jaffa in July 1192, Richard responded with characteristic brilliance. Richard rushed south from Acre with a tiny force of only 55 knights and crossbowmen at the head of a sea borne counter attack. Despite being heavily outnumbered Richard ordered his men to attack and was one of the first to wade ashore at the head of his small army. The surprise of his attack turned the battle around and gave the Crusaders an improbable and dramatic victory. The Muslim troops themselves were overawed by Richard's courage and nerve. Richard's highly disciplined and organised army had again proved too much for Saladin's men and they retreated.

- Richard ability as a military tactician was shown by his caution on the march to Jerusalem. To ensure his advance on Jerusalem could be properly sustained, Richard carefully rebuilt several fortresses along the route.
- Richard also demonstrated his strategic competence when he withdrew twice from Jerusalem, realising that once recaptured, Jerusalem would be impossible to defend due to insufficient manpower and the possibility that their supply lines to the coast could be cut off by the Muslims. Despite his personal desire to march on Jerusalem, Richard was a general and knew that military sense told him that his depleted force of 12,000 men and lack of resources couldn't hold Jerusalem against Saladin's vast army drawn from across the Muslim world.
- That Richard was a military strategist of the highest order was also demonstrated on his journey to the Holy Land when he captured Cyprus and sold part of it to the Templars. Richard recognised the long term importance of Cyprus as a base for crusading armies to use when supplying and reinforcing expeditions to the Holy Land.
- Richard also realised that Egypt was the key to Saladin's wealth and resources. Ever the military strategist Richard wanted to take the mighty fortress of Ascalon which would threaten Saladin's communications with Egypt. Richard was aware that in order to keep Jerusalem after it was captured; Egypt would need to be conquered first. Richard wrote to the Genoese asking for a fleet to support a campaign in the summer of 1192 but the Crusader army was not interested in Jerusalem and wanted to proceed to Jerusalem. Richard reluctantly agreed to march on Jerusalem before campaigning in Egypt.
- Although the Third Crusade failed in its ultimate aim of the recovery of Jerusalem, Richard's leadership played a crucial role in providing the Crusaders with a firm hold on the coastline which would provide a series of bridgeheads for future crusades. Compared to the situation in 1187, the position of the Crusaders had been transformed.

Richard's military weaknesses

- Richard was ultimately unable to recapture Jerusalem, the main objective of the Third Crusade.
- Richard also failed to draw Saladin into battle and inflict a decisive defeat. He failed to comprehensively defeat Saladin.

Saladin's military strengths

- Saladin counter attacked at Acre. Saladin's troops launched fierce attacks on the Crusaders at given signals from the Muslim defenders and launched volley after volley of Greek fire putting Richard on the defensive as all three of his giant siege towers went up in flames. Saladin also sent a huge supply ship with 650 fighting men in an attempt to break into Acre's harbour. After destroying a number of English vessels, it was scuttled to prevent its cargo falling into Christian hands.
- On the march south to Jaffa, Saladin's army unleashed a relentless series of forays and inflicted constant bombardment, tempting the Christians to break ranks. Saladin's skilled horsemen made lightning strikes on the Crusaders showering the men and their horses with arrows and cross-bow bolts. The Crusaders lost a large number of horses and the Crusaders themselves resembled pincushions with as many as ten arrows or crossbow bolts protruding from their chain mail.
- Saladin massed his forces from Egypt and all across Syria and launched an intense bombardment on the Crusaders which tested the Crusader knights' discipline and patience, not to react, to the absolute limits.

- At the Battle of Arsuf, despite the devastating impact of the Crusader charge, Saladin's own elite Mamluk units rallied and offered fierce resistance.
- To prevent the Crusaders taking Ascalon, Saladin made the decision to pull down Ascalon's walls and sacrifice the city.
- While the Crusaders remained in Jaffa and strengthened its fortifications Saladin took the opportunity to destroy the networks of Crusader castles and fortifications between Jaffa and Jerusalem.
- In October 1191 as the Crusaders set out from Jaffa and began the work of rebuilding the Crusader forts along the route to Jerusalem, they were repeatedly attacked by Saladin's troops.
- At the end of July Saladin decided to take advantage of the Crusaders' retreat from Jerusalem by launching a lightening attack on Jaffa in an attempt to break the Christian stranglehold on the coast. In just four days the Muslim sappers and stone throwers destroyed sections of Jaffa's walls which left only a small Christian garrison trapped in the citadel. Saladin's forces blocked help coming from overland which meant that relief could only arrive by sea.
- Arguably Saladin's greatest military achievement was to gather and hold together (despite divisions) a broad coalition of Muslims in the face of setbacks at Acre, Arsuf and Jaffa. Although the consensus is that Saladin was not a great battlefield general (it could be argued that his triumph at Hattin was down more to the mistakes of the Crusaders than his own skill), Saladin was still able to inspire his troops and fight back. Saladin's continued resistance had ensured that Jerusalem remained in Muslim hands.

Saladin's military weaknesses

- Saladin found it increasingly difficult to keep his large army in the field for the whole year round. In contrast to the Crusading army, many of his men were needed back on their farms or were only expected to provide a certain number of days' service.
- Saladin's authority was ignored when the garrison at Acre struck a deal with Conrad of Montferrat to surrender. Saladin lost control of his men at Jaffa.
- The stalemate at Jaffa showed that Saladin was incapable of driving the Crusaders out of southern Palestine.

Richard's diplomatic strengths

- During the siege of Acre and despite his illness Richard opened negotiations with Saladin showed his willingness to use diplomacy.
- That Richard was skilled in the art of diplomacy was shown in his negotiations with Saladin's brother, Al-Adil. A bond was forged between them and Richard even offered his sister Joan to be one of al-Adil's wives as part of a deal to divide Palestine between the Crusaders and the Muslims. Richard's connection with Al-Adill was enough of an incentive for Saladin to agree to a truce with Richard.
- Richard negotiated a five year truce over Jerusalem.

Richard's diplomatic weaknesses

- Richard showed poor diplomacy towards his allies. After the victory at Acre, Richard's men pulled down the banner of Count Leopold of Austria, claiming his status did not entitle him to fly his colours alongside the king of England, even though Leopold had been fighting at Acre for almost two years. This resulted in Leopold leaving Outremer in a rage, taking his German knights with him (Eighteen months later he imprisoned Richard after the king was captured returning through Austria).

- Richard also failed to show subtlety in his dealings with King Philip. Richard's inability to share the spoils taken during his attack on Cyprus with Philip helped persuade the ill king of France that he was needed at home. The one thing Richard had wished to do was keep Philip with him on the Crusade; now he had to worry about French incursions into his Angevin Empire.
- Against advice Richard backed Guy de Lusignan to become King of Jerusalem, against the popular Conrad of Montferrat, perhaps because he was the favourite of Philip. This continued support of Guy resulted in a compromise that no one liked. The assassination of Conrad was even whispered by some to be Richard's fault. The end result was the withdrawal of the support of Conrad's forces and those of the Duke of Burgundy's remaining French knights.

Saladin's diplomatic strengths
- During the siege of Acre and alongside the military skirmishes as the Crusaders set out on their march to Jerusalem, Saladin and Richard were engaged in diplomacy. Both sides were willing to find areas of agreement at the same time as engaging in brutal combat.
- Following Richard's victory at Jaffa, Saladin knew he could not maintain such a level of military struggle indefinitely. He recognised the need to make a truce with Richard. On 2 September 1192, the Treaty of Jaffa was agreed which partitioned Palestine in return for a three year truce. While Saladin was to retain control of Jerusalem, the Crusaders were allowed to keep the conquests of Acre and Jaffa and the coastal strip between the two towns. Christian pilgrims were also allowed access to the Church of the Holy Sepulchre in Jerusalem.

Saladin diplomatic weaknesses
- Saladin faced increasing discontent from his Muslim allies.
- Saladin negotiated a five year truce over Jerusalem despite his strong position.

Any other relevant factors.

33. **The outcome of the Fourth Crusade was the sacking of Constantinople, the Christian capital city of the Byzantine Empire leading to the claim that by 1204 enthusiasm for reclaiming the Holy Land had begun to wane. The self interest of many of the nobles on the Fourth Crusade was also far removed from the religious ideals of the early crusaders.**

Co-existence of Muslim and Crusading states
- There were many attempts at peace between Muslim and the Crusading states during the reign of Baldwin IV, before his death and the fall of Jerusalem.
- Other examples include the treaty of mutual protection signed between King Alric of Jerusalem and the Emir of Damascus prior to the Second Crusade.

The corruption of the crusading movement by the Church and nobles
- There are many examples of nobles using the Crusade for their own ends. Examples include Bohemond and Baldwin in the First Crusade and arguably Richard in the Third Crusade. The greed of many nobles on the Fourth Crusade was a far cry from the religious ideals of the early crusaders.
- At the end of the Fourth Crusade, the Pope accepted half of the spoils from the Crusaders despite his earlier excommunication of them.

Effects of trade
- Trade links directly into the Fourth Crusade and the influence of Venice.
- The Italian city-states (Genoa, Pisa and Venice) continued to trade with various Muslim powers throughout the crusading period.
- Pisa and Genoa both had a lot of influence in events during the Third Crusade; they both had favoured candidates for the vacant throne of Jerusalem for example and used trade rights as a bargaining chip to get what they wanted.

The Fourth Crusade
- The initial inspiration of the Fourth Crusade had a strong crusading ideology behind it. Pope Innocent III was a highly effective pope. He had managed to settle the problem of the Investiture Contest with Germany, and hoped to sort out the issue of the Holy Lands as well. Innocent believed that the inclusion of medieval monarchs had caused the previous two Crusades to fail, unlike the First Crusade that was nominally under the command of Bishop Adhemar. This Crusade would fall under the command of six papal legates. These men would hold true to the ideal of the Crusade and not be bound by earthy greed of politics.
- However, the Fourth Crusade has also been described as the low point of the crusading ideal. Hijacked by the Venetians, the Crusade instead became a tool for their growing political and economic ambitions.
- While attacking Zara, Alexius, son of the deposed emperor of Byzantium, arrived with a new proposal for the Crusaders. He asked them to reinstate his father, who had been imprisoned by his brother, and if they agreed they would be handsomely rewarded. He also promised to return control of the Byzantine Church to Rome. The Church was against such an attack on another Christian city, but the prospect of wealth and fame led the Crusade to Constantinople.
- When the Crusaders discovered that Alexius and his father could not, or would not, meet the payment as agreed, the Crusaders stormed the city. The murder, looting and rape continued for three days, after which the Crusading army had a great thanksgiving ceremony.
- The amount of booty taken from Constantinople was huge: gold, silver, works of art and holy relics were taken back to Europe, mostly to Venice. Most crusaders returned home with their newly acquired wealth. Those that stayed dividing up the land amongst themselves, effectively creating several Latin Crusader States where Byzantium had once stood.

Role of Venice
- By 1123 the city of Venice had come to dominate maritime trade in the Middle East. They made several secret trade agreements with Egypt and North African emirs, as well as enjoying concessions and trade agreements within the Kingdom of Jerusalem. Byzantium however, remained a constant rival for this dominance of trade and in 1183 Venice was cut off from the lucrative trading centres of the empire.
- Venice's participation in the Crusade was only secured when the Pope agreed to pay huge sums of money to Venice for the use of its ships, and supplies as well as half of everything captured during the Crusade on land and sea.
- Venice's leader, the Doge Enrico Dandolo, had sold the Crusaders three times as much supplies and equipment as required for the Crusade. The crusading leader, Boniface

of Montferrat, found that he was unable to raise enough money to pay, and the Crusaders were all but imprisoned on an island near Venice. Dandolo's proposal to pay off the Crusaders' debt involved attacking Zara, a Christian city that had once belonged to Venice but was now under the control of the King of Hungary, a Christian monarch. Thus the Crusade had become a tool of the Venetians.

- The Fourth Crusade's intended target, Egypt, was totally unsuitable from a Venetian perspective. Thus when the Pope's representative approached the Venetians in 1201 they agreed to help transport the Crusaders, hoping to divert the Crusade to a less friendly target. The final target for the Fourth Crusade was therefore determined by politics and economics.

Any other relevant factors.

Part B: The American Revolution, 1763–1787

34. Since the 1600s, the thirteen colonies of North America had been part of the British Empire. However, on 4 July 1776 the Continental Congress met in Freedom Hall, Philadelphia and issued the Declaration of Independence. This historic event, the turning point in the American Revolution, came after over ten years of opposition by colonists to British rule. The action by the delegates in Philadelphia led to the American War of Independence.

Punishment of Massachusetts and Quebec Act

- The British response to the Boston Tea Party, was a series of measures between March and June 1774, known to colonists as the Intolerable Acts and the British as the Coercive Acts – the Port of Boston Act closed the port, denying valuable revenue to the city, the constitution of the Massachusetts Assembly was altered reducing its powers, the Quartering Act billeted British troops in colonial homes, and trial by jury was suspended. In addition, the Quebec Act, passed in June, allowed French-speaking Catholics to settle in the Ohio valley with local law-making powers that were now being denied to Massachusetts. These legislative measures enraged colonists such as Thomas Jefferson of Virginia who proclaimed that "the British have a deliberate plan of reducing us to slavery".
- The Virginia Assembly was now motivated to call for unity amongst the thirteen colonies to discuss the current crisis and the 1st Continental Congress, with delegates from all colonies except Georgia, met on 5 September in Philadelphia. There it issued the Declaration of Rights and Grievances which, although proclaiming loyalty to George III, dismissed the Coercive Acts as null and void and rejected the supremacy of the British Parliament.

Taxation and the Stamp Act

- Indirect taxation appeared in 1764 with the Sugar Act which controlled the export of sugar and other items which could now only be sold to Britain. This was to be enforced through greater smuggling controls. Colonist merchants protested on the grounds of their reduced income and the idea that there should be no taxation of colonists who had no representation in the British Parliament.
- Also, the Stamp Act, passed by Grenville's administration in 1765, was the first direct taxation on colonists. It stated that an official stamp had to be bought to go on printed matter such as letters, legal documents, newspapers, licences pamphlets and leases. Many colonists subsequently refused to pay the tax, with

James Otis of Boston arguing that "taxation without representation is tyranny".

- While the British argued that taxation would contribute to the costs of Seven Years War and pay for the continued presence of British Army in America, colonists claimed that they already paid financial dues to British through the Navigation Acts and other trading restrictions, and also that they had their own militia and did not need the British Army to protect them.
- The slogan "No Taxation without Representation" was a familiar protest during this time, and due to inability to enforce the Stamp Act, Prime Minister Rockingham oversaw its repeal in March 1766. At the same time he passed the Declaratory Act, supporting any future taxation of the colonies. To underline opposition to any taxation by Britain, the secret organisation Sons of Liberty was founded in February 1766 by colonist like John Adams and Patrick Henry, who proclaimed loyalty to the king but opposition to Parliament.
- In 1767, new Prime Minister William Pitt proposed indirect taxation in the form of duties against imports into the colonies. Chancellor of the Exchequer Lord Townshend introduced taxes on glass, tea, paper and lead. These were opposed by those such as Boston merchant John Hancock whose ships, including the "Liberty", were regularly raided by Customs Board officials acting on behalf of new Prime Minister Grafton, and there were riots across Massachusetts.

Boston Massacre

- On 5 March 1770, during a riot in Boston in opposition to the Townshend Duties, forces sent by General Gage, the British Commander-in-Chief in North America, to quell resistance opened fire on a crowd on the orders of Captain Preston, killing three people instantly, injuring eleven others, and fatally wounding two more. Preston and four soldiers were charged with murder. Many Bostonians were horrified at what they perceived as the brutal actions of the British Army.
- Committees of Correspondence, which had been established during the 1760s, quickly spread news of the massacre around the thirteen colonies, and Paul Revere, a Boston silversmith, depicted the event in an engraving which shocked colonists viewing prints of it. The soldiers were represented at the trial in October by John Adams after he volunteered to ensure there was a fair hearing, and the result was the acquittal of all defendants. This outcome outraged colonists as it suggested that British soldiers had a free hand to kill Americans.
- Committees of Correspondence would later prove effective after the Gaspee Incident in the summer of 1772, when a Royal Navy schooner was captured off Rhode Island and burned by smugglers who resented its enforcement of the Navigation Acts. Britain resolved to transport any culprits to England for trial. Subsequently, all the thirteen colonies' Committees worked together to investigate the legality of all British actions towards them from now onwards.

Proclamation of 1763

- The Proclamation, made by George III, forbade anyone from settling beyond the Frontier, which was a line drawn in the map along the Appalachian Mountains. When it passed through Parliament and became the Proclamation Act, it caused anger amongst colonists of a bold and adventurous nature who were now to be kept within the jurisdiction of British authorities.

- In addition, the Proclamation enforced the re-imposition of the Navigation Acts, restricting colonist trade with European merchants. This meant Royal Navy cutters patrolling the east coast for smugglers collaborating with the French, Dutch or Spanish. Colonist traders greatly resented this curtailment of their economic activities which had gone unhindered for over 40 years during the Whig Ascendancy of the mid-1700s.

The Tea Act

- In 1773, tea duties in the colonies were reduced by the Tea Act, designed by the Lord North's government to give the British East India Company a monopoly in North America to help ease it out of financial difficulty. Although this also benefited colonist tea merchants, many felt not only that Britain may extend this monopoly to other commodities. The key effect of the act was to lead many to suggest that accepting the cheap tea symbolised acceptance of Britain's right to tax America.
- In Boston, crowds of colonists organised blockages of loading bays to prevent the unloading of tea cargoes. On 16 December 1773, in what became known as the Boston Tea Party, hundreds of people, co-ordinated by Samuel Adams, boarded three British East India Company ships and threw £10,000 worth of tea into the harbour. This destruction of British government property was an expression of colonist frustration at policies.

Events at Lexington and Bunker Hill

- On 19 April 1775 British troops encountered colonial militia at Lexington Green in Massachusetts after General Gage sent a force of 700 men to Concord to seize a store of military supplies held by local militia, and were intercepted on the way by Lexington's "minutemen". Eight colonists were killed, and reports of the skirmish raised issues about the conduct of British officers, as there were questions about warnings not being given before firing. This incident was significant because it was the first blood spilled in a military engagement between colonist and British in the developing conflict in America, and led to a series of attacks by various New England militia groups on British forts.
- The Battle of Bunker Hill over 16-17 June 1775 saw the British defeat 1,200 militia on high ground overlooking Boston, but although the colonists suffered over 400 casualties, the British sustained over 1,000, including 200 dead. This was an important development as colonists took heart and attacked more British posts in New England and even Canada, and the 2nd Continental Congress, which had met on 10 May, decided in June to form the Continental Army in June with George Washington of Virginia appointed as its Commander.

Rejection of Olive Branch Petition

- The 2nd Continental Congress had written an appeal to the King in June 1775, known as the Olive Branch Petition, which pledged colonists' allegiance to the crown but expressed bitterness towards Parliament, Lord North and the King's ministers. Congress requested Constitutional Union, which would allow the colonies to legislate for themselves and raise their own taxes but remain within the British Empire under royal authority, yet this last hope of compromise fell on deaf ears as George III rejected the petition in October, declaring the colonists to be in rebellion.

Events of 1775–6

- Congress's Trade Declaration stated that the colonies would no longer obey the Navigation Acts. In response, General Gage requested further military support in the colonies, including the hiring of foreign troops, but thousands of German mercenaries in place of regular soldiers offended colonist sensibilities as Britain was underestimating the Continental Army.
- In November 1775, Governor Dunmore of Virginia formed a regiment of black soldiers in the South, promising freedom to slaves, and this brought many indignant Southerners, previously reluctant to become involved in the conflict, on board the movement towards independence.
- In January 1776 the British republican writer Thomas Paine produced his pamphlet 'Common Sense' which advocated war in order for the colonies to free themselves from British rule. This sold 100,000 copies and influenced many middle-class, educated colonists.
- British intransigence and uncompromising attitudes in the face of continued colonist protest and pleas for compromise, as well as a perception in America of Parliamentary ignorance of the spirit and determination of the colonists, irked many in the colonies.
- On 4th July 1776 Congress met to sign the Declaration of Independence, which had been drafted by Jefferson and Franklin to state that "all men are created equal", and they have "inalienable rights" amongst which are "life, liberty and the pursuit of happiness". It expressed the "right of the people" to abolish their own government if they so desire. Lord North immediately ordered more troops to America in preparation for war.

Any other relevant factor.

35. **The American War of Independence took place between 1776 and 1781, between Britain and its thirteen colonies of North America. For many colonists, this was a revolutionary conflict fought by people fighting for freedom against tyranny, monarchy and the threat of enslavement. The war was fought not only on American soil, but on the high seas and across the world once other European Powers became involved.**

Washington's military capability

- Washington was aware that the British forces would hold the advantage in open battle, so he fought using guerrilla warfare effectively, for example at the significant crossing of the Delaware River in December 1776. This was part of a surprise raid on British posts which resulted in Washington's small bands of men crossing the river back to their positions in Pennsylvania with captured supplies and arms. Guerrilla warfare, therefore, was an effective weapon in Washington's armoury.
- In addition, Washington taught his troops to fire accurately from a distance on those occasions when they were engaged in open battle, particularly in the fight to control the New Jersey area in the first half of the war. During the attack on Princeton in January 1777 and the Battle of Monmouth in June 1778, Washington's forces successfully drove the British from the battlefield.
- Washington's "scorched earth" campaign during the summer of 1779 was aimed at Iroquois settlements in New York in revenge for their co-operation with the British early in the war. This policy deterred further collaboration between Native Americans and the British Army. Although brutal, this strategy increased colonists' chances of winning the war on land.
- Moreover, Washington had experience of serving with the British Army during the Seven Years War, and had been a leading figure in the British capture of Pittsburgh in 1758. He was aware of British military practice and the weaknesses in the chains of communication between

London and North America. This meant he was well-placed to second-guess British manoeuvres during the War of Independence.

Washington's leadership

- He was a self-made Virginian who had become a successful tobacco planter in the 1760s and involved himself in local politics as a member of the Virginia legislature. As a military hero from the Seven Years War, his choice as Commander of the Continental Army in 1775 gave heart to many. So Washington's business and political reputation were key features of his authority during the war.

- His personal qualities included the ability to give speeches to his troops, emphasising the incentive of independence if they won the war. Washington was aware of the political aspect of the conflict, and turned military defeats, of which he suffered many, into opportunities to inspire his forces to fight on. Therefore, this motivational aspect of his nature, an asset which the British did not possess, was an important advantage to the colonists.

- Washington's leadership at Valley Forge during the winter of 1777-8 saw him preserve the morale of his 10,000-strong army in terrible conditions, particularly by his allowing soldiers' families, known as Camp Followers, to remain with the troops. His appointment of celebrated Prussian drill sergeant Baron Friedrich von Steuben to maintain discipline meant firearms skills stayed of a high quality; his promotion of Nathaniel Greene through the ranks from Private to Quartermaster-General meant regular food for the soldiers as well as adequate supplies of ammunition and uniforms, including boots; and the trust he showed in the French General Lafayette led to Congress commissioning Lafayette into the Continental Army before the French entered the war, allowing him an important role in strategic planning. These astute decisions were vital to the colonists' war efforts, both practically and militarily.

French entry into the war

- The Franco-American Treaty of Alliance was signed by Franklin and Louis XVI at Versailles in February 1778. This formalised French recognition of the United States, the first international acknowledgement of American independence. The agreement cemented the colonists' autonomy and provided much-needed help in the fight against the British.

- From this period onward, the French guaranteed the colonists abundant military support in the form of troops sent to fight on land and a naval contribution on the Eastern seaboard, around Britain and across the world. In addition, France provided the Continental Army with ammunition, uniforms, expertise, training and supplies. This meant that the colonists were better equipped to tackle the British successfully in America.

- Importantly, the forces under the command of Count Rochambeau who landed at Rhode Island in 1780 hampered the British army's attempts to dislodge colonist strongholds in Virginia throughout 1780 and 1781. Rochambeau's co-operation with the colonist General Lafayette and the clear lines of communication he established between himself and de Grasse led to the trapping of Cornwallis at Yorktown and the French navy's arrival in Chesapeake Bay. Thus, the French army significantly contributed to the ending of the war on land.

French contribution worldwide

- The strength of the French navy meant Britain had to spread its forces worldwide, particularly as France attacked British colonies in the Caribbean Sea and Indian Ocean. In addition, there were attempts to raid Portsmouth and Plymouth in order to land soldiers on the British mainland. Although these failed, French naval activity worldwide reduced the efforts which Britain could make to defend its North American possessions.

- Admiral d'Orvilliers defeated the Royal Navy in the Battle of Ushant in the English Channel in July 1778, weakening British defences in preparation for further attacks on the south-coast of England. Admiral de Grasse successfully deceived British fleets in the Atlantic to arrive at Chesapeake Bay in September 1781 prior to the Yorktown surrender. It is clear, therefore, that leading French naval figures planned a strategy to divide British maritime forces, thus exposing their hold on the colonies to greater threat from the Continental Army and American Navy.

- The entry of France into the conflict encouraged Spain and Holland to follow suit within next two years, declaring war against Britain in June 1779 and December 1780 respectively. French action against the Royal Navy gave these European Powers confidence to attack British interests in India and the southern colonies.

British military inefficiency

- On several occasions British generals did not act appropriately to instructions, such as when Lord George Germain, the British Secretary of State for America, hatched a plan to separate the New England colonies from the others in mid-1777. This involved General Howe moving his forces north from New York, but Howe misinterpreted his orders and moved south during August, rendering the plan futile. This demonstrates a costly incompetence on the part of the leading British military figure in North America.

- Meanwhile, General Burgoyne, commander of British forces in Canada, had received orders to march south into the Hudson Valley towards Ticonderoga in early 1777. Burgoyne, however, was left isolated in the Hudson Valley after capturing Ticonderoga because Howe had gone south and General Clinton was too slow to move north in place of Howe, and so, confronted by large American forces, Burgoyne was forced to surrender his 3,500 men and equipment at Saratoga in October 1777.

- Furthermore, changes in personnel hindered operations, as politicians such as Lord North and Lord Germain promoted or appointed officers frequently, causing inconsistency and lack of stability at command level. Petty jealousies amongst military leaders also obstructed progress, so that even after military campaigns had been waged successfully or battles had been won, there was no co-operation, leading to the British losing land gained, particularly after French entry in 1778.

Local knowledge

- The main theatre of the land war was on American soil, with the main battles being fought out in Massachusetts, the Middle Colonies and Virginia. Even if the British gained ground, the revolutionary forces knew the terrain well enough to find ways of re-occupying lost territory. This gave the Continental Army an obvious advantage over their British enemies.

- Key colonist victories such as the Battle of Princeton on 3 January 1777, the Battle of King Mountain on 7 October 1780, and the Battle of Yorktown between September and October 1781 were in no small part due to colonist forces' ability to utilise local geography to advantage. British forces constantly found themselves having to react to the movement of the Continental Army. This meant that the British found it hard to go on the attack in the field.

- Furthermore, as witnessed in British victories such as the Battle of New York City between August and October 1776, the Battle of Fort Ticonderoga on 6 July 1777, and the Battle of Brandywine on 25 August 1777, colonist troops had intimate knowledge of the surrounding areas and were able to avoid capture, and so withdrew to safety in order to fight another day. This meant it was difficult for the British to reduce the size of their enemy's numbers.
- On occasions, such as during the Saratoga campaign, local people burned their crops rather than let them fall into British hands. The distance between Britain and the colonies already meant that supplies were slow in arriving at the front. Therefore, the behaviour of locals further reduced the potential supplies for the British army.

Other worldwide factors

- Spain entered into the war in June 1779, intent on mounting an attack on the British mainland. Dutch entry into war came in December 1780, providing another threat of invasion. These European Powers stretched British resources even further and made the British less effective in their overall military effort.
- The Armed League of Neutrality was formed in December 1780. The involvement of Russia, Denmark and Sweden in an agreement to fire on the Royal Navy, if provoked, placed extra pressure on Britain.
- The war at sea was a vital feature of Britain's weaknesses. British concentration was diverted from maintaining control of the colonies on land towards keeping control of maritime access to its wider Empire. Ultimately, with the surrender at Yorktown, it was loss of control of the sea which led to the eventual British defeat.

Any other relevant factors.

36. **The American War of Independence took place between 1776 and 1781, between Britain and its thirteen colonies of North America. When the colonists drew up their constitution they built in a separation of powers that would be essential to the government of the new United States.**

Separation of power

- When the colonists drew up their Constitution, they built in a separation of powers providing checks and balances within the political system, influenced by the thinking of the French philosopher Montesquieu. This was driven through by Alexander Hamilton and James Madison who had disapproved of the too-powerful Continental Congress. The separation of powers, in its division of authority between branches of government in a modern industrialising nation, is, therefore, considered to be the most revolutionary aspect of the Constitution.
- The Constitution stated that no branch of government should ever be subordinate to any other. The Executive, Legislature and Judiciary had to remain apart, with no one person allowed to participate in more than one branch at any one time. This prevented, for example, the administration of justice being subject to outside influence from anyone with political interest.
- This separation of power would be essential to the government of the United States. The President could not take a seat in Congress, Congressmen could not be part of the Supreme Court, and members of the Supreme Court could only be appointed by an agreed confirmation between President and Congress. This secured the separation of powers as a vital component of the Constitution.
- The separation of powers had a built-in system of checks and balances, whereby each branch of government could be kept in line by the other two. The Philadelphia Convention had arranged this to ensure that no single branch could establish tyrannical authority. This meant that the Legislature and Judiciary could check the power of the Executive if necessary.
- The President and his Cabinet, Congressmen and Supreme Court judges could all lose their jobs if they acted improperly. Each strand of government acted independently of each other. This system thus ensured that no one person could rule tyrannically.

Executive

- Executive power was vested in the elected President, and his Vice-President and Cabinet. The first President, George Washington, was elected in February 1789, and could make all key decisions and establish policy. This gave Washington and future Presidents clearly defined powers within the American political system.
- Members of the Executive, including the President, or Thomas Jefferson, who became the USA's first Secretary of State, could be removed from office by the electorate in four-yearly elections. Other branches of government could also remove Executive members from office if it was felt they were not doing their job appropriately. This meant that even the most powerful were kept in check by others in government.

Legislature

- Legislative power lay in the hands of an elected Congress which was divided into two Houses, the Senate and Representatives. The Senate was set up with each state equally represented and the House of Representatives was set up with states represented proportionately to size and population. This was an attempt to divide power equally amongst those representing the electorate.
- The job of Congress was to pass laws and raise taxes. In addition, Congress was given responsibility for international trade, war and foreign relations. This presented Senators and Representatives with significant powers within the country as well as influence around the world.
- No-one in the legislature could serve in the judiciary or executive without first resigning from the legislature. In addition, Congressional elections were held regularly to ensure that Congressmen remained in touch with the people they served. Therefore, the views of the American people would be represented as faithfully as possible amongst those setting taxes and enacting laws.

Judiciary

- The newly formed Supreme Court of Justice, consisting of nine judges, would hold judicial power in the United States. The Supreme Court was formed in order to prevent legal matters becoming entwined with political ones. Therefore, this Judiciary also had a plain role to act out in the country.
- The Supreme Court could be called upon to debate the legality of new laws enacted by Congress. It also acted as the highest court of appeal in the United States. It can be seen, therefore, that one of the key functions of the Supreme Court was to protect individual citizens from unconstitutional behaviour on the part of law-makers and law-enforcers.
- Supreme Court judges were nominated by the President upon advice from his Cabinet and political staff. New appointments had to be ratified by Congress after a rigorous vetting process. This design led to the Supreme Court representing a mix of views on various legal issues.

Bill of Rights

- The Bill of Rights was drawn up in 1791 as the first ten amendments to the Constitution, after several states refused to ratify the Constitution as it stood. These states' delegates at Philadelphia wanted greater protections for citizens against the federal government. Therefore, the Bill of Rights became an important document that set out the limitations of the power of Congress.
- The Bill of Rights established liberty for individual citizens in states within a federal union of all states, and set out clear lines of authority between federal government and individual states. Central government controlled matters of national importance, and state assemblies were to be responsible for local government and administration. This meant that the Constitution would prevent central government from exerting a controlling power over people's lives.
- In addition, the Bill of Rights stated that neither Congress nor the government could pass laws which established religion as a part of state institutions, for example within the education system. School prayer was, therefore, prohibited. This meant that religion was disestablished in the United States.
- Moreover, the Bill of Rights protected the freedom of the press, freedom of speech, and the right to peaceable assembly. Also it set out the rights of citizens who were under investigation or being tried for criminal offences; for example, no-one could be compelled to give evidence which might incriminate them. This was designed to prevent the government from assuming too much power over individuals.
- Furthermore, any powers which had not been written into the Constitution as being delegated to the federal government would be delegated to state governments. This meant that any future disputes over certain powers, for example, the power to abolish slavery, which had not been envisaged at the time of the Revolution, would be ceded to states automatically and, therefore, taken out of the hands of Congress and central government.

Democratic ideals

- The hierarchy of colonial government which had existed under rule by Britain was altered drastically by the Constitution. The Constitution stated that "all men are created equal" and that everyone was entitled to "life, liberty and the pursuit of happiness". This established, therefore, a new approach to the rights and position of ordinary citizens within the processes of government.
- From now on, people would be asked to ratify many of the stages within democratic processes at state and national level. This meant ordinary citizens were involved in the election of various offices from local education boards to state governors. The Constitution was thus ensuring government by the people.
- However, women and blacks were excluded from the franchise, and in reality only one-fifth of eligible voters turned out for national elections. Forces of vested interest were too strong. This suggests that democracy was more of an ideal than an actuality.
- Moreover, the Philadelphia Convention introduced an elitist system of electors in Presidential elections voting for an electoral college. The electoral college consisted of educated men who would vote for the President, a system which still exists today. The electoral college system implies an institutional distrust of ordinary citizens, which is an undemocratic practice.

The experience of rule by Britain

- As part of the British Empire, colonists had been ruled by the King and the British Parliament, who together made key policy decisions, set laws and taxes, and enforced the law. As a result there had been no checks and balances on executive, legislative and judicial processes. This created a need for a Constitution which had built in safety mechanisms to prevent tyrannical behaviour on any ruler's part.
- The notion of "No Taxation without Representation" had been a source of much of the original resentment towards British colonial policy. After 1787, representation would be a key feature of the new system of politics. This meant that the new branches of government were to be predominantly elective, to ensure participation of the people.
- During their experience of being ruled by Britain, colonists had learned to be suspicious of all forms of government, and they feared the potentially tyrannical power of a monarch. They designed the Constitution to thwart any future attempts of American heads of state to act in a similar manner as George III. Therefore, the separation of powers was devised.

Other features

- The Articles of Confederation had been written in 1776, signed in 1781, and acknowledged in 1787, to declare that states would retain individual sovereignty and provided for state representatives to Continental Congress. This led to states rights being fiercely guarded by states in the future.
- In relation to religion, the church was separated from the state in order to ensure equality was extended to include freedom of belief for everyone. The church was thus disestablished.
- Regarding the question of slavery, in northern states measures were taken for the practice, already declining, to be gradually abolished, although pro-slavery sentiment in the South intensified simultaneously.

Any other relevant factors.

Part C: The French Revolution, to 1799

37. **By 1789 the problems of the Ancien Regime were coming to a head. A series of foreign wars had led the state into debt. The demands for more cash, attempts to reform the taxation system, demands for political change, the influence of the Enlightenment and an ineffectual monarch all led to pressures on the Ancien Regime, which was put into stark relief by the economic crisis of 1788/9.**

Influence of the Enlightenment

- The Enlightenment encouraged criticism, and freedom of thought, speech and religion, and was seen as the end of man's self-imposed irrationality at the hands of the Church in particular.
- Ideas of Philosophes like Voltaire who attacked God, Montesquieu who favoured a British system of government and Rousseau who put forward the idea of direct democracy.
- Very much appealed to the middle-classes, who led the revolution.

Other factors

The economic crisis of 1788/9

- Bad harvests and grain shortages inspired unrest among the peasantry and the urban workers in Paris and in provincial cities throughout France, exerting critical pressures on the Ancien Regime.

- There was less demand for manufactured goods, which led to unemployment increasing amongst the urban workers.
- The nobility were increasingly blamed as peasants started to take political action.
- The economic crisis clearly created an environment in which the Ancien Regime was struggling to survive.

Financial problems of the Ancien Regime

- Because of exemptions the crown was denied adequate income. The privileged orders were an untapped source of revenue but it would require reforms to access it.
- This created resentment amongst the Third Estate
- Exacerbated divisions that already existed between the Estates.
- Tax - farming meant not all revenues were reaching the government.
- By the 1780s France faced bankruptcy due to heavy expenditure and borrowing to pay for wars.
- Government failed to gain agreement on tax reform.
- This was arguably the biggest threat facing the Ancien Regime. The opposition which this generated not only led to Calonne's dismissal in 1787 but more importantly to the convocation of the Estates General in 1788. When it met in May 1789 the long-standing divisions between the three Estates unleashed forces which culminated in the overthrow of the Ancien Regime.

The American Revolution

- This war contributed to the financial crisis which came to a head in France post-1786 as the French had to finance both their navy and army fighting America.
- For many in France at the time they also represented the practical expression of the enlightened views of the Philosophes in terms of the rights of the individual, no taxation without representation and freedom from tyrannical government.
- The wars inspired many of the lesser nobility and the bourgeoisie to seek the same freedoms.

The political crisis of 1788/9

- The convocation of the Estates General in August 1788 sharpened divisions between the three Estates which came to a head between May and August 1789.
- The Cahiers des Doleances revealed the depth of dissatisfaction with the existing order, especially among the bourgeoisie and the peasantry.
- The creation of the National Assembly, the abolition of feudalism and the Declaration of the Rights of Man and the Citizen all contributed to a revolutionary change in French government, society and economy.

Actions of Louis XVI

- Louis was largely under the influence of his wife, Marie Antoinette who, although strong minded, failed to grasp the serious nature of the situation and was also unpopular as she was Austrian.
- Louis XVI's handling of the Estates-General contributed towards the start of the Revolution. He wanted to make reform difficult by making the three Estates meet separately, in the hope that the First and Second Estates would vote the Third down.
- This backfired: opposition to the King grew, the Third Estate refused to act separately, and many of the clergy changed sides, changing the balance of power.
- Louis allegedly closed the meeting halls, which led to the Tennis Court Oath from members of the Third Estate.

He later agreed to a constitution when the Third Estate representatives occupied the royal tennis courts.

- The King had lost more political ground than if he had just listened to the grievances of the middle classes and the Third Estate from the start.

Role of Bourgeoisie

- As part of the Third Estate resented paying the taxation.
- Dominated the Third Estate representatives in the Estates-General.
- Were outside the political process unless they bought a noble title: wanted access to power.
- Very attracted to ideas of a constitutional monarchy as advocated by people like Montesquieu.
- Provided the leadership for the Revolution.

Any other relevant factors.

38. **French military performance in 1798 and 1799 led to the eventual collapse of the Directory. The British encouraged Royalist insurrection in the south of France, further complicating matters. Subsequent political intrigue by Sieyes backed by the military reputation of Bonaparte led to the coup that established the Consulate.**

Role of Sieyes

- Afraid that France would descend into anarchy as a result of the on-going political conflict and deeming the 1795 constitution unworkable, Sieyes enlisted the aid of Bonaparte in mounting a coup against it.
- The Convention, the Directory and the legislative councils had run their course and few, if any, mourned their passing.

Other factors

Increasing intervention of the army in politics

- Even before the 1795 constitution was ratified the army had been used to quell sans-culottes insurgents who sought to invade the Convention and to repel an émigré invasion at Quiberon.
- Napoleon's use of a 'whiff of grapeshot' to put down the disturbances in October merely underlined the parlous nature of politics at the time.
- The deployment of the army in May 1796 to put down the left-wing Babeuf Conspiracy was followed by the Coup of Fructidor in September 1797 when the first 'free' Convention elections returned a royalist majority.

Political instability

- In the late summer of 1794 France was emerging from two years of increasing radicalisation and resulting bitterness between opposing factions.
- The Jacobins under Robespierre had been overthrown and a 'White Terror' was soon to sweep the country in revenge for the excesses of the radical left during the Terror.
- France had been torn apart by civil war, threatened by foreign armies egged on by émigré nobles seeking to overthrow the Revolution and riven by religious conflict occasioned by the State's opposition to the primacy of the Catholic Church.

The Constitution of 1795

- Policy-makers framed a new constitution which sought to reconcile the bitterness of the preceding years by imposing checks and balances against the emergence of one dominant individual, group or faction. In so doing, many historians argue that the new constitution was a recipe for instability in the years which followed.
- A bi-cameral legislature was established wherein each chamber counter-balanced the power of the other. By so doing it inhibited strong and decisive government.

- To ensure continuity, the new Convention was to include two-thirds of the outgoing deputies from the old. This enraged sections of the right who felt that the forces of left-wing radicalism still prevailed in government.
- The resulting mass protests in October 1795 were put down by the army under Bonaparte. The principle of using extra-parliamentary forces to control the State had been established with Bonaparte right at the heart of it. It was to prove a dangerous precedent.
- Annual elections worked against consistent and continuous policy-making
- So did the appointment of an Executive — the Directory — one of whose members rotated on an annual basis.
- Again, the counter-balance between the legislature and the executive may have been commendable but it was to prove inherently unstable in practice.

Role of Bonaparte
- A supreme self-propagandist, he seemed to offer the strength and charisma which the Directory and the legislative councils singularly lacked.
- Afraid that his spectacular victories in Italy during 1795 might be jeopardised by the election of a right-wing government less sympathetic to conducting a war against monarchical states, Bonaparte threw his support behind the Directory who effectively annulled the election results by purging right-wing deputies.
- The 1788 and 1799 elections were similarly 'adjusted'.
- The Consulate — with Bonaparte as First Consul — came into being. A notably more authoritarian constitution was promulgated by referendum, supported by a populace tired of weak and ineffectual government and the instability it had brought between 1795 and 1799.

Any other relevant factors.

39. **The effects of the French Revolution were profound and lasting. In particular the impact was felt by the French Aristocracy and Clergy. However, there was also an impact on the peasantry, the middle class and urban workers.**

The impact of the Revolution on the First Estate
- The Catholic Church was a key pillar of the Ancien Regime. The Upper Clergy (usually drawn from the ranks of the traditional nobility) enjoyed considerable wealth and status based on a raft of privileges and tax exemptions. These privileges and exemptions were swept away by the Revolution and the position of the Catholic Church within France by 1799 was far less assured than it had been under the Ancien Regime.
- The Civil Constitution of the Clergy (July 1790) polarised attitudes towards the place of the Catholic Church within French society and promoted conflict between opposing factions through the rest of the period to 1799. In November 1789 Church lands were nationalised, stripping the Church of much of its wealth. The net result of all of this was that the Church never regained its primacy within the French state and can be seen to have lost far more than it gained.

The impact of the Revolution on the Second Estate
- The aristocracy had enjoyed similar privileges and tax exemptions to those of the Catholic Church under the Ancien Regime. Advancement in the key positions of the State, the Army and, indeed the Church, depended more often on birth than merit. The traditional nobility monopolised these key positions and sought at all times to defend its favoured position. Again, the Revolution swept away aristocratic privilege even more completely than that of the clergy.

- The ending of feudalism in August 1789 marked the prelude to a decade when the status of the nobility in France effectively collapsed. In 1790 outward displays of 'nobility' such as titles and coats of arms were forbidden by law and in 1797, after election results suggested a pro-royalist resurgence, the Convention imposed alien status on nobles and stripped them of French citizenship.
- The Revolution brought in a regime where careers were open to talent regardless of birth or inheritance and the traditional aristocracy simply ceased to exist. Having said that, some nobles simply transformed themselves into untitled landlords in the countryside and continued to exercise significant economic and political power.

The impact of the Revolution on the Third Estate

The peasantry
- In contrast to the Catholic Church and the nobility the position of the peasantry was in many ways strengthened by the Revolution. The ending of feudalism in August 1789 removed many of the legal and financial burdens which had formed the basis of peasant grievances in the Cahiers des Doleances presented to the Estates-General in 1789.
- The revolutionary land settlement, instigated by the nationalisation of church lands in November 1789, had transferred land from the nobility and the clergy to the peasantry to their obvious advantage.
- Not all peasants benefited equally from the land settlement. Only the well-off peasants could afford to purchase the Church lands which had been seized by the National Assembly.

The bourgeoisie
- The Revolution instigated a fundamental shift in political and economic power from the First and Second Estates to the bourgeoisie.

  The ending of feudalism in August 1789 heralded profound social and economic change (eg facilitating the development of capitalism) whilst the Declaration of the Rights of Man and the Citizen later in the month did the same for political life. In both cases the main beneficiaries were the bourgeoisie.
- Successive constitutions and legislative reforms throughout the1790s favoured the bourgeoisie above all other social groups by emphasising the notion of a property-owning democracy with voting rights framed within property qualifications, whilst the ending of trade restrictions and monopolies favoured an expanding business and merchant class.
- France had moved from a position of privileged estates to one where increasingly merit was what counted. It was the educated bourgeoisie who were best placed to benefit from this change in French society.

The urban workers
- At key points throughout the Revolution overt demonstrations of discontent by the urban masses- particularly in Paris - impacted on key events as successive regimes framed policy with an eye to appeasing the mob.
- The modest gains by the urban poor were short-lived. A decade of almost continuous wars in the 1790s had created shortages and inflation which hit the urban poor particularly hard.
- The passing of the Chapelier Law in May 1791, by a bourgeois-dominated National Assembly protecting the interests of industrialists, effectively banned the formation of trade unions and thereafter the Revolution brought few tangible economic or political gains for urban workers.

Any other relevant factors.

Part D: Germany, 1851–1939

40. German nationalism, the desire for a united Germany, was already in existence in 1815 as a response to the ideas of the French Revolution and due to resentment of French domination under Napoleon. However, the lack of popular support for nationalism — especially amongst the peasants — and the political repression coordinated by Metternich meant there were still many factors unfavourable to German nationalism.

Evidence that nationalism had made significant progress in their aims:

- Cultural nationalism — work of poets, musicians, writers and their effects on Germans. Impact largely on educated Germans and not everyone was interested in such ideas. Not considered vital to the everyday lives of the ordinary people.
- *Vormarz* period — evidence suggests that workers were starting to take a real interest in politics and philosophy, but only in relatively small numbers.
- Nationalism remained largely middle-class before 1848.
- In 1815 there were tens of thousands of people, especially among the young, the educated and the middle and upper classes, who felt passionately that the Germans deserved to have a fatherland.
- 1840 — French scare to German states. Ordinary Germans were now roused to the defence of the fatherland. This was not confined to the educated classes — spread of nationalist philosophy to large numbers of ordinary Germans. Enhanced reputation of Prussia among German nationalists.
- Economic nationalism — middle class businessmen pushed the case for a more united Germany in order to be able to compete with foreign countries. Benefits evidenced by the Zollverein to German states. Arguments that 'economic' nationalism was the forerunner to political nationalism.

Evidence that nationalists had not made significant progress

- Growth of the *Burschenschaften* — dedicated to seeing the French driven from German soil. Nationalist enthusiasm tended to be of the romantic type, with no clear idea of how their aim could be achieved. Much of the debate in these societies was theoretical in nature and probably above the comprehension of the mass of ordinary Germans.
- Political nationalism — virtually non-existent between 1820 and 1848. Suppressed by the Karlsbad Decrees and the Six Acts. Work/success of Metternich in suppressing such a philosophy.
- Work of the German Confederation and the rulers of the autonomous German states to suppress nationalism.
- Troppau Congress — decision taken by the representatives of Austria, Prussia and Russia to suppress any liberal or nationalist uprisings that would threaten the absolute power of monarchs. This was a huge blow to nationalists within the German states.
- German *Bund* remained little more than a talking shop. Austrian domination of the *Confederation* and the *Bund* stifled political change. 'The French spread liberalism by intention but created nationalism by inadvertence' (Thomson). The French united these German states in a common feeling of resentment against them.

- 1848 Revolutions and the Frankfurt Parliament. No agreement was reached on a grossdeutsch or a kleindeutsch solution. German rulers regained authority. Divided aims of revolutionaries. Self-interest of the rulers of the German states led to their opposition to Frankfurt Parliament. Frederick William of Prussia backed down in face of Austrian pressure at Olmutz and the humiliation of Prussia. German nationalism was arguably a spent force.

Any other relevant factors.

41. In 1933 Hitler became Chancellor of Germany. His ability to tap into German resentment towards the Treaty of Versailles aided his rise to power.

Resentment towards the Treaty of Versailles

- The Treaty of Versailles: acceptance by Republic of hated terms.
- Land loss and accepting blame for the War especially hated.
- Led to growth of criticism; 'November Criminals', 'Stab in the back' myth.

Other factors

Weaknesses of the Weimar Republic

- A Republic without Republicans/a Republic nobody wanted — lack of popular support for the new form of government after 1918.
- Peasants in a palace — commentary on Weimar politicians.
- Divisions among those groups/individuals who purported to be supporters of the new form of government eg the socialists.
- Alliance of the new government and the old imperial army against the Spartacists — lack of cooperation between socialist groups — petty squabbling rife.
- The Constitution/Article 48 ('suicide clause') - arguably Germany was too democratic.
- Proportional representation led to weak coalition governments.
- Lack of real, outstanding Weimar politicians who could strengthen the Republic, Stresemann excepted.
- Inability (or unwillingness) of the Republic to deal effectively with problems in German society.
- Lukewarm support from the German Army and the Civil Service.

Social and Economic difficulties

- Over-reliance on foreign investment left the Weimar economy subject to the fluctuations of the international economy.
- 1922/23 (hyperinflation) - severe effects on the middle classes, the natural supporters of the Republic; outrage and despair at their ruination.
- The Great Depression of the 1930s — arguably without this the Republic might have survived. Germany's dependence on American loans showed how fragile the recovery of the late 1920s was. The pauperisation of millions again reduced Germans to despair.
- The Depression also polarised politics in Germany — the drift to extremes led to a fear of Communism, which grew apace with the growth of support for the Nazis.

Appeal of the Nazis after 1928

- Nazi Party attracted the increasingly disillusioned voting population: They were anti-Versailles, anti-Communist [the SA took on the Red Front in the streets], promised to restore German pride, give the people jobs etc.
- The Nazis put their message across well with the skilful use of propaganda under the leadership of Josef Goebbels.

- Propaganda posters with legends such as "Hitler — our only hope" struck a chord with many.
- The SA was used to break up opponents' meetings and give the appearance of discipline and order.
- Gave scapegoats for the population to blame from the Jews to the Communists.

The role of Hitler

Hitler was perceived as a young, dynamic leader, who campaigned using modern methods and was a charismatic speaker.

- He offered attractive policies which gave simple targets for blame and tapped into popular prejudice.

Weaknesses and mistakes of others

- Splits in the Left after suppression of Spartacist revolt made joint action in the 1930s very unlikely.
- Roles of von Schleicher and von Papen. Underestimation of Hitler.
- Weakness/indecision of Hindenburg.

Any other relevant factors.

42. **The Nazis used a variety of methods to stay in power. These ranged from policies that pleased the German people to the development of State terror.**

Fear and terror

- Opponents liable to severe penalties, as were the families.
- The use of fear/terror through the Nazi police state; role of the Gestapo.
- Concentration camps set up; the use of the SS.

Other factors

Success of economic policies

- Nazi economic policy — attempted to deal with economic ills caused by the Great Depression affecting Germany, especially unemployment.
- Nazis began a massive programme of public works; work of Hjalmar Schacht.
- Nazi policy towards farming eg Reich Food Estate — details of various policies.
- Goring's policy of 'guns before butter'. Popular once foreign policy triumphs appeared to justify it.

Social policies

- Attempts to create the *Volksgemeinschaft* (national community).
- Nazi youth policy.
- Nazi education policy.
- Nazi policy towards the Jews-first isolate, then persecute and finally destroy.
- Nazi family policy — Kinder, Kirche, Kuche.
- Kraft durch Freude programme.
- A Concordat with the Catholic Church was reached; a Reichsbishop was appointed as head of the Protestant churches.

Success of foreign policy

- Nazi success in foreign policy attracted support among Germans; Rearmament, Rhineland, Anschluss.
- Much of Hitler's popularity after he came to power rested on his achievements in foreign policy.

Establishment of totalitarian state

- Political parties outlawed; non-Nazi members of the civil service were dismissed eg Enabling Act following the Reichstag Fire.

- Nazis never quite able to silence opposition to the regime.
- Speed of takeover of power and ruthlessness of the regime made opposition largely ineffective.
- Anti-Nazi judges were dismissed and replaced with those favourable to the Nazis.
- Acts Hostile to the National Community (1935) — all-embracing law which allowed the Nazis to persecute opponents in a 'legal' way.

Crushing/weakness of opposition

- Opponents liable to severe penalties, as were their families.
- Opponents never able to establish a single organisation to channel their resistance – role of the Gestapo, paid informers.
- Opposition lacked cohesion and a national leader; also lacked armed supporters.
- Lack of cooperation between socialists and communists.
- The Night of the Long Knives removed internal opposition, removed the unpopular SA and earned the gratitude of the Army.

Propaganda

- Use of Nuremburg Rallies.
- Use of radio.
- Cult of the Leader: the Hitler Myth.
- Use of the Cinema: Triumph of the Will, the Eternal Jew, etc.
- Role of Goebbels.

Any other relevant factors.

Part E: Italy, 1851—1939

43. **By 1850 the forces of nationalism had grown in Italy. The Revolutions of 1848 showed this, but they also illustrated the tensions within the nationalist movement and the continued strength of Austria.**

Supporters of nationalism

Educated middle class

- Risorgimento saw 'patriotic literature' from novelists and poets including Pellico, and Leopardi. These inspired the educated middle class.
- Gioberti, Balbo and Mazzini promoted their ideas for a national state, this inspired nationalism amongst the middle classes.

Liberals

- Some liberals and business classes were keen to develop an economic state. Napoleon Bonaparte had built roads and encouraged closer trading. One system of weights, measures and currency appealed.

Popular sentiment

- French revolutionary ideals had inspired popular sentiment for a national Italian state.
- There was a growing desire for the creation of a national state amongst students; many joined Mazzini's 'Young Italy'.
- Operas by Verdi and Rossini inspired growing feelings of patriotism.
- The use of Tuscan as a 'national' language by Alfieri and Manzoni spread ideas of nationalism.
- Membership of secret societies such as the Carbonari grew. Members were willing to revolt and die for their beliefs which included desire for a national state.

Opponents

Austria and her dependent duchies

- Resentment against Austria and its restoration of influence in the Italian peninsula and their use of spies and censorship, helped increase support for the nationalist cause. However, any progress made by nationalists was firmly crushed by the Austrian army. Strength of the Quadrilateral. Austrians never left Italian soil. Carbonari revolts in Kingdom of Naples 1820–1821, Piedmont 1821, Modena and the Papal States 1831 all crushed by Austrian army. During 1848 revolutions, Austrian army defeated Charles Albert twice – Custoza and Modena, retook Lombardy and destroyed the Republic of St Mark.

Italian princes and rulers

- Individual rulers were opposed to nationalism and used censorship, police and spies as well as the Austrian army, to crush revolts 1820–1821, 1830 and 1848.

Attitude of the peasants

- The mass of the population were illiterate and indifferent to politics and nationalist ideas. They did revolt during bad times as can be seen in 1848 – but their revolts were due to bad harvests and bad economic times and were not inspired by feelings of nationalism.

Position of the Papacy

- Pope Pius IX. Nationalist movement had high hopes of New Pope Pius IX, initially thought of as a liberal and sympathetic to nationalist cause. Hopes dashed when Pope

Pius IX denounced the nationalist movement during and after 1848 revolutions.

Failures of 1848 revolutions

- These showed that nationalist leaders would not work together, nor did they seek foreign help thus hindering progress. Charles Albert's 'Italia farad a se' declared that Italy would do it alone – she did not. Lombardy and Venetia suspected Charles Albert's motives and were reluctant to work with him. Venetians put more faith in Manin.
- All progress was hampered when Pope Pius IX denounced nationalism.
- Charles Albert hated Mazzini and would not support the Roman Republic.
- Austrian military might based on the Quadrilateral defeated Charles Albert twice – at Custoza and Modena, retook Lombardy and destroyed the Republic of St Mark.
- The French crushed the Roman Republic.

Any other relevant factors.

44. By 1925, Mussolini and the Fascists had gained power in Italy. A number of factors contributed to Mussolini's rise to power, including the economic difficulties facing Italy after the First World War.

Economic difficulties

- The First World War imposed serious strain on the Italian economy. The government took huge foreign loans and the National Debt was 85 billion lira by 1918. The lira lost half of its value, devastating middle class savers. Inflation was rising; prices in 1918 were four times higher than 1914. This led to further major consequences:
  - no wage rises
  - food shortages
  - two million unemployed 1919
  - firms collapsed as military orders ceased.

Weaknesses of Italian governments

- Parliamentary government was weak – informal 'liberal' coalitions. Corruption was commonplace (trasformismo). Liberals were not a structured party. New parties formed: PSI (socialists), PPI (Catholic Popular Party) with wider support base threatening existing political system.
- WWI worsened the situation; wartime coalitions were very weak. 1918; universal male suffrage and 1919 Proportional Representation; relied on 'liberals' – unstable coalitions. Giolitti made an electoral pact with Mussolini (1921); fascists gained 35 seats then refused to support the government. Over the next 16 months, three ineffective coalition governments.
- Fascists threatened a 'March on Rome' – King refused to agree to martial law; Facta resigned; Mussolini was invited to form coalition. 1924 Acerbo Law.

Resentment against the Peace Settlement

- Large loss of life in frustrating campaigns in the Alps and the Carso led to expectation that these would be recognised in the peace settlement; Wilson's commitment to nationalist aims led to the creation of Yugoslavia and a frustration of Italian hopes of dominating the Adriatic.
- 'Mutilated victory' – Italian nationalists fuelled ideas that Italy had been betrayed by her government.

Role of the King

- The King gave in to fascist pressure during the March on Rome. He failed to call Mussolini's bluff.
- After the Aventine Secession the King was unwilling to dismiss Mussolini.

Appeal of the Fascists

- They exploited weaknesses of other groups by excellent use of Mussolini's newspaper 'Il Popolo D'Italia'.
- The Fascio Italiano di Combattimento began as a movement not a political party and thus attracted a wide variety of support giving them an advantage over narrower rivals.
- By 1921 fascism was anti-communist, anti-trade union, anti-socialist and pro- nationalism and thus became attractive to the middle and upper classes.
- Fascism became pro-conservative, appealed to family values, supported church and monarchy; promised to work within the accepted political system. This made fascism more respectable and appealing to both the monarchy and the papacy.
- Squadristi violence was directed against socialism so it gained the support of the elites and middle classes.
- Violence showed fascism was strong and ruthless. It appealed to many ex-soldiers.
- Fascists promised strong government. This was attractive after a period of extreme instability.
- Fascists promised to make Italy respected as a nation and thus appealed to nationalists.
- Fascist policies were kept deliberately vague to attract support from different groups.

Role of Mussolini

- Key role in selling the fascist message: Powerful orator-piazza politics.
- He seized his opportunities. He changed political direction and copied D'Annunzio.
- He used propaganda and his newspaper effectively and had an ear for effective slogans.
- He dominated the fascist movement, kept support of fascist extremists (Ras).
- He relied on strong nerve to seize power and to survive the Matteotti crisis.

- Mussolini manipulated his image, kept out of violence himself but exploited the violence of others.

Weaknesses and mistakes of opponents

- D'Annunzio's seizure of Fiume was not stopped by the government.
- Government failed to get martial law to stop fascist threat. Some liberals supported the Acerbo Law.
- Socialist General Strike July 1922 — failed. Socialists' split weakened them; refused to join together to oppose fascism.
- Liberals fragmented into four factions grouped around former PMs. They were too weak to effectively resist. Hoped to tame fascists.
- PPI was divided over attitude to fascism—right wing supported fascism. Aventine Secession backfired; destroyed chance to remove Mussolini.

Any other relevant factors.

45. **By 1925, Mussolini and the Fascists had achieved power in Italy. The establishment of the Fascist State had in part been achieved by economic and social policies, which were important in maintaining power up to 1939.**

Economic and social policies

- Fascists tried to develop the Italian economy in a series of propaganda-backed initiatives eg the 'Battle for Grain'. While superficially successful, they did tend to divert resources from other areas.
- Development of transport infrastructure, with building of autostrade and redevelopment of major railway terminals eg Milan
- One major success was the crushing of organised crime. Most Mafia leaders were in prison by 1939.
- Dopolavoro had 3.8 million members by 1939. Gave education and skills training; sports provision, day-trips, holidays, financial assistance and cheap rail fares. This diverted attention from social/economic problems and was the fascist state's most popular institution.

Crushing of opposition

- Liberals had divided into four factions so were weakened.
- The Left had divided into three—original PSI, reformist PSU and Communists—they failed to work together against fascists.
- Pope forced Sturzo to resign and so PPI (Catholic Popular Party) was weakened and it split.
- Acerbo Law passed. n1924 elections—fascists won 66% of the vote.
- Opposition parties failed to take advantage of the Matteotti crisis. By walking out of the Chamber of Deputies (Aventine Secession) they gave up the chance to overthrow Mussolini; they remained divided—the Pope refused to sanction an alliance between PPI and the socialists. The King chose not to dismiss Mussolini.
- Communists and socialists did set up organisations in exile but did not work together. Communist cells in northern cities did produce some anti-fascist leaflets but they suffered frequent raids by OVRA.
- PPI opposition floundered with the closer relationship between Church and State (Lateran Pacts).

Fear and intimidation

- Mussolini favoured complete State authority with everything under his direct control. All Italians were expected to obey Mussolini and his Fascist Party.
- The squadristi were organised into the MVSN Milizia Voluntaria per la Sicurezza Nazionale the armed local Fascist militia (Blackshirts). They terrorised the cities and provinces with tactics such as force-feeding with toads and castor oil.
- After 1925-6 around 10,000 non-fascists/opposition leaders were jailed by special tribunals.
- The secret police, OVRA was established in 1927 and was led by Arturo Bocchini. Tactics included abduction and torture of opponents. 4,000 people were arrested by the OVRA and sent to prison.
- Penal colonies were established on remote Mediterranean islands such as Ponza and Lipari. Conditions for those sentenced to these prisons were primitive with little chance of escape.
- Opponents were exiled internally or driven into exile abroad.
- The death penalty was restored under Mussolini for serious offences but by 1940 only ten people had been sentenced to death.

Establishment of the Fascist state

- Nov/Dec 1922 Mussolini was given emergency powers. Nationalists merged with PNF 1923. Mussolini created MSVN (fascist militia) — gave him support if the army turned against him — and Fascist Grand Council — a rival Cabinet. These two bodies made Mussolini's position stronger and opposition within PNF weaker. The establishment of a dictatorship began:
- 1926 — opposition parties were banned. A one party state was created.
- 1928 — universal suffrage abolished.
- 1929 — all Fascist Parliament elected.

Social controls

- Workers were controlled through 22 Corporations, set up in 1934; overseen by National Council of Corporations, chaired by Mussolini.
- Corporations provided accident, health and unemployment insurance for workers, but forbade strikes and lock-outs.
- There were some illegal strikes in 1930s and anti-fascist demonstrations in 1933 but these were limited.
- The majority of Italians got on with their own lives conforming as long as all was going well. Middle classes/ elites supported fascism as it protected them from communism.
- Youth knew no alternative to fascism, were educated as fascists and this strengthened the regime. Youth movements provided sporting opportunities, competitions, rallies, camps, parades and propaganda lectures — 60% membership in the north.

Propaganda

- Press, radio and cinema were all controlled.
- Mussolini was highly promoted as a 'saviour' sent by God to help Italy - heir to Caesar, world statesman, supreme patriot, a great thinker who worked 20 hours a day, a man of action, incorruptible.

Foreign policy

- Mussolini was initially extremely popular, as evidenced by huge crowds who turned out to hear him speak.
- Foreign policy successes in the 1920s, such as the Corfu Incident, made him extremely popular. He was also able to mobilise public opinion very successfully for the invasion of Abyssinia.
- Mussolini's role in the Munich Conference of 1938 was his last great foreign policy triumph.
- As Mussolini got more closely involved with Hitler his popularity lessened. His intervention in Spain proved a

huge drain on Italy's resources. The invasion of Albania was a fiasco.

Relations with the Papacy

- Lateran treaties/Concordat with Papacy enabled acceptance of regime by the Catholic majority.
- Many Catholics supported Mussolini's promotion of 'family values'.

Any other relevant factors.

Part F: Russia, 1881—1921

46. By 1905 Russia's problems had led to open opposition to the Tsarist state. Poor military performance in the war with Japan exposed the social, economic and political weaknesses of the state.

Military defeat

- Land battle: decisive defeat at Mukden.
- Sea battle: defeat at Tsushima Strait. They sailed 18,000 miles before being defeated in under an hour.
- The Russo-Japanese War was disastrous for Russia. Defeats by Japan were humiliating and led to discontent in Russia over the Tsar's leadership, the incompetence of the Tsar's government and the inadequate supplies and equipment of Russia's armed forces.
- Russian soldiers and sailors were unhappy with their poor pay and conditions.
- The incompetence of their leaders and their defeats led to low morale.
- Naval mutiny in the Black Sea fleet, battleship *Potemkin*, over poor conditions and incompetent leadership threatened to spread and weakened support for the Tsar.

Other factors

Economic problems

Working-class discontent

- Russia had been experiencing a number of economic problems in the period before 1905. Russia had started the process of industrialisation, however its cost meant that Russia used foreign loans and increased taxes to fund it.
- The working and living conditions in the cities were very poor and this, along with long working hours and low pay, led to discontent.

Peasantry discontent

- The vast majority of Russians were peasant farmers who lived in poverty and were desperate to own their own land. Many peasants were frustrated at paying redemption payments and at the unwillingness of the government to introduce reforms. An economic slump in Russia hurt the newly-created Russian industries and, coupled with famine in 1902/1903, led to food shortages.
- There was an outcry when Russian grain was still being exported to pay for the foreign loans.

Political problems

- Growing unhappiness with Tsarist autocratic rule. The middle class and the industrial workers were calling for a constitutionally-elected government as they were so frustrated at the incompetence of the Tsar's government, especially during the war with Japan. During 1905, workers set up groups called soviets to demand better pay and conditions. The Russian nobility feared a revolution if moderate reforms were not introduced.
- Tsar Nicholas II was seen as being too weak and unable to make good decisions for Russia in a crisis.

- National minorities hated the policy of Russification as it ignored their language, customs and religion and many felt so isolated that the desire for independence intensified.
- As the war with Japan progressed there were a growing number of protests from different parts of Russian society calling for the war to end and the Tsar to share his power.

Events

- Bloody Sunday, on Sunday 9 January 1905, led by Father Gapon. Troops fired on the unarmed crowd which led to strikes in all major towns and cities.
- Terrorist acts followed towards government officials and landowners.
- Peasant violence in the countryside when peasants took over land and burned landowners' estates started after the government threatened to repossess the land of those behind with their redemption payments.

Any other relevant factors.

47. In 1917, the Bolsheviks successfully overthrew the Provisional Government. A reason for this was the appeal of the Bolsheviks under the leadership and organisation of Lenin.

Appeal of the Bolsheviks

- Lenin returned to Russia announcing the April Theses, with slogans such as "Peace, Land and Bread" and "All Power to the Soviets" which were persuasive.
- Lenin talked of further revolution to overthrow the Provisional Government and his slogans identified the key weaknesses of the Provisional Government.
- The Bolsheviks kept attending the Petrograd Soviet when most of the others stopped doing so and this gave them control of the Soviet, which they could then use against the Provisional Government.
- The Bolsheviks did not return their weapons to the Provisional Government after they defeated Kornilov.
- Bolsheviks were able to act as protectors of Petrograd.

Other factors

Weaknesses of the Provisional Government

- The Provisional Government was an unelected government; it was a self-appointed body and had no right to exercise authority, which led it into conflict with those bodies that emerged with perceived popular legitimacy.
- The Provisional Government gave in to the pressure of the army and from the Allies to keep Russia in the War.
- Remaining in the war helped cause the October Revolution and helped destroy the Provisional Government as the misery it caused continued for people in Russia.
- General Kornilov, a right wing general, proposed to replace the Provisional Government with a military dictatorship and sent troops to Petrograd.
- Kerensky appealed to the Petrograd Soviet for help and the Bolsheviks were amongst those who responded.
- Some Bolsheviks were armed and released from prison to help put down the attempted coup.

Dual power — The role of the Petrograd Soviet

- The old Petrograd Soviet re-emerged and ran Petrograd.
- The Petrograd Soviet undermined the authority of Provisional Government especially when relations between the two worsened.
- Order No. 1 of the Petrograd Soviet weakened the authority of the Provisional Government as soldiers were not to obey orders of Provisional Government that contradicted those of the Petrograd Soviet.

Economic problems

- The workers were restless as they were starving due to food shortages caused by the war.
- The shortage of fuel caused lack of heating for the workers in their living conditions.
- The shortage of food and supplies made the workers unhappy and restless.

The Land Issue

- All over Russia peasants were seizing nobles land and wanted the Provisional Government to legitimise this.
- The failure of the Provisional Government to recognise the peasants' claims eroded the confidence in the Provisional Government.
- Food shortages caused discontent.

Any other relevant factors.

48. **In order to secure power the Bolsheviks had to fight a vicious Civil War with their opponents. That they won was due to their strengths, such as the role of Trotsky as well as disunity among their enemies.**

Role of Trotsky

- Trotsky had a completely free hand in military matters.
- HQ was heavily armed train, which he used to travel around the country.
- He supervised the formation of the Red Army, which became a formidable fighting force of three million men.
- He recruited ex Tsarist army officers and used political commissars to watch over them, thus ensuring experienced officers but no political recalcitrance.
- He used conscription to gain troops, and would shoot any deserters.
- Trotsky helped provide an army with great belief in what it was fighting for, which the whites did not have.

Other factors

Disunity among Whites

- The Whites were an uncoordinated series of groups whose morale was low.
- The Whites had a collection of different political beliefs who all wanted different things and often fought amongst themselves due to differences. All of the Whites shared a hatred of Communism but other than this they lacked a common purpose.
- No White leader of any measure emerged to unite and lead the White forces whereas the Reds had Trotsky and Lenin.

Organisation of the Red Army

- The Red Army was better organised than the White army and better equipped and therefore able to crush any opposition from the White forces.
- Use of ex-officers from old Imperial Army.
- Reintroduction of rank and discipline.
- Role of Commissars.

Superior Red resources

- Once the Reds had established defence of their lines they were able to repel and exhaust the attacks by the Whites until they scattered or surrendered.
- By having all of their land together it was easier for the Reds to defend. With the major industrial centres in their land (Moscow and Petrograd) the Reds had access to factories to supply weapons etc and swiftly due to their control of the railways.

- Control of the Railways meant they could transport troops and supplies quickly and efficiently and in large numbers to the critical areas of defence or attack.
- The decisive battles between the Reds and Whites were near railheads.
- The Reds were in control of a concentrated area of western Russia, which they could successfully defend due to the maintenance of their communication and supply lines.
- Having the two major cities of Moscow and Petrograd in their possession meant that the Reds had the hold of the industrial centres of Russia as well as the administrative centres.
- Having the two major cities gave the Reds munitions and supplies that the Whites were unable to therefore obtain.

Use of Terror (Cheka)

- The Cheka was set up to eradicate any opposition to the Reds.
- There was no need for proof of guilt for punishment to be exacted.
- There was persecution of individual people who opposed the Reds as well as whole groups of people, which helped to reduce opposition due to fear, or simply eradicate opposition.
- The Cheka group carried out severe repression.
- Some of the first victims of the Cheka were leaders of other political parties.

Foreign Intervention

- The Bolsheviks were able to claim that the foreign "invaders" were imperialists who were trying to overthrow the revolution.
- The Reds were able to stand as Champions of the Russian nation from foreign invasion.
- The help received by the Whites from foreign powers was not as great as was hoped for.
- The Foreign Powers did not provide many men due to the First World War just finishing and their help was restricted to money and arms.

Propaganda

- Whites were unable to take advantage of the brutality of the Reds to win support as they often carried out similar atrocities.
- The Whites were unable to present themselves as a better alternative to the Reds due to their brutality.
- The Reds kept pointing out that all of the land that the peasants had seized in the 1917 Revolution would be lost if the Whites won. This fear prevented the peasants from supporting the Whites.

Leadership of Lenin

- Introduction of War Communism
- By forcing the peasants to sell their grain to the Reds for a fixed price the Reds were able to ensure that their troops were well supplied with and well fed.
- The Whites' troops were not as well supplied and fed as the Reds' troops.
- Skilled delegation and ruthlessness

Any other relevant factors.

Part G: USA, 1918–1968

49. Between 1918 and 1941 the USA was a racist society to a large extent. Black Americans faced hostility due to racist attitudes. Such racism was underpinned by a lack of political influence, legal sanction, social attitudes and organisations that persecuted black Americans.

Lack of political influence
- 1890s: loopholes in the interpretation of the 15th Amendment were exploited so that states could impose voting qualifications.
- 1898 case of Mississippi v Williams – voters must understand the American Constitution.
- Grandfather Clause: impediment to black people voting.
- Most black people in the South were sharecroppers they did not own land and some states identified ownership of property as a voting qualification.
- Therefore black people could not vote, particularly in the South, and could not elect anyone who would oppose the Jim Crow Laws.

Activities of the Ku Klux Klan
- Racist organisation formed in 1860s to prevent former slaves achieving equal rights. Suppressed by 1872, but in the 1920s there was a resurgence.
- Methods horrific: included beatings, torture and lynching.
- Roosevelt refused to support a federal bill to outlaw lynching in his New Deal in 1930s - feared loss of Democrat support in South.
- Activities took place at night — men in white robes, guns, torches, burning crosses.
- The 'second' Klan grew most rapidly in urbanising cities which had high growth rates between 1910 and 1930, such as Detroit, Memphis, Dayton, Atlanta, Dallas, and Houston.
- Klan membership in Alabama dropped to less than 6,000 by 1930. Small independent units continued to be active in places like Birmingham, where in the late 1930s members launched a reign of terror by bombing the homes of upwardly mobile African- Americans.
- Their activities in the 1930s led to continued migration of black Americans from the South to the North.

Legal impediments
- 'Jim Crow Laws' — separate education, transport, toilets etc — passed in Southern states after the Civil War
- 'Separate but Equal' Supreme Court Decision 1896, when Homer Plessey tested their legality
- Attitudes of Presidents eg Wilson 'Segregation is not humiliating and is a benefit for you black gentlemen'.

Divisions in the black community
- Booker T. Washington, accommodationist philosophy, regarded as an 'Uncle Tom' by many.
- In contrast W. E. B De Bois founded the NAACP — a national organisation whose main aim was to oppose discrimination through legal action. 1919 he launched a campaign against lynching, but it failed to attract most black people and was dominated by white people and well off black people.
- Marcus Garvey and Black Pride — he founded the UNIA (Universal Negro Improvement Association) which aimed to get blacks to 'take Africa, organise it, develop it, arm it, and make it the defender of Negroes the world over'.

Popular prejudice
- Since the institution of slavery the status of Africans was stigmatized, and this stigma was the basis for the anti-African racism that persisted.
- The relocation of millions of African-Americans from their roots in the Southern states to the industrial centres of the North after World War I, particularly in cities such as Boston, Chicago, and New York (Harlem). In northern cities, racial tensions exploded, most violently in Chicago, and lynchings increased dramatically in the 1920s.

Any other relevant factors.

50. After 1945, the Civil Rights Movement was active in campaigning to improve the lives of African-Americans. There are many reasons why this mass movement developed after 1945 and the role of Martin Luther King is a significant factor.

The role of Martin Luther King
- Martin Luther King — inspirational. Linked with SCLC. Peaceful non-violence and effective use of the media. 'I have a dream' speech.
- 1957 Martin Luther King and other black clergy formed the Southern Christian Leadership Conference (SCLC) to coordinate the work of civil rights groups.
- King urged African-Americans to use peaceful methods.
- Leadership during Montgomery Bus Boycott 1955.
- Use of media to gain publicity for the cause.

The emergence of effective black leaders
- Malcolm X — inspirational, but more confrontational. Articulate voice of Nation of Islam.
- Stokely Carmichael — Black Power and rejection of much on MLK's non-violent approach. A 'direct ideas' descendant of Marcus Garvey.
- All leaders attracted media coverage, large followings and divided opinion across USA.
- Black Panthers attracted attention but lost support by their confrontational tactics.
- Other leaders and organisations eclipsed by media focus on main personalities.

The formation of effective black organisations
- 1960: groups of black and white college students organised Student Non-violent Coordinating Committee (SNCC) to help the civil rights movement.
- They joined with young people from the SCLC, CORE and NAACP in staging sit-ins, boycotts, marches and freedom rides.
- Combined efforts of the civil rights groups ended discrimination in many public places including restaurants, hotels, and theatres.

Continuation of prejudice and discrimination
- The experience of war emphasised freedom, democracy and human rights yet in USA Jim Crow laws still existed and lynching went unpunished.
- The Emmet Till murder trial and its publicity.
- Education: 1954 Brown v Board of Education of Topeka; 1957 Little Rock Central High School.
- Transport: 1955 Rosa Parks and the Montgomery Bus Boycott.

The experience of black servicemen in the Second World War
- Black soldiers talked about 'the Double-V-Campaign': Victory in the war and victory for Civil Rights at home.

- Philip Randolph is credited with highlighting the problems faced by black Americans during World War Two.
- Planned March on Washington in 1941 to protest against racial discrimination.
- Roosevelt's response — Executive order 8802.
- Roosevelt also established the Fair Employment Practices Committee to investigate incidents of discrimination.
- Creation of the Congress of Racial Equality (CORE) 1942.
- Beginning of a mass movement for Civil Rights.

Any other relevant factors.

51. **After 1945, the Civil Rights Movement was active in campaigning to improve the lives of black Americans. This mass movement was successful, in part, in solving the problems facing black Americans, up to 1968.**

Aims of the Civil Rights Movement
- Was mainly pacifist and intended to bring Civil Rights and equality in law to all black Americans.
- More radical segregationist aims of Black Radical Movements.

Role of NAACP
- Work of NAACP in the Brown v Topeka Board of Education, 1954.
- Work of NAACP in the Montgomery Bus Boycott, 1955.

Role of CORE
- Organised sit-ins during 1961 and freedom rides.
- Helped organise march on Washington.
- Instrumental in setting up Freedom Schools in Mississippi.

Role of SCLC and Martin Luther King
- Emergence of Martin Luther King and the SCLC.
- Little Rock, Arkansas — desegregation following national publicity.
- Non-violent protest as exemplified by Sit-ins and Freedom Rides.
- Birmingham, Alabama 1963: use of water cannon: Reaction of Kennedy.
- March on Washington, August 1963 — massive publicity.
- Martin Luther King believed that the Civil Rights Act of 1964 'gave Negroes some part of their rightful dignity, but without the vote it was dignity without strength'.
- March 1965, King led a march from Selma to Birmingham, Alabama, to publicise the way in which the authorities made it difficult for black Americans to vote easily.

Changes in Federal Policy
- Use of executive orders: Truman used them to appoint black appointments, order equality of treatment in the armed services: Kennedy signed 1962 executive order outlawing racial discrimination in public housing, etc
- Eisenhower sent in federal troops and National Guardsmen to protect nine African-American students enrolled in a Central High School: Kennedy sent troops to Oxford, Mississippi to protect black student: James Meredith
- Johnson and the 1964 Civil Rights Act banning racial discrimination in any public place, Voting Rights Act of 1965: by end of 1965 over 250,000 Blacks newly registered to vote, Affirmative Action, etc

Social, economic and political changes
- Civil Rights Acts of 1964 and 1965 irrelevant to the cities of the North.
- Economic issues more important in the North.
- Watts Riots and the split in the Civil Rights movement.
- King and the failure in Chicago.

- Urban poverty and de facto segregation still common in urban centres — failure of King's campaign to attack poverty.

Rise of black radical movements
- Stokely Carmichael and Black Power.
- Malcolm X publicised the increasing urban problems within the ghettos of America. The Black Panthers were involved in self-help schemes throughout poor cities.
- Kerner Commission 1968 recognised US society still divided.

Any other relevant factors.

Part H: Appeasement and the Road to War, to 1939

52. **By its nature the fascism espoused by Hitler and Mussolini was expansionist in nature. However, the methods used to fulfil their aims varied owing to the circumstances faced by the fascist powers. There was considerable skill on display as well as the ability to use opportunity when it arose. However, the inevitable end of such actions was war.**

Military agreements, pacts and alliances
- The German-Polish Non-Aggression Pact between Nazi Germany and Poland signed on January 26, 1934 — normalised relations between Poland and Germany, and promised peace for 10 years. Germany gained respectability and calmed international fears.
- Anglo German Naval Treaty 1935 — Germany allowed to expand navy. Versailles ignored in favour of bi-lateral agreements. A gain for Germany.
- Rome-Berlin axis — treaty of friendship signed between Italy and Germany on 25 October 1936.
- Pact of Steel — an agreement between Italy and Germany signed on May 22, 1939 for immediate aid and military support in the event of war.
- Anti-Comintern Pact between Nazi-Germany and Japan on November 25th, 1936. The pact directed against the Communist International (Comintern) but was specifically directed against the Soviet Union. In 1937 Italy joined the Pact Munich Agreement — negotiations led to Hitler gaining Sudetenland and weakening Czechoslovakia.
- Nazi Soviet Non-Aggression Pact August 1939 - Both Hitler and Stalin bought time for themselves. For Hitler it seemed war in Europe over Poland unlikely. Poland was doomed. Britain had lost the possibility of alliance with Russia.

Other Factors

Fascist strategies: use of Military threat and force
- Italy's naval ambitions in the Mediterranean — 'Mare Nostrum'.
- Italian invasion of Abyssinia — provocation, methods, and relatively poor performance against very poorly equipped enemy.
- German remilitarisation of Rhineland — Hitler's gamble and timing, his generals' opposition, lack of Allied resistance.
- Spanish Civil War — aid to Nationalists, testing weapons and tactics, aerial bombing of Guernica.
- Anschluss — attempted coup 1934; relations with Schuschnigg; invasion itself relatively botched militarily; popularity of Anschluss in Austria.
- Czechoslovakia — threats of 1938; invasion of March 1939.
- Italian invasion of Albania — relatively easy annexation of a client state.

- Poland — escalating demands; provocation, invasion.
- The extent to which it was the threat of military force which was used rather than military force itself — eg Czechoslovakia in 1938; and the extent to which military force itself was effective and/or relied on an element of bluff — eg Rhineland.

German Rearmament

- Open German rearmament from 1935.
- The speed and scale of rearmament, including conscription.
- The emphasis on air power and the growing threat from the air.
- By 1939, Hitler had an army of nearly 1 million men, over 8,000 aircraft and 95 warships.
- Germany's perceived military strength may have had an effect on other countries. Britain, for example feared aerial power, especially after the bombing of Guernica by the German Condor Legion.

Fascist diplomacy as a means of achieving aims:

- Aims can be generally accepted as destruction of Versailles, the weakening of democracies, the expansion of fascist powers and countering communism.
- Diplomacy and the protestation of 'peaceful' intentions and 'reasonable' demands.
- Appeals to sense of international equality and fairness and the righting of past wrongs eg Versailles.
- Withdrawal from League and Disarmament Conference.
- Prior to Remilitarisation of Rhineland Hitler made offer of 25 year peace promise. Diplomacy used to distract and delay reaction to Nazi action.

Fascist strategies: Economic

- Use of economic influence and pressure, eg on south-eastern European states.
- Aid supplied to Franco (Spain) was tactically important to Hitler. Not only for testing weapons but also access to Spanish minerals.

Any other relevant factors.

53. **Czechoslovakia was created by the break-up of Austria-Hungary, at the end of World War One, by the Treaty of St Germain. It was a successful democracy in Eastern Europe, though there was a significant minority of Sudeten Germans. This Germanic population became very restless after relentless Nazi propaganda. Hitler threatened invasion to 'protect' the 'persecuted' German minority. In September of 1938 Chamberlain flew out to meet Hitler directly at Berchtesgaden in order to avoid war. He met with Hitler again at Bad Godesberg and finally at a four-power conference in Munich, conceding the Sudetenland 'peace for our time'.**

Munich Agreement was a reasonable settlement

- Czechoslovakian defences were effectively outflanked anyway following the Anschluss.
- Britain and France were not in a position to prevent German attack on Czechoslovakia in terms of difficulties of getting assistance to Czechoslovakia.
- British public opinion was reluctant to risk war over mainly German-speaking Sudetenland.
- Military unpreparedness for wider war – especially Britain's air defences.
- Lack of alternative, unified international response to Hitler's threats:
  - Failure of League of Nations in earlier crises

- French doubts over commitments to Czechoslovakia
- US isolationism
- British suspicion of Soviet Russia
- Strong reservations of rest of British Empire and Dominions concerning support for Britain in event of war.
- Attitudes of Poland and Hungary who were willing to benefit from the dismemberment of Czechoslovakia.
- Munich bought another year for rearmament which Britain put to good use.
- Views of individuals, politicians and media at this time.

Munich Agreement was not a reasonable settlement

- A humiliating surrender to Hitler's threats.
- Another breach in the post-WW1 settlement.
- A betrayal of Czechoslovakia and democracy.
- Czechoslovakia wide open to further German aggression as happened in March 1939.
- Further augmentation of German manpower and resources.
- Furtherance of Hitler's influence and ambitions in Eastern Europe.
- Further alienation of Soviet Union.
- Poland left further exposed.
- A British, French, Soviet agreement could have been a more effective alternative.
- Views of individuals, politicians and media at this time.

Any other relevant factors.

54. **The Nazi occupation of the Sudentenland could be justified in the eyes of Appeasers as Hitler was absorbing fellow Germans into Greater Germany. However, by the time of the Nazi-Soviet Pact, any illusion of justified grievances had evaporated.**

Importance of Nazi-Soviet Pact

- Pact – diplomatic, economic, military co-operation; division of Poland.
- Unexpected — Hitler and Stalin's motives.
- Put an end to British-French talks with Russia on guarantees to Poland.
- Hitler was freed from the threat of Soviet intervention and war on two fronts.
- Hitler's belief that Britain and France would not go to war over Poland without Russian assistance.
- Hitler now felt free to attack Poland.
- But, given Hitler's consistent, long-term foreign policy aims on the destruction of the Versailles settlement and lebensraum in the east, the Nazi-Soviet Pact could be seen more as a factor influencing the timing of the outbreak of war rather than as one of its underlying causes.
- Hitler's long-term aims for destruction of the Soviet state and conquest of Russian resources — lebensraum.
- Hitler's need for new territory and resources to sustain Germany's militarised economy.
- Hitler's belief that British and French were 'worms' who would not turn from previous policy of appeasement and avoidance of war at all costs.
- Hitler's belief that the longer war was delayed the more the balance of military and economic advantage would shift against Germany.

Other factors

Changing British attitudes towards appeasement

- Czechoslovakia did not concern most people until the middle of September 1938, when they began to object to a small democratic state being bullied. However, most press and population went along with it, although level of popular opposition often underestimated.

- Events in Bohemia and Moravia consolidated growing concerns in Britain.
- The anti-appeasement movement gained more support as Hitler's intentions became clearer.
- German annexation of Memel [largely German population, but in Lithuania] further showed Hitler's bad faith
- Actions convinced British government of growing German threat in south-eastern Europe.
- Guarantees to Poland and promised action in the event of threats to Polish independence.

The occupation of Bohemia and the collapse of Czechoslovakia

- British and French realisation, after Hitler's breaking of Munich Agreement and invasion of Czechoslovakia in March 1939, that Hitler's word was worthless and that his aims went beyond the incorporation of ex-German territories and ethnic Germans within the Reich.
- Promises of support to Poland and Rumania.
- British public acceptance that all attempts to maintain peace had been exhausted.
- <u>Prime Minister Chamberlain</u> felt betrayed by the Nazi seizure of Czechoslovakia, realised his policy of appeasement towards Hitler had failed, and began to take a much harder line against the Nazis.

British diplomacy and relations with the Soviet Union

- Stalin knew that Hitler's ultimate aim was to attack Russia.
- Lord Halifax, the British Foreign Secretary was invited by Stalin to go to Russia to discuss an alliance against Germany.
- Britain refused as they feared Russian Communism, and they believed that the Russian army was too weak to be of any use against Hitler.
- In August 1939, with war in Poland looming, the British and French eventually sent a military mission to discuss an alliance with Russia. Owing to travel difficulties it took five days to reach Leningrad.
- The Russians asked if they could send troops into Poland if Hitler invaded. The British refused, knowing that the Poles would not want this. The talks broke down.
- This merely confirmed Stalin's suspicions regarding the British. He felt they could not be trusted, especially after the Munich agreement, and they would leave Russia to fight Germany alone. This led directly to opening talks with the Nazis who seemed to be taking the Russians seriously by sending Foreign Minister von Ribbentrop and offering peace and land.

The position of France

- France had signed an agreement with Czechoslovakia offering support if the country was attacked. However, Hitler could all but guarantee that in 1938, French would do nothing as their foreign policy was closely tied to the British.
- French military, and particularly their air force, allowed to decline in years after 1919.
- After Munich, French more aggressive towards dictators and in events of 1939 were keen on a military alliance with the Soviet Union, however despite different emphasis on tactics were tied to the British and their actions.

Developing crisis over Poland

- Hitler's long-term aims for the destruction of Versailles, including regaining of Danzig and Polish Corridor.

- British and French decision to stick to their guarantees to Poland

Invasion of Poland

- On 1 September 1939, Hitler and the Nazis faked a Polish attack on a minor German radio station in order to justify a German invasion of Poland. An hour later Hitler declared war on Poland stating one of his reasons for the invasion was because of "the attack by regular Polish troops on the Gleiwitz transmitter."
- France and Britain had a defensive pact with Poland. This forced France and Britain to declare war on Germany, which they did on September 3.

Any other relevant factors.

Part I: The Cold War, 1945–1989

55. **Although Soviet motives in creating a buffer zone of states with sympathetic pro-Stalinist governments made sense to the Russians many of those in the satellite states did not see it that way. Resentment within the satellite states grew, especially when the standard of living did not rise. The death of Stalin seemed to offer an opportunity for greater freedom. However, Soviet tolerance of change only ran so far.**

The international context

- 1955 — emergence of Nikita Khrushchev as leader on death of Stalin. He encouraged criticism of Stalin and seemed to offer hope for greater political and economic freedom across the Eastern European satellite states.
- Speech to 20th Party Congress, Feb 1956: Khrushchev attacked Stalin for promoting a cult of personality and for his use of purges and persecution to reinforce his dictatorship. Policy of de-Stalinisation.
- Development of policy of peaceful co-existence to appeal to the West.
- Development of policy of different roads to Socialism to appeal to satellite states in Eastern Europe who were becoming restless.

Demands for change and reaction: Poland (1956)

- Riots sparked off by economic grievances developed into demands for political change in Poland.
- On the death of Stalinist leader Boleslaw Bierut in 1956 he was replaced by Wladyslaw Gromulka, a former victim of Stalinism which initially worried the Soviets.
- Poles announced their own road to Socialism and introduced reforms.
- Release of political prisoners (incl. Cardinal Wyszynski, Archbishop of Warsaw); collective farms broken up into private holdings; private shops allowed to open, greater freedom given to factory managers.
- Relatively free elections held in 1957 which returned a Communist majority of 18.
- No Soviet intervention despite concerns.
- Gromulka pushed change only so far. Poland remained in the Warsaw Pact as a part of the important 'buffer zone'. Political freedoms were very limited indeed. Poland was a loyal supporter of the Soviet Union until the 1980s and the emergence of the Solidarity movement. Limited challenge to Soviet control.

Demands for change and reaction: Hungary (1956)

- Hungarians had similar complaints: lack of political freedom, economic problems and poor standard of living.
- Encouraged by Polish success, criticism of the Stalinist regime of Mátyás Rákosi grew and he was removed by Khrushchev.

- Popular upsurge of support for change in Budapest led to a new Hungarian government led by Imre Nagy, who promised genuine reform and change.
- Nagy government planned multi-party elections, political freedoms, the withdrawal of Hungary from the Warsaw Pact and demands for the withdrawal of Soviet forces.
- Nagy went too far. The Soviet Union could not see this challenge to the political supremacy of the Communist Party and the break-up of their carefully constructed buffer zone. They intervened and crushed the rising brutally.
- Successful intervention against a direct challenge to Soviet control, but lingering resentment from mass of Hungarian people, through some economic flexibility allowed the new regime of Janos Kadar to improve economic performance and living standards.

Demands for change and reaction: Berlin (1961)

- Problem of Berlin — a divided city in a divided nation.
- Lack of formal boundaries in Berlin allowed East Berliners and East Germans to freely enter the West which they did owing to the lack of political freedom, economic development and poor living standards in the East.
- Many of those fleeing (2.8 million between 1949 and 1961) were skilled and young, just the people the communist East needed to retain. This was embarrassing for the East as it showed that Communism was not the superior system it was claimed to be.
- Concerns of Ulbricht and Khrushchev: attempts to encourage the Western forces to leave Berlin by bluster and threat from 1958 failed.
- President Kennedy spoke about not letting the Communists drive them out of Berlin. Resultant increase in tension could not be allowed to continue.
- Building of barriers: barbed wire then stone in August 1961 to stem the flood from East to West.
- Success in that it reduced the threat of war and the exodus to the West from the East to a trickle. To an extent it suited the West as well as they did not like the obvious threat of potential conflict and escalation that Berlin represented.
- Frustration of many in East Germany. Propaganda gift for the US and allies, though Soviets had controlled the direct challenge.

Military and ideological factors

- Buffer zone could not be broken up as provided military defence for Soviet Union.
- Use of force and Red Army to enforce control in late 40s and early 50s.
- Need to ensure success of Communism hence policy.

Domestic pressures

- Intention to stop any further suffering of Soviet Union in aftermath of WW2 made leadership very touchy to change.
- Some economic freedoms were allowed, but at the expense of political freedoms.
- Need to stop spread of demands for change.

Any other relevant factors.

56. **Events during the Cuban Missile crisis had concentrated the minds of the superpowers leaders and led to a more conciliatory relationship between the USSR and USA. However, each side also had its own reasons for engagement. The USSR wished to restructure its economic focus from weapons production and heavy industry to more consumer goods. The USA felt that there were other ways to contain Communism and wished for more engagement in the context of their involvement in Vietnam.**

Economic cost of arms race

- Developments in technology raised the costs of the arms race.
- The development of Anti-Ballistic Missile technology and costs of war led to SALT 1, and the ABM treaty
- Limiting MIRV and intermediate missile technology led to SALT 2.
- The cost of 'Star Wars' technology also encouraged the Soviet Union to seek better relations.
- Khrushchev's desire for better relations between the superpowers in the 50s and 60s was, in part, about freeing up resources for economic development in the USSR. He hoped this would show the superiority of the Soviet system.
- Gorbachev wanted to improve the lives of ordinary Russians and part of this was by reducing the huge defence budget eg Intermediate Nuclear Forces Treaty, December 1987.

Other factors

Mutually Assured Destruction

- The development of vast arsenals of nuclear weapons from 1945 by both superpowers as a deterrent to the other side; a military attack would result in horrific retaliation.
- So many nuclear weapons were built to ensure that not all were destroyed even after a first-strike, and this led to a stalemate known as MAD. Arms race built on fear.

Dangers of military conflict as seen through Cuban Missile Crisis

- In this it worked as the threat of nuclear war seemed very close on the discovery of Soviet nuclear missiles on Cuba in 1962. Before Khrushchev backed down nuclear war was threatened. It also illustrated the lack of formal contact between the superpowers to defuse potential conflicts.
- Introduction of a 'hot-line' between the Kremlin and White House in order to improve communication between the superpowers. Khrushchev and Kennedy also signed the Limited Nuclear Test Ban Treaty, the first international agreement on nuclear weapons.

Technology: The importance of verification

- American development of surveillance technology (U2 and satellites) meant that nuclear weapons could be identified and agreements verified.
- Example of U2 flight over Cuba where Anderson photographed nuclear sites.
- Also U2 and satellite verification to make sure the Soviets were doing as promised at the negotiating table.
- Some historians think Arms Control would never have taken root, but for the ability of the sides to verify what the other was doing.

Co-existence and Détente

- Policies of co-existence and détente developed to defuse tensions and even encourage trade.
- Role of others like Brandt in West Germany in defusing tension through their policies of Ostpolitik, etc.

Any other relevant factors.

57. Ronald Reagan became President of the United States in 1981. He brought an aggressive anti-Communism to Cold War relations. This showed itself through new defence initiatives as well as tough talk. By 1985 Mikhail Gorbachev had become General Secretary of the Communist Party in Soviet Russia. He was very aware of the economic problems building up for Russia and sought reform at home and engagement abroad.

Actions of President Ronald Reagan

- Unlike many in the US administration Reagan actively sought to challenge Soviet weakness and strengthen the west in order to defeat Communism. In 1983 he denounced the Soviet Union as an 'Evil Empire'.
- Programme of improving US armed forces, including nuclear weapons and he proposed a Star Wars missile shield to challenge the belief in MAD (SDI).
- He was very charming when he met Gorbachev and visited the Soviet Union.

Other factors

Failure of Communism in Eastern Europe

- Strong Polish identity and history of hostility with Russia. By 1970s, Poland in economic slump. Emergence of opposition around Gdansk in 1980: industrial workers strike led by Lech Walesa, who argued for the creation of an independent trade union. Solidarity grew to nine million members in a matter of months. Movement suppressed in 1981 by General Jaruzelski's government.
- Multiparty elections in Poland, after Soviet troops left, victory for Solidarity.
- Czechoslovakia, political prisoners released in November 1989 and by the end of the month, the communist government had gone. No Soviet intervention.
- Opening of the Berlin Wall: division of Germany finally came to an end.
- Soviet domination ended.
- Perestroika and Glasnost and end of Communist rule in USSR.

Role of President Mikhail Gorbachev

- Gorbachev saw that the USSR could not afford a new arms race. The Soviet economy was at breaking point. Commitments to the arms race and propping up allied regimes meant consumer goods and other things such as housing that mattered to Russian people were neglected.
- Gorbachev implemented policies of Perestroika and Glasnost which aimed to reform the Soviet economy and liberalise its political system.
- Gorbachev worked to improve relations with the USA. He took ideology out of his foreign policy, as exemplified by arms agreements to allow the USSR to concentrate on internal matters: Intermediate Nuclear Forces Treaty, Dec 1987, Nuclear Weapons Reduction Treaty, 1989.
- Gorbachev told leaders of the satellite East European states in March 1989 that the Soviet army would no longer help them to stay in power.

Western economic strength

- Allowed America to embark on the Star Wars weapons programme.
- Perception of the affluent West through television and consumer goods undermined Communist claims of the superiority of their economic system.

Withdrawal of the Soviet Union from Afghanistan

- Symptom of the problems of Soviet Union
- Intervention in Dec 1979: conflict with the Mujahidin. Russian army morale crumbled when over 20,000 Soviet soldiers died, as did support at home.
- The conflict showed the weaknesses of the Soviet economy. War led to a slump in living standards for ordinary Russians.
- Russians began to question the actions of their own government. Gorbachev withdrew troops in 1988.

Any other relevant factors.

Acknowledgements

Permission has been sought from all relevant copyright holders and Hodder Gibson is grateful for the use of the following:

An extract from 'Kings and Queens of Scotland' by Richard Oram, published by The History Press Ltd 2006 (Model Paper 1 page 3);

An extract from 'Medieval Scotland Kingship and Nation' by Alan Macquarrie, published by The History Press Ltd 2004 (Model Paper 1 page 4);

An extract from 'History of the Reformation in Scotland' by John Knox. Public Domain (Model Paper 1 page 5);

An extract from 'Mary Queen of Scots: A Study in Failure' by Jenny Wormald, published by Hamlyn 1988 © I.B. Tauris & Co. Ltd. (Model Paper 1 page 5);

An extract from 'Scotland James V to James VII, History of Scotland' by Gordon Donaldson, published by Oliver & Boyd 1965 © The Estate of Gordon Donaldson (Model Paper 1 page 6);

An extract from 'The History Of The Union Of Great Britain' by Daniel Defoe, published by The Heirs Of Anderson 1709. Public Domain (Model Paper 1 page 7);

An extract from 'The Scottish Nation 1700-2000' by T.M. Devine (Allen Lane and the Penguin Press 1999, Penguin Books 2000). Copyright © T.M. Devine, 1999 (Model Paper 1 page 7);

An extract from 'The Scots and the Union' by Christopher A. Whately, published by Edinburgh University Press 2007 (Model Paper 1 page 8);

An extract from 'Irish Catholics in the West of Scotland', in the book 'New Perspectives on the Irish in Scotland' by Martin J. Mitchell, published by John Donald/Birlinn Ltd. 2008 (Model Paper 1 page 9);

An extract from 'Settlers: New Zealand Immigrants from England, Ireland and Scotland, 1800-1945' by Jock Phillips and Terry Hearn, published by Auckland University Press 2008 (Model Paper 1 page 9);

An extract from the diary of Private Thomas McCall, taken from 'Everyman at War', edited by C.B. Purdom, published by J.M. Dent, London 1930 (public domain) (Model Paper 1 page 11);

An extract from 'In War's Wake' by Nicholas Morgan, taken from 'The Sunday Mail Story of Scotland', Vol 4 part 44 © Scottish Daily Record and Sunday Mail Ltd (Model Paper 1 page 11);

An extract from 'The Flowers of the Forest: Scotland and the First World War' by Trevor Royle, published by Birlinn Ltd. 2006 (Model Paper 1 page 11);

An extract from 'Scottish Journey' by Edwin Muir, published by Mainstream 1996 © The Random House Group Ltd (Model Paper 1 page 12);

An extract from 'Robert Bruce' by G.W.S. Barrow, published by Edinburgh University Press 1988 (Model Paper 2 page 3);

An extract from 'Kings and Queens of Scotland' by Richard Oram, published by The History Press Ltd 2006 (Model Paper 2 page 4);

An extract from 'John Knox' by Rosalind K. Marshall, published by Birlinn Ltd. 2000 (Model Paper 2 page 5);

An extract from 'The Scottish Reformation' by Ian B. Cowan, published by St Martin's Press 1982 © Macmillan Education (Model Paper 2 page 6);

An extract from 'The Scots and the Union' by Christopher A. Whatley, published by Edinburgh University Press 2006 (Model Paper 2 page 7);

An extract from 'The History Of The Union Of Great Britain' by Daniel Defoe, published by The Heirs Of Anderson 1709. Public Domain (Model Paper 2 page 7);

An extract from 'The Union of 1707' by Paul Henderson Scott, published by The Saltire Society 2006 (Model Paper 2 page 8);

An extract from The Scotsman, 20 February 1923, 'Emigration boom in the Hebrides' © The Scotsman Publications Ltd. (Model Paper 2 page 9);

An extract from 'New Arrivals' by Tony Jaconelli taken from www.ourglasgowstory.com (Model Paper 2 page 9);

An extract from 'Irish Immigrants and Scottish Society in the Nineteenth and Twentieth Centuries', edited by T.M. Devine, published by John Donald/Birlinn Ltd. 1991 (Model Paper 2 page 10);

An extract from 'Private 12768: Memoir of a Tommy' by John Jackson, published by The History Press Ltd 2004 (Model Paper 2 page 11);

An extract from The Glasgow Herald, 29th October 1915 © Herald & Times Group (Model Paper 2 page 11);

An extract from 'Scottish Popular Politics: From Radicalism to Labour' by W. Hamish Fraser, published by Edinburgh University Press 2000 (Model Paper 2 page 12);

An extract from 'Robert the Bruce's Rivals: The Comyns, 1212-1314' by Alan Young, published by Tuckwell Press Ltd./Birlinn Ltd. 1997 (Model Paper 3 page 3);

An extract from 'The Scottish Civil War: The Bruces and Balliols and the War for Control of Scotland 1286-1356' by Michael Penman, published by The History Press Ltd 2002 (Model Paper 3 page 3);

An extract from 'The Age of Reformation: The Tudor and Stewart Realms 1485—1603 (Religion, Politics and Society in Britain)' by Alec Ryrie, published by Longman 2009 © Pearson Education (Model Paper 3 page 5);

An extract from 'Mary, Queen of Scots, and the Murder of Lord Darnley' by Alison Weir, published by Vintage, 2008 ©

The Random House Group Ltd (Model Paper 3 page 5);

An extract from 'The Union of 1707' by Paul Henderson Scott, published by The Saltire Society 2006 (Model Paper 3 page 7);

An extract from 'The Scots and the Union' by Christopher A. Whatley, published by Edinburgh University Press 2006 (Model Paper 3 page 7);

An extract from 'The History Of The Union Of Great Britain' by Daniel Defoe, published by The Heirs Of Anderson 1709 (public domain) (Model Paper 3 page 8);

An extract from 'Glencoe and the Indians' by James Hunter, published by Mainstream 1996 © The Random House Group Ltd. (Model Paper 3 page 9);

An extract from The Ayr Advertiser, 1849 © Clyde and Forth Press Ltd (Model Paper 3 page 9);

An extract from 'Red Scotland!: The Rise and Fall of the Radical Left, c. 1872 to 1932' by William Kenefick, published by Edinburgh University Press 1999 (Model Paper 3 page 11);

An extract from 'The Flowers of the Forest: Scotland and the First World War' by Trevor Royle, published by Birlinn Ltd. 2006 (Model Paper 3 page 11);

An extract from 'The Wars of Scotland 1214–1371' by Michael Brown, published by Edinburgh University Press 2004 (2015 page 4);

An extract from 'Under the Hammer: Edward I and Scotland, 1286-1307' by Fiona Watson, published by Tuckwell Press/Birlinn Ltd. 1998 (2015 page 4);

An extract from 'Edward I' by Michael Prestwich, published by University of California Press. Copyright © 1988 Michael Prestwich (2015 page 4);

An extract from 'Scotland: A New History' by Michael Lynch, published by Pimlico 1992 © The Random House Group Ltd (2015 page 6);

An extract from 'The life and impact of Scottish Reformer John Knox' by T. Booher 2012, taken from http://tulipdrivenlife.blogspot.co.uk/2012/02/church-history-life-and-impact-of.html (2015 page 6);

An extract from 'Scotland Re-formed 1488–1587' (New Edinburgh History of Scotland, Volume 6) by J.E.A. Dawson, published by Edinburgh University Press 2009 (2015 page 6);

An extract from 'The History Today Companion to British History' by Juliet Gardiner and Neil Wenborn, published by Collins & Brown 1995 (2015 page 8);

An extract from 'Last of the Free: A History of the Highlands and Islands of Scotland' by James Hunter, published by Mainstream 1999 © The Random House Group Ltd (2015 page 10);

An extract from 'The Mineworkers' by Robert Duncan, published by Birlinn Ltd. 2005 (2015 page 10);

An extract from 'The Flowers of the Forest: Scotland and the First World War' by Trevor Royle, published by Birlinn Ltd. 2006 (2015 page 12);

An extract from the Glasgow Herald, 1st February 1919 © Herald & Times Group (2015 page 13).

Hodder Gibson would like to thank SQA for use of any past exam questions that may have been used in model papers, whether amended or in original form.